FUNDAMENTALS OF COMPUTING I

Logic, Problem Solving, Programs, and Computers

C++ Edition

McGraw-Hill Series in Computer Science

Senior Consulting Editor

C.L. Liu, *University of Illinois at Urbana–Champaign*

Consulting Editor

Allen B. Tucker, *Bowdoin College*

Fundamentals of Computing and Programming
Computer Organization and Architecture
Computers in Society/Ethics
Systems and Languages
Theoretical Foundations
Software Engineering and Database
Artificial Intelligence
Networks, Parallel and Distributed Computing
Graphics and Visualization
The MIT Electrical Engineering and Computer Science Series

Fundamentals of Computing and Programming

* Co-published by the MIT Press and McGraw-Hill, Inc.

FUNDAMENTALS OF COMPUTING I

LOGIC, PROBLEM SOLVING, PROGRAMS, AND COMPUTERS

C++ EDITION

Allen B. Tucker
Bowdoin College

Andrew P. Bernat
University of Texas at El Paso

W. James Bradley
Calvin College

Robert D. Cupper
Allegheny College

Greg W. Scragg
SUNY Geneseo

McGRAW-HILL, INC.

New York St. Louis San Francisco Auckland Bogotá Caracas
Lisbon London Madrid Mexico City Milan Montreal New Delhi
San Juan Singapore Sydney Tokyo Toronto

FUNDAMENTALS OF COMPUTING I
Logic, Problem Solving, Programs, and Computers

C++ Edition

This book is printed on acid-free paper.

2 3 4 5 6 7 8 9 0   DOC/DOC   9 9 8 7 6 5

ISBN 0-07-065506−5

The editor was Eric M. Munson;
the production supervisor was Kathryn Porzio.
R. R. Donnelley & Sons Company was printer and binder.

Figure Credits:
1–1 Left: Portrait by Phillippe de Champaign / The Bettman
        Archive. Right: Smithsonian Institution Collection.
1–2 BBC Hulton Picture Library / The Bettmann Archive.
1–3 The Institute for Advanced Studies, Princeton, N.J.
1–4 The Bettmann Archive.
1–7 NCR Corporation

Library of Congress Catalog Card Number: 94–77818

ABOUT THE AUTHORS

Allen B. Tucker is Professor of Computer Science at Bowdoin College; he held similar positions at Colgate University and Georgetown University. He earned a BA in mathematics from Wesleyan University in 1963 and an MS and Ph.D. in computer science from Northwestern University in 1970. Professor Tucker is the author or coauthor of several books and articles in the areas of programming languages, natural language processing, and computer science education. He recently served on the ACM Task Force on the Core of Computing and as cochair of the ACM/IEEE-CS Joint Curriculum Committee Task Force that developed the report *Computing Curricula 1991*. He is a member of ACM, IEEE-CS, CPSR, and the Liberal Arts Computer Science Consortium (LACS).

Andrew P. Bernat is Professor and Chair of the Computer Science Department at the University of Texas at El Paso. He earned a BS from Harvey Mudd College and an MS and Ph.D. from the University of Texas at Austin. Professor Bernat is the author of articles in the areas of programming languages, computer vision, concurrent processing and computer science education. His scholarly interests are in concurrent and real-time systems and computer science education. Professor Bernat is a member of IAU, ACM, and IEEE-CS.

W. James Bradley is Professor of Mathematics and Computer Science at Calvin College. He graduated from MIT with a major in mathematics in 1964 and completed a Ph.D. from the University of Rochester in 1974. Professor Bradley also earned an MS in computer science from the Rochester Institute of Technology in 1982. He has authored papers on game theory and computer science curriculum, as well as an introductory text in discrete mathematics. His current scholarly interests are in formal methods in decision making, database systems, ethical and social issues in computing, and computer science education. Professor Bradley is a member of MAA, ACM, CPSR, and LACS.

Robert D. Cupper is Professor and Chair of the Department of Computer Science at Allegheny College. He received a BS from Juniata College and a Ph.D. from the University of Pittsburgh. At Allegheny, Professor Cupper developed one of the first computer science major programs for a liberal arts college, a program that helped motivate the design of the liberal arts model curriculum in 1986. He has been an active member of ACM for several years, having served as chair of the Student Chapters Committee and as secretary-treasurer of the Special Interest Group on Computer Science Education (SIGCSE). Professor Cupper has written and spoken on the economics of computing, curriculum development, and program accreditation. He is a member of ACM and a cofounder of LACS.

Greg W. Scragg is Professor and Chair of the Computer Science Department at the State University of New York at Geneseo. He earned his BA in mathematics at the University of California at Riverside in 1969 and his MS and Ph.D. in computer science at the University of California at San Diego in 1974. Professor Scragg is the author or coauthor of three previous books and numerous articles in the areas of natural language processing, human factors, and computer science pedagogy. He is a member of ACM and LACS.

To our students

CONTENTS

PREFACE

The discipline of computer science and engineering, or *computing*, is an extraordinary one in many ways. More than any other field of study or professional engagement, the process of solving computational problems and designing computational devices evolves with relentless speed. And so must the undergraduate curriculum that prepares students to confront the challenges that will await them.

This text, together with its accompanying laboratory manual and software, is designed for the first course in computing (CS1). In its revised edition, this text aims to capture and present to beginning students some of the "essence" of the discipline of computing. We do this in a way that is more broadly-based, deeply engaging, and therefore more representative of the richness of the discipline than most other introductory texts. This is done in the belief that students should leave the first course with not only a strong mastery of problem solving and programming but also a clear sense of the interdependence among the mathematical, scientific, engineering, and societal points of view that are embodied in the whole discipline of computing. While programming is a central activity, the discipline is far richer and broader in its content and methodology than that which is implied by a course where students learn *only* programming.

For instance, this text not only helps students begin to develop concrete problem solving and programming skills, it also introduces them to the elements of mathematical logic and functions. Why? Because logic is the language through which computational problems are specified and computer hardware is designed, and functions provide a clear and universal model for computation at both the software and hardware levels. To ignore these fundamental ideas within a first course in computing can lead students to the false conclusions that programming is a loosely-conceived and intuition-driven pastime, and that software and hardware design has no theoretical or abstract underpinnings at all.

Thus, the heart of this text (chapters 2–6) prominently develops MAPS, an elementary methodology for algorithmic problem solving and programming using C++. A series of laboratory exercises, presented in a separate laboratory manual, is carefully coordinated with this development, enabling students to gain mastery of C++ syntax and programming skills in three major application areas—mathematical, text processing, and graphical. This development, combined with an introduction to logic and functions, typically requires 9–10 weeks in a 14–week semester course. Those sections which may optionally be skipped are marked in the table of contents with an asterisk (*).

The next 2–3 weeks of the course (chapter 8 *or* 9) develop fundamental ideas of computer organization, illustrating how the principles of logic and C++ program structure support and motivate the design of computers themselves. Again, the laboratory manual provides exercises and a simple machine simulator called MARINA that give students hands-on experimental work with elementary logic design and machine language program execution.

The last 1–2 weeks of the course (chapters 10–11) engage students with broader societal and professional issues that uniquely confront the discipline of computing. For instance, what is software piracy, and what are its technical, legal, and ethical dimensions? Who is responsible when a software error causes injury or other loss? In this part of the course, students should be challenged to read one or more contemporary articles and write a short paper on a pertinent issue. Ideally, the laboratory in this part of the course can be turned into a seminar in which students grapple with these issues more actively.

This text supports a variety of other course organizations beyond the one suggested above. For instance, a more traditional CS1 course would spend more time with Chapters 1–6 and cover chapters 7–11 only briefly. A course that emphasizes more of the hardware aspects of computing would cover both chapters 8 and 9 and give less time to the problem solving methodology developed in chapters 2–7. A course that emphasizes more of the social and professional issues surrounding computing would devote more time to chapters 8 and 9. A course that emphasizes the mathematical foundations of computing would include a more thorough treatment of proof methods and program verification from chapter 7. A course taught in a 10-week term would necessarily sacrifice some of the breadth of discipline coverage or some of the depth of programming that appears in the suggested course outline. Any of these alternatives can be effectively followed and still give students a broad and substantive introduction to the discipline of computer science.

Programming Language for the First Course We believe that the particular programming language used in the first course is far less important than the particular mix of subject matter that the course covers. For that reason, and because wise persons continue to disagree over what might be an "ideal" first language in the curriculum, we separate the teaching of C++ language-specific details from the subject matter in the text itself. Also, it is important to mention that a Scheme edition is also contemplated at this writing. We believe that, in principle, this text's emphasis on problem-solving, rigor, and breadth of discipline coverage is portable to any one of a number of alternative "first languages" without losing its basic message.

However, it is also important not to overwhelm students with unnecessary amounts of language detail in the first course. This is a particular hazard for a language like C++, which has a vast number of features, facilities, and libraries. For this reason, we have carefully defined a subset of C++ that we believe to be adequate for the CS1 course, and we use only that subset in our programming examples and software. Roughly speaking, that subset mirrors the basic features of Pascal that are found in a CS1 course. Notably, it includes only stream I/O, parameter passing only by reference and by value, and it excludes pointers. A more detailed summary of the C++ subset we use is given in Appendix B of this text and laboratory manual.

Student Audience and Goals This text has been used successfully for a first course in computer science in colleges of arts and sciences, liberal arts colleges, and engineering colleges. These different points of view are, in fact, particularly well-served by the text's broad subject matter coverage and integration of diverse, yet fundamentally interrelated, topics.

While no prior computing experience is assumed by this course, more and more students do enter with some programming experience. Students who have AP credit in computer science from secondary school may place out of this course, but in doing so they may miss some fundamental material that is not covered by the standard AP curriculum.

It is important to note that this text has also been used successfully in courses having a mixed enrollment of majors and nonmajors. For such a course, we find it useful to create two parallel "tracks" in the syllabus, beginning at week 9 or 10. One track follows the laboratory sequence suggested in the table below, while the other allows students the alternative of substituting a 7–10 page paper in place of the labs for weeks 10, 12, and 14. This paper would reflect a student's reading three or more outside articles on a contemporary social issue in computing and discussing that issue at some depth.

This alternative track allows many nonmajors to opt out of the more difficult programming exercises near the end of the course and substitute some work that may relate better to their major field of study. Nonmajors, therefore, can leave the course with a much better appreciation for the breadth and richness of the discipline than they would in either a traditional CS1 course that teaches only programming or a traditional service course that teaches *no* programming. This text's approach to the first course, therefore, provides a versatile vehicle that can be used in different ways to introduce the richness of the discipline of computing for majors and nonmajors alike.

Coordination of Laboratory Work On the following page is a typical one-semester (14-week) schedule that shows how the text and laboratory materials can be effectively coordinated. Each weekly laboratory assignment requires students to complete a problem-solving exercise that either illustrates or builds upon ideas introduced in lectures.

To complete a lab assignment, students must solve a problem, exercise and test a program, and answer a series of questions related to the problem. All of this work is described in the laboratory manual.

At the beginning of each laboratory session, the instructor can present technical material from the laboratory manual that students will need to understand before completing the lab assignment. Having a scheduled weekly laboratory session guarantees a dedicated time period and computing facilities for students to begin working on the assignment itself. Some of these assignments can be completed by the end of the laboratory period; others are longer and can be completed later in the week at students' convenience.

A TYPICAL SCHEDULE FOR LECTURES AND LABORATORY ASSIGNMENTS

Lab Week	Technical Material	Problem for the Assignment	Text Chapter(s)
1	Basic C++ syntax, I/O, functions, types	Enter and execute a simple C++ program	1, 2
2	C++ expressions, assignment, sequencing	Develop a program that invokes a function	3
3	Boolean expressions, if statements, assertions, for loops	Analyze the logic of a simple program	4
4	While and repeat loops	Design an iterative solution to a problem	4
5	*Test #1 -- no lab this week.*		
6	Specifications for strings and the list class	Solve a list problem, like finding the smallest element	5
7	Functions and parameters	Solve a problem like sorting, using a function and MAPS	5
8	Recursion, specifications for grids class	Solve a strings problem like "Ghost" using MAPS	6
9	Arrays, separate compilation, using class libraries	Solve a Grids problem using MAPS, ensuring robustness	6
10	Integrating the elements of MAPS	Solve a complete problem using MAPS	6
11	*Test #2 -- no lab this week.*		
12	MARINA machine language	Analyze a simple machine language program	9
13	MARINA assembly language and programming	Develop a simple assembly language program	9
14	Reprint of a recent article on a social issue	Discuss a contemporary social issue in a 2-3 page paper	10, 11

The software required for completing these assignments includes the specific classes `list` and `grid`, data files, miscellaneous sample programs, and the MARINA machine simulator. This software runs on the PC (Turbo), Macintosh (Symantec), and Unix (Gnu) C++ environments, and accompanies the instructor's manual on a separate disk. The software can also be obtained through the Internet by sending e-mail to `allen@polar.bowdoin.edu`.

Similarity with the Revised Pascal Edition This text is an emulation of the Revised Pascal Edition of *Fundamentals I*, published earlier this year. The main difference between these two editions, beyond the switch to C++, is that this text conspicuously introduces elements of object-oriented programming to students in the first course. Specifically, we introduce the notions of *class* and *object*. Two detailed classes—the `list` and the `grid`—are provided so that students can appreciate these ideas and become active clients of class libraries as they learn about programming and problem solving in C++. The remaining complexities of class design, inheritance, and other intricate features of C++ and object-oriented programming are left for the second course. Those topics are, in fact, addressed in *Volume II* of the *Fundamentals of Computing* series (see below).

Instructors who used or participated in the class-testing for the original Pascal edition of this text (published in 1992) will notice that, while the overall subject matter is similar, extensive organizational and pedagogical changes have been made. Principally, these changes include an expanded presentation of problem solving and programming, a better integration of logic and functions into key areas of problem solving and computer organization, and a laboratory manual with a more robust introduction to C++ and a greater selection of laboratory exercises than the manual that accompanied the original edition.

The Breadth–First Curriculum: The Fundamentals of Computing Series Readers may know that the course for which this text has been developed is the first in a collection of courses proposed in *Computing Curricula 1991* and labeled as the "breadth–first" curriculum. The general goal of these courses is to provide a broad view of the major subjects in the discipline of computing, an integration of the theory with the practice of computing, and a rigorously-defined laboratory component. We hope to achieve a curriculum that has much the same goals and style as a two- or three-semester introduction to another science, such as chemistry or biology.

This text is therefore the first in a series that are being developed to support the breadth-first approach for the first four courses in the introductory curriculum. At this time, the second text in this series is also available (in Pascal and C++ editions), while the third and fourth are planned for development over the next two or three years. The titles of these texts, which are collectively called the *Fundamentals of Computing Series*, are as follows:

Volume I: Logic, Problem Solving, Programs, and Computers
Volume II: Abstraction, Data Structures, and Large Software Systems
Volume III: Levels of Languages, Architecture, and Applications
Volume IV: Algorithms, Concurrency, and the Limits of Computation

The prerequisite structure assumed here is similar to that which is followed by their counterparts in a more conventional curriculum. That is, the course using

Volume I is a prerequisite for all the others, and the course using *Volume II* is a prerequisite for the course using *Volume IV*.

Any of these texts can be used interchangeably with other alternative texts for any of the first four courses in the curriculum. For instance, this text can be used in the first course and some alternative for *Volume II* can be used in a more traditional data structures course, or vice versa. In short, the *Fundamentals Series* is a "loosely coupled" collection of teaching materials designed to cover one or more of the the first four courses in the computer science curriculum in a wide range of institutional settings.

Acknowledgments This work results from the toil, suggestions, and support of many people—too numerous to mention individually. Since it represents a fundamentally new approach to introducing computer science at the undergraduate level, we cannot overstate the value of the comments we have received from the many instructors and students who have class-tested earlier versions of this material. We hope that this edition will reward those efforts by providing an exciting teaching and learning experience.

The following reviewers deserve credit for their many contributions to the development of this text: John Barr (Ithaca College), Mary Bivens (Allegheny College), Richard Close (U.S. Coast Guard Academy), Robert Harlan (St. Bonaventure University), Kenneth Lambert (Washington and Lee University), Ralph Morelli (Trinity College), William Richardson (U.S. Air Force Academy), Richard Salter (Oberlin College), and Antonio Siochi (Christopher Newport University). Finally, we thank Brian Davies for developing the C++ laboratory software that accompanies this text, as well as Bowdoin College for providing a computing environment that supports this effort.

Allen B. Tucker, Andrew P. Bernat, W. James Bradley,
Robert D. Cupper, Greg W. Scragg

References

1. P. Denning, D. Comer, D. Gries, M. Mulder, A. Tucker, A. Turner, and P. Young, "Computing as a Discipline," *Report of the ACM Task Force on the Core of Computer Science*, ACM Press, New York, 1988. Portions reprinted in *Communications of the ACM 32* (1) (January 1989) and *Computer* (March 1989).

2. A. Tucker (ed), B. Barnes, R. Aiken, K. Barker, K. Bruce, J. Cain, S. Conry, G. Engel, R. Epstein, D. Lidtke, M. Mulder, J. Rogers, E. Spafford, and A. Turner, *Computing Curricula 1991*, ACM/IEEE–CS Joint Curriculum Task Force, ACM Press and IEEE–CS Press, New York, 1991. Portions reprinted in *Communications of the ACM* (March 1991) and *IEEE Computer* (November 1991).

3. A. Tucker and D. Garnick, "A Breadth-First Introductory Curriculum in Computing," Computer Science Education 3 (1991), 271–295.

FUNDAMENTALS OF COMPUTING I

Logic, Problem Solving, Programs, and Computers

C++ Edition

CHAPTER 1

COMPUTING AS A HUMAN ENTERPRISE

The discipline of *computing* is known by various titles, such as "computer science," "computer science and engineering," "computing sciences," "informatics," and so on. Under any of these headings, we understand the name "computing" to mean something like the following:

Definition *Computing* is the study of systematic processes that describe and transform information: their theory, analysis, design, efficiency, implementation, and application. The fundamental question underlying all computing is, What can and cannot be automated? (adapted from Denning et al., "Computing as a Discipline," *Communications of the ACM*, January, 1989).

Whenever we use the term *computing* in this text, we understand it to encompass all these possible labels and the above definition.

Our study of computing begins with a brief historical sketch of key events in its history, followed by an introduction to three *processes*, or general ways of looking at the discipline—through mathematics, science, and engineering—and an identification of their applicability to the historical events. Third, we look at the discipline of computing in a more modern framework, identifying its *nine major subject areas* as well as its *social and professional* dimensions. Four of these areas—algorithms and data structures, architecture, programming languages, and software methodology—are emphasized throughout this text. Fourth, we conclude this chapter with two illustrations that introduce, in familiar day-to-day terms, some of the discipline's basic ideas that will be valuable throughout the remainder of the text.

A BRIEF HISTORY OF COMPUTING

Computing is an ancient discipline, with roots that can be traced to the Greek, Babylonian, and Egyptian civilizations. It is rooted in two quests that have motivated thinkers for thousands of years—the quest to systematize reasoning and the quest to develop means to make computations accurate and efficient. The modern electronic digital computer is the most recent advance in this chain of development. Although you will see a lot of names and dates in the next few pages, be patient; in the next section, we use them to illustrate the different modes of thought—called *theory*, *abstraction*, and *design*—that characterize the modern discipline of computing.

Ancient Greece made an enormous contribution to the systematization of reasoning. The Greeks developed the axiomatic method in mathematics; for instance, they developed geometry as a logico-deductive system. That is, rather than doing experiments on circles and gathering data, Greek mathematicians stated formal axioms, precisely defined the concept of circle, and derived the properties of circles by formal reasoning. The Greeks also did a great deal to clarify patterns of valid reasoning. Aristotle presented this example:

All persons are mortal.
Socrates is a person.
Therefore Socrates is mortal.

This pattern of reasoning is called *modus ponens*. It can also be written as follows:

If one is a person, then one is mortal.
Socrates is a person.
Therefore Socrates is mortal.

In this alternative "If-then" form, *modus ponens* is a basis for much of contemporary mathematical reasoning and is commonly used in everyday conversation. A slightly different pattern of reasoning, which is called *modus tollens*, is illustrated in the following variation:

All persons are mortal.
Zeus is not mortal.
Therefore, Zeus is not a person.

This pattern is also widely used in mathematics and everyday discourse. Aristotle's work provided the foundation of formal logic; no truly revolutionary advances beyond it were made until the nineteenth century.

The Babylonians and Egyptians were not systematic reasoners like the Greeks. Instead, they developed a number of computational methods that were intended to save people considerable labor, primarily by trial-and-error methods. For instance, they developed multiplication tables, tables of squares and square roots and cubes and cube roots, tables of reciprocals, and exponential tables for finding compound interest. They found a formula for solving quadratic equations and discovered the method for completing the square.

The Babylonians and Egyptians also used a number of *approximate* methods and formulas. For instance, they developed a method to compute the area of a circle by taking the square of eight-ninths of the circle's diameter. This is equivalent to setting $\pi = 3.1604\ldots$, an estimate which was probably close enough at that time to the true value of $3.14159\ldots$ but which was nevertheless not correct. Unlike the Greeks, the Babylonians and Egyptians lacked a systematic method to test the correctness of their results.

Improvements in computational methods continued for many centuries in different parts of the world. For example, our modern word *algorithm* is derived from the name of a famous Persian textbook author, Abu Ja'far Mohammed ibn Mûsa al-Khowârizmî, who lived about A.D. 825. The word was originally written as *algorism* and referred to the process of carrying out arithmetic computations using Arabic numerals, which was the subject of al-Khowârizmî's book.

The next major discoveries of interest to computing burst forth in the late sixteenth and early seventeenth centuries. François Viète (1540–1603) originated the subject of algebra by introducing letters for unknowns around 1580. John Napier (1550–1617) invented logarithms as a calculational aid in 1614; Edmund Gunter (1581–1626) invented a forerunner of the slide rule in 1620. The slide rule itself was invented around 1630. Galileo (1564–1642) undertook the mathematical formulation of the physical sciences. This provided a concise, compact, and unambiguous way to express scientific insights. René Descartes (1596–1650) discovered analytic geometry, thus making it possible to apply algebra to geometric problems and subsequently to problems involving physical motion.

Wilhelm Schickard designed and built in 1623 what is believed to be the first digital calculator. It did addition and subtraction automatically and partially automated multiplication and division. Unfortunately, Schickard and all his family died in a plague, and his invention fell into obscurity. Blaise Pascal (1623–1662) is often credited with this invention, but his calculator was built about 20 years after Schickard's and was less advanced. Pascal's calculator (See Figure 1–1) could only add and subtract. It depended on a sequence of interlocking gears that performed the carries of addition and the borrows of subtraction; however, the technology of the time could not manufacture these gears with sufficient consistency to allow reliable production of Pascal's adder.

Another important figure of this era was Gottfried Wilhelm Leibniz (1646–1716). Leibniz was both a great theoretician and an outstanding practical thinker. He was the coinventor (with Isaac Newton) of calculus. Leibniz wrote:

> *It is unworthy of excellent [persons] to lose hours like slaves in the labor of calculation which could be safely relegated to anyone else if machines were used.*

Drawing on Pascal's work, he invented a device known as the *Leibniz wheel*. This device did addition, subtraction, multiplication, and division automatically. Machines based on Leibniz's concepts played a major role as recently as

FIGURE 1–1   Blaise Pascal and his calculator.

World War II, and some are still in use. Leibniz was also the first Western thinker to investigate binary arithmetic. He had a vision for reducing reasoning to calculation and was the first person to propose the idea that a machine could be used to test hypotheses. These ideas subsequently became the foundation for symbolic logic.

The next period of major advancement in computation was the nineteenth century. Once again there were theoretical advances in systematizing reasoning and practical advances in improving computational methods. One of the most important figures of this time was Charles Babbage (1791–1871). Babbage was a founding member of the Royal Astronomical Society in England, and he was the first recipient of its gold medal, for the work "Observations on the Application of Machinery to the Computation of Mathematical Tables." He developed the concepts for two machines, the "difference engine" and the "analytic engine," which were both steam-powered computers. Ada Byron, Countess of Lovelace (see Figure 1–2), was Babbage's colleague who developed the first "programs" for these computers; she is often recognized for this work as the world's first computer programmer. Byron also wrote the following about these computers and their capabilities:

The Analytical Engine has no pretensions whatever to originate anything. It can do whatever we know how to order it to perform. It can follow analyses; but it has no power of anticipating any analytical relations or truths. Its province is to assist us in making available what we are already acquainted with.

FIGURE 1–2   Ada Byron, Countess of Lovelace.

A Swedish printer, Pehr George Scheutz, succeeded in building a difference engine, which was displayed in London in 1854.

The difference engine was a highly specialized machine, designed only to assist in the computation of mathematical tables. It did this by using a polynomial to approximate the function to be tabulated and then computing the value of the polynomial. The analytic engine was much closer in concept to a modern general-purpose computer. It consisted of a "store" (now called memory) and a "mill" (now called a central processor). It operated by means of punched cards that contained a series of operations (i.e., a program) and data. Babbage's idea of using cards came from observing an invention that revolutionized weaving—the Jacquard loom—which used punched cards that encoded weaving patterns to automate the weaving process. Babbage, like Pascal, was limited by the imprecise technology of his time and also by his own temperament. He never succeeded in developing a working model of the analytic engine.

A relatively recent theoretical advancement of Aristotle's original work on reasoning was made by George Boole (1815–1864). Boole was born in London of lower-middle-class parents and was largely self-educated. He taught himself Latin and Greek by the time he was 16 and subsequently learned French, Italian, and German. Boole also taught himself mathematics, mastering virtually all the mathematics of his time. His major contribution was *An Investigation of the Laws of Thought*, published in 1854. In this work he set out to do for reasoning what algebra had done for arithmetic—that is, he wanted to identify fundamental operations and variables and represent them symbolically. For example, he denoted the logical operator **or** by + and **and** by *. He introduced variables that had only two values—1 for **true** and 0 for **false**—and he made a thorough study of the algebra of expressions that contain such variables. Although little was done with Boole's ideas for over 50 years, they became a foundation for the modern study of formal logic. Boole's notions again bore fruit nearly 100 years later when they formed the basis for the fundamental circuitry of the arithmetic-logic unit of a digital computer. Today these expressions are known as *Boolean expressions*, and they are so prevalent in the discipline of computing that we shall study them in various parts of this text and laboratory work.

Practical computational needs increased during the nineteenth and twentieth centuries. The advance of science produced increasingly complex equations that required considerable time and effort to solve. Another kind of computational need arose in the U. S. Census Bureau. Prior to 1890 the census had been tabulated by hand. However, the rapid growth of the U.S. population in the nineteenth century made hand tabulation of the census no longer feasible. In 1890, a new punched-card technology invented by a mechanical engineer, Herman Hollerith, was used to tabulate the census. Hollerith's technology proved much faster than manual methods and also made it possible to ask more questions on the census form, thus providing more useful information. This success led Hollerith to set up his own company, the Tabulating Machine Company, in 1896. Later this company became International Business Machines, Inc. (IBM).

During the nineteenth century, mathematicians made great headway in applying the Greeks' axiomatic method in the study of geometry and arithmetic to many other areas of mathematics. Building on this foundation, early-twentieth-century mathematicians made major theoretical breakthroughs. A most influential mathematician of the time was David Hilbert (1862–1943), who proposed that mathematicians find a single logico-mathematical axiomatic system from which all mathematics could be derived. He believed that such a system would be consistent, in the sense that it could never lead to the proof of two contradictory assertions. However, Kurt Gödel (1906–1978) proved in 1931 that Hilbert's proposal could never be realized. Gödel showed that *any* formal system sufficiently general to contain the arithmetic of the natural numbers either must be inconsistent or must contain statements that can be neither proved nor disproved. *That is, there are mathematical problems which are inherently unsolvable.* Thus, the ancient problem of systematizing reasoning had been advanced to the point where a limit to reasoning itself had been discovered. Gödel's work revolutionized mathematicians' views of their discipline.

Gödel's discovery also had an immediate practical effect by forcing mathematicians and logicians to address the question of what exactly it means to say that we have a method for solving a problem. Several answers to this question were proposed; the most influential was one published in 1936 by an English logician, Alan Turing (1912–1954). In this paper he showed that an "effective computation" could be represented in the form of a particular kind of abstract machine, which has subsequently come to be called a *Turing machine*. Although the Turing machine was a major theoretical development, its greatest impact occurred about 10 years later, when it influenced the design of the digital computer.

Simultaneous with these theoretical advances, major advances occurred as well in the design of computational equipment. In 1893, Leonardo Torres y Quevedo (1852–1936) proposed an electromechanical machine based on Babbage's concepts. By 1928, Hollerith's punched-card tabulator was being used to make tables of the moon's position in the sky; thus, what had been designed as a business machine was now being used for scientific purposes. The need for more effective scientific calculating equipment led Wallace J. Eckert (1902–1971), who was trained as an astronomer, to propose to IBM several extensions to their business tabulating machines for scientific uses. Another person who was actively involved in the design of electromechanical digital computers was Howard T. Aiken (1900–1973). In 1937, Aiken identified four capacities of computing equipment that would be needed in the sciences but were not available on the business machines of his time:

- The ability to handle both positive and negative numbers

- The ability to utilize various mathematical functions

- The ability to operate fully automatically

- The ability to carry out long calculations in their natural sequence

Collaborating with a group of IBM engineers, Aiken and his associates designed and built a machine with these capabilities in 1944. This machine, the Mark I, was electromechanical; it could multiply two numbers in about 6 seconds and divide two numbers in about 12 seconds. It was controlled by a paper tape on which its instructions were written. A similar machine was built by Bell Telephone Laboratories between 1937 and 1940. Several larger versions were subsequently produced. They were built using electromechanical switches called relays.

Another important breakthrough during this period appeared in a master's thesis written by Claude E. Shannon at the Massachusetts Institute of Technology. Shannon showed how the analysis of complicated switching circuits could be carried out by the use of Boolean algebra. This provided an important link between the *theory* of computation and the *design* of computing machines, opening the way to a systematic approach to the design of switching circuits.

The first fully electronic digital computer was designed by the physicist John V. Atanasoff (1903–), an associate professor at Iowa State University, with the assistance of a graduate student named Clifford E. Berry. Atanasoff was concerned with finding an efficient means for solving systems of simultaneous linear equations. The ABC (*A*tanasoff *B*erry *C*omputer), a vacuum tube machine, was built in 1940 to assist with this problem. It used binary arithmetic and was specialized for one purpose. Although it never became a serious computing tool, the ABC was a major breakthrough. It had a direct influence on the thinking of John W. Mauchly, who designed ENIAC, the first large-scale fully electronic digital computer. ENIAC was designed in late 1943 and early 1944 and was completed in late 1945. Its design was quite similar to the electromechanical machines which had gone before it; it contained about 18,000 vacuum tubes and 1500 relays.

During the development of the ENIAC, John von Neumann (1903–1957), a mathematician at the Institute for Advanced Study at Princeton University, became interested in computer design. Von Neumann earned his Ph.D. in mathematics, minoring in experimental physics and chemistry, at the young age of 22. By the time he reached 23, von Neumann had already become a world-renowned mathematician. He had substantial training in formal logic and worked with David Hilbert in his efforts to axiomatize mathematics. But von Neumann also had significant interests in applied mathematics, especially in problems of fluid flow. Mathematical models for fluid flow require the use of nonlinear partial differential equations; this type of equation is particularly hard to solve algebraically. Methods existed for approximating solutions to these equations, but they required extensive and time-consuming calculations. Thus von Neumann's interests united both the ancient quests mentioned earlier—the quest to systematize logic and the quest to find a means to carry out calculations quickly and accurately.

Von Neumann began to work with the ENIAC project in August 1944 (see Figure 1–3). He took part in discussions about the design of a new machine, to be called EDVAC, that would correct some of the deficiencies of ENIAC. Von Neumann quickly assumed responsibility for designing the logical structure of EDVAC. He made several major contributions during his work on this project that set the course of computing for many years to come; his standard for logic design served as a model for many subsequent developments. These contributions included:

- A notation for describing the logical aspects of computer circuitry (adapted from a notation that had been used earlier in medicine to describe the nervous system).

- A detailed instruction set for EDVAC.

- The *stored program concept*—the notion that a program and the data it uses can be stored in memory.

FIGURE 1–3   John von Neumann and the ENIAC computer.

- The first stored program, which sorted and merged numbers in a list.

- The notion of *serial operation*—the idea that since a computer operates very quickly, a task can be broken down into a sequence of steps performed one at a time. Since only one step needed to be done at a time, EDVAC's circuitry was greatly simplified over that of ENIAC.

- Binary arithmetic. Unlike ENIAC, which used decimal arithmetic, ED-VAC used binary notation to store and manipulate numbers and instructions.

These contributions were so influential, in fact, that we still use the term *von Neumann machine* to describe that class of modern computers that possesses these basic operational characteristics.

Computer design has evolved rapidly in many directions since the development of EDVAC. The *first generation* of computer "hardware" (until approximately 1959) used vacuum tubes; hence, these early machines were expensive, large, and somewhat unreliable, and they consumed great amounts of energy. The *second generation* (roughly 1959–1964) saw the replacement of vacuum tubes with transistors. These machines were smaller, cheaper, and more reliable than their predecessors. The *third generation* (roughly 1965–1970) was characterized by the introduction of integrated circuits—miniaturized circuits containing many transistors. The *fourth generation* of computers uses LSI (large-scale integration) or VLSI (very large-scale integration) circuitry. Memory has also changed considerably—from the delay lines of ENIAC and EDVAC to magnetic cores to high-speed semiconductor technology.

Software has also changed dramatically in the four decades since EDVAC. Early machines had to be programmed in *machine language*, which has a tedious binary representation. For example, the following machine language program adds two integers:

```
10100101   00000001
01100101   00000010
10000101   00000011
```

In the early 1950s, symbolic machine languages, called *assembly languages*, were developed. In assembly language the program that adds two integers can be written:

```
LOAD A
ADD  B
STO  C
```

In the late 1950s and early 1960s the first *high-level languages* were developed. FORTRAN (*for*mula *trans*lator) was the first of these, developed by John Backus in 1954. Other higher-level languages include COBOL (*com*mon *b*usiness-*o*riented *l*anguage), developed by Grace Murray Hopper (see Figure 1–4) and others in 1960; and C++, developed by Kernighan, Ritchie, and Stroustrup in the 1980s. A C++ statement to compute the sum C of two integers, A and B, can be written:

```
C = A + B ;
```

You will learn the C++ language in great detail as you study Chapters 2 through 7 in this text and the accompanying laboratory manual.

The field of computing remains dynamic in the 1990s. One special area is the design of *parallel processors*. This is a move away from the von Neumann design. As computers become applied to larger and larger problems, von Neumann's assumption that electronic speed was sufficiently fast that all steps could be done sequentially has proved to be invalid. Thus there is much interest in designing machines that can carry out many operations simultaneously. Programming languages have also developed considerably in recent years. For instance, *object-oriented languages*, which allow the programmer to isolate different parts of a program from one another, enable the development of more

FIGURE 1–4   Grace Murray Hopper.

reliable software. In fact, C++ supports object-oriented programming, and we shall explore some of these features also in this text. Computer networking is also a more focused area of development. Computers no longer exist in isolation; rather, many computers share resources and can communicate with each other in increasingly complex and useful ways.

THEORY, ABSTRACTION, DESIGN, AND THE SOCIAL CONTEXT

The discipline of computing can be viewed as comprising three distinct *paradigms*, or modes of approach, which are called *theory*, *abstraction*, and *design*. Moreover, all three paradigms exist within a very definite social context. That is, computation and the artifacts that surround it exist most generally for the purpose of enabling social, scientific, governmental, business, and international systems to work effectively and accomplish things that they could not otherwise accomplish. Computer scientists, more than professionals in the other sciences, are more keenly influenced in their work by this social context in which modern-day computation finds itself.

A person who works within the *theory* paradigm tends to take the mathematician's point of view, and therefore is concerned with formal definitions, axioms, theorems, and proofs as underlying media for the exploration of ideas and thoughts about computation. The process of *abstraction* is rooted in the sciences. Like the study of physics, chemistry, and biology, the scientific point of view of computing is engaged with the formation of hypotheses, construction of models, making predictions, running experiments, and testing results. *Design* has roots in engineering. The engineering point of view of computing is interested in system feasibility, costs, efficiency, and alternatives. The engineering-oriented computer professional will therefore be engaged with such activities as assessing requirements, formulating specifications, preparing and implementing a design, and testing and evaluating that design.

These three paradigms are complementary and interdependent whenever they are used in computing. That is, solving most computing problems requires some combination of theory, abstraction, and design. Thus, computer scientists and computer engineers are best served when they develop at least an appreciation for all three of these paradigms, even though they may eventually specialize in only one or two.

In retrospect, we can see examples of all three of these modes of thought throughout the history of computing. The ancient Greeks used theory when they developed the axiomatic method and studied the formal patterns of reasoning, and they used abstraction when they took ordinary reasoning, observed patterns in it, and formulated other patterns. The Babylonians and Egyptians, in contrast, preferred abstraction and design over theory. They used abstraction in formulating problems in standard forms, such as compound interest problems, and they used design in developing methods for solving such problems.

Viète's introduction of algebra involved abstraction (rendering problems in symbolic form); Napier's invention of logarithms involved theory; and the invention of the slide rule involved design. Galileo's work involved both abstraction and theory—abstraction in that he used mathematical tools to model events and processes in the physical world and gathered data to test models and theory insofar as he used mathematical techniques to work with those models. Schickard's and Pascal's efforts in building early computational devices were triumphs of design, as was Babbage's work. Boole's work is a good example of both theory and abstraction: In attempting to model reasoning using symbols, he was using abstraction, and in working with the model to deduce conclusions, he was using theory. Quevedo, Hollerith, Eckert, Aiken, and Atanasoff all made major contributions to design. Hilbert, Gödel, and Turing made major contributions to theory.

It is important to note, though, that two important figures in the history of computing—Leibniz and von Neumann—utilized all three modes of thought in significant ways. Leibniz used theory in investigating binary arithmetic. His vision for reducing reasoning to calculation was an attempt to model reasoning symbolically, and thus it involved abstraction. And his development of the Leibniz wheel is an example of design. Similarly, von Neumann's knowledge and use of the work of Gödel and Turing contributed to theory. His formulation of the stored program concept and the sequential operation of the central processor are examples of abstraction. And his rendering of these notions in a detailed proposal for the instruction set and logical circuitry of EDVAC are instances of design.

In this text, we explore all three methods of thought. Our goal is to provide a repertoire of intellectual tools that will enable you to appreciate and solve a variety of problems relating to computing. In the next six chapters you will use theory, abstraction, and design as we develop MAPS—a *m*ethod for *a*lgorithmic *p*roblem *s*olving. In Chapters 8 and 9, we examine what happens "behind the scenes" when a computer executes a program. In Chapters 10 and 11 we consider some of the social, ethical, and professional issues that confront the discipline of computing today and in the future.

THE NINE SUBJECT AREAS OF COMPUTING

The processes of theory, abstraction, and design, along with their social context, influence work in nine different major subject areas that make up the discipline of computing, as depicted in Figure 1–5.

The nine subject areas identified in the oval area in the figure encompass a wide range of topics, far wider than can be covered in a single introductory text. However, some areas contain topics that are more central to a beginning study of the discipline, and these are placed in the inner oval in Figure 1–5. We introduce these four central subject areas as follows.

- **Algorithms and data structures**   Specific methodologies and models are used for representing information and solving computational problems. As mentioned above, we develop a specific methodology for solving algorithmic problems in the next six chapters; we use two simple data structures, lists and arrays, in Chapters 4, 5, and 6.

- **Programming languages**   In order to represent solutions to algorithmic problems, programmers use an "artificial" style of language that can be both understood by humans and interpreted by computers. We use the C++ language as a vehicle in this text for representing programs. Most chapters in this text and laboratory manual are full of expressions in this notational style.

- **Architecture**   We need to learn how computers are organized and designed so that they can efficiently and accurately carry out the steps of a program. The von Neumann machine is an early example of a particular computer architecture. Chapters 8 and 9 discuss a modern descendant of this architecture.

- **Software methodology and engineering**   Programmers need methods designed for effectively creating reliable, efficient, and safe software systems on computers. Chapters 2 through 7 introduce some basic principles of software methodology, including both formal and informal methods for ensuring reliability of software. Chapter 10 discusses the important social issue of software error control and risk management.

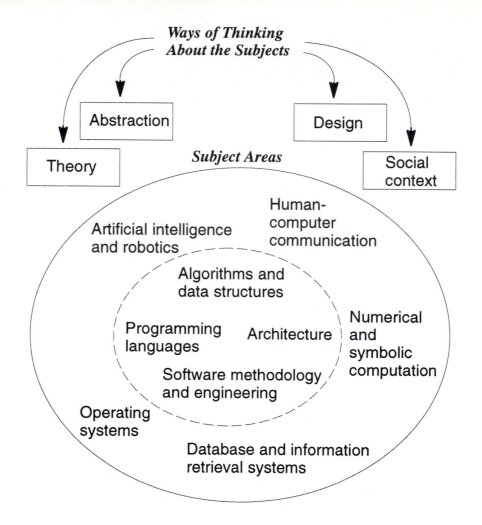

FIGURE 1–5   The nine subject areas, three processes, and social context of the discipline of computing.

COMPUTERS, PROGRAMS, AND DAILY LIFE

Before we begin our formal study of computing, we need to take a look at the real world; it is important to convince ourselves that the principles and practices that this text explores are strongly related to everyday life. History has already shown us that computing has existed in one form or another since the ancient Greeks. Our daily experience tells us, furthermore, that computers, algorithms, problem-solving, and programs are ubiquitous and have fundamental effects on how we conduct ourselves.

We often hear or utter the phrase "I've been programmed" in reference to tasks performed slavishly in the same way over and over again—tasks like taking out the garbage every Wednesday, washing the dishes every evening, following a recipe to cook a meal, or conducting a bank transaction at an automatic teller machine (ATM).

For example, the act of following the steps of a recipe in *Betty Crocker's Picture Cookbook*, we are effectively being "programmed" to perform a task, such as preparing fried chicken (see Figure 1–6).

HOW TO PREPARE CHICKEN FOR FRYING

Cut in halves, quarters, or pieces.

Wash, dry well, and flour pieces by shaking several at a time in a paper bag containing . . .

1 cup GOLD MEDAL flour
2 tsp. salt
1/4 tsp. pepper
1/2 tsp. celery salt
1 tsp. paprika (if desired)

FRIED CHICKEN

Crisp and tender . . . according to the best Southern traditions.

Prepare *young, tender* Fryers as above. Place halves, or quarters (in heavy deep skillet) in 1/2" hot fat (part butter) skin side down. Brown on both sides and cover tightly. Cook over very low heat until tender (35 to 40 min.). To crisp the crust . . . remove the cover and cook 5 to 10 min. longer. Use the leftover flour plus extra, if needed, to make cream gravy (p. 356).

FIGURE 1–6   A recipe for preparing fried chicken. (Source: *Betty Crocker's Picture Cookbook*, General Mills, 1950, p. 283)

In the vernacular of computing, the recipe itself is called the "program," the process of preparing fried chicken from this recipe is called "program execution," and the person who actually prepares the chicken is playing the role of the "computer."

In general, a program can be viewed as a series of steps to be performed in a particular order to accomplish the goal. In the case of preparing fried chicken, we see that the recipe calls for the following steps to be carried out in order:

Step 1: Prepare fryers.
Step 2: Brown on both sides.
Step 3: Cook until tender.
Step 4: Crisp the crust.
Step 5: Make cream gravy.

Failure to carry out these steps in the given order will have a result different from that which is commonly known as fried chicken.

The authors of the recipes in a cookbook are themselves the "programmers," and as such they have tested their recipes for "correctness." For example, they took steps to ensure that the fried chicken recipe, when properly executed, does indeed guarantee a dish that resembles fried chicken in the way that we understand it.

In this text, you will play the role of the designers of recipes for others to follow. However, there will be a major difference between the programs that you design and the recipes that appear in the *Cookbook*. That is, programs are designed so that they can be executed by a computer rather than a person. Thus, the language we use to describe programs is constrained by the limits of the vocabulary of a computer rather than that of a person. Nevertheless, we shall see that our programs will often be able to model activities that might just as well have been carried out by a person instead of a computer.

In this sense, computer programs are *simulations* of a human problem-solving that can be done either more accurately or more efficiently by a computer than by a person. For example, consider the ubiquitous ATM, which is programmed to simulate the work of a bank teller in performing simple transactions—withdrawals and deposits—for customers (see Figure 1–7). Thus, the program is a series of steps that are controlled through a dialogue with a customer. For instance, the first question asked, in effect, is:

What is your account number?

In response, the customer enters her ATM identification card. The next question is:

Do you want to make a withdrawal or a deposit?

Depending on the answer, the program guides the ATM through a series of steps that assist the customer in completing the transaction, with questions like:

What is the amount of your deposit?

and

Would you like to make another transaction?

FIGURE 1–7   An automatic teller machine.

Each of these individual actions is quite simple, and thousands of them are performed each day in every bank. Each one, however, must be carried out reliably and efficiently, so that the integrity of the banking process is maintained. The computer program that controls the activities of an ATM, therefore, must be designed with care and precision. We shall write programs later in this course that simulate some of the ATM's activities.

WHY STUDY COMPUTING?

Thus, the study of computing is more than learning to program the operation of a machine. Rather, it is the study of a mode of human thinking that has been evolving for thousands of years. The resulting discipline of computing has had enormous impact on our culture and our daily lives. In the past fifty years, computing has enabled many advances in the sciences and professions that would not otherwise have been possible. Understanding the underlying thought process that characterizes the application of computers to daily life, becoming skilled in that thought process, and being able to reflect on its overall potentials and limitations can be enjoyable and exciting experiences as we prepare to meet the challenges of contemporary society.

This text is designed to introduce the breadth and vitality of the discipline of computing. Whether you intend to major in computer science or take a laboratory-intensive, broader study of the discipline, this text offers a unique level of engagement. You should look for four major themes as you study various parts of this text and the accompanying laboratory material:

- The discipline of computing is firmly grounded in mathematical logic. It is also helpful to have a basic understanding of mathematical functions, since many computational paradigms use the notion of a function as their model. Chapter 2 introduces the fundamental ideas, Chapter 3 shows how logic and problem solving are interrelated, and Chapter 8 shows how logic and the design of computers are interrelated.

- The development of reliable and effective programs (software) involves a systematic approach to problem solving. We shall introduce this approach, which we call MAPS, at the end of Chapter 2. We then carefully develop and illustrate its various facets in Chapters 3 through 7. This is the central part of the course and is fully supported by weekly C++ programming work, as covered in the laboratory manual.

- The study of computing as a discipline would be incomplete without gaining a basic understanding of how computers are designed and how they carry out the steps of the programs that we write. This is the subject of discussion in Chapters 8 and 9. Appropriate laboratory work supports this area, too, in the form of a simulated computer called MARINA.

- Finally, the study of computing cannot take place in isolation from the social and professional context in which the discipline is embedded, and which supplies it with a reason for being. In Chapter 10, we engage two fundamental areas where computing and social issues come together: (1) software and intellectual property issues and (2) sofware reliability.

Hopefully, this introduction has piqued your interest in this fascinating and dynamic field of study. The remainder of this text takes a very broad view of the discipline. While you will gain a rigorous programming experience, both here and in the laboratory parts of this course, the message that computing is an enormously dynamic and rich discipline will also come through. Enjoy your work, and think often about the larger issues that the various exercises in this text suggest!

SUMMARY

This discussion provides a historical overview of the development of the discipline of computer science and computer engineering, or *computing*. The points of view of *theory, abstraction, design,* and *social context* originated with the ancient Greeks and Babylonians. The discipline of computing can be viewed as an application of these points of view to nine distinct subject areas. Four of these areas—*algorithms and data structures, programming languages, architecture,* and *software methodology and engineering*—are central to the discipline and form a basis for this text. The notion of programming has many analogies in day-to-day life, and effective procedures for solving computational problems are all around us.

EXERCISES

1–1 Decide whether each of the following is an example of theory, abstraction, or design:

a. Gunter's invention of the forerunner of the slide rule
b. Descartes' discovery of analytic geometry
c. The invention of the Jacquard loom
d. Shannon's master's thesis
e. Mauchly's work on ENIAC
f. Hopper's development of COBOL
g. Von Neumann's efforts to solve the equations of fluid flow problems
h. Byron's programs for the analytic engine

1–2 Use the information in Figure 1–6 and the following recipe for braised chicken to make a list of all the steps that would be needed in order to prepare braised chicken.

BRAISED CHICKEN

The fried chicken of the Middle West.

Prepare as for Fried Chicken–*except* use a Larger Fryer and cut in serving pieces. After browning, add 3 tbsp. water. Cover; cook over low heat on top of stove, or bake in a preheated oven . . . 325° (slow mod.) until tender (45 to 60 min.). In either case, remove cover the last 10 min. to crisp crust.

Source: *Betty Crocker's Picture Cookbook*, General Mills.

1–3 Identify at least two specific activities in your own life in which you were primarily involved in each of the modes of thought—theory, abstraction, and design.

1–4 In programming, we use the terms *input* and *output*, respectively, to characterize the items of information that go into a program's execution and the items of information that result after all the steps have been carried out. For instance, for the fried chicken recipe, the input is the list of ingredients—flour, salt, pepper, celery salt, paprika, and the fryer—and the output is the plate of fried chicken itself.

    a.   What is the input for the braised chicken recipe? What is the output?

    b.   What is the input for the ATM? What is the output?

1–5 Which of the following processes are algorithmic? Which not? Explain why.

    a.   Changing a flat tire.

    b.   Brushing your teeth.

    c.   Falling in love.

    d.   Drawing a geometric figure with straight edge and compass.

    e.   Deciding whether an event A was caused by another event B.

1–6 Identify two processes in your life which are primarily algorithmic and two which are not. Explain why you classified each as you did.

CHAPTER 2

COMPUTERS AND PROBLEM SOLVING

The range of problems that can be solved using computers is very broad indeed. Many of these problems, such as the ATM example in the previous chapter, are *mathematical* in nature and therefore involve computation with numbers and the application of mathematical principles. Others are *graphical* in nature and involve the manipulation of graphic objects, such as points, lines, rectangles, and circles. Still others involve the manipulation of English-language *text* and therefore use alphabetic characters and words as basic units of information.

More often than not, however, the most interesting and useful computational problems require that the computer manage information in *all three* of these domains—mathematics, graphics, and text. For example, when using a computer to simulate the moves of a tic-tac-toe game, we wish not only to see the sequence of moves (represented as text) but also to view a display of the board after each move is played (represented graphically).

A fundamental reason for studying a mixture of mathematical, graphical, and text-processing problems in a first course in computing is that the problem-solving principles and techniques learned in any one of these areas apply equally to problems in the other two areas. This suggests that there is an underlying and unifying set of ideas that govern how computers and programs behave. These ideas, in turn, influence our thinking when we approach a particular problem to be solved with a computer. This unifying set of ideas combine into a process known as *algorithmic problem solving*.

In this chapter, we begin the study of algorithmic problem solving by exploring how the *theory* of mathematical sets and functions helps to explain the basic structure of computers and computer programs. We also learn about the *design* of computers and how that design is used to model the solutions to algorithmic problems. Finally, we begin to look at the process of *abstraction* by presenting MAPS, a methodology for modeling solutions to algorithmic problems in the form of computer programs. Thus, in these ways, we may begin to appreciate how the three processes of theory, abstraction, and design complement each other indispensibly in the study of computing.

ALGORITHMS AND PROBLEMS

The concepts of algorithmic problems, algorithms, algorithmic language, and algorithmic behavior are fundamental to the activity of problem solving with computers and therefore are central to the entire discipline of computing. Thus, we need to develop a strong grasp of what an algorithm is, and isn't, and what an algorithmic problem is in order to engage in effective problem-solving activities. The following definitions serve as a starting point for our discussion:

Definition An *algorithmic problem* is any problem whose solution can be expressed in a list of executable instructions. By executable we mean an instruction which an independent executor (human or machine) can actually perform, or carry out, in a step-by-step manner.

Algorithmic problems have many (often an infinite number of) *instances*. That is, consider the problem of processing a transaction at an ATM. Each different transaction represents a particular instance of the ATM problem, since it may be either a deposit or a withdrawal, it may affect the balance in any one of a million different bank accounts, and it may involve a distinct amount of money.

Definition An *algorithm* is a list of instructions specifying a precise description of a step-by-step process that is guaranteed to terminate, after a finite number of steps, with the correct answer for every particular instance of an algorithmic problem that may occur.

Examples of algorithmic problems and algorithms occur everywhere in day-to-day life, both inside and outside the discipline of computing. Table 2–1 lists some additional examples.

TABLE 2–1   SOME ALGORITHMIC PROBLEMS AND ALGORITHMS

Algorithmic problem	Algorithm
Preparing fried chicken	Any particular recipe for preparing fried chicken
Knitting a sweater	Any set of instructions for knitting a sweater
Traveling around the world	Any itinerary for traveling around the world
Completing a college degree	Any program of study to complete a college degree

An algorithm is always designed, therefore, for the purpose of solving a problem in *all* its instances. However, for any particular problem there are usually several alternative algorithms that can serve as solutions to that problem. For example, a particular recipe for preparing fried chicken is one of several alternative algorithms for solving the general problem of preparing fried chicken. A student who majors in computer science will follow a very different algorithm for completing a college degree than a student who majors in environmental science or philosophy.

Nevertheless, each of the algorithms in Table 2–1 exhibits the four fundamental characteristics given in the definition:

- Exactness ("specifying a precise description")

- Effectiveness ("guaranteed to give a correct answer")

- Guaranteed termination ("terminate after a finite number of steps")

- Generality ("every particular instance")

Some algorithms, when carried out, can be completed in a short time, while others can take a very long time. Yet all algorithms terminate. Therefore, any description of a step-by-step process that does not terminate is not an algorithm. For example, the process of listing all the positive integers, one by one, is not an algorithm since it goes on forever.

Of course, in the discipline of computing, we associate the notion of algorithm with a process to be carried out by a computer rather than by a person. In principle, every algorithm we describe for a computer could effectively be carried out by hand (given enough time and chalkboard space). We rely upon the computer to carry out the steps of an algorithm because it can complete the task in a fraction of the time that we could and because it is not as error-prone as people are when carrying out these tasks. That is, computers are *fast* and they are *accurate*.

However, not all algorithms can be carried out by computers. A computer can carry out only those algorithms whose individual steps involve tasks it can understand and execute. For example, the preparation of fried chicken requires tasks like "turn on the oven" and "debone the chicken," tasks which a computer is ill-prepared to carry out. We therefore must first understand the kinds of fundamental tasks that a computer *can* carry out, so that we can effectively build algorithms that contain only these kinds of tasks.

As a starting point, consider the simple model of computation shown in Figure 2–1. In this model, a computation is viewed as having three parts: an *input*, a *process*, and an *output*. The *input* is a collection of information that is required for the algorithm's steps to be effectively carried out; that is, it represents the starting point for an algorithm. For example, the input to the ATM could be any particular account number, transaction type, and amount of money. The *process* is a complete list of the steps that represent the algorithm itself. The *output* is the result that would be obtained by carrying out these steps with the given input.

Here is a more concrete example. Let's consider the algorithm we would follow to calculate a grade point average (GPA). In this case, the input can be any list of numeric grades in the range 0 to 4 (0 = F, 1 = D, 2 = C, 3 = B, and 4 =

FIGURE 2–1   The input-process-output model of computation.

A). The output is the average of those grades (that is, the quotient of their sum and their count), and the process is a description of the individual steps that are required to carry out the algorithm. If someone asked us to perform this algorithm by hand, we could follow a series of steps like those in the following process description:

```
Step 1.   Obtain the input list of grades.
Step 2.   Compute n = the number of grades in the list.
Step 3.   Compute Sum = the sum of the grades in the list.
Step 4.   Compute GPA = Sum / n.
Step 5.   Report the resulting GPA.
```

Any particular collection of grades, like

```
2 3 3 2 1 4 3 2
```

represents an *input* fo the GPA problem. If the steps are carried out carefully, the number

```
2.5
```

represents the *output* for this particular input. Together, this input and output represents one particular *instance* of the GPA problem.

When we write such process descriptions, we make some tacit assumptions about the behavior of the input-process-output model of Figure 2–1. Our first assumption is that the number of grades in the input cannot be predicted by the algorithm, though it must always be finite. Our second assumption is that in order to compute anything about these grades, the algorithm needs to obtain them—that is, to transfer them physically into the process part of the model from the input part. This physical transfer is called *reading*, in the vernacular of computing. Finally, in order to reveal the results of the computation, we must physically transfer them from the process part of the model to the output part. This physical transfer is called *writing*.

A diagram of the various units of the computer that support the input-process-output model is shown in Figure 2–2. When we use a computer to assist in solving this algorithmic problem, the instructions for the individual steps in the process description, along with the numerical values of Sum, n, and GPA, are physically stored in a place called the *memory* of the computer (see Figure 2–2). The *central processing unit* (CPU) of the computer contains the circuitry that carries out the steps in the process description. All input and output information originates in places that are physically distinct from the CPU. These include a keyboard, a display screen, a diskette, and a printer.

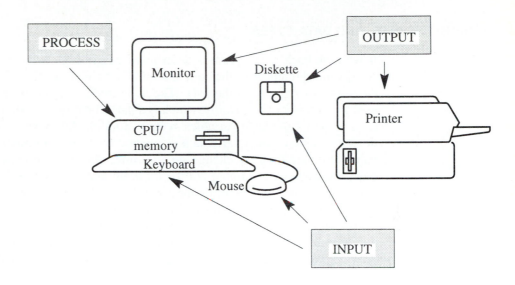

FIGURE 2–2   A computer realization of the input-process-output model.

Our third assumption is that the individually numbered steps in the process description will be carried out in the same order in which they are written. For example, we could not very well carry out step 5 before steps 1 through 4 have been completed and still claim that we were computing a GPA.

Our fourth assumption is that each individual step itself is effective—that it includes only those capabilities that the computer has within its repertoire. For example, we have assumed that "Display" (step 5) is within the computer's repertoire of capabilities. Thus, whenever a step containing the word *display* is carried out, output information will appear on the monitor, regardless of where that step occurs within the algorithm.

These four assumptions are, in fact, fundamental for all algorithms that are developed for computers. Computers carry out the steps in an obedient fashion, beginning with the first, and will only carry out steps that are intelligible to them—that is, steps which describe tasks that are within their repertoire.

EXERCISES

2–1 Describe an algorithmic problem that you have encountered in your day-to-day life that is similar to those discussed in this section. Give two alternative algorithms that will solve this problem.

2–2 For the problem that you described in Exercise 2–1, describe its input and its output in general. Give two particular instances of that input and output.

VARIABLES, SETS, AND DATA TYPES

If we look back at the process description describing our GPA algorithm, we see several references to the computation of a value (e.g., Step 2. Compute $n = $ the number of grades in the list). The assignment implicit in these statements uses the concept of a *variable*, which is a named entity that can take on a value (n, Sum, and GPA are all variables in our example). Although in these computations the value of each variable is computed only once, in many situations the value of a variable may change several times during the computation. Moreover, the value of a variable will be different and, in general, is unpredictable from one instance of executing the algorithm to the next. For example, the value of the variable n will likely be different each time we execute the GPA algorithm. In order to understand the capabilities of computers, it is fundamental that we understand variables and the related *sets* of values that they may have. A set of values that a particular variable can have in an algorithm is called a *type*.

Variables

A variable is a notational device borrowed from mathematics that allows a powerful idea to be represented by a single symbol, creating brevity, clarity, and accuracy. Often we read phrases like, "Let x denote any letter of the alphabet." Thereafter, we can use the symbol x and understand precisely what we mean, because that symbol has been previously defined to stand for the precise notion "any member of the set $L = \{a, b, \ldots, z\}$." When used in this way, x is known as a "variable," since its particular value can vary among several different alternative values (26, to be exact).

> **Definition**   A *variable* is a symbol that is associated with a single value, which in turn can be any particular member of a well-defined set. During the steps of a computation, a variable's value can change from one member to another member of that set. The set upon which a particular variable is defined is called the *type* of that variable. In some programming contexts, the idea of a variable and its type is referred to as an *object* and its *class*.

For example, the variable x we just defined has type L. The variable n in our GPA example has type *positive integer*, since the number of grades that can be averaged may be 1, or 2, or 3, and so on.

In our definition of variable, we used the notion of a "member of a well-defined set." Before we continue, we take a look at the mathematical concept of a set.

Sets

Collections of objects or numbers are commonplace. We might think of the collection of people in a classroom, the collection of digits and letters on an automobile's license plate, or the collection of the names of the airlines that use the Chicago O'Hare airport. Mathematically, such collections are called *sets*. We can explain this notion more precisely as follows.

> **Definition**   A *set* is any well-defined collection of objects. Often the objects of a set share some common characteristic. A *member* of a set is any one of its constituent objects. A member of a set is said to *belong to* that set. If S is a set that contains the member x, we write $x \in S$ to denote that x belongs to S.

When we describe a set, we enclose its members between braces, { and }. The empty set, which has no members, is denoted either by { } or by ϕ. For example, the set whose members are the five days of the working week can be described as follows:

{ Monday, Tuesday, Wednesday, Thursday, Friday }

Some more examples of sets are given in Equations 2.1 through 2.6:

(2.1)   { 0, 1, 2, 3, 4, 5, 6, 7, 8, 9 } is the set whose members are the decimal digits.

(2.2)   { 0, 1 } is the set of digits for writing binary numbers.

(2.3)   { a, b, c, … , z } is the set of all lowercase letters of the alphabet.

(2.4)   { +, −, *, / } is the set of the four major arithmetic operations (addition, subtraction, multiplication, and division, respectively).

(2.5)   { 1, 2, …, 100 } is the set of integers from 1 to 100, inclusive.

(2.6) ϕ is the set of all oranges which are blue (presumably there aren't any such oranges!).

Notation   Note the use of commas and ellipses. Commas separate individual members of a set, while ellipses (…) denote continuation of a clearly established pattern, as in Equations 2.3 and 2.5.

Sets can also be written by stating the properties that all their elements have in common, for instance:

(2.7) $\{\, x \mid x \text{ is an integer and } 1 \le x \le 100 \,\}$

This notation requires a variable at the beginning, a vertical bar, and a description of the elements at the end. Equation 2.7 is read, "the set of all x such that x is an integer from 1 to 100, inclusive." Thus, this example defines, in an alternate style, the same set as in Equation 2.5. Equation 2.8 is another example of this alternative style of description:

(2.8) $\{\, p \mid p \text{ is a polynomial of degree 2} \,\}$

Typical members of the set described in Equation 2.8 are polynomials such as:

$$x^2 + 2x + 1$$
$$.01n^2 - 100n - 3$$
$$8000y^2 - 67$$

Some sets are finite in size, whereas others have an infinite number of members. For example, the sets described in Equations 2.1 through 2.7 are finite, while the set described in Equation 2.8 is infinite.

Definition   The *cardinality* of a finite set is the number of members of the set. The *empty set* contains no members, so it has cardinality 0, and is denoted by $\{\}$ or ϕ.

For example, the cardinality of the finite set described in Equation 2.3 is 26.

There are four sets that have special importance in computing as well as in mathematics:

$\mathbf{N} = \{\, 0, 1, 2, 3, \dots \,\}$	*Natural numbers*
$\mathbf{Z} = \{\dots, -3, -2, -1, 0, 1, 2, 3, \dots \}$	*Integers*
$\mathbf{R} = \{\, x \mid -\infty < x < +\infty \,\}$	*Real numbers*
$\mathbf{Z}_n = \{\, 0, 1, 2, 3, \dots, n-1 \,\}$	*Integers modulo n*

The first three of these are infinite. The last is finite and has cardinality n. For example, the set $\mathbf{Z}_2 = \{\, 0, 1 \,\}$ has cardinality 2; the set $\mathbf{Z}_{10} = \{\, 0, 1, \dots, 9\}$ has cardinality 10.

Because size of memory for representing the value of a variable is finite, the type of a variable, which is the set of values that the variable can take on, must also be finite. When we begin to write C++ programs in the laboratory, we shall encounter the types `int` and `float`, and we shall often use variables with these types. However, these types are not equivalent to the mathematical concepts of integer and real, as described above, precisely because the latter are infinite sets. Thus, in C++, the range of the `int` type is restricted, as is the range and precision of the `float` type. We will further discuss this restriction later.

Set Relationships

The order in which members appear when a set is listed does not matter; furthermore, duplicate occurrences of members are redundant. That is, $\{a, b, c\}$ and $\{b, a, c, a\}$ both represent the same set.

It often happens that all the members of one set are members of another set. For example, all the members of the set $V = \{a, e, i, o, u\}$ are also members of the set $L = \{a, b, \ldots, z\}$. The following definition formalizes these notions.

> **Definition**   If two sets A and B have the same members, then they are *equal*, which is denoted by $A = B$. If every member of A is also a member of B, then A is a *subset* of B, denoted by $A \subset B$. If A is a subset of B, then B is a *superset* of A, denoted by $B \supset A$. If both $A \subset B$ and $A \neq B$, then A is a *proper subset* of B. If *all* the members of a set or collection of sets are selected from some common set, that common set is called a *universal set.*

Note the distinction between *member* and *subset*. For example, let $A = \{0, 1, 2, 3, 4, 5, 6, 7\}$. Then the digit 0 is a member of A (denoted by $0 \in A$), and the set $\{0\}$ is a subset of A (denoted by $\{0\} \subset A$). It would be improper to say that 0 is a subset of A, since 0 itself is not a set. Similarly, it would be improper to say that $\{0\}$ is a member of A.

We often represent sets using Venn diagrams (see Figure 2–3). A *Venn diagram* is a drawing in which sets are depicted as labeled circles inside a rectangular box that represents the universal set from which their members are drawn.

Set Operations and Their Properties

Consider the following sets:

$S = \{\, 0, 1, 01, 10, 11, 00 \,\}$
$T = \{\, 1, 10, 100, 1000, 10000 \,\}$

The numbers 1 and 10 are the only numbers that are members of both sets, but there are nine other numbers in one or the other of S and T. The concepts of set intersection, union, and difference help us describe common members of sets in various ways.

> **Definition**   Let A and B be sets. The *union* of A and B, denoted by $A \cup B$, is the set whose members are in at least one of A or B. The *intersection* of A and B, denoted by $A \cap B$, is the set whose members are in both A and B. The

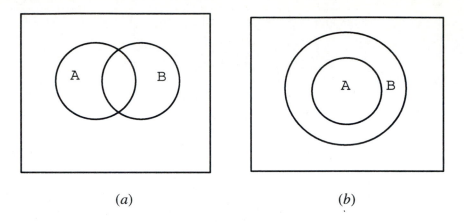

(a)   (b)

FIGURE 2–3   Venn Diagrams. (a) Two sets A and B which may have some members in common; (b) The relationship A ⊂ B.

difference (or *relative complement*) of A and B, denoted by $A \setminus B$, is the set whose members are in A but not in B.

Figure 2–4 shows Venn diagrams whose shaded areas represent the union, intersection, and difference of A and B. We can also write out some examples using set notation.

Let $A = \{1, 3, 5, 7, 9\}$ and $B = \{-3, -1, 1, 3, 5\}$. Then the following relationships hold:

$$A \cap B = \{1, 3, 5\}$$
$$A \cup B = \{-3, -1, 1, 3, 5, 7, 9\}$$
$$A \setminus B = \{7, 9\}$$

As another example, assume the following:

$A = \{\, p \mid p$ is a polynomial of the form $n^2 + bn$ and b is any
real constant $\}$

$B = \{\, p \mid p$ is a polynomial of the form $n^2 + c$ and c is any
real constant $\}$

Typical members of A are $n^2 + n$ and $n^2 + 45n$, while typical members of B are $n^2 - 3$ and $n^2 + 7$. Then the following hold:

$$A \cap B = \{\, n^2 \,\}$$

$A \cup B = \{\, p \mid p$ is a polynomial of the form $n^2 + bn + c$, where
$b = 0$ or $c = 0 \,\}$

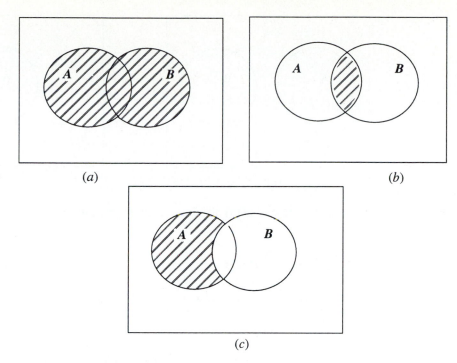

FIGURE 2–4   Venn Diagrams. (*a*) Union, (*b*) intersection, and (*c*) difference of sets *A* and *B*.

$$A \setminus B \ = \ \{ \, p \mid p \text{ is a polynomial of the form } n^2 + bn, \text{ where } b \ne 0 \, \}$$

The empty set ϕ turns out to be very useful. For example, if C is the set of consonants (not including the letter y) and V is the set of vowels (including the letter y), then $C \cap V = \phi$.

Definition   If the intersection of two sets is the empty set, they are called *disjoint* sets.

Definition   The *complement* of a set S is the set of all members of the universal set U that are not in S, and is denoted by S'.

For example, if C and V denote the consonants and the vowels, respectively, and U is the entire alphabet, then $C' = V$ and $V' = C$. That is, all letters that are not consonants are vowels, and conversely. (This assumes that the letter y is a vowel.) Figure 2–5 illustrates the notions of disjoint sets and complement in the form of Venn diagrams.

Example 2.1   Suppose x and y are integers. Let S be the set consisting of all possible pairs of integers (x, y). If we define the sets $A = \{(x, y) \mid x \ge 0$

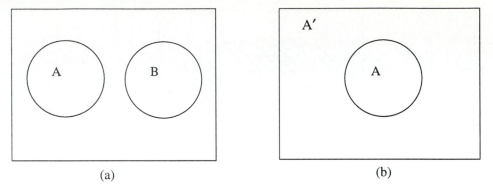

(a)   (b)

FIGURE 2–5   Venn diagrams representing (*a*) disjoint sets and (*b*) complement.

and $y \geq 0$} and $B = \{(x, y) \mid x < 0 \text{ and } y < 0\}$, then A and B are disjoint. This is illustrated in Figure 2–6, where the shaded areas represent the sets A and B. Note furthermore that $B \neq A'$, since $A' = \{(x, y) \mid x < 0 \text{ or } y < 0\}$.

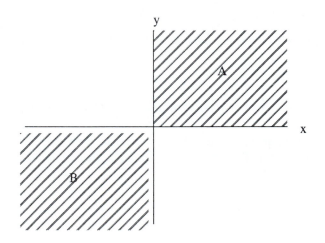

FIGURE 2–6   Two disjoint sets.

Properties of set operations   Arithmetic operations with numbers have certain properties, such as associativity, commutativity, inverses, and so forth. We use these properties automatically whenever we do arithmetic or simplify an algebraic equation. Sets and their operators have similar properties, and we often use these properties to help simplify complex set operations. The main properties of set operations are summarized in Table 2–2.

TABLE 2–2 PROPERTIES OF SETS AND THEIR OPERATIONS (*A* and *B* are any sets; *U* is the universal set upon which *A* and *B* are defined.)

Commutativity

$$A \cap B \equiv B \cap A$$

$$A \cup B \equiv B \cup A$$

Associativity

$$A \cap (B \cap C) \equiv (A \cap B) \cap C$$

$$A \cup (B \cup C) \equiv (A \cup B) \cup C$$

Distributivity

$$A \cap (B \cup C) \equiv (A \cap B) \cup (A \cap C)$$

$$A \cup (B \cap C) \equiv (A \cup B) \cap (A \cup C)$$

De Morgan's laws

$$(A \cap B)' \equiv A' \cup B'$$

$$(A \cup B)' \equiv A' \cap B'$$

Property of negation

$$(A')' \equiv A$$

Law of the excluded middle

$$A \cup A' \equiv U$$

Law of contradiction

$$A \cap A' \equiv \phi$$

$\cup$-simplification

$$A \cup A \equiv A$$

$$A \cup \phi \equiv A$$

$$A \cup U \equiv U$$

$\cap$-simplification

$$A \cap A \equiv A$$

$$A \cap U \equiv A$$

$$A \cap \phi \equiv \phi$$

Complementarity

$$U' \equiv \phi$$

$$\phi' \equiv U$$

Sets of strings   The type `string` is an important one in computing. Informally, a "string" is understood to be any contiguous sequence of characters from a predefined universal set, known as the *alphabet*. The standard alphabet in computer science is known as the ASCII (American Standard Code for Information Interchange) character set. Other alphabets exist, including EBCDIC for IBM mainframe computers. Here are some examples of sets whose members are strings:

Example 2.2   The set {aa, ab, ba, bb} is the set of all possible two-character strings from the alphabet {a, b}.

Example 2.3 M = {abc, acb, bac, bca, cab, cba} is the set of all strings that are a particular arrangement, or *permutation*, of the three letters a, b, and c. Note that there are six such permutations.

Example 2.4 S = {0, 1, 01, 001, 100, 0100} is a set of strings over the alphabet {0, 1}. There are many other sets of strings over this alphabet, such as {1, 10, 100, 1000, 10000} and {0, 1} itself. We can put various restrictions on such sets. For example, {0, 1, 01, 10, 11, 00} is the set of all strings over {0,1} that have length 1 or 2.

Example 2.5 F = {abcd, abdc, acbd, acdb, adbc, adcb, bacd, badc, bcad, bcda, bdac, bdca, cabd, cadb, cbad, cbda, cdab, cdba, dabc, dacb, dbac, dbca, dcab, dcba} is the set of all permutations of the four letters a, b, c, and d. This can also be written as F = {p | p is a permutation of abcd}. Note that there are 24 such permutations.

Example 2.6   If A = {s | s is a string over {0, 1} that begins with 1}, then A' = {ε} ∪ {s | s is a string over {0, 1} that begins with 0}. Here, the symbol ε denotes the *empty string*, which has no characters. The notation {ε} means "the set containing a single member, which is the empty string ε." The empty set, ϕ, on the other hand, contains no strings.

Example 2.7   Let D denote the set of all permutations of abcd that end with d. Then D = {abcd, acbd, bacd, bcad, cabd, cbad}. If N = {p | p is a permutation of abcd}, then D is a proper subset of N, so that the intersection of D and N is D and the union of D and N is N.

Example 2.8   Let U = { u | u is any string over the alphabet {0, 1}, including the empty string ε}. Then U is a natural universal set for various sets of strings over the same alphabet, such as the set S = {ε, 0, 1, 00, 01, 10, 11} and T = {0, 01, 001, 0001, ...}. Note that S is not a subset of T, nor is T a subset of S. In most situations, the universal set over which particular sets of strings are defined is obvious and won't need to be explicitly mentioned.

Example 2.9   Suppose we have the following two sets of strings:

A = {p | p is a permutation of the string abcd that begins with a}
    = {abcd, abdc, acbd, acdb, adbc, adcb}

D = {p | p is a permutation of the string abcd that ends with d}
    = {abcd, acbd, bacd, bcad, cabd, cbad}

Then the intersection, union, and difference operations yield the following strings:

$$A \cap D = \quad \{\text{abcd, acbd}\}$$

$$A \cup D = \quad \{\text{abcd, abdc, acbd, acdb, adbc, adcb, bacd, bcad, cabd,}$$
$$\text{cbad}\}$$

$$A \setminus D = \{\text{abdc, acdb, adbc, adcb}\}$$

Note that each of A and D has 6 members and $A \cup D$ has only 10 members rather than 12, since abcd and acbd are members of both A and D.

EXERCISES

2–3 Express each of the following in set notation:

a. The strings over the alphabet $\{0, 1\}$ with length less than 5 and containing one or two 0s

b. The even integers

c. The set of all strings over the alphabet $\{a, b, c\}$ that have no duplicate symbols

d. The set of all permutations of the string 012

e. The set of all polynomials of degree 3 or less that have x as a factor

2–4 Let $A = \{(x, y) \mid x \geq 0 \text{ and } y \geq 0\}$ and $B = \{(x, y) \mid x \leq 1 \text{ and } y \leq 1\}$. Identify each of the following on an xy graph by shading the appropriate area.

a. $A \cap B$

b. $A \cup B$

c. $A \setminus B$

d. A'

e. U

2–5 Suppose s and t are strings over the alphabet $\{a, b, \ldots, z\}$. Then we can define strcat(s,t) as the string that results from concatenating s and t together. For example, if $s = $ abc and $t = $ xy, then str-

$\mathrm{cat(s,t)} = \mathrm{abcxy}$. Furthermore, if S and T are *sets* of such strings, we can define $\mathrm{strcat(S,T)}$ as the set of all strings that result from concatenating an arbitrary string s from S with an arbitrary string t from T. Suppose, for example, that $S = \{\varepsilon, \mathrm{x}, \mathrm{xy}, \mathrm{xyy}\}$ and $T = \{\varepsilon, \mathrm{y}, \mathrm{yx}, \mathrm{yxx}\}$. Find each of the following:

a. $\mathrm{strcat(S,T)}$

b. $\mathrm{strcat(T,S)}$

c. $S \cup T$

d. $S \cap T$

e. $S \setminus T$

f. $T \setminus S$

2–6 Suppose S and T are sets of strings. Find two examples of pairs S and T such that $\mathrm{strcat(S,T)} = S \cup T$.

2–7 Draw a Venn diagram for sets A and B, and then shade in the portion corresponding to each of the following sets:

a. $(A' \cap B') \cup (A \cap B)$

b. $(A \cup B)' \cup (A \setminus B)$

2–8 How many strings are there with length 2 or less, over the set $\{0, 1\}$? With length 3 or less, over the same set? With length n or less?

2–9 Determine whether each of the following is **true** or **false**.

a. $\{2,3,4\} \cup \{2,4,5,6\} = \{2,3,4,5,6\}$

b. $\{2,3,5\} \cap \{2,4,5,6\} \subset \{2,3,6\}$

c. $\{3,4,6,8\} \setminus \{2,4,7,8\} \supset \{3\}$

d. $(\phi \cap \{3,5,7,8\}) \cup \{3,7\} = \{3,5,7,8\}$

e. $\{2,3,5\} = \{5,2,3,2\}$

f. $\{2,4,5\} \subset \{1,2,4,5,6\}$

g. $\{3,4,5\} \subset \{1,2,4,5,6\}$

    h. $\{1, 2, 6\} \supset \{1, 2, 4, 5, 6\}$

    i. $\phi \subset \{2, 5\}$

2–10 Suppose that

$$S = \{1, 2, 3, 4, 5\}$$
$$T = \{x \mid 0 < x < 10 \text{ and } x \text{ is odd}\}$$
$$U = \mathbf{Z}_{16}$$

List the members of each of the following sets:

    a. $S \cap T$

    b. $(S \cup T)'$

    c. $(S \cup T) \setminus S$

2–11 The following sets are expressed as rules. Rewrite them in list form.

    a. $\{x \mid x \; \varepsilon \; \mathbf{N}, \; x \le 10, \text{ and } x \text{ is even}\}$

    b. $\{p \mid p \text{ is a permutation of the string } 012\}$

Sets and Data Types

Previously we said that the set of possible values of a variable defined the *type* of the variable. We also discussed several specific sets including the integers **Z** and the reals **R**. The reason that the type of the variable is so important is that different types may be manipulated in different ways. For example, it makes no sense to speak of the remainder after division unless we are dealing with integers; it makes no sense to speak of the fractional portion of the quotient after division when dealing with the integers. It would not make sense to speak of any mathematical operation for the set of characters.

    It does make sense to speak of addition, multiplication or subtraction for both reals and integers. Thus each type will have a corresponding set of valid manipulations or operations which may be performed on the members of that type.

    Definition   A *data type* is a set of possible values together with a set of operations which may be performed on the members of that set. Sometimes, a data type is referred to as a *class*.

It is not required that each operation be valid for every member of the set. An example is when the data type includes division, which is not valid when the divisor is 0.

Besides the integers **Z** and the reals **R**, three other types will be of immediate interest to us: **C** the set of characters (we identify **C** with the ASCII character set discussed earlier), **B** the set of booleans (the set consists of only two values, **true** and **false**; we will discuss booleans further in Chapter 3) and the *list* data type (see below).

There is a further complication. As previously discussed, the cardinality of the mathematical sets **Z** and **R** is infinite. That is, we can count forever and never run out of integers or reals. But computers do not have infinite storage and hence cannot represent an infinite set. Both **Z** and **R** are therefore restricted to finite sets when they are represented in the computer.

The cardinality of these set representations will depend upon the particular computer and particular language implementation you are using. In C++, two primary data types serve to represent **Z** and **R**: they are int and float, respectively. Since computer memory is finite, the set of values for type int is also finite. In most C++ implementations, type int covers the range {–32768, –32767, ..., 0, ..., 32766, 32767}. A discussion of the set of values for float is complicated by the fact that it is not possible to represent a potentially infinite number of decimal digits (such as $1/3 = 0.3333333\ldots$) in the finite computer. This will be discussed further in Chapter 8. More details concerning the implementation of the C++ float data type can also be found in the laboratory manual.

A summary of the basic C++ data types is given in Table 2–3, where we also show several C++ operations that are associated with these data types: * represents the product, / represents the quotient, and % the remainder under integer division; strcat concatenates two strings, strcpy makes a copy of a string; and &&, | |, and ! are logical connectives which will be studied in Chapter 3. In addition, relational operations (>, >=, =, <=, <) may be applied to each of these types; we will illustrate those in the next chapter as well.

TABLE 2–3 BASIC DATA TYPES IN COMPUTING

Data type	Mathematical equivalent	C++ equivalent	Some operations
integers	**Z**	int	{+, –, *,/ , %}
reals	**R**	float	{+, –, *, /}
character strings	**C**	char	{strcat, strcpy}
Booleans	**B**	int (1=true, 0=false)	{&&, | |, !}

In our discussions of algorithmic problems and their solutions, we will frequently refer to the class (data type) `list`, which is any sequence of `float` values. For example, the grades used in the GPA problem can be represented as a list. Thus, we will assume the existence of the additional class `list` of `float`. All members of a single list must be of the same type; we cannot have a mixed-type list of `float` and `char` values, for instance. We will also assume that lists have specific operations associated with them, such as

`length`   to return the number of elements in the list

`read`   to read an entire list from input

`write`   to display an entire list on output

Since this is a fairly complex idea, we will further discuss and illustrate the list class in Chapter 4.

THE STRUCTURE OF COMPUTERS

We are now ready to discuss the capabilities of computers from an operational (but not actual hardware) point of view. Fundamentally, a computer has hardware to implement the following functions:

- Read input from an input device (keyboard, mouse, diskette) into memory.

- Write output from memory to an output device (monitor, diskette, printer).

- Perform operations (arithmetic, comparison, etc.) on values stored in memory.

- Control the sequence in which the above actions are carried out, or executed.

The utility of the computer for solving problems is that it can accomplish these simple functions extremely quickly and extremely accurately. Later in this text (Chapters 8 and 9) you will begin to explore how these actions are implemented as electronic circuits. However, for the next few chapters, we look at these actions from an operational point of view, so that we may better understand how to combine them to solve various kinds of algorithmic problems.

Input and Output

At the simplest hardware level, computers are capable of inputting or outputting a single character. Additions have been made to this capability through software in the operating system and C++ language to allow the input and output of aggregate quantities such as whole numbers or strings of characters. Thus computers have the ability to input or output a value for a variable, regardless of the type of the variable.

External sources or destinations into which data input and output occur are best viewed as *streams*.

> **Definition**   A *stream* is a sequence of values which are normally accessed in sequential order. That is, to access the nth value in a stream, the preceding $n - 1$ values must first be accessed. Here the term access applies to both reading a value and writing a value.

That is, a stream may be either a source of values (input) or a destination for values (output), but never both at the same time. In addition, the direction of flow in a data stream may not be reversed. That is, if we have read a value from input, the next time we read data from a stream we will obtain the value that follows behind the one just read. Values may neither be reread nor skipped. If we wish to retain a value, we must do so explicitly by storing it in a separate variable in memory. Similarly, once we have written a value to the output stream, it will appear on the monitor.

In C++, we can specify the input or output of the value of a variable using the operators >> (for keyboard input) and << (for screen output), respectively. The names `cin` and `cout`, when used with these operators, designate the keyboard input stream and the display screen output stream, respectively. The laboratory manual explains the exact syntax and meaning of these operators, showning several examples of their use.

Memory and State

On the hardware level, computer memory is made up of a large number of electronic circuits. Memory is used to store individual data values while a program is running, as well as the instructions that comprise the program itself. Each individual data value is associated with a distinct memory location. Operationally, we can visualize the memory as containing a number of uniquely named locations, each of which is identified with a different *variable* in the program.

A basic notion in computing is that of state, which is a snapshot description of the values of all the variables contained in memory at a particular instant while the program is running. For example, a chess-playing program has many possible states—one for each possible arrangement of the pieces on a chessboard. A graphical program might control a million "pixels" (dots on a display screen, each of which can be illuminated in any one of an extensive set of colors). The state of this program at any given moment is the complete set of pixel values (colors) for each of the 1 million pixels. We define the notion of state more formally as follows:

> **Definition**   Suppose we have a list of variables $x_1, x_2, \ldots, x_n$ whose types are defined by the sets $S_1, S_2, \ldots,$ and S_n, respectively. Suppose also that

the value of x_1 is $s_1 \in S_1$, the value of x_2 is $s_2 \in S_2$, and so on. Then the expression

$$x_1 == s_1 \text{ and } x_2 == s_2 \text{ and } \ldots \text{ and } x_n == s_n$$

is said to be the *state* of the variables x_1, x_2, ..., and x_n. The set of all possible states of x_1, x_2, ..., x_n is known as the *state space* for these variables. (Note here that the symbol pair == denotes the C++ expression of equality. The traditional equals sign, =, has an entirely different meaning in C++.)

The state of a computation can also be represented graphically if there are only two or three variables being represented, or diagrammatically if there are more. Figure 2–7 shows a diagrammatic representation of a program's state.

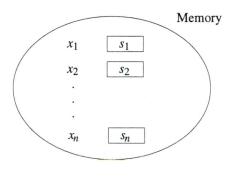

FIGURE 2–7   Diagrammatic representation of the state of a computation.

Examples 2.10 through 2.12 illustrate these important notions:

Example 2.10   Suppose that a computer program has two variables, i and j, used for counting. Then they both have the natural numbers **N** as their type. The initial state of the program might be:

$$i == 0 \text{ and } j == 0$$

A subsequent state might be:

$$i == 5 \text{ and } j == 6$$

This change of state can be illustrated graphically as shown in Figure 2–8a.

Example 2.11   If the pixels controlled by a graphics program are identified by the variables x_1, x_2, ..., $x_{1000000}$, a state of the program would have a million entries, one for each of these variables. The expression

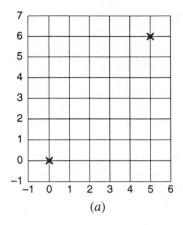

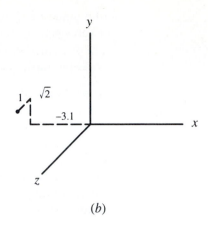

(a)   (b)

FIGURE 2–8   Visualizing the state of a program graphically. (*a*) Two states in the state space of Example 2.10; (*b*) one state in the state space of Example 2.12.

$x_1 ==$ red and $x_2 ==$ red and... and $x_{1000000} ==$ red

describes that particular state in the program where the entire screen is red.

Example 2.12   Consider a program with three variables, x, y, and z, all having type `float` (the programming analogue to the mathematical set **R**). Three possible states of this program are:

$x == 0.0$ and $y == 0.0$ and $z == 0.0$

$x == -3.1$ and $y == \sqrt{2}$ and $z == 1.0$ (See Figure 2–8*b*.)

$x == -1.0$ and $y == \frac{\pi}{2}$ and $z == 1.789$

A graphical representation for the second of these states is shown in Figure 2–8*b*, while a diagrammatic representation is shown in Figure 2–9.

When we have only two or three variables in a program, its state can be represented as a single point on the graph which is its state space. For example, the points in Figure 2–8*a* represent two states in the state space that correspond to Example 2.10. The three-dimensional graph in Figure 2–8*b* represents the state space of Example 2.12, again with one of the states marked as a point on that graph. In a computer program, whenever the value of one variable changes, the effect is to move from one point in the state space to another. A diagrammatic representation of the state of a computation is useful when there are several variables involved, rather than two or three.

The operational view of a computation is simply that the contents of memory, input, and output define the current state of the program. Programs will typically have extremely large, but never infinite, state spaces. That is, the `int` and `float` data types do not have infinite cardinality in computers (as do **Z** and **R** in mathematics), since the amount of available memory space for each individual value is fixed in size.

Operations on Memory

Being able to input and output information to and from memory gives the computer an ability to interact with its environment. But it is the power to manipulate the information stored in memory that allows computers to solve such a wide variety of problems. The operations that computers can perform are very limited:

- *Arithmetic* operations, using the values of integer or real variables

- *Relational* (logical) operations, such as comparing the values of two variables

- *Moving* a value from one memory location to another, called *assignment*

- *Control* operations, which can be used to vary the sequence in which steps are executed, depending on the nature of the data

Recall that not all operations may be performed on every value. That is, each value is a member of a data type which determines the valid operations for that value.

Note that computers have no built-in operations to do things like "look at a picture and recognize the scene," "put a list of books into alphabetical order by title," etc. Yet computers can be programmed to accomplish each of these complex tasks by breaking them into a (large) number of very simple steps. *Abstraction*, as we will see, is the process of giving a group of ideas a single name and then referring to the entire group of ideas by simply using that name.

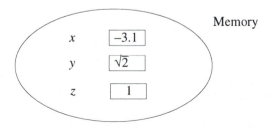

FIGURE 2–9   Diagrammatic representation of the state $x == -3.1$ and $y == \sqrt{2}$ and $z = 1$.

Assignment   Consider a program with three `float` variables *x*, *y*, and *z* (`float` *variable* means the same thing as *variable of type* `float`). Suppose the program contains a statement of the form

```
x = 1.0 ;
```

This C++ statement assigns the value 1.0 to the variable `x`. (Note again that the use of = does not denote a mathematical test for equality in C++. The pair of symbols == is reserved for the purpose of testing equality, as suggested in the foregoing discussion of state.) If no further restrictions have been placed on the other two variables *y* and *z*, the entire plane *x* == 1 is the set of all possible states for this program after this statement is executed (see Figure 2–10).

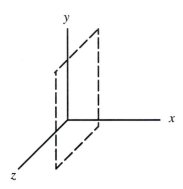

FIGURE 2–10   The state `x  ==  1.0` in a program with three `float` variables *x*, *y*, and *z*.

Furthermore, if we wanted to assign a copy of the value of variable *x* to the variable *y*, we would write the assignment `y = x`. Now the possible program states are as shown in Figure 2–11.

Diagrams for Representing Change of State

Because the number of variables in a computation is typically much larger than two or three and because the nature of a computation, its input, and its output is often complex, programmers tend to use diagrammatic models to help convey the meaning of a computation.

As an example, the so-called spider diagram in Figure 2–12 shows some of the basic statements in C++ that affect the transfer of data between memory, input, and output. The state of the computation is represented by the particular variables that are in memory along with their respective values. In this exam-

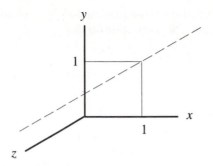

FIGURE 2–11   The state x == 1.0 and y == 1.0 in a program with three float variables *x*, *y*, and *z*.

ple, the circled elements represent locations in memory, while the labels on the arrows represent C++ input, output, and assignment statements. Thus, this diagram represents the state x == 1 and y == 2 after the two assignment statements x = 1; and y = 2; have been executed.

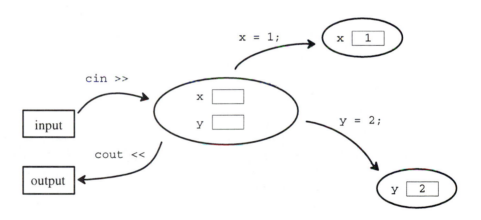

FIGURE 2–12   A spider diagram representation of C++'s basic input, output, and computational capabilities.

EXERCISES

2–12 Assume that the state i == 1 && j == 1 exists initially. Describe the state that will occur *after* each of the groups of assignment statements in *a* through *c* is executed. Draw a two-dimensional *xy* graph, and locate a point on that graph that represents that initial state along with each of the three alternative final states that result from the groups of C++ assignment statements in *a* through *c*.

a.   ```
i = 2;
   j = i;
```

*b.*   ```
i = i + 1;
   j = j + 2;
```

c.   ```
j = j + 1;
   i = i + 1;
   j = j + i;
```

**2–13**  Draw a spider diagram representation for the assignment statements in Exercise 2–12*a*.

## Control

Being able to input and output information in memory and to manipulate the values of the variables in memory is not sufficient to achieve powerful computational abstractions. Control of the sequencing and selection of which assignments are made is also important.

Consider the following C++ sequence:

```
i = 10 ;
k = 100 ;
```

It makes no difference in which order we execute these two assignments, since two different variables are affected. No matter in which order they are executed, the resulting state i == 10 and k == 100 is the same.

Now consider the following fragment:

```
i = 0 ;
i = 5 ;
j = 10 / i ;
```

Here, the order of execution of the last two statements has a great impact on the resulting state. Executed in the indicated order, we have the state i == 5 and j == 2. But if we reverse the order of execution, then the state is undefined (since the assignment j = 10/0 cannot be computed).

Consider too the problem of assigning the larger value of two variable values to a third variable:

```
if (var1 > var2)
  var3 = var1 ;
else
  var3 = var2 ;
```
```

That is, we wish to execute a different assignment depending upon the present state of memory (the present values of `var1` and `var2`). Thus the end state will depend upon the starting state (one possible end state is `var3 == var1`, while the other is `var3 == var2`).

These examples indicate that we need to be able to control the flow of our programs; that is, programs must have a means of sequencing the various statements which manipulate the values of variables in memory. The last operational feature of computers is this ability.

There are three fundamental control statements:

- *Sequence*. This is the default; statements are normally executed sequentially, in the order in which they appear in the program listing.

- *Selection*. This form of control statement allows us to make a choice between one or more possibilities. For example, we can determine the absolute value of variable `var1` by using the C++ selection statement

```
if (var1 < 0.0)
    absvalue = -var1 ;
else
    absvalue = var1 ;
```

- *Iteration* (or repetition). This form of control statement allows us to repeat a series of statements 0 or more times, depending upon a condition. For example, if we wish to count down from 10 to 0 we would write:

```
Count = 10 ;
while (Count >= 0)
{
    cout << Count << "\n" ;
    Count = Count - 1 ;
}
```

Much of the programming process is concerned with understanding the differences between these three forms of control.

Computers and the GPA Problem

Let's now return to the GPA example and see how the functionality described above can be used to implement the steps in the algorithm:

```
Step 1.  Obtain the input list of grades.
```

- Input to memory

```
Step 2.  Compute n = the number of grades in the list.
```

- Operations on memory

```
Step 3.   Compute Sum = the sum of the grades in the list.
```

- Operations on memory

- Control (must repeat the operation on memory for each grade in the list)

```
Step 4.   Compute GPA = Sum / n.
```

- Operations on memory

```
Step 5.   Display GPA.
```

- Memory to output

We can also describe the state of our system after each step in the execution of the algorithm:

- The values of Sum, GPA, and n are undefined.

```
Step 1.   Obtain the input list of grades.
```

```
Step 2.   Compute n = the number of grades in the list.
```

- n now has a value; Sum and GPA have no assigned values.

```
Step 3.   Compute Sum = the sum of the grades in the list.
```

- n and Sum now have values; GPA has no assigned value.

```
Step 4.   Compute GPA = Sum / n.
```

- n, Sum and GPA now have assigned values.

```
Step 5.   Display GPA.
```

COMPUTERS AND FUNCTIONS

In the previous section, we discussed the operational view of the computer in terms of the general properties which computers possess. We distinguished this view from a more hardware-oriented one, in which we would have explored electronic signals and how they are used to design computers. This functional view of computers is closely related to the mathematical notion of a function which, in turn, is fundamental to all computing. We will make great use of functions as we learn the programming process; in this section we introduce some basic notions.

In its simplest form, a *function* is just a table with two columns that shows a correspondence between values in the first column and values in the second.

Example 2.13   Consider the following table:

1	2
2	5
3	10
4	17

This is a function that relates each of the first four integers to a corresponding integer. If we were to extend this function, it would not be hard to infer a fifth row with the pair 5 and 26. That is, there is a pattern suggested by the four lines in this table that can be generalized so that any number of pairs can be listed.

Example 2.14   The following table is quite different:

1	2
2	5
1	7
3	2
2	6

Because some of the numbers on the left are duplicated, this table appears to represent an unstable or unreliable relationship. It seems not to embody any rule by which a value on the left can be used to compute a unique value on the right.

Unambiguous behavior—that for each distinct value in the first column there is a unique value in the second column—is the basis for the idea of a function.

Figure 2–13 illustrates two more functions, this time using an xy graph rather than a table. Note that in Figure 2–13a, each x corresponds to one y, and coincidentally, each y corresponds to one x. In Figure 2–13b, each x corresponds to one y, but different x's correspond to the same y. Both these graphs, however, represent functions because they have the property that each distinct x value corresponds to *no more than* one y value. To work effectively with functions, we need to define the concept more precisely. Let's clarify the ideas about correspondence that are discussed in these examples.

Basic Concepts

A function is always defined on the basis of two corresponding sets.

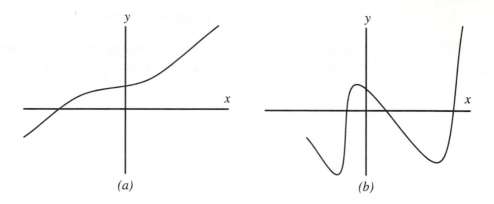

FIGURE 2–13   Two functions represented graphically. (*a*) Each *x* corresponds to one *y*; (*b*) each *x* corresponds to one *y*, but some *y*'s are duplicated.

Definition   Let X and Y be sets. The notation (x, y) where $x \in X$ and $y \in Y$ is called an *ordered pair*. The *cross product* of X and Y, denoted $X \times Y$, is the set $\{(x, y) \mid x \in X \text{ and } y \in Y\}$. That is $X \times Y$ is the set of all ordered pairs (x, y) for which $x \in X$ and $y \in Y$.

Example 2.15   Let $X == Y == \mathbf{R}$. Then $X \times Y$ is the *xy* coordinate system shown in Figure 2–14*a*.   If $I == J == \mathbf{Z}$, then $I \times J$ is the collection of all points in the Cartesian plane whose coordinates are integers. The points of $I \times J$ are thus all the intersections of the vertical and horizontal lines shown in Figure 2–14*b*.

A function is a particular kind of cross product. That is, it is a set of pairs in which no two pairs have the same first member. Formally, a function can be defined as follows:

Definition   Let X and Y be sets. A *function* is a subset f of $X \times Y$ such that each $x \in X$ has precisely one $y \in Y$ paired with it. X is called the *domain* of the function f, and Y is called the *range* of f.

In the context of a tabular representation, as in Example 2.13, we can think of the domain of a function as the first column in the table and the range as the second column. The function itself is the correspondence between the numbers in the two columns. Similarly, when viewing the graphical representation of a function, we identify the *x* axis as the domain, the *y* axis as the range, and the function as the set of pairs (x, y) that appears on the graph (e.g., as shown in Figure 2–13). In either case, the requirement that each *x* has only one y paired with it captures the notion of dependability or stability in that correspondence.

Example 2.16   Suppose $X == \{1, 2, 3, 4\}$ and $Y == \{2, 4, 6, 8\}$. Also suppose we have the set of pairs $f == \{(1, 2), (2, 4), (3, 6), (4, 8)\}$. Then f is a function; the set $\{1, 2, 3, 4\}$ is its domain; and $\{2, 4, 6, 8\}$ is its range. Note that each $x \in X$ has one and only one $y \in Y$ paired with it. Note also that this particular correspondence can also be represented by the state $y == 2x$.

Suppose again that $X == \{1, 2, 3, 4\}$ and consider the set $g == \{(1, 2), (2, 4), (3, 6)\}$. In this case, g is not a function with domain X, since there are members of the domain X for which g is not defined. Sets that have all the properties of functions except that they are not defined over their entire domain are called *partial functions*. Partial functions are often useful in computing.

Although a function requires that every x in its domain must have a value y in its range associated with it, it is not necessary that every y in the range correspond to some x. For instance, if $Y == \{1, 2, 3, 4\}$ and we define the function $y = 4$ for all $x \in \{2, 4, 8\}$, then the values 1, 2, and 3 in Y correspond to no x in X. Finally, let $h == \{(1, 2), (2, 4), (3, 6), (1, 8), (4, 10)\}$. The set h is also not a function since there is an x that corresponds to two distinct y's.

The following terms are also often used in connection with functions.

Definition   Let f be a function with domain X and range Y. We often denote this relationship by $f: X \rightarrow Y$. When the domain and range have been so specified, we write $y == f(x)$ to denote the relationship that f represents between any member x of the domain X and a corresponding value y of the range Y. In this notation x is called the *independent variable* and y the *dependent variable*. The set of all pairs $\{(x, f(x)) \mid x \in X$ and $f(x) \in Y\}$ is used to define the *graph* of the function f.

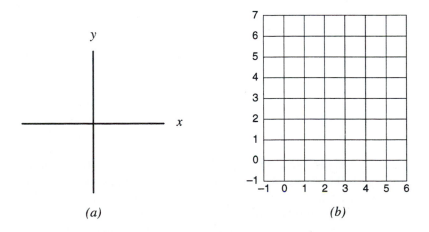

(a)   (b)

FIGURE 2–14   Graphical representation of (a) the cross product of reals and (b) the cross product of integers.

Example 2.17   If $X == Y == \mathbf{R}$ and $y == f(x) == 2x - 1$, x is the independent variable and y is the dependent variable. The graph of f is given in Figure 2–15.

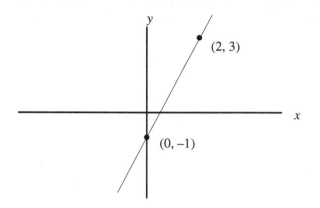

FIGURE 2–15   Graph of the function $f(x) == 2x - 1$.

Continuous and Discrete Functions

Functions are often categorized by whether they can be displayed using a continuous, unbroken line or not. If not, the function has "gaps" in its xy graph, and is called a *discrete function*.

Example 2.18   Let $X == Y == \mathbf{R}$. The *absolute value* function, given by $y == |x|$, can be defined by the rule

$$|x| \quad\; == \quad x \quad \text{when } x \geq 0$$
$$== -x \quad \text{when } x < 0$$

Figure 2–16a presents the graph of $y == |x|$ when the domain and range of the function is $\mathbf{R}$ (giving a *continuous* function). If its domain and range were the integers (i.e., $X == Y == \mathbf{Z}$), this function would appear quite differently, as shown in Figure 2–16b (a *discrete* function).

Example 2.19   The *floor function* $\lfloor x \rfloor$ is defined as the greatest integer less than or equal to x. It has domain $\mathbf{R}$ and range $\mathbf{Z}$. Thus if $x == n \cdot d_1 d_2 d_3 \ldots$ (where n is any integer and each d_i is any digit), then $\lfloor x \rfloor == n$ when $x \geq 0$ or x is an integer, and $\lfloor x \rfloor == n - 1$ otherwise. For positive real numbers, therefore, $\lfloor x \rfloor$ is the result of dropping the decimal part of x; for negative real numbers that are not already integers, $\lfloor x \rfloor$ is the result of dropping the decimal part and subtracting 1. The graph of $y == \lfloor x \rfloor$ is given in Figure 2–17. A related function, the *ceiling function* $\lceil x \rceil$, is defined as the least integer great-

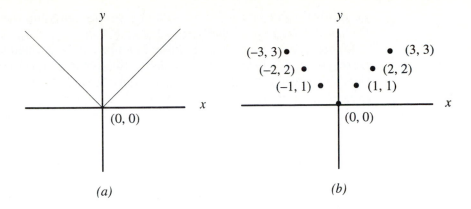

(a)   *(b)*

FIGURE 2–16   Graph of $y == |x|$. *(a)* A continuous function; *(b)* a discrete function.

er than or equal to x. It is computed by dropping the decimal part of x and, if x is not itself an integer, adding 1. The floor and ceiling functions are sometimes called the *greatest integer* and *least integer* functions, respectively.

The absolute value function can be directly computed in C++ by using the expression `abs(x)`, where x can be any `int` or `float` variable or expression. The floor and ceiling functions also have exact analogues in C++; they are called `floor` and `ceil`, respectively, and can be found in the C++ library `<math.h>` (see *Laboratory Manual* for more details). Thus, `floor(3.14)` == 3 and `floor(-3.14)` == −4.

A slightly different outcome from that of the floor function is realized by the C++ expression `int(x)`, which converts the value of the `float` variable x to

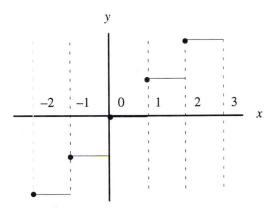

FIGURE 2–17   The floor function $y == \lfloor x \rfloor$.

the nearest lower or equal `int` value by simply dropping the decimal digits. Thus, `int(3.14) == 3` and `int(-3.14) == -3`.

In this section, we have seen how a function can be defined in several different ways: using a formula, an xy graph, a two-column table, or a set of ordered pairs. They can be implemented in a variety of ways in C++, whether they are already in a C++ library or not. We shall have many occasions in this text to implement functions in C++. Functions can be defined in several other ways, too, as we shall also see later in the text.

EXERCISES

2–14 Which of the following sets of ordered pairs are functions?

    a. $\{(1, 1), (1, \pi), (1, 100)\}$

    b. $\{(2, 1), (3, 7), (5, 13), (4, 19)\}$

    c. $\{(-1, 1), (0, 1), (1, 1), (2, 1), (3, 1)\}$

    d. $\{(x, y) \mid x \geq 0 \text{ and } y = x\}$

    e. $\{(1, a), (2, b), (3, a), (4, b), (5, c)\}$

    f. $\{(1, a), (2, b), (1, c), (2, d), (3, e)\}$

    g. $\{(1, e), (2, d), (3, c), (4, b), (5, a)\}$

2–15 Determine the domain and range for each of the following functions.

    a. $h(x) == x \% 17$, for $x == 0, 16, 17, 32,$ and 69 (% is a function that computes the integer remainder when dividing its first argument by its second)

    b. $b(x) == (-1 \leq x \leq 10)$, for $x = -2, -1, 0, 10,$ and 15

    c. $\lfloor x \rfloor$ for $x == 10, \pi, 0$, and -1.5

    d. $|x|$ for $x == -1, 0, 1, -49.5,$ and $\dfrac{\pi}{6}$

2–16 Define functions that accomplish each of the following:

    a.   Take a positive integer x and compute the remainder after division by 67.

    b.   Truncate a positive real number x to the next lower tenth (e.g., 19.567 becomes 19.5).

2–17 Consider the function f(x) == (x % 2 == 0).

    a.   What is the domain of this function?
    b.   What is its range?

One-to-one Functions and Inverses

Suppose f is a function with domain X and range Y. Then, as we saw in Figure 2–13b, each x corresponds to one and only one y, but two distinct x's can correspond to the same y. Thus, Figure 2–18a represents a function. However, if we were to try to "reverse the process" by starting from Y, the result would not be a legitimate function. That is, one y would correspond to two distinct x's, and some y's would have no x's corresponding to them. The function pictured in Figure 2–18b is different—in this case we *can* reverse the process and still have a function. This is because each x is mapped to a *distinct y*. The following definition formalizes these ideas.

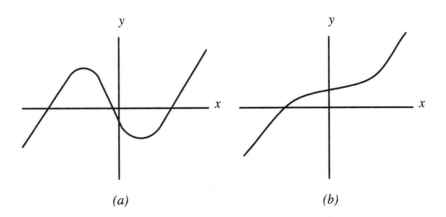

(a)   (b)

FIGURE 2–18   (*a*) Non-one-to-one function; (*b*) one-to-one function.

Definition   Let $f: X{\rightarrow}Y$ be a function. Then f is a *one-to-one function* if distinct x's correspond to distinct y's for every $x \in X$ and $y \in Y$. Two sets, X

and *Y*, are said to be in *one-to-one correspondence* if there is a function *f*: *X*→*Y* which is one-to-one.

Example 2.20   Functions that are permutations provide important examples of one-to-one correspondences. For example, consider the string abcd and its permutation bdac. If we let $X = Y = \{a, b, c, d\}$, this permutation can be viewed as the function *p*, defined as follows:

```
p(a) == c
p(b) == a
p(c) == d
p(d) == b
```

That is, *p* reveals the position to which each member of {a, b, c, d} will move for an arbitrary string of a's, b's, c's, and d's. This function *p* is also a one-to-one function, since distinct *x*'s map to distinct *y*'s and the range of $p = \{a, b, c, d\} = Y$.

Definition   Let *f*: *X*→*Y* be a one-to-one function. Then f^{-1} is a function with domain *Y* and range *X* such that if $y == f(x)$ then $x == f^{-1}(y)$. The function f^{-1} is called the *inverse* of *f*.

Not every function has an inverse. For example, suppose $X == Y == \{a, b, c, d\}$, and $f(a) = b, f(b) = c$, and $f(c) = f(d) = d$, as shown in Figure 2–19. Then for the inverse of *f* to exist, $f^{-1}(d)$ would have to equal both c and d, which would prevent f^{-1} from being a legitimate function. In order for a function to have an inverse, it must therefore be a one-to-one function.

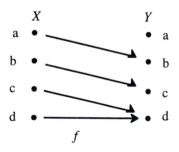

FIGURE 2–19   A function *f* that is not one-to-one, and hence has no inverse.

Example 2.21   In Example 2.20, since *p* is a one-to-one function, it has an inverse. That inverse, p^{-1}, can be defined as follows:

```
p⁻¹(a)  ==  b
p⁻¹(b)  ==  d
p⁻¹(c)  ==  a
p⁻¹(d)  ==  c
```

Note that $p^{-1}(p(\text{a})) == p^{-1}(\text{c}) == \text{a}$. In general, for any invertible function p: $X \rightarrow Y$ and any $x \in X$, $p^{-1}(p(\text{x})) = \text{x}$. Likewise, for any $y \in Y$, $p(p^{-1}(\text{y})) == \text{y}$.

Example 2.22   One-to-one functions and inverses are often used in coding. The American Standard Code for Information Interchange (ASCII) defines a numerical equivalent between 0 and 127 for each regular character or control character that can be typed at a standard computer keyboard. This function is one-to-one, and is realized in C++ by using the name `int`. That is, for any character x that appears on the keyboard, `int(x)` is an integer in the range 0 through 127 that corresponds to it in the ASCII set. Some ordinal values of familiar keyboard characters are given below:

```
int('0')  ==  48
int('A')  ==  65
int('=')  ==  61
int('a')  ==  97
```

A full listing of the ASCII characters and their corresponding integer values is given in Appendix A.

The `int` function therefore exploits the uniform ASCII coding scheme for the keyboard characters. This scheme is followed by most manufacturers of computer hardware and software. The existence of such a standard facilitates the smooth interchange of information among different types of computers.

Note that, to work properly, `int` has to be a one-to-one function; if one character were assigned two distinct numerical codes, there would be no consistent way to decipher the code. Since `int` is one-to-one, it has an inverse function in the C++ language called `char` (for *char*acter). If n is an integer in the range 0 through 127, then the expression `char(n)` delivers the corresponding keyboard character for that integer. For example:

```
char(48)  ==  '0'
char(65)  ==  'A'
char(61)  ==  '='
char(97)  ==  'a'
```

Note that, since `int` and `char` are inverses of each other, the following are always true in C++:

```
char(int(x))  ==  x       and
int(char(n))  ==  n
```

for any integer n in the range 0 through 127 and any keyboard character x.

Example 2.23   Cryptography (the encoding of secret messages) is an area of computing that uses many of the principles we have discussed. For example, consider the *Caesar cipher*, a coding scheme in which each letter of a message is replaced by a different letter in the alphabet, say the third letter following it. Thus, the message

```
SERGEANT PEPPERS LONELY HEARTS CLUB BAND
```

is encoded in the Caesar cypher as

```
VHUJHDQW SHSSHUV ORQHOB KHDUWV FOXE EDQG
```

The Caesar cipher is therefore a permutation of the letters of the alphabet and thus is a one-to-one function whose domain and range is the uppercase roman alphabet. Decoding such a message is the equivalent of discovering the inverse of the function that was used to encode it in the first place.

A disadvantage of the Caesar cipher is that it is relatively easy to decode. We can devise a code that is more difficult to decode by using a random permutation and substituting based on it. Using the substitution table

```
ABCDEFGHIJKLMNOPQRSTUVWXYZ
```

```
JSATERNICFHPLUGWVYDZOMXQBK
```

allows us to encode the message

```
SERGEANT PEPPERS LONELY HEARTS CLUB BAND
```

as

```
DEYNEJUZ WEWWEYD PGUEPB IEJYZD APOS SJUT
```

If the encoded message is long enough, even a random cipher can be decoded by counting the frequency of the letters and matching them to the known frequency of occurrence of letters in English. Some more sophisticated encryption systems apply coding functions to blocks of letters.

The concept of one-to-one correspondence provides a way to precisely define the notion of two sets having the same number of members and also to define the size of a set.

Definition   Two sets A and B have the *same number of members* if they are in one-to-one correspondence. A set which is in one-to-one correspondence with $\mathbf{Z}_n$, for some natural number n, is said to have *cardinality n*. Such a set has n elements, and is called a *finite* set. Sets that do not have cardinality *n* for any integer *n* are called *infinite* sets.

Most sets that we will encounter in computing are finite sets. For example, the ASCII character set discussed in Example 2.22 has cardinality 128. Even the set of integers used in computing is finite—for many computers it has cardinality 2^{16}, or 65,536. This is the type `int` that is used in C++ programming, which differs from the mathematical notion of integers, **Z**, for exactly this reason. That is, the range of integers in mathematics is infinite, but the range of values of type `int` in programming is finite. We will pursue this point in Chapter 4.

Using a Program to Define a Function

Functions can also be defined by designing a program that, in effect, describes how the corresponding range value of the function can be calculated for any predetermined value in its domain. Following the input-process-output model of computation shown in Figure 2–1, we can view a program as a well-defined sequence of steps that transforms some input (from some specified allowable set of inputs) into a corresponding output. That is, the algorithm defines how to evaluate a function *f(x)* for any particular value *x* taken from its domain.

Example 2.24   For example, Figure 2–20 shows a program written in the C++ language that computes the value of the function *GPA(L)*, where the domain is a set of lists `L` `==` (e_1 e_2 ... e_n) of real numbers and the range is the set **R**. The function *GPA* can be defined mathematically by the expression *GPA*(`L`) `==` (e_1 + e_2 + ... + e_n) / `n`. When defined as a program, the input can be any list *L*, while its output is the resulting average computed by the following definition. That definition can also be stated in the form of a complete C++ program or function.

While the details of the C++ program in Figure 2–20 will be unfamiliar to readers, its five major steps are the same ones that appeared in the discussion of computer organization earlier in this chapter. Each of these steps is clearly annotated by a *comment* in the program, which is a text beginning with the characters `//`. Comments are generally useful in programming as a device for annotating ideas directly within the code. We shall use them for that purpose throughout this text.

In general, when a program is used to realize a function, its set of allowable *inputs* (all lists `L` in this case) corresponds to the function's domain; its set of *outputs* (**R** in this case) corresponds to the function's range; and its *steps* define procedurally the rule of correspondence between each individual member of the domain and an individual member of the range.

computation at each step. Identify the control relationships among these steps. That is, what steps must precede other steps, what steps are constituents of larger steps, what steps must be repeated within a loop, and so on. Document each step by writing a brief description of its own (local) expectations. Assign an appropriate name and a clear purpose to each new variable and object that you discover for each new step. The five steps that comprise the solution to the GPA problem are documented in the five lines that begin

```
// Step
```

in Figure 2–20.

Stage 4: Defining abstractions. Determine which of these steps you have seen before in other algorithmic problem-solving situations, recall the appropriate functions, variables, and objects that were used in those situations, and adapt those routines for reuse in this new problem's solution. Often this activity will require combining two or more functions to form a new one, or else tailoring a function to fit its specialized new use.

Stage 5: Coding. Translate each of the individual steps in your solution into C++, identify new functions, classes, and objects, and reuse old ones as appropriate to accomplish each individual step. Connect the steps with appropriate control structures in a way that agrees with your discoveries in Stage 3. The remaining lines in Figure 2–20 are examples of the C++ code needed to solve the GPA problem.

Stage 6: Testing and verification. Systematically test, or validate, your C++ program by running it once for each set of input values in a suite of alternatives that exploit the full range allowed by the problem's input specifications. For each run, check that the program's output satisfies the output specifications. Alternatively, verify some or all of the program's constituent steps by using proof techniques when appropriate.

Stage 7: Presentation. Add commentary at the beginning (the "top") of your program to clarify the purpose of the program, note its authorship and date, and identify the use of routines that were developed for other purposes (and often by other programmers). Prepare a printed listing of your program, along with a printed copy of one or more sample outputs.

We will repeatedly use these stages in the MAPS methodology to solve various problems throughout the text. In the next chapter, we explore Stages 1 and 2 by discussing how to develop specifications which clearly define *what* we need to accomplish in order to solve a problem. Subsequent chapters explore Stages 3, 4, and 5 by seeing how we use specifications to develop and implement an algorithm and Stages 6 and 7 by focusing on how we ensure that our software is correct, usable, and maintainable.

EXERCISES

2–20 Describe in English the steps of an algorithmic process that would calculate and display the number of grades that are above the average for an arbitrary list of grades. (Hint: Consider this problem as an extension of the GPA problem. What additional variables do you need?)

2–21 What is the state of the variables at the beginning of the process that you just described in Exercise 2–20? At the end? Give a sample input list and output that would be displayed by your algorithm.

SUMMARY

In this chapter, we began our study of how to solve problems with a computer. We discussed the concept of an algorithm to solve a problem, of the operational capabilities of computers, and of how an algorithm may be expressed in terms of these capabilities. Of particular importance are the concepts of type, variable and of the state of a variable. The idea of a computer program as a representation of a mathematical function was also introduced, and the identification of a program's input and output with the corresponding function's domain and range was established.

This chapter lays important groundwork for subsequent chapters. It introduced MAPS, a systematic problem-solving methodology that can be used for a wide range of application areas. We later develop the individual stages of MAPS to take us from an initial problem statement to a complete solution. The program which results from that solution will have dual utility; it will be readable by others and executable by computers.

LOGIC AND PROBLEM SOLVING

Chapters 3 through 7 provide a comprehensive discussion of all seven steps in the MAPS process. Altogether, this discussion develops a general strategy for solving problems using the computer. As examples of MAPS, we will be developing the solution to the GPA problem that was introduced in Chapter 2, as well as three other algorithmic problems from the numeric, text processing, and graphics problem solving domains.

PROBLEM DEFINITION AND THE DIALOGUE

The first step in the MAPS methodology for solving problems is *The Dialogue*, during which we ask questions in order to gain a complete and clear understanding of the problem. While it may seem obvious that we cannot solve a problem until we understand all of its details, sometimes it is not as easy to clarify those details as it seems. Consider the following examples.

Example 3.1   Suppose you know that a stream of characters will be given as input, and the task is to develop an algorithm that displays the longest word in the stream.

In order to proceed, more information is required. For instance, we need to understand how the algorithm will recognize an individual word in the text. Are contractions one word? How about hyphenated words such as "look-out?" Should sequences of digits and other nonblank, nonalphabetic symbols be considered legal as (part of) a word? Moreover, what if two or more words are the same length? Should the program display only one or all of them? What can be assumed by the program as the maximum possible length of a word, and can such assumptions be used to simplify the algorithm's design?

Example 3.2   The following problem statement appears verbatim in a text on programming: "Calculate the square root of the prime numbers from 3 to 97 and print in three columns."

Suppose we try to develop such a program. What is meant by "the square root of the prime numbers?" Since 'square root' is singular, we probably need to infer that what is *really* requested is the square root of *each* prime number in the range 3 to 97. But still that is not clear enough. Do we mean "3 to 97 inclusive" or "between 3 and 97?" Different interpretations will lead to different solutions for this problem statement.

Example 3.3   You are to develop a program that computes the sum of a list of numbers.

Before you begin to develop a solution you need to answer such questions as the following. What is the form of the numbers (integers, reals, rational numbers, complex numbers)? How is the list presented as input? Is there a known upper bound to the sum (recall the discussion of C++'s type `int` vs. the mathematical definition of the integers $\mathbf{Z}$)? How does the program know when it is at the end of the input list? How should the output be displayed?

In the problems discussed in this text, we will always need to know all the necessary information in a problem statement before beginning Stages 2 through 7 in the MAPS methodology. But it is not uncommon to be tempted to jump ahead into one of these stages—often Stage 5: Coding—before we get stuck, discover we need more information before we can proceed, and retreat to an earlier stage. We caution readers to avoid this temptation as much as possible. That is, one should complete each stage in MAPS before moving on to the next stage.

On the other hand, it is often not possible to gather all the information about a problem and its solution before we proceed to later stages in the MAPS process. So it would be simplistic to think that MAPS is always a linear sequence of stages; often an earlier stage is repeated after some experience has been gained in later stages of developing the solution.

OTHER ALGORITHMIC PROBLEMS AND THE DIALOGUE

In this section, we introduce three new algorithmic problems. As we move through the steps in the MAPS methodology in later chapters, we will often return to these problems as illustrations. Each of the problem statements given below can be considered as an *incomplete* problem statement. That is, if we exercise *stage 1: the dialogue* using any of these, we should arrive at a more detailed description of exactly what the solution should be expected to produce, and what it should not.

Computing a^b

Let's consider developing a program named `Power` that will compute and display the *b*th power of *a*, or a^b, where *a* and *b* are integers and the result is a real number. For example, written as a C++ function, `Power(2,3)` would compute the value of $2^3 = 8$.

In the *dialogue*, we explore the computational and mathematical limits under which this function should work correctly. For example, we need to worry about the outcome in unusual cases, such as the state `a == 0` and `b == -1`. What is the largest result that can be computed and displayed?

Counting Words in a Text

The numeric data types `int` and `float` are used in almost all algorithmic problems. However, a large class of problems is not well-served by these types alone. Many problems deal with strings of ASCII characters as data, and their solution requires the use of a set of operators that can manipulate variables of this type. In C++, the notion of a string is defined as follows:

> **Definition**   A *string* is a finite sequence of zero or more ASCII characters. When written within a C++ program, a string is enclosed within quotes (″) to distinguish it from the program statements that surround it. When stored, a string occupies $n+1$ memory locations—n for the characters that make up the string and one for the "null character" \0 that marks the end of the string.

For example, the following input prompt

```
"Enter a list of grades"
```

is a string. Extending this notion, C++ allows us to declare a *string variable* to be of type `char[n]` (n a constant denoting the number of memory locations reserved for storing the value of a string variable, including the null character \0) when we want it to have string values, rather than numeric values, during the program's execution.

Strings are the basic data types that text processing programs use. Consider the problem of developing a program that takes as input any string `s` and returns a count of the number of words in that string.

In the *dialogue* stage of solving this problem, we may decide that a *word* is any string of nonblank characters, whether or not it has a meaning in the sense of ordinary English usage. For simplicity, we might also assume that punctuation marks, such as periods, commas, and so on, also are counted as part of the word to which they are appended. Thus, each of the following three strings is a word:

```
"these"
"know."
"World!"
```

Monitoring a Tic-Tac-Toe Game

Although the numeric and string data types cover a wide variety of algorithmic problems, they do not address problems that require the representation of *graphical* information. Such problems include the display and analysis of x-ray images, satellite photographs, chess and other board game configurations, and the various charts and graphs that are commonly used in business and scientific computing.

To illustrate this area of algorithmic problem solving, let's look at the familiar game of tic-tac-toe. Suppose we are asked to develop an algorithm that monitors the individual moves in a single game of tic-tac-toe, displaying the result of each move (X or O) on a rectangular grid on the computer screen.

In the *dialogue*, we need to establish the nature of the input and the output for this problem. Each "move" in the game, by X or O, might be indicated by a pair of integers that gives the row and column number on the board where the X or O should be placed (see Figure 3–1). The output would be a display of the board that shows the result of all moves made so far (Figure 3–1).

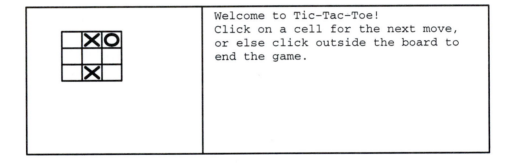

FIGURE 3–1   Series of three moves in tic-tac-toe.

THE NEED FOR PROBLEM SPECIFICATIONS

In an earlier section, we discussed the first stage in MAPS, *The Dialogue*, which allows us to clearly understand the problem to be solved—especially its input and output requirements.

During the second stage, *the specifications*, we describe precisely what must be accomplished in order to affect a solution. We give this description in terms of state descriptions of where things are at crucial times during the program's execution, such as immediately before the first step of the program and immediately after the last. For example, three different states of the process described in Section 2.1 would be a snapshot of its input just before Step 1 has been executed, a snapshot of the values of variables Sum and n just after Step 3, and a snapshot of its output after Step 5.

The two most crucial states of a program's execution are its initial state and final state. The initial state is a description of the input before the first step of the algorithm is executed and is thus called the algorithm's *precondition* (*pre* for short). The final state is a description of the input and output after the last step of the algorithm is executed and is called its *postcondition* (*post* for short). When written in a program, the precondition and postcondition appear as comments (lines that begin with //) and are placed just after the beginning and just before the end of the program's body executable statements, as illustrated in Figure 3–2.

```
#include <iostream.h>
void main ()
{
// pre: input == an expression describing all possible inputs
//    that can occur for the problem

    declarations and statements

// post:  input == empty and output == a description of all
//    possible outputs that can occur for any of these inputs
}
```

FIGURE 3–2   Style of a precondition and postcondition when written inside a program.

The precondition precisely describes, in most general terms, what must be true before our algorithm begins. That is, the precondition describes the entire region in state space from which our program may start. Before any given execution of our algorithm our program will be located at a single point in state space; the region described encompasses all such possible starting points. Similarly, the postcondition describes what we know to be true when our algorithm ends execution. Since the desired solution lies in the region of state space satisfying this postcondition, we must ensure that our algorithm ends in a state satisfying the postcondition.

To illustrate, consider again the GPA problem. If we let $grades_1$ denote the first grade in a list, $grades_2$ denote the second, and so forth, then the following is a precise description of that problem in the form of a precondition and postcondition:

```
// pre:  input == (grades₁, grades₂, ..., gradesₙ) and
//       n is at least 1 and
//       every grade gradesᵢ is in the range 0 through 4 inclusive

// post:  input == empty and
//       output == the sum of all grades divided by n
```

Technically, the precondition and postcondition are examples of what is known as an *assertion* about the state of a process.

One of the problems which you may see in this approach to writing specifications is the cumbersome and sometimes vague wording of these assertions. We had to say that "... every grade grades$_i$ is within the range 0 through 4 inclusive" to assure that the program will read as input only numbers which are valid grades. Similarly, we had to eliminate the possibility that there would be no grades at all in the input by declaring that n must be at least 1. If we had omitted this part of the precondition, then a perfectly legal beginning state would be one in which the input was empty. In that case, Step 4 would be left in the awkward position of dividing by zero. Furthermore, it is not clear in the postcondition if we are dealing with "...the sum of all the grades" which is then divided by n, or the sum of the result of dividing each grade separately by n. In this particular example, the end result is the same, but there are numerous occasions in which different interpretations would lead to different outcomes.

The difficulty in general with using English for specifications is that English is an inherently ambiguous language. Humans normally resolve this ambiguity because they understand the context or "world" in which the statement is said. This latitude is not available to us as we specify algorithmic problems, since

- The computer has no concept of context, and

- The user of the program may be working in an entirely different context than the person who defines the problem or writes the program.

Thus, we need to utilize a more formal system of expression that has well-defined rules. The language of logic allows this level of expressive precision and conciseness that we cannot usually reach when we use a more informal language (such as English) to describe the states of the computation. The next section introduces the elements of logic that will be used for writing program specifications, preconditions, and postconditions for programs.

INTRODUCTION TO LOGIC

Logic has come to play an increasingly important role in computing. In fact, some would go so far as to view computing as applied logic. In this text, logic has four important and distinct uses: writing pre- and postconditions and other assertions about the behavior of programs; the use of logical expressions in programming; reasoning about program correctness; and designing computers themselves. The first two of these roles are introduced in this chapter, and then utilized throughout Chapters 3 through 6. The third role is introduced and discussed in Chapter 7, and the fourth is presented in Chapter 8.

In the following sections, we introduce propositional logic, which is a system for reasoning and making calculations with propositions. Propositional logic began with the work of George Boole between 1847 and 1854. Boole observed a similarity between the properties of the logical operations **and** and **or** and the arithmetic operations multiplication and addition. He developed a system for manipulating logical statements that would be as precise for these statements as is arithmetic for manipulating numbers.

Finally, we extend the notion of propositional logic to a broader idea known as predicate logic. This extension allows us to use logic in a wide range of constructive ways in computing. We shall illustrate, for example, the idea that the use of so-called logical quantifiers is closely connected with the idea of loops in programs, as introduced in chapter 2.

Propositional Logic

Boole's basic strategy was to study patterns of logical arguments, using symbols to represent both individual statements and the patterns themselves. This approach to logic is known as *propositional logic* (or sometimes *symbolic logic*). A statement (or *proposition*) in propositional logic can have either of two truth values, **true** or **false** (represented in C++ by the `int` values 1 and 0, respectively). The following are typical propositions:

- The area of an isosceles right triangle with hypotenuse of length $\sqrt{2}$ is 1/2.

- All elements of the list (1 3 5 7 6 4) are less than 10.

- $3 + 5 == 7$

- The text "The quick brown fox jumps over the lazy dog" contains at least one occurrence of every letter in the English alphabet.

- No student in Computer Science 151 at Calvin College in the fall of 1993 earned a B+.

Note that although the third proposition is **false**, it is still a proposition. In order to express statements like these in a precise way, we use a formal style for writing propositions.

Definition   A *proposition* is any expression that can be formed according to the following rules:

Rule 1:   **true** and **false** are propositions.
Rule 2:   Any variable whose type is {**true, false**} is a proposition.
Rule 3:   If p is a proposition, so is $(\sim p)$.
Rule 4:   If p and q are propositions, so are $(p \lor q)$, $(p \land q)$, $(p \Rightarrow q)$, and $(p \Leftrightarrow q)$.

Table 3–1 lists the *logical operators* that are listed in Rules 3 and 4 for writing propositions, along with their C++ equivalent representations and their meanings. Recall that, in C++ programs, the values **true** and **false** are represented respectively by the integers 1 (technically, *any* nonzero value) and 0, and hence all propositional variables are declared to have type int inside a C++ program.

Note that this definition is recursive. That is, rules 3 and 4 define a proposition in terms of one or more existing propositions and *logical operators*, and each of these propositions can be formed using rules 3 and 4 again. However, because there are elementary propositions, formed by rules 1 and 2, that do not use the word *proposition*, the process of finding propositions using these rules does not go on indefinitely; that is, the definition is not circular.

For the moment, when we work within propositional calculus we will use variables and will not be concerned with any particular propositions that they might symbolize. Later, we will apply various interpretations to variables that are appropriate within the realm of programming and computer design.

TABLE 3–1   THE LOGICAL OPERATORS

Mathematical Representation	C++ equivalent	Meaning
$\sim$	!	Negation
$\vee$	||	Disjunction
$\wedge$	&&	Conjunction
$\Rightarrow$	(none)	Implication
$\Leftrightarrow$	(none)	Equivalence

We will apply other interpretations to these operators after we have looked at a few examples in the abstract.

Example 3.4   If p, q, and r are Boolean variables, then the following are examples of valid propositions. Their C++ equivalents are shown on the right:

p	p
q	q
$(\sim p)$	! p
$(p \vee q)$	(p || q)
$(p \vee (q \vee r))$	(p || (q || r))
$(p \Rightarrow (q \vee (r \Rightarrow (p \Leftrightarrow q))))$	not applicable in C++

The first three of these are clearly propositions, following directly from rules 2 and 3. The fourth follows directly from rules 2 and 4. For the fifth statement, we can apply rule 4 repeatedly:

p, q, and r are propositions, from rule 2
$(q \lor r)$ is a proposition, from rule 4
$(p \lor (q \lor r))$ is a proposition, from rule 4

A similar line of reasoning justifies that the sixth example above is a proposition.

p, q, and r are propositions, from rule 2
$(p \Leftrightarrow q)$ is a proposition, from rule 4
$(r \Rightarrow (p \Leftrightarrow q))$ is a proposition, from rule 4
$(q \lor (r \Rightarrow (p \Leftrightarrow q)))$ is a proposition, from rule 4
$(p \Rightarrow (q \lor (r \Rightarrow (p \Leftrightarrow q))))$ is a proposition, from rule 4

Example 3.5   The following are not propositions because there is no sequence of applications of rules 1 through 4 that lead to any one of them.

(p)
$(p\ q)\ p)$
$\sim (p)$

As Example 3.5 shows, if we adhere strictly to the four rules, parentheses play an important role in determining whether an expression is a proposition. However, we can drop them whenever the meaning is clear without them. For example, we can write $\sim p$ in place of $(\sim p)$, $p \lor q$ in place of $(p \lor q)$, and so on.

Careless dropping of parentheses can, however, lead to ambiguities. For example, it is not clear whether $p \lor q \land r$ means

$$((p \lor q) \land r) \qquad \text{or} \qquad (p \lor (q \land r))$$

To avoid ambiguity, the following priorities are assigned to the five operators: $\sim$ has the highest priority; $\land$ has the next highest; and $\lor$, $\Rightarrow$, and $\Leftrightarrow$ follow in that order. The same priority rules apply in C++ among the operators **not, and,** and **or**. Thus, $p \lor q \land r$ is always interpreted as $(p \lor (q \land r))$. This is similar to the priority of multiplication over addition in mathematics, allowing the equation $a + 2b$ to be interpreted as as the sum of a and $2b$ rather than the product of $a + 2$ and b.

Logic and the English Language

It is not always possible to represent arbitrary sentences symbolically using propositions. That is, many sentences are not declarative statements and thus have no truth value. For instance, "Close the door!" is a command, and "Did you attend Professor Davidson's anatomy lecture today?" is a question. However, there are a great many statements that can be represented by propositions, and even more that can be represented by predicates. For computing, most statements we might want to represent symbolically are declarative, have an unambiguous truth value, and are expressible as propositions or predicates.

Note that there are only five operators in propositional logic. In fact, only one is really necessary, since each of the others can be shown to be equivalent to an expression that uses just one (see the exercises). The English language offers an enormous variety of ways to express the same idea; thus, in representing statements by propositions, we omit many shades of meaning and focus on the logical structure of statements. Also, we will use the same logical structure to express many different forms in English. For example, if we represent the proposition "Phogbound is running for senator" by the variable p, we can then represent either of the following sentences by the proposition $\sim p$:

Phogbound is not running for senator.
It is not the case that Phogbound is running for senator.

Similarly, we can represent any of the following sentences as $p \wedge q$, when suitable assignments of the variables p and q are made:

The number n is a prime number less than 100.
$10 \leq x \leq 100$
Henry Higgins was a confirmed bachelor, but Eliza Doolittle won his heart.
Although he had been a slave merchant, John Newton became a great opponent of slavery.

The first of these sentences consists of two phrases—"n is a prime number" and "n is less than 100"—but they are collapsed, using a common stylistic device for abbreviation. The second also contains two hidden phrases—"$10 \leq x$" and "$x \leq 100$"—but these are abbreviated in a mathematical style. In the third, the word *but* has logically the same meaning as *and*; it adds an element of contrast that we need not distinguish symbolically in the propositional expression. In the fourth sentence, the word *although* also indicates the presence of an *and* along with a note of contrast.

We can represent the sentence

Some are born to greatness, some achieve greatness, and some have greatness thrust upon them

either as $((p \wedge q) \wedge r)$ or as $(p \wedge (q \wedge r))$. In Chapter 7 we shall see that these two logical expressions are equivalent and the parentheses can be dropped, yielding $p \wedge q \wedge r$. In the English sentence, the first comma therefore stands for the logical operator $\wedge$.

The logical operator $\vee$ can have either of two slightly different meanings in English that we need to distinguish from each other. By the sentence

> *This bank will give free checking to anyone maintaining an average checking account balance over $500 or having a certificate of deposit over $5000.*

the bank certainly does not intend to exclude people who satisfy both conditions. In contrast, we can imagine a parent saying to a child "You may go on the swing or the slide" and meaning "You can go on one or the other, but not both." The bank's use of *or* is the *inclusive* **or**, meaning "either or both possibilities are accepted." The parent's use is the *exclusive* **or**, meaning "Either one possibility or the other is accepted, but not both." In propositional logic, we usually use the inclusive **or** rather than the exclusive **or**.

In propositions of the form $p \Rightarrow q$, p is called the *antecedent* and q the *consequent*. An English example of logical implication is

> *If Phogbound is elected, then we will be in a real mess*

although the *then* is often dropped in normal discourse. If we let p denote "Phogbound is elected" and q denote "we will be in a real mess," the entire sentence can be represented as $p \Rightarrow q$ (meaning "p implies q"). Alternatively, we can word this sentence as

> *We'll be in a real mess if Phogbound is elected.*

and we can still represent it as $p \Rightarrow q$.

Consider the distinction between two different uses of the word *if* in sentences like the following:

> *I will get tickets if Our Town is being performed.*
> *I will get tickets only if Our Town is being performed.*

If r denotes the proposition "*Our Town* is being performed" and s denotes the proposition "I will get tickets," the first sentence can be denoted by $r \Rightarrow s$. A person uttering this sentence is not saying whether or not she would get tickets if *MacBeth* is being performed. The latter sentence has quite a different meaning, and is denoted by $s \Rightarrow r$. That is, it could be reworded as "If I get tickets then *Our Town* is being performed"; the performance of *Our Town* is the only circumstance under which the person will get tickets. The proposition $s \Rightarrow r$ is called the *converse* of $r \Rightarrow s$.

Another important property of $p \Rightarrow q$ is that *causality* is not necessarily assumed between p and q. For instance, when we say

> *If George plays the viola well, then he will be selected for the orchestra*

we implicitly assume that selection for the orchestra is caused by George's playing well. The statement

If 1 + 1 = 2, then the sun is the center of the solar system

is also represented as $p \Rightarrow q$ and, from the point of view of logic, is just as valid as our prior statement about George and the orchestra. Causality is another of the concepts we can express in natural language that we cannot express in propositional calculus.

The expression $p \Leftrightarrow q$ is used to indicate that two propositions are logically equivalent; that is, either one implies the other. A typical example is the following:

Let T be a triangle with sides a, b, and c. Then $a^2 + b^2 = c^2$ if and only if T is a right triangle.

If p denotes "$a^2 + b^2 = c^2$" and q denotes "T is a right triangle," then the phrase "$a^2 + b^2 = c^2$ if and only if T is a right triangle" is denoted $p \Leftrightarrow q$. That is, both $p \Rightarrow q$ and $q \Rightarrow p$ are **true** simultaneously.

Example 3.6   Entire statements can be represented as propositions. Let's consider a relatively complicated example: "If Dynamic Systems or Metadyne is awarded the contract, van Alstyne or Liu will be assigned to do both the analysis and design, Frederick will not be assigned the analysis, and Thompson will be fired." To write an equivalent proposition for this statement, we first associate variables with its constituent phrases:

DS	= Dynamic Systems is awarded the contract
MD	= Metadyne is awarded the contract
VAA	= van Alstyne will be assigned the analysis
LIUA	= Liu will be assigned the analysis
VAD	= van Alstyne will be assigned the design
LIUD	= Liu will be assigned the design
FRA	= Frederick will be assigned the analysis
TF	= Thompson will be fired

This entire statement can then be represented by the following proposition:

$$(DS \lor MD) \Rightarrow$$
$$(((VAA \land VAD) \lor (LIUA \land LIUD)) \land \sim FRA \land TF)$$

Evaluating Propositions: Truth Values

Recall from Chapter 2 that we defined the notion of state for a set of variables. This notion can be applied to propositions as well.

Definition   Let $p_1, \ldots, p_n$ be all the variables in a proposition. Then the *state* of these variables $p_1, \ldots, p_n$ is the result of assigning the Boolean value **true** or **false** to each of them.

For example, suppose we have the proposition $p \vee q$. Since there are only two variables, each of which can only take on two possible values (**true** or **false**), there are only four possible states for the variables in $p \vee q$. Thus, unlike types with infinite cardinalities (such as **N** or **R**), $p \vee q$ has such a small state space that we can tabulate its value for all four possible states of its variables. Such a tabulation is called a *truth table*. The truth table for $p \vee q$ is given in Figure 3–3.

p	q	$p \vee q$
true	true	true
true	false	true
false	true	true
false	false	false

FIGURE 3–3   Truth table for $p \vee q$.

Here, we see that the value of the function is **true** whenever either one or both of its variables are **true**; otherwise, it is **false**. This definition of the proposition is consistent with our intuition about disjunction that was illustrated previously. That is, suppose the variables p and q are assigned as follows:

$p ==$ "You have an average checking account balance over \$500."
$q ==$ "You have a certificate of deposit over \$5000."

Then the proposition $(p \vee q)$ is **true** whenever either p is **true**, q is **true**, or both p and q are **true**; otherwise, $(p \vee q)$ is **false**.

Truth tables for the other operators in propositional logic can be constructed in a similar fashion, as shown in Figure 3–4. Most of the truth values are consistent with the intuitive ideas discussed earlier.

The implication operator deserves a bit more discussion, especially for the case when p is **false**. It is not hard to see the rationale for this assignment if we consider a specific example:

If Our Town is being performed, then I will buy tickets.

This statement is represented by $p \Rightarrow q$. If, in fact, *Our Town* is not being performed, the variable p is **false**. However, there is no guarantee that I won't buy tickets even if *Our Town* is not being performed; that is, I might buy tickets

p	$\sim p$
true	false
false	true

(a)

p	q	$p \wedge q$
true	true	true
true	false	false
false	true	false
false	false	false

(b)

p	q	$p \Rightarrow q$
true	true	true
true	false	false
false	true	true
false	false	true

(c)

p	q	$p \Leftrightarrow q$
true	true	true
true	false	false
false	true	false
false	false	true

(d)

FIGURE 3–4   Truth tables for propositions. (*a*) Negation; (*b*) conjunction; (*c*) implication; (*d*) equivalence.

to *A Chorus Line* instead. Since the falsity of p in the proposition $p \Rightarrow q$ does not guarantee the falsity of q, we must allow the entire proposition in this case to be **true**.

Truth tables can be constructed for propositions of arbitrary complexity. When a proposition has more than one operator, the truth assignments are made in the order in which the operators are interpreted. This is illustrated in Example 3.7.

Example 3.7   We construct the truth table for $(p \vee q) \Rightarrow \sim p$ by starting with p and q, deriving the table for each subproposition $(p \vee q)$ and $\sim p$, and then combining those results using the original truth table for $\Rightarrow$. We usually work from left to right, as shown below:

p	q	$p \vee q$	$\sim p$	$(p \vee q) \Rightarrow \sim p$
true	true	true	false	false
true	false	true	false	false
false	true	true	true	true
false	false	false	true	true

The number of rows in a truth table grows exponentially with the number of variables in the proposition. That is, if a proposition has one variable, like $\sim p$, then its truth table will have two rows (one for each possible value of p). Two-variable propositions, like $p \vee q$, will have four rows. Three-variable propositions will have eight rows, since there are $2^3 = 8$ different ways to assign the two values **true** and **false** to three variables. In general, the size of a truth table with n variables will therefore be 2^n rows. Hence, if we have more than three or four variables, the size of a truth table can become unwieldy.

EXERCISES

3–1 Which of the following are propositions?

   a.   There are precisely 512 words on this page.

   b.   314159 is a prime number.

   c. $x^2 + 2x + 1 = 13E = mc^2$

   d.   The age of the universe is over 17 billion years.

   e.   Shoot the piano player.

   f. $x - y = 0$

   g.   Why is the sky blue?

   h.   The hypotenuse is the shortest side of a right triangle.

3–2 Build the following propositions from variables, applying one rule from the definition at each step.

   a. $(p \Rightarrow (p \wedge q))$

   b. $(((\sim p) \Leftrightarrow q) \wedge (\sim r))$

   c. $(((p \vee (\sim q)) \wedge (p \vee q)) \Rightarrow p)$

3–3 Represent the following statements symbolically using propositions. Indicate what each variable stands for.

   a. $-1 \leq x \leq 1, -1 \leq y \leq 1$

   b.   Although Manderson had a fine analytic mind and great wealth, he was hopelessly insane.

   c. Either Trent was in Paris while Mabel was in London or Trent was in Venice while Mabel was in Paris.

   d. A definition is recursive only if it includes an initialization step and an induction step.

   e. Whenever Thomas and Dumars are shooting well, the Pistons will win unless Rodman is out with an injury and Laimbeer fouls out, in which case the Pistons will lose.

   f. If the design group made the error, they are primarily responsible and everyone else bears a secondary responsibility; if the programming team made a coding error then Ted's group or Louis's group has primary responsibility; if it was a testing error, both FouSen's and Rita's group were primarily responsible.

3–4 According to the definition, which of the following are valid propositions?

true
(*true*)
$\sim p \wedge q$
$p \Rightarrow \sim q)$
$(p \vee ((\sim p) \wedge q))$
$(p \Rightarrow p) \wedge ((\sim q) \Rightarrow q)$

3–5 Construct truth tables for each of the following expressions.

   a. $((p \Rightarrow q) \wedge p) \Rightarrow q$

   b. $((p \Rightarrow r) \wedge (q \Rightarrow \sim r)) \Rightarrow (p \wedge q)$

   c. $p \wedge (q \vee r) \Rightarrow s$

   d. $(((p \Rightarrow q) \wedge (q \Rightarrow r)) \Rightarrow (p \Rightarrow r))$

   e. $((p \Rightarrow (q \wedge \sim q)) \Rightarrow p)$

   f. $(p \Rightarrow q) \vee (p \Leftrightarrow \sim q)$

3–6 Show that $\sim (p \vee q)$ and $(\sim p \wedge \sim q)$ have the same truth table (this is known as DeMorgan's Law).

3–7 Consider the proposition $((p \lor q) \land \sim p) \Rightarrow q$. Show that it is equivalent to the following statement by assigning appropriate variables to each of the phrases.

Either the Red Sox are better than the A's or the Pirates are better than the Reds. The Red Sox are not better than the A's. Therefore, the Pirates are better than the Reds.

Predicate Logic

Now that we have explored propositional logic, the question arises as to whether it is sufficient for the purposes of specifying the preconditions, postconditions, and other intermediate states of an algorithmic problem. Unfortunately, the answer is no. Propositional logic is deficient in the following ways:

- It cannot express universal truths. There is no general way to express a concept that is true for every member of a set. For example, we would like to express that every grade input to the GPA program is in the range 0 through 4 inclusive.

- It cannot express relationships if we wish to use numerical variables. There is no way to express that two variables have the same value, or that the value of a variable is greater than a constant, etc. For example, we would like to be able to state that the number of grades in the input is at least one, that is, $n \geq 1$.

- It cannot express mathematical functions. We would like to be able to develop a function which would test a property of an object and return **true** or **false**; for example, *even* (*num*) returns **true** or **false** depending upon whether or not the variable *num* is a multiple of 2.

To express these ideas, we must turn to a more robust expressive notation, called *predicate logic*.[1]

Example 3.8   Suppose we want to develop specifications for a program that rearranges a list of 30 integers so that they are in ascending order (a process called *sorting*). We can informally (i.e., using English rather than a logic expression) describe the inputs and outputs for such a program in the following style:

---

1.   Similarly, predicate logic is not powerful enough to express all concepts of interest in computing. For example, if we are developing a real-time program to control the flight of an airplane, we would like to be able to express issues concerned with timing and deadlines for programmed events, like lowering the landing gear. To express such concepts we need a so-called *temporal logic*. The development of logics in general is an active area of research.

```
// pre:  input  ==  Any list of thirty integers
// post: output ==  The original 30 integers arranged in
//            ascending order
```

However, this style of description is not precise enough to be used as a basis for defining a problem. For example, it doesn't give a criterion for determining that the integers are arranged in ascending order. This might seem to be a trivial point, since we all have a good idea about what is meant by "ascending order." But that is only because we share enough common experience that we can take this information for granted. A computer, however, does not have this luxury, so at some point in the programming process we must specify exactly how to determine whether or not a list of integers is in ascending order. A more precise description, therefore, is this:

```
// pre:  input  ==  Any list A == (e₁ e₂ ... e₃₀) of integers
```
$$// \text{ pre: input } == \text{ Any list } A == (e_1\ e_2\ ...\ e_{30}) \text{ of integers}$$
$$// \text{ post: output } == \text{ Any list } B == (e_1'\ e_2'\ ...\ e_{30}'), \text{ a } permutation$$
$$// \quad\quad\quad \text{ of } A \text{ for which } e_{i+1}' \geq e_i' \text{ for every integer } i \text{ in}$$
$$// \quad\quad\quad \{1,\ ...,\ 29\}$$

This alternative description more precisely spells out the relationship between the input and the output, and it provides an unambiguous definition of what we mean by the phrase "in ascending order."

While our second description is more precise than the first, it is still too wordy. We need to have a more compact notation for expressing the input states, the output states, and other intermediate states of a program. Such a notation is called "predicate logic," and is a simple extension of the propositional logic discussed earlier.

The input and output descriptions that appear in the above examples, in fact, are informal examples of predicates. Informally, we can think of a predicate as a statement that includes variables and which, when its variables are in any particular state, has a truth value.

Definition   A *predicate* is an expression that is either **true** or **false** for each state of its variables. It can include constants (integers, real numbers, and truth values **true** and **false**); arithmetic and Boolean variables and function references; arithmetic operators ($+$, $*$, etc.); relational operators ($<$, $\leq$, $\geq$, $>$, $=$, $\neq$), and logical operators ($\vee$, $\wedge$, $\sim$).

In C++, these kinds of predicates are known as *relational expressions*, and they have many uses in programming. The relational operators, however, have different representations in C++ than in mathematics (see Table 3–2).

Earlier, we defined propositions using precise syntax rules. We could do the same for predicates; however, we will instead use our intuition and experience with these types of expressions in other mathematical settings along with our new knowledge of propositions themselves. We start by noting that every proposition is also a predicate.

TABLE 3–2   THE RELATIONAL OPERATORS

Mathematical representation	C++ equivalent	Meaning
<	<	Less than
≤	<=	Less than or equal
>	>	Greater than
≥	>=	Greater than or equal
=	==	Equal
≠	!=	Not equal

Example 3.9   The following are mathematical representations for predicates. Equivalent C++ relational expressions are shown on the right.

$$x < 10$$
$$i^2 + j^2 = 25$$
$$a_1 < a_2 \land a_2 < a_3$$

```
x < 10
i*i + j*j == 25
a[1] < a[2] && a[2] < a[3]
```

The third item of Example 3.9 illustrates the use of precedence rules that govern the order in which different operators are applied in a predicate. In particular, the relational operators have higher precedence than the logical operators (both in mathematics and in C++). Thus, the expression `a[1] < a[2] && a[2] < a[3]` is equivalent to `(a[1] < a[2]) && (a[2] < a[3])`, which is the normal interpretation.

The following are *not* predicates:

$$i + 1$$
$$y^2 < 10 \neq$$
```
x = x + 1
```

$i + 1$ is not a predicate since it has no truth value; it is simply an arithmetic expression that has numerical value which is one greater than the value of i. $y^2 < 10 \neq$ would be a predicate if there were another expression to the right of $\neq$, but as written it is syntactically meaningless. The expression `x = x + 1` happens to be a C++ assignment, but it is not normally treated as an expression that has a truth value.

We can evaluate a predicate by replacing all of its variables by their values in a specific state, and then computing the result using the familiar rules of arithmetic. Thus, the predicate x < 10 is evaluated as **true** in the state x == 1 and **false** in the state x == 11. We say that x == 1 *satisfies* the predicate x < 10. A predicate that has states for which it can be satisfied is called *satisfiable*. For instance, the predicate 11 < 10 is not satisfiable.

Definition   A predicate that is satisfied in every state is said to be *valid*.

For example, if i is an integer variable the predicate $i \geq 0 \vee i \leq 1$ is valid, since it is **true** for every possible integer value of the variable i.

Example 3.10   Predicates are often used in the definitions of sets. For instance, in each of the following definitions, the set defined contains all states that satisfy the predicate that appears at the right of the vertical bar. The variables in all the definitions use the natural numbers **N** as their domain.

a. $\{(i,j) \mid i < j\}$
b. $\{(i,j) \mid i^2 + j^2 == 25\}$
c. $\{(a_0, a_1, a_2) \mid a_0 == \max(a_1, a_2)\}$
d. $\{(i,j) \mid i < j \vee j == 0\}$
e. $\{(i,j) \mid i^2 + j^2 == 25 \ \wedge \ j > 2\}$

Testing for membership in each of these sets can be done using a C++ conditional expression with the set-defining predicate as its condition. Each of the following statements sets the int variable result to 1 or 0 (effectively, **true** or **false** in C++), depending on whether or not the indicated predicate is satisfied by the values of the variables i, j, a0, a1, and a2.

a.   `result = i < j ;`

b.   `result = i*i + j*j == 25 ;`

c.   `result = (a0 >= a1 && a0 >= a2 && (a0 == a1 || a0 == a2));`

d.   `result = (i < j || j == 0) ;`

e.   `result = (i*i + j*j == 25 && j > 2) ;`

Note that each of these statements that encloses its conditional expression in parentheses could just as well have been writtend without the enclosing parentheses. That is because the priority of the assignment operator in C++ yields precedence to the other (relational and arithmetic) operators that appear in the statement. The outermost parentheses are thus included only for clarification and readibility.

The universal and existential quantifiers   Recall that we can describe the output of some programs as a *list* of the form

$$B = (e_1' \; e_2' \; \dots \; e_{30}')$$

which is a permutation of another list A and has the property that, for every i between 1 and 29 inclusive, $e_{i+1}' \geq e_i'$. This particular statement is actually called a *conjunction* of two predicates. The first, "B is a permutation of A," is a predicate with 30 variables. The second, "for every i between 1 and 29 inclusive, $e_{i+1}' \geq e_i'$," contains 29 predicates of the form $e_{i+1}' \geq e_i'$, one for each of the integers 1 through 29. That is, it serves as a shorthand for the predicate

$$e_2' \geq e_1' \wedge e_3' \geq e_2' \wedge \dots \wedge e_{30}' \geq e_{29}'$$

Because statements like "for every," "for all," and "for each" occur so frequently in mathematics and logic, they are abbreviated by the special symbol $\forall$, called the *universal quantifier*. In this example, we write the phrase

"for every i between 1 and 29 inclusive, $e_{i+1}' \geq e_i'$"

in the following shorthand form:

$$\forall \, i \in \{1, 2, \dots, 29\}: e_{i+1}' \geq e_i'$$

where the symbols $\forall i \in$ are followed by a set representation of the domain of the variable i and a predicate that describes what is true for *every* value of that variable in its domain. The domain of a variable is like its *type*—that is, the set of values whose members may be assigned to that variable.

More generally, the following predicate can be composed out of predicates $R(i)$ and $P(i)$:

$$\forall \; R(i) \; : \; P(i)$$

Here, $R(i)$ is used to describe the domain of i and $P(i)$ must be satisfied for every value of i in its domain in order for the complete predicate $\forall \; R(i) \; : \; P(i)$ to be valid—i.e., to be **true** in all cases. This kind of predicate can therefore be used as a shorthand for the conjunction $P(i_1) \wedge P(i_2) \wedge \dots$, where $i_1, i_2, \dots$ denote all the values of i that satisfy R.

Predicates with the universal quantifier can be tested in a C++ program by writing a loop. In general, for the predicate

$$\forall \; i \in \{1, \; \dots, \; n\} \; : \; P(i)$$

can be tested by the following loop structure, where the int variable result will be set to **true** or **false** (1 or 0 in C++) depending respectively on whether or not the predicate is satisfied.

```
result = 1 ;
for (i = 1; i<=n; i++)
  if ( ! P(i) )
    result = 0 ;
```

This loop assumes the predicate will be 1 at the outset of loop execution, and then for each value of the variable i tests to see if it can determine that one particular P(i) is false.

Recall that a multiple conjunction is true only if all of its operands are true simultaneously. If only one is false, then the entire conjunction is false. That is the spirit in which this loop is written. The following examples show some of the many uses for quantified predicates in describing the state of a computation, along with the corresponding loops that can be used to test whether or not the predicate is satisfied.

Example 3.11   Each of the statements below is followed by its representation as a predicate that uses the universal quantifier:

a.   Every list element e_i from e_1 to e_{21} is distinct from 9:

$$\forall\, i \in \{1, 2, \ldots, 21\}: e_i \neq 9$$

```
result = 1;
for (i=1; i<=21; i++)
  if (! (e[i] != 9))
    result = 0 ;
```

(Note that the conditional statement can be written more simply instead as if (e[i] == 9)...)

b.   The point (a, b) is above and to the right of every point (i, j) in some rectangular region G of the xy plane (see Figure 3–5):

$$\forall\, (i, j) \in G: i < a \wedge j < b$$

(This one doesn't have an equivalent C++ loop, since the set of points G is not made up of integer pairs.)

c.   All e_j's between e_m and e_n are positive numbers:

$$\forall\, j \in \{m, m+1, \ldots, n\}: e_j > 0$$

```
result = 1 ;
for (j=m; j<=n; j++)
  if (! (e[j] > 0))
    result = 0 ;
```

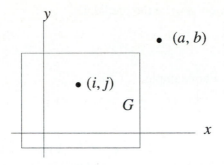

FIGURE 3–5   Graphic representation for a region G that satisfies the predicate $\forall\,(i, j) \in G\colon i < a \wedge j < b$.

d.   In a list $A = (e_1\ e_2\ ...\ e_n)$, the elements up to but not including the jth are arranged in increasing order (see Figure 3–6):

$\forall\,i \in \{1, 2, \ldots, j-2\}\colon e_i \leq e_{i+1}$

```
result = 1;
for (i=1; i<=j-2; i++)
   if (! (e[i] <= e[i+1]))
      result = 0 ;
```

Note that there is no claim that any of these statements is true for all possible values of the variables; the claim is only that they are true whenever a particular set of values falls within the stated domain.

There are times when the range for the quantified predicate can be omitted if that range is clear from context—that is, if it is a universal set which has been clearly specified. For instance, if we know that i is an integer (which is often the case), we can write

$\forall\,i : i < i + 1$

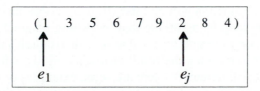

FIGURE 3–6   Example of the predicate $\forall\,i \in \{1, 2, ..., j-2\}\colon e_i \leq e_{i+1}$.

Similarly, we can always rewrite the predicate

$$\forall \ R(i) : P(i)$$

as $\forall \ i : R(i) \Rightarrow P(i)$. For example,

$$\forall \ i \in \{1, ..., 21\} : e_i \neq 9$$

is the same as $\forall \ i : 1 \leq i \leq 21 \Rightarrow e_i \neq 9$. Literally, this says that "if i is in the range from 1 to 21, then e_i is not equal to 9." Thus, it is equivalent to the statement, "for all i in the range 1 to 21, e_i is not equal to 9."

A second quantifier of interest to us is the so-called *existential quantifier*, denoted mathematically by the symbol $\exists$. It can be read, "there exists," "there is," or "for some." It is used to abbreviate multiple occurrences of the disjunction operator when several similar predicates are joined by it.

The existential quantifier, like the universal quantifier, is just a shorthand notation. For instance, $\exists \ i \in \{1, ..., n\} : e_i = = 0$ is a shorthand notation for $(e_1 == 0) \vee (e_2 == 0) \vee ... \vee (e_n == 0)$. That is, just as the universal quantifier is a shorthand for a sequence of $\wedge$'s, the existential quantifier is a shorthand for a sequence of $\vee$'s. Note that the existential quantifier does not tell us which value (or values) makes the predicate **true**, just that there exists at least one value for which the predicate is satisfied.

A test for an existentially-quantified predicate can also be constructed using a loop. To do this for the general predicate

$$\exists \ i \in \{1, ..., n\} : P(i)$$

we write a loop in the following basic form:

```
result = 0 ;
for (i=1; i<=n; i++)
  if ( P(i) )
    result = 1 ;
```

This construction follows a reverse sort of logic from the loop representing the universal quantifier. Recall that for a disjunction of predicates to be **true** (1), we need only find *one* of its constituent predicates to be **true**. The only case in which the whole disjunction will be **false** (0) is if *every* constituent is **false**.

So, we start the loop by assuming that the whole disjunction will be 0, and then we use the loop to search for a value of i that satisfies the predicate *P(i)*. If we find one (or more) then the result of evaluating the whole predicate will be 1; otherwise, it will remain 0. Here are some examples of using the existential quantifier in a predicate, along with the corresponding C++ loops that will test whether the predicate is satisfied by the current values of the variables in question.

Example 3.12   The following sentences are shown with their representations using the existential quantifier:

a.   There is a member of the list $L = (e_1 \ e_2 \ ... \ e_n)$ which is zero.

$$\exists \ i \ \in \ \{1, ..., n\} : e_i \ = \ = \ 0$$

```
result = 0;
for (i=1; i<=n; i++)
   if (L.element(i) == 0)
      result = 1 ;
```

b.   Some point (i, j) in the planar set R is in the third quadrant (i.e., both coordinates are negative).

$$\exists \ (i,j) \in R : i < 0 \wedge j < 0$$

(This one doesn't have an equivalent C++ loop, since the set of points G is not made up of integer pairs.)

c.   The elements of the list $L = (e_1 \ e_2 \ ... \ e_n)$ are not in ascending order.

$$\exists \ j \ \in \ \{1, ..., n - 1\} : e_{j+1} < e_j$$

```
result = 0;            .
for (j=1; j<=n-1; j++)
   if (L.element(j+1) < L.element(j))
      result = 1 ;
```

d.   There are nonzero integers a, b, and c such that $a^3 + b^3 \ = \ = \ c^3$.

$$\exists \ a, b, c \neq 0 : a^3 + b^3 = c^3$$

(This one doesn't have an equivalent C++ loop, since the set of nonzero integer triples a, b, and c is limitless.)

e.   There is some row on the checkerboard that has no pieces on it.

$$\exists \ \text{row } R \text{ on the checkerboard: } R \text{ has no pieces on it}$$

(See Exercise 3–12 for building this sort of C++ loop.)

f.   There is a sentence in this text with at least one spelling error.

$$\exists \ \text{sentence } S: S \text{ is in this text and } S \text{ has at least one spelling error}$$

(This one is too complex to be done in C++ so soon in the text; stay tuned!)

It is often the case that the universal and existential quantifiers are both needed to represent a single predicate.

Example 3.13   For example, suppose we want to express symbolically that $B = \{e_1'\ e_2'\ ...\ e_{30}'\}$ is a permutation of $A = \{e_1\ e_2\ ...\ e_{30}\}$. Suppose also that all the e_i's are distinct. We can express this as follows:

perm $(B, A) == \forall i \in \{1, ..., 30\}\ \exists j \in \{1, ..., 30\} : e_i' == e_j.$

In English, this says that B is a permutation of A if, for every element e_i' of B there is an identical element e_j in A, though not necessarily in the same position (that is, the indexes i and j do not need to be identical for $e_i' == e_j$ to be **true**). If the e_i's are not all distinct, the situation is more complicated because we must express the concept that all of the original members of A appear in B. The above formulation would allow duplicate members of A to not appear in B at all.

Further Quantifiers   In addition to $\exists$ and $\forall$, five other quantifiers are so often used in computing that they should be introduced here. These are written in mathematical logic as follows:

Num *R(i): P(i)*
Min *R(i): P(i)*
Max *R(i): P(i)*
Sum *R(i): f(i)*
Prod *R(i): f(i)*

Num *R(i): P(i)* gives the *num*ber of values of i in the range given by R which satisfy the predicate P. **Min** yields the *min*imum value of i for which $P(i)$ is **true**, with i restricted to the range specified by R. **Max** is the same as **Min** but yields the *max*imum value. **Sum** is used to express the result of adding together all values of $f(i)$ where i takes on all possible values in the domain specified by R. In mathematics, **Sum** is often abbreviated Σ. **Prod** is the same as **Sum** but denotes the *prod*uct rather than the sum (sometimes in mathematics the product is denoted by the Greek letter $\prod$). Note that none of these quantifiers results in a boolean value and that several require that a function rather than a proposition be evaluated for each value of the index i.

Like the other quantifiers, these five quantifiers can be used in predicates that are implemented in the form of a C++ loop. These predicates and their C++ loop equivalents are illustrated in the following example.

Example 3.14   The evaluations of these expressions are shown on the right, and the equivalent C++ loop is shown below each one:

a. **Num** $i \in \{0, \ldots, 3\} : i^2 > i$ $== 2$

```
count = 0 ;
for (i=0; i<=3; i++)
  if (i*i > i)
    count++ ;
```

(Note: the variable `count` is used to keep track of the number of times the predicate `i*i > i` is **true**, for all the values of `i` in the range 0 to 3. Each time a value of `i` satisfies this predicate, `Count` is incremented by 1.)

b. **Min** $i \in \{0, \ldots, 3\} : i^2 > i$ $== 2$

```
smallesti = -1;
for (i=0; i<=3; i++)
  if (i*i > i && smallesti == -1)
    smallesti = i ;
```

(Note: the variable `smallesti` is used to keep track of the smallest value of i for which the predicate `i*i > i` is 1, for all the values of i in the range 0 to 3. The *first* time a value of i satisfies this predicate, `smallesti` is assigned the value of i; for other values of i that satisfy this predicate, `smallesti` is not reassigned a value. This is guaranteed by the condition `smallesti == -1` in the conditional statement, and `smallesti` is initially assigned the value −1 to signal the fact that it has not yet been assigned *any* value of i in the desired range. If it turns out that none of these values of i satisfies the predicate, then `smallesti` will be left with the value −1 to so designate that outcome.)

c. **Max** $i \in \{0, \ldots, 3\} : i^2 > i$ $== 3$

```
largesti = -1 ;
for (i=0; i<=3; i++)
  if (i*i > i)
    largesti = i ;
```

(Note: This loop uses a reverse strategy from the one above. That is, by the order in which each different value of i is assigned for each subsequent repetition of the loop, the largest value of i will be there for the last repetition of the loop.) Alternatively, we could write this as a while loop as follows:

```
largesti = -1 ;
i = 0 ;
while (i <= 3)
{
   if (i*i > i)
      largesti = i ;
   i++ ;
}
```

   d. **Sum** $i \in \{0, \ldots, 3\} : i^2 - i \quad == 0 + 0 + 2 + 6 == 8$

```
sum = 0 ;
for (i=0; i<=3; i++)
  sum = sum + (i*i - i) ;
```

(Note: Each time this loop is repeated, another value is added to the variable sum, which is keeping track of the running total. The parentheses in this assignment are added for emphasis, though they are not technically needed.)

   e. **Prod** $i \in \{1, \ldots, 4\} : i^2 \quad == 1 \times 4 \times 9 \times 16 == 576$

```
product = 1;
for (i=1; i<=4; i++)
  product = product * (i*i) ;
```

(Note: Each time this loop is repeated, another value is multiplied by the variable product. The parentheses in this assignment are also not needed. Note also that this loop does not need to be repeated for the value i = 1, since multiplication of any variable by 1 does nothing for the result.)

Free and Bound Variables   Compare the expression

$$e_{i+1}' \leq e_i'$$

with the quantified expression

$$\forall\, i \in \{1, \ldots, 29\} : e_{i+1}' \leq e_i'$$

In the first case, i is unrestricted; it can take on any value from whatever domain it happens to be defined over. Thus, i is called a *free variable*. In the second case, however, i is restricted by the universal quantifier to take on all values in the specified range. In this case, i is called a *bound variable*.

In general, variables whose values are restricted to a domain by application of a quantifier are bound; variables which are not bound are free. (We shall see that the distinction between free and bound variables has an analogy with global and local variables, respectively, when we define functions in programming.)

Consider the expression

$$\forall\, i \in \{m, \ldots, n\} : e_i \leq K$$

In this expression, i is bound, but m, n, and K are free. It is not unusual for free and bound variables to occur together.

Predicates and Programs

We will frequently use predicates as we discuss programs and problem solving. Fundamental to these uses is the idea of a predicate defining the exact conditions under which a program will run. Also fundamental is the correspondence between quantified predicates and program loops. We develop the first idea here and continue it in Chapter 5; the second idea is further developed in Chapter 6.

The State of a Computation   Earlier we introduced pre- and postconditions for programs in general. That is, a precondition is a predicate that describes all allowable input states before program execution, and a postcondition is one that describes all possible outputs that correspond to those inputs for the algorithm under consideration.

We can now affirm that pre- and postconditions can be inserted before and/or after *any* statement within a program. For instance, suppose that we have the following statement:

```
i = 0 ;
```

which assigns the value 0 to the variable i. Suppose also that this is a simple program with only two variables, i and j. We can use a predicate to describe the set of all states of the program *after* execution of this statement. For instance, the predicate

```
i == 0
```

is called a *postcondition* for the statement i = 0; . Suppose further that before this statement is executed, we know that $i > j \land j > 10$. That predicate is called a *precondition* for the statement i = 0, because it describes a set of states that can occur *before* that statement is executed. Preconditions and postconditions for a statement are written as comments immediately before and after that statement in the program, as illustrated below for the above assignment statement.

```
// i > j and j > 10
   i = 0 ;
// i == 0 and j > 10
```

In this case, the assignment changed only the value of i, so that the value of j in the postcondition satisfies the same predicate that it did before the assigment is executed.

Definition   A *postcondition* for a statement or group of statements in a program is a predicate that describes the set of all states in which those statements can terminate after they are executed, and is written as a comment immediately *after* that group of statements in the program text. A *precondition* for such a group of statements is a predicate that describes the set of all states in a program immediately prior to execution of a statement or group of statements, and is inserted as a comment immediately *before* that group of statements. An *assertion* is a logical statement describing a truth about the computation at the point in the program where it appears.

Preconditions and postconditions, then, represent special cases of the concept of assertion. Further we can think of the postcondition as being a predicate describing the *target set*, or the goal at which the program is aiming. Later we will see how to use assertions, postconditions and preconditions to assist in the development and verification of programs.

EXERCISES

3–8 Evaluate the following predicates in each of states I and II:

(I) $i = 0 \land j = 1 \land k = -1$ (II) $i = -1 \land j = 1 \land k = 0$

    a. $i < 10 \land j < 10$
    b. $-1 < j \le i$
    c. $i + j > k$
    d. $i^3 = j^3 = k^3$

3–9 For each of the predicates in Exercise 3–8, write a C++ conditional statement that will evaluate it and set the value of the int variable result to 1 or 0 (denoting **true** or **false**), accordingly.

3–10 Evaluate each of the following predicates. Assume the domain of all variables is **N**.

    a. $\forall\, i : i < i + 1$
    b. $\forall\, i : i^2 < i$
    c. $\forall\, i, j : i^2 + j^2 > 0$
    d. $\exists\, i : i^2 = 5i - 6$
    e. $\exists\, i, j : i^2 + j^2 \le 25$
    f. $\forall\, i \,\exists\, j : i + j = 0$
    g. **Max** $i \in \{1, ..., 100\} : i + 2 = 101$
    h. **Min** $i \in \{1, ..., 6\} : (i^2 - 6i) = 3$

    i. $\forall\, i \,\exists\, j : i - j = 0$
    j. $\exists\, i \,\forall\, j : i - j = 0$
    k. $\forall\, i \,\exists\, j : i \times j = 0$
    l. **Sum** $i \in \{1, ..., 10\} : i - 5$
    m. **Prod** $i \in \{1, ..., n\} : i$

3–11 For each of the predicates in Exercise 3–10, write a C++ loop that will evaluate it.

3–12 Suppose a chessboard is defined as $\{(i, j) \mid 1 \le i \le 8 \land 1 \le j \le 8\}$. Suppose the pair (1, 1) represents the square in the lower lefthand corner of the board, that square is black, and white initially occupies the lower two rows of the board. Let p denote a function which assigns to any square on the board, the name of the piece on it. Thus, if square (4, 7) is empty, we write $p(4, 7)$ = empty; if square (1, 5) contains the white king, we write $p(1, 5)$ = WK. Write predicates to describe each of the following:

a. The white queen has been captured.
b. Black has retained both of her bishops.
c. A white rook is in the same row as the black queen.
d. A black pawn is attacking the white king.
e. A white rook is attacking the black queen.
f. A black bishop is attacking the white king.

3–13 Write C++ **if** statements or loops that test each of the predicates you wrote for Exercise 3–12.

3–14 Identify the free and bound variables in the following expressions.

a. $\forall\ i \in \{0, ..., n\} : i^3 - i^2 < 100$
b. $\exists\ i \in \mathbf{N} : \forall\ n \in \{1, ..., i\} : n^2 = i$
c. $(0 \leq m \leq p) \land (\forall\ w \in \mathbf{R} : w < m \land w^2 < p)$

3–15 Consider the board configuration for the game of tic-tac-toe (sometimes alternately called "naughts and crosses") shown below. Suppose the notation $s(i, j) = v$ means that the square in row i and column j contains the value v (where v may be X, O, or *empty*).

a. Write a predicate that describes the particular configuration shown above.
b. Write a predicate that describes O's next best move.
c. Write a predicate that describes all states in which X threatens to win in the middle column; i.e., all states in which X has two squares in column 2 and the other square is *empty*.
d. Write a quantified predicate that describes the impossibility of X

winning in the second column.

    e. Write another that describes the impossibility of *X* winning in any column.

    f. Write a predicate that describes the impossibility of *X* winning at all.

3–16 Describe the following situations using predicates and quantifiers. Assume that $A = (e_1\ e_2\ ...\ e_n)$ is a list of single ASCII characters.

    a. All characters in the list are identical.

    b. The letter *x* does not appear in the list

    c. Some character in the list is a *z*.

    d. The list is arranged alphabetically from smallest to largest.

    e. No two characters in the list are alike.

    f. Some pairs of characters in the list are alike.

    g. The letter *y* appears exactly twice in the list.

    h. List $B = (b_1\ b_2\ ...\ b_m)$ is a sublist of *A*.

    i. The variable `Kount` tells the number of semicolons in *A*.

    j. List *B* is identical with list *A*.

    k. List *B* is identical with *A*, except that somewhere in the list a zero has been replaced by the letter *o*.

    l. The number 3621 is not prime.

A LOGIC-BASED SPECIFICATION LANGUAGE

In the previous section we spent a considerable amount of time introducing the field of mathematical logic, time which may seem wasted as we study computer science. But recall our motivation: We need a concise, correct method of describing exactly what we are attempting to accomplish in our computer solutions. Mathematical logic provides us with the best-known technique for developing such a method. We will use mathematical logic as the basis for our specifications of the problem.

Good design principles suggest the use of formal specifications for two reasons: to aid us in the problem-solving process and to provide guidance for readers or users of our programs. The foregoing discussion suggests that these specifications take the form of assertions about the state of our system: preconditions, postconditions, and intermediate assertions placed strategically among the statements of our program as comments.

In this section we discuss the specification language that we will be using in this text. While our specification language is based upon mathematical logic, we will often use English phrases when their meaning is clearer (simpler) than a formal logic statement. While mathematically rigorous formal specification languages are regularly used in the design and maintenance of large systems, they often lack the simplicity and clarity of informal specifications.

Specifying the State of the Computation

Earlier we introduced the concept of *state*, which is the set of variables and their values upon which the computation is operating at some specific time. We also introduced the concept of an assertion, which is used to express properties of the program's state at such a time. Here are some examples of assertions as they might be written inside the text of a program:

Example 3.15   `// num_students is defined`

This asserts that the variable `num_students` has a value.

Example 3.16   `// num_students >= 0 && num_students <= 100`

This assertion states that the variable `num_students` has a value at least 0 and at most 100. This assertion also implies that `num_students` is defined. Note that C++ representations of the operators are used rather than their mathematical representations, since most of the mathematical symbols used in predicates are not available in the ASCII character set (see Appendix A). The equivalent expression using formal predicate logic symbols would have been written $num\_students \geq 0 \wedge num\_students \leq 100$.

Example 3.17
```
// (letter_grade == 'A' || letter_grade == 'B' ||
//   letter_grade == 'C') && average >= 70.0
```

This assertion states that the variable `letter_grade` has the value `'A'`, `'B'`, or `'C'`, and that the value of `average` is at least 70. Note the use of parentheses to specify the order in which the logical connectives are computed. Without them, the higher precedence of `&&` over `||` would force a different meaning on this expression.

Example 3.18
```
// letter_grade in {'A', 'B', 'C'} && average >= 70.0
```

This assertion is equivalent to the previous one; the word `in` denotes set membership and is equivalent to the mathematical symbol $\in$. Also, the braces that are used in mathematics to enclose the members of a set are also used in our assertions for describing sets. However, neither the operator `in` nor the set braces { and } are directly usable as such in C++ programs.

Example 3.19
```
// grade_sum == sum i in {1,..., n}: grades[i]
```

This assertion states that the value of the variable `grade_sum` is the sum of the list elements `grades[i]` for all `i` in the range between 1 and n inclusive. Note that brackets are also used in programs to distinguish an index (in this case, i) in a list, rather than a subscript.

Table 3–3 summarizes how the logical symbols should be typed when they are represented within C++ programs. *Readers should note that the symbols flagged with asterisk (*) in the righthand column are not part of the C++ language itself; they should only be used within comments.*

TABLE 3–3 ASCII SUBSTITUTES FOR FORMAL LOGICAL SYMBOLS

Symbol	Meaning	ASCII substitute
$grades_i$	Selection of the ith element in a list	`grades[i]`
∅	Empty set	`empty` *
Σ or `sum`	Summation	`sum` *
≤	Less than or equal	`<=`
≥	Greater than or equal	`>=`
≠	Not equal	`!=`
=	Equal	`==`
∀	Universal quantifier	`for all` *
∃	Existential quantifier	`there is` *
∧	Conjunction ("and")	`&&`
∨	Disjunction ("or")	`||`
~	Negation	`!`
{ and }	Set braces	`{ and }` *
∈	Set membership	`in` *

Specifying Input Processing

External sources of data, such as the keyboard or external files, are viewed as *streams*. A stream is a sequence of characters. We use the notation \n to denote the *new line* character that designates returning to the beginning of the next line for keyboard input (it corresponds to the <return> or <enter> key) and for text files that are organized as a sequence of lines. In general, if a << function processes input from the keyboard or an external file, then the specifications that are associated with that statement should describe the effect of that input upon the state of the variables referenced by that statement. The symbol `input` is used to refer generically to input from either of these two sources.

The examples that follow show preconditions and postconditions for processing inputs of various kinds from various sources.

Example 3.20

```
// input == aReal
   cin >> grade ;
// input == empty && grade == aReal
```

The precondition for this C++ statement says that the input stream has a single real value, denoted by `aReal`. The postcondition states that the input stream is empty after this statement executes and the variable `grade` now contains the value `aReal`.

Recall that the symbol `input` can refer to the stream of values coming in from the user at the keyboard. We will generally use symbols such as `aReal`, `aChar`, `anInteger`, and so forth to indicate the particular type of value (a real number, a character, an integer, etc.) that is expected in the input stream.

Example 3.21

```
// input == aString \n aReal \n
   cin >> Name >> grade ;
// input == empty && Name == aString && grade == aReal
```

The precondition states that the input stream contains a string on one line followed by a real value on the next line (the symbol `\n` , when used in a C++ program, represents the ASCII carriage return character). The postcondition states that the input is empty (since both `aString` and `aReal` have been read by the time the program is completed), the variable `Name` contains the value `aString`, and the variable `grade` contains the value `aReal`.

Example 3.22   Here, `grade` is used as a `list` rather than a `float`.

```
// input == anInteger aReal[1] aReal[2] ... aReal[N]
   cin >> N ;
   for (i=1; i<=N; i++)
     cin >> grade.element(i) ;
// input == empty && N == anInteger &&
//   for all i in {1, ..., N}: grade[i] == aReal[i]
```

The precondition for this loop states that the input stream contains an integer `N` followed by `N` real values. The `i`th real value is denoted by `aReal[i]`. The postcondition states that the input stream has been completely read by this loop (`input == empty`), that the variable `number_of_grades` has the value `anInteger` (the first value in the input stream), and that the `list` variable `grade` has the last `N` input values as its values.

In addition, the predicate beginning with the universal quantifier `for all` is used to explain the correspondence between the N real values in the input stream and the individual variables `grade.element(i)` in the list `grade`. In fact, the postcondition states that the N real values in the input stream are read and stored sequentially into the elements of the list `grade`, so that each `grade.element(i)` now contains the ith input value `aReal[i]`.

Specifying Output Generation

The generation of output from a program is specified very much like the processing of input. Output is viewed as a stream of numbers and strings, separated from each other by blank spaces and end-of-line characters. Output may be sent either to the computer screen or to an external file. The special symbol `output` is used to refer generally to either of these. Again, the symbol \n is used to specify the new line character. Here are some examples of output statements and loops, together with their preconditions and postconditions.

Example 3.23

```
// output == empty && number_of_grades >= 0 &&  for all i in
//   {1,..., number_of_grades}: grade[i] == aReal[i]
      for (i=1; i<=number_of_grades; i++)
         cout << grade.element(i) << "\n" ;
// output == aReal[1] \n ... \n aReal[number_of_grades] \n
```

The precondition states that the output stream (normally the computer display) is empty, that the list elements `grade[i]` are all defined and that `number_of_grades` is at least 0 (there can't be a negative number of grades). If `number_of_grades` is 0, then the set {1, ..., number_of_grades} is interpreted as the empty set. In this case, the assertion

```
for all i in {1, ..., number_of_grades}: grade[i] == aReal[i]
```

is surely true and no new data is sent to the output stream. In the more general case, the postcondition states that the output consists of all the values of `grade[i]` for i in the set {1, ..., number_of_grades}, and furthermore that each grade appears on a separate line.

Specifying Control Flow

Recall that computers, and therefore C++ programs, can modify the sequential nature of statement execution; that is, they are able to control the flow of programs using conditional and loop statements. In writing specifications, the disjunction operator, ||, is related to the C++ conditional statement, while the quantifiers `for all` and `there is` generally signal the existence of a C++ loop. The following example shows specifically how these logical operators are related to C++ program statements for searching a list.

Example 3.24

```
// number_of_grades >= 0 and search_key == aReal
    result = 0 ;
    for (i=1; i<=number_of_grades && result==0; i++)
      if (grade.element(i) == search_key)
        result = i ;
// (there is i in {1,..., number_of_grades}: search_key ==
//   grade[i]) && result == i ||
// (for all i in {1, ..., number_of_grades}: search_key !=
//   grade[i]) && result == 0
```

These specifications describe a loop that searches through the list `grade` for the value of `search_key`. The precondition says that `number_of_grades` is at least 0 and that `search_key` is defined. The postcondition is interesting because it states two alternative results of the loop. If there is a match for `search_key` in the list of grades, the result is a value for i for which the match occurs. If there is no match for `search_key`, the result is 0.

EXERCISES

3–17 This problem presents preconditions and postconditions for program segments. In each case, give an English language description of what the program segment should do, and then add appropriate C++ statements that will accomplish that outcome. Assume that `Addem` and `MinVal` are **real** variables.

a.
```
// pre:  input == N aReal[1] ... aReal[N]
// post: input == empty &&
//         Addem == sum i in {1,..., N}: aReal[i]
```

b.
```
// pre: N > 0 &&
//     for all i in {1 ... N}: A[i] == aReal[i]
// post: MinVal == min i in {1,..., N}: A[i]
```

3–18 Give preconditions and postconditions for each of the following problems:

a. Given a list A with N elements, where N is at least 1, the value of the variable `average_element` should contain the average of the N elements of A.

  b. Given a list A with N elements and a list B with M elements, C should contain the result of copying the N elements of A into C followed by the M elements of B. The number of elements in C will be N + M. The relative order of elements in A and B are preserved in C.

  c. This problem is similar to part *b*, except that the lists A and B are initially sorted and the elements are merged into C so that the elements in the list C are also sorted.

Example: Specifying the GPA Problem

We now finally return to our GPA example. A reasonable assumption based upon the anticipated use of our program is that the GPA problem definition excludes the case of zero integers as a valid input possibility. Thus, the program solution for this problem can ignore making provision for that case. Figure 3–7 shows the solution that we've developed.

```
// pre: input == (grades[1] grades[2] ... grades[n]) && n > 0
//    && for all i in {1,..., n}: grades[i] in {0,..., 4}

Step 1. Obtain the input list of grades
Step 2. Compute n = number of grades in the list
Step 3. Compute Sum = sum of the grades in the list
Step 4. Compute GPA = Sum / n
Step 5. Display GPA

// post: input == empty &&
//    output == (sum i in {1,..., n}: grades[i]) / n
```

FIGURE 3–7 Uniting a process description with its specifications.

Recall that the designation input == empty in the postcondition means that, at the end of the process, all scores in the input have been read and cannot be reread. This aspect of the final state reflects the stream notion by which input and output are processed during a program's execution. The act of obtaining input consists of a series of discrete steps in which:

1. a value cannot be obtained again after it has been obtained once, and

2. the individual input values are obtained in exactly the order in which they are entered at the keyboard.

Intermediate states of a computation: introducing variables The state resulting from each of the intermediate steps in a computation is described by a predicate. Unlike the precondition and postcondition, however, intermediate predicates need to take into account additional intermediate values that are computed en route to the final state, as well as the changes in the input itself as its individual values are incorporated into the computation. For example, in the GPA algorithm, the necessary intermediate values are identified by the variable n (the number of scores); Sum (the sum of the individual scores grades[i] for all i in {1, ..., n}); and GPA (the resulting grade point average).

These intermediate values are identified as variables because they cannot be predicted in advance of any particular run of the algorithm's steps. For example, one run may compute the average of 3 scores (and thus n = 3), while another may compute the average of 24 scores (n = 24). The same variability can be expected for the values of the scores themselves, and hence for their sum, from one run of the algorithm to another. Thus we identify the *variable* idea of the sum by an appropriate name, such as Sum. The names Sum, n, and GPA are therefore used to identify the key variables that occur during any particular run of the program.

We can use an algorithm's variables whenever we want to describe an intermediate state of the computation. For example, we can insert the predicate

```
// input == empty && Sum == sum i in {1,..., n}: grade[i]
```

to describe the state of the computation after steps 1, 2, and 3 have been completed. This is a convenient shorthand for saying, "the input has been obtained, the size of the input (n) has been determined, and the sum of the input values has been computed as the value of the variable Sum."

In order to precisely locate the place within the process where this assertion should hold, we insert it just after that step that will cause it to become **true**. An augmented process description for the GPA algorithm might look like this:

```
Step 1. Obtain the input list of grades
Step 2. Compute n = number of grades in the list
Step 3. Compute Sum = sum of the grades in the list

// input == empty && Sum == sum i in {1, ..., n}: grade[i]

Step 4. Compute GPA = Sum / n
Step 5. Display GPA
```

In general, an assertion can be placed between any two adjacent steps in the description of a process, and it can say as much or as little about the state of the computation as is needed for annotation. Assertions that are inserted before the first step and after the last step should be logically consistent with, and usually identical to, the algorithm's pre- and postconditions themselves. Thus, a complete set of intermediate assertions, together with the original pre- and postconditions, can be inserted to provide full annotation for an algorithm's process description, as shown in Figure 3–8.

However, the level of detail shown in Figure 3–8 for the intermediate assertions is excessive, since much of the information in one assertion can be found

```
// pre: input == (grades[1] grades[2] ... grades[n]) &&
// n > 0 && for all i in {1,...,n}: grades[i] in {0,...,4}

  Step 1. Obtain the input list of grades
// input == empty
  Step 2. Compute n = number of grades in the list
// input == empty && n > 0
  Step 3. Compute Sum = sum of the grades in the list
// input == empty && Sum == sum i in {1,..., n}:grades[i]
  Step 4. Compute GPA = Sum / n
// input == empty && Sum == sum i in {1,..., n}: grades[i]
//    && GPA == Sum / n
  Step 5. Display GPA

// post: input == empty &&
//    output == (sum i in {1,..., n}: grades_i) / n
```

Intermediate assertions

FIGURE 3–8   Adding intermediate assertions to fully annotate the GPA process description.

directly in a neighboring assertion. That is, there is *too much* redundant information in this level of description to be useful. For example, each occurrence of input == empty in the assertions after steps 2 through 4 can be eliminated, since it is redundant with the same information in the assertion that appears after step 1. More globally, an entire intermediate assertion can be eliminated when its content is directly inferred from a neighboring assertion.

A more useful level of specification, process description, and annotation is shown in Figure 3–9. The purpose of using intermediate assertions to annotate the steps in a process description is twofold. First, the assertions provide assistance for readers who need to understand the effects of individual steps on the state of the computation. Second, they provide a vehicle for verifying the correctness of these steps as a solution for the original problem that was defined by the preconditions and postconditions. Note that there is a strong correspondence between this style of description for an algorithmic process and the original input-process-output model of an algorithm that appeared at the beginning of the previous chapter. That is, the precondition corresponds to the input, the steps of the algorithm describe the process, and the postcondition characterizes the output.

EXERCISES

3–19 Describe in English the steps of an algorithmic process that would calculate and display the number of grades that are above average for an

```
// pre: input == (grades[1] grades[2] ... grades[n]) &&
//   n > 0 && for all i in {1,...,n}: grades[i] in {0,...,4}

   Step 1. Obtain the input list of grades

// input == empty && n > 0
   Step 2. Compute n = number of grades in the list

   Step 3. Compute Sum = sum of the grades in the list
// input == empty && Sum = sum i in {1,..., n}: grades[i]
//   && GPA == Sum / n

   Step 4. Compute GPA = Sum / n

   Step 5. Display GPA

// post: input == empty &&
//   output == sum i in {1,..., n}: grades_i / n
```

FIGURE 3–9   A partially annotated version of the GPA process description.

arbitrary list of grades. Consider this problem as an extension of the GPA problem. Be very general in describing the steps of this process. What additional variables do you need?

3–20 What are the preconditions and postconditions for the process that you just described in Exercise 3–19? Give a sample input list and output that would be displayed by your algorithm.

SPECIFYING OTHER ALGORITHMIC PROBLEMS

In this section, we return to the three algorithmic problems that were introduced previously. Having conducted the Dialogue for each one, we now turn to developing their specifications; that is, the preconditions and postconditions that will more formally define their expected inputs and outputs.

Computing a^b

In specifying this problem, we must first be precise about not only the expected result but also the range of integers for which the program is well-defined— that is, its preconditions. In particular, we must specify that certain pairs of values of a and b, such as $a == 0$ and $b == -1$, be excluded because they would lead to computational errors. (That is, `Power(0,-1)` would represent 0^{-1} or $1/0$, which is undefined mathematically.)

We should also take into account the limitations of the programming language in which we express the algorithm. For example, many versions of C++ restrict the range of integer values to the range $-2^{15} \ldots 2^{15}-1$. If we identify these values as MININT and MAXINT respectively, then the preconditions for Power should also disallow values of *a* and *b* that would yield a result in excess of MININT or MAXINT. For example, $a = 2$ and $b = 16$ would yield 2^{16}, which exceeds MAXINT for those versions of C++.

Keeping these considerations in mind, the following preconditions and postconditions might be appropriate for designing the Power program:

```
// pre: input == a b && a and b are integers &&
//     (a != 0 || (a == 0 && b > 0)) &&
//     MININT <= a^b <= MAXINT
// post: output == a^b
```

For values of *a* and *b* that do satisfy this precondition, the result a^b can be computed using the following definition.

Definition a^b $== 1$ if $b == 0$

$== \textbf{prod}\ i\ \text{in}\ \{1,...,b\}:a$ if $b > 0$

$== 1\ /\ (\textbf{prod}\ i\ \text{in}\ \{1,...,b\}:a)$ if $b < 0$

This definition, which uses the quantifier **prod**, comes directly from mathematics. Since it is a quantified expression, we can expect from our earlier experience that the programmed solution will involve writing a loop.

Who checks the preconditions?   When we look at a solution for an algorithmic problem, such as the GPA program or computing a^b, it is fair to ask, where does the responsibility lie for checking the preconditions—with *the program* or with *the user* of the program? We would ideally like to have some sort of operational guarantee that no input besides that for which the problem was originally designed can creep in and contaminate the integrity of the program itself.

Consider the Power program, with its precondition that for given values of a and b, the result a^b must lie within the allowable range of integer values that the computer can recognize. Unfortunately, this particular precondition cannot be explicitly checked by the Power program, since the act of computing a^b for invalid input values will result in a run-time error; a message like integer overflow will appear on the screen and execution will immediately and abruptly end.

The clause (a != 0 || (a == 0 && b > 0)) in the precondition could have been checked explicitly by the Power program and an error message displayed for cases where the precondition is violated.

In general, we have a choice between two rather extreme strategies when we decide about who will check the preconditions:

- *Strategy 1:*   Design the program to check *none* of the preconditions; develop the program to conform to the preconditions and postconditions, but if it solves a more general problem (that is, if it does something—including crashing—for input cases that are outside the range prescribed by the preconditions), then so be it. That is, we assume that the user will not be offended if the program does something unpredictable when given input that is not specified by its preconditions.

- *Strategy 2:* Design the program to check *all* the preconditions that can possibly be checked before proceeding to compute and display the output. Develop a convention for displaying useful diagnostic information to the user in cases where the input fails to conform to the preconditions.

Strategy 1 can be characterized as *passive programming*: programs that follow this strategy are correct, but not necessarily well-suited for general use. Strategy 2 is often called *defensive programming*: programs that follow it are called "robust." In an advanced programming course or professional software development setting, Strategy 2 is always favored over Strategy 1. In an introductory course, where many other fundamentals are being introduced for the first time, it is often expedient to temporarily accept Strategy 1 — develop programs that are correct, but may not necessarily be robust. However, the issue of software reliability is important and pervasive. We will raise it again in Chapter 6 (where we discuss the difference between the notions of a program's correctness, robustness, and user-friendliness) and in Chapter 10 (where we discuss the larger social implications of software reliability).

No matter which strategy we choose, we should always enter the preconditions and postconditions for a problem at the top and bottom of the program text before we begin writing the code. That is, the human reader should never be left in the dark about the precise nature of the problem the program solves, even though the computer may not ever need this information.

Counting Words in a Text

Recalling the dialogue we had earlier in this chapter about the word counting problem, the following specifications might be appropriate.

```
// pre: input == a series of characters c[1] c[2] ... c[n] &&
//     n >= 0 && for all i in {1,..., n}: c[i] in ASCII

// post: input == empty && output == the word count
```

Here, we have used a mixture of logic and English to express the preconditions and postconditions for this problem. Note that before solving this problem we shall need to express more clearly what we mean by a "word" in the computational sense. At the moment, the precondition only expresses that the input is a stream of ASCII characters. We shall revisit this problem, taking into account the use of specific C++ facilities for handling text input, in the next chapter.

Monitoring a Tic-Tac-Toe Game

From the foregoing dialogue, we can write the following specifications for this problem. Note that these specifications are more informally stated than those for the other problems.

```
// pre:  input == a series of tic-tac-toe moves
// post:  input == empty &&
//   output == a display of these moves on a tic-tac-toe board
```

A more formal level of description would necessarily involve the details of a graphical board layout, which will be developed for C++ in the next chapter.

EXERCISES

3–21 We have shown different levels of precision in writing pre- and post-conditions in this chapter. When is it more appropriate to use a more precise style, and when might it be more appropriate to use a less precise style?

3–22 Writing detailed predicates for problem specifications seems to be a lot of work without much reward, when considering the fact that predicates are just glorified C++ comments. Can't we accomplish the same effect by just writing a few English-language comments at the beginning of a program? Why or why not?

SUMMARY

In this chapter, we introduced the general idea of algorithmic problems and their accompanying solutions. We emphasized the importance of writing precise specifications for problems, in the form of preconditions and postconditions, as a precursor and guide to the program coding process itself.

Certainly the view of computer science as a theoretical process (see Chapter 1) is emphasized in this chapter as well. We have spent considerable time developing mathematical logic, including propositions, predicates, and formal specifications. At this point it might seem that we have neglected computers entirely! But take a closer look. We follow the abstraction process every time we introduce logic to express a requirement; we use symbols to represent real-world objects. Similarly, we have pointed out how C++ programming constructs such as loops are related to logical statements such as quantifiers. This will eventually become part of the program design process. Thus, theory, abstraction, and design are tightly interwoven in problem solving.

In Chapter 4 we continue this line of development by using the specifications to help us break down algorithmic problems. The coding and presentation stages of MAPS are finally discussed and illustrated in Chapter 5.

PROBLEM BREAKDOWN
AND ABSTRACTION

In Chapter 3, we discussed the use of statements expressed in formal logic to describe the state of a computation. Two states were of particular interest: the state describing the starting point and the state describing the termination point (as expressed by the precondition and the postcondition, respectively). Any state satisfying the precondition is a possible starting point for the computation, and any state satisfying the postcondition is a possible termination of our computation.

An immediate question arises: how do we figure out getting from a state satisfying the precondition to one satisfying the postcondition? Answering this question is the subject of this chapter. That is, what are all the possible paths that lead a computation from a state that satisfies its precondition to one that satisfies its postcondition, and how do we develop programs that describe these paths?

In this chapter, we develop a strategy for breaking down a problem specification into a series of steps that can eventually be coded in the form of an effective C++ program. In the vernacular of the MAPS methodology, this chapter addresses stages 3 (the breakdown) and 4 (defining abstractions). To support this development, we discuss the process of designing loops as well as the idea of recursion. We introduce the idea of class and object-oriented design, using lists and grids as examples of classes. These ideas are illustrated through the development of actual problems: computing a GPA, monitoring a tic-tac-toe game, and recording transactions at an ATM.

An optional section at the end of the chapter presents additional information about mathematical functions and their role in the discipline of computing. This material is provided as an example of important domain knowledge that computing professionals bring to bear on the process of algorithmic problem solving. It is also important for students who continue their study of computing beyond the first course to obtain a solid grounding in mathematics.

Here, again, the themes of theory, abstraction, and design complement each other within the overall process of algorithmic problem solving: *theory* provides mathematical functions as a foundation for modeling problems and their solutions, *abstraction* provides a vehicle for making generalizations about data types and related operations, and *design* is epitomized in the process of breaking down a problem specification en route to a complete solution.

EFFECTIVE SOLUTION DESIGN

How do we design an effective solution to a well-specified algorithmic problem? That is, given a set of preconditions and postconditions, how do we develop a series of computational steps leading to a program that satisfies the postconditions for all possible inputs that satisfy the preconditions? Consider the following example.

> **Example 4.1** Develop an algorithm to input a list of names and output this list in alphabetical order. That is, we want a program that satisfies the following specifications:

```
// pre:  input == aName₁ aName₂ ... aNameₙ
// post: input == empty &&
//       output ==  aName'₁ aName'₂ ... aName'ₙ
//       (a permutation of input) &&
//       for all i in {1,..., n}: aName'ᵢ <= aName'ᵢ₊₁
//       where aName' is the value in output
```

One way to do this is to break down the solution into the following three major steps:

1. Input all names.

2. Sort them.

3. Output them.

An alternative effective breakdown for the solution is the following:

1. Repeat until there are no more names:
    a. Input a single name.
    b. Merge it, in alphabetical order, into the list of names already read.

2. Output the list of names.

Each of these alternative solutions will satisfy the postcondition; each has advantages and disadvantages. Part of the joy of computer science is in the process of choosing among alternative solution strategies.

In addition to our knowledge of the problem statement, as expressed in the pre- and postconditions, we have other constraints as we develop a solution to an algorithmic problem. Recall from Chapter 2 that knowledge of the functional nature of computers is required for this process as well. That is, we must understand what computers are capable of accomplishing and utilize only those capabilities in each step of the solution. Clearly any solution which will be implemented on a computer must use only the capabilities the computer can fulfill. Recall that these capabilities are:

- *Input* from an external device to memory

- *Output* from memory to an external device

- *Operations* on the values in memory: addition, comparison, etc.

- *Control* of the above: sequence, selection, iteration, etc.

Finally, we wish to design programs that satisfy certain minimum performance criteria. That is, programs must be *correct*, *clearly written*, and *efficient*. These criteria embody the following ideas:

- *Correctness*. For any input state that satisfies the precondition, our solution must terminate in a state that satisfies the postcondition.

- *Clarity*. Our solution must be understandable by our human readers. Many software systems are maintained and used for years after the programming is finished. New programmers are hired to modify or correct the software. If the program is not intelligible to these maintainers, the system will fail.

- *Efficiency*. Our solution must meet certain standards of efficiency in terms of execution time and hardware requirements. For the purposes of this text, efficiency is not of great importance; for the purposes of computer professionals, it is of major importance. (Volume II of this series treats software efficiency in great detail.)

We emphasize that the solution development strategy described below is not a panacea. The quality of the computer scientist directly determines the quality of the solution developed. What we describe is an approach, rather than a formula, for developing solutions to algorithmic problems. After all, if we had a formula which could guarantee correct, efficient, understandable solutions to all problems, then we wouldn't need software designers at all!

THE BREAKDOWN

It is usually difficult to go directly from a problem statement and its pre- and postconditions to an implementable algorithm. That is, solutions are more easily developed if we look at the big picture without worrying about details. Of course we must eventually worry about details but only after we have developed the broad outline of a solution.

To begin the breakdown process, we start in a state described by the precondition; call this state *pre*. Our goal is to arrive at a state described by the postcondition; call this state *post*. Our solution is a path, or a sequence of steps, that allow the computer to navigate through the state space between *pre* and *post*. Each of these steps starts from a state and ends in another state; call the start state for the ith step $initial_i$ and the ending state for the ith step $final_i$. Suppose we have n steps in our solution. For a valid solution, the sequence of steps must satisfy the following:

```
// pre ( = initial₁)

Step 1.

// final₁ = initial₂

Step 2.

// final₂ = initial₃

Step 3.
   .
   .
   .

// finalₙ₋₁ = initialₙ

Step n.

// (finalₙ = ) post
```

That is, the initial step must start in the state described by the precondition, each step must end in a state which is a valid initial state for the subsequent step, and the ending state of the last step must be described by the postcondition. In general, we have

```
// finalᵢ₋₁ = initialᵢ, for all i in {2,..., n}

Step i.
```

If we have done this breakdown carefully, our n steps will constitute a correct algorithm for solving the problem, since it systematically changes the state from one described by the precondition to one described by the postcondition. This process of "breaking down" our solution into a sequence of steps is why we call stage 3 of MAPS *the breakdown*. (As you may have realized, our $final_i$ and $initial_i$ logical state descriptions are written in the form of assertions, as discussed in Chapter 3.)

Identifying the intermediate assertions in this sequence can often present difficulties. The temptation is to duck the whole issue and write down something like "Solve the problem", which certainly would generate a correct solution! But it is not sufficiently detailed to provide guidance. Similarly, we might go to the other extreme and list very detailed statements in terms of the manipulation of bits in the computer (see Chapter 8), but this approach would be lost in details. We must strike a balance between providing sufficient detail to make progress toward the solution and our limited ability to keep track of all the details at one time. Our guiding rules for choosing steps in the breakdown will be:

- Each step should accomplish one task and only one task. This keeps the solution clear and we are more easily able to judge the correctness of our solution.

- Each step should make progress toward the solution. Otherwise the step is wasted effort.

- Each step should be clearly understandable. Otherwise it would be difficult to judge the correctness and appropriateness of the step.

- Each step should not be too detailed. Otherwise we will quickly become overwhelmed with details at a time when we should be looking more globally at the sequence of steps.

Sometimes the steps to be chosen are fairly obvious, particularly after you have gained experience in solving problems. Often the best way to solve a problem is to use the solution of a similar one from a different context! Thus it is very important to expand your repertoire by trying many problems; the more you have solved the more experience you will have to draw upon as you solve new problems. Sometimes others will have solved the problem for you and you can just use their work; we return to this idea later in this chapter.

It is exceedingly important to carefully study the series of steps which you have just generated. Ask yourself: Do these steps constitute a correct solution? Do they really describe a path from all states described by the precondition to the postcondition? Have you taken care of, allowed for, all possible states described by the precondition? Are you confident that someone else who follows your algorithm will generate a correct solution under all conditions without asking you questions about it? If you cannot answer an enthusiastic **Yes!** to these questions, then return to your sequence of steps and refine them. Do not overlook inconsistencies. These steps are the foundation upon which your solution is going to be built; and, of course, without a solid foundation your program won't be stable.

When we follow these rules we have a series of n steps and we are confident that if anyone (or any computer) follows these steps she will generate a correct solution too. The steps "flow" in the sense that the final state of each step is identically the initial state of the next. We have not worried about details. However, we also know that ultimately, in order to have a computer algorithm for solving the problem, each of our steps must match some functional capability of the computer. How to proceed? By taking each one of our n steps and looking at it separately as a new problem. Thus, for each step i in our algorithm we consider

```
// prei = initiali

Step i.

// posti = finali
```

as describing a new and independent problem and apply the same strategy to generate a series of steps to affect a solution of this problem. We choose the steps in the same way that we chose the original n steps. While we are working on this new problem, we completely forget about the rest of the overall solution. That is, we look at this as a new and completely independent problem for us to solve. By doing so, we again are handling the overall complexity by ignoring the other steps in the overall problem. When we are done, we will have created a series of "sub-steps" for each of the original steps. And if any of these sub-steps are not sufficiently detailed, we apply the process again to these sub-steps to generate sub-sub-steps; this approach is called stepwise refinement. When do we stop subdividing? When we have reached a sufficient level of detail that we have expressed our algorithm in terms of the functional capabilities of the computer.

This process of breaking down an algorithmic problem may itself be described as shown in Figure 4–1. Indeed this is an algorithm as it is guaranteed to generate a correct solution and it will terminate. The only caveat is that we must choose the sub-steps for each problem carefully.

It is extremely important to note that correctly determining the pre- and postconditions is absolutely vital to ensuring the correctness of the whole solution. That is, the pre- and postconditions are the glue which holds our solution together. If we are not careful to match the postcondition of step i with the precondition of step $i+1$, then we are unlikely to generate a correct algorithm. Above we said that you should consider each step as separate and independent from the others as you broke it down into sub-steps. This process works, but only if you are careful with the pre- and postconditions.

This process also lets us deal with the problem of complexity by focussing our attention on only the important steps in problem solution. We are able to think at a "higher level" and just assume that the solution to each step will be available when we need it. The collecting together of many details under a single name which summarizes them is called *abstraction*. For example, in your programming assignments you have been able to make use of the C++ `cin>>` expression without worrying about how the data was actually to be read into the computer. Yet you knew that the computer was actually involved in electronic signals, bits and bytes, etc. You abstracted the details and didn't think about them; C++ thus provides you with a very convenient abstraction to

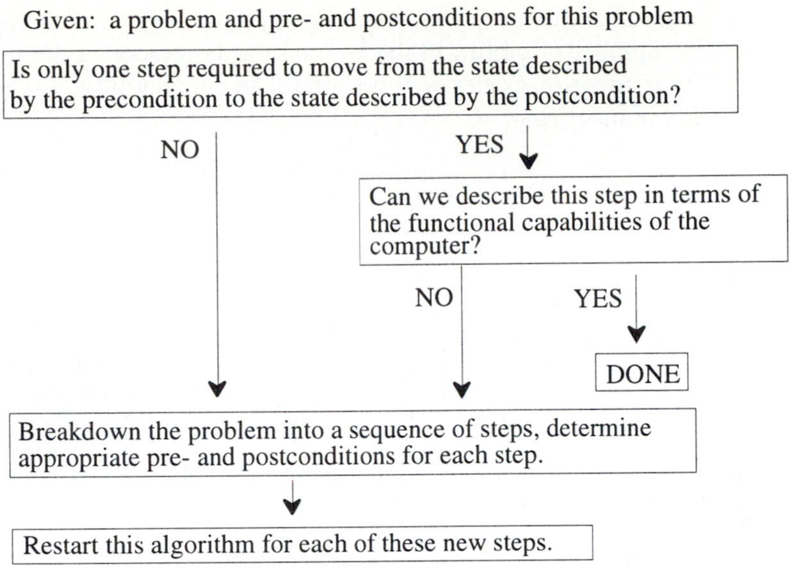

Given: a problem and pre- and postconditions for this problem

Is only one step required to move from the state described
by the precondition to the state described by the postcondition?

NO   YES

Can we describe this step in terms of
the functional capabilities of the
computer?

NO   YES

DONE

Breakdown the problem into a sequence of steps, determine
appropriate pre- and postconditions for each step.

Restart this algorithm for each of these new steps.

FIGURE 4–1   The Breakdown Process

facilitate your efforts. Much of developing algorithmic solutions to problems
consists of determining the appropriate abstractions, and levels of abstraction,
to use. We will spend much of this chapter on the abstraction process.

For an example of using this breakdown strategy on solving a real problem,
we return to the GPA problem introduced in Chapter 2 and dialogued in Chapter 3. Recall that the problem starts in a state where the input consists of a
non-empty list of valid grades and ends in a state where the (correctly calculated) GPA has been output.

Given that a computer must have values in memory before it can manipulate
them, the obvious first step is to obtain the input list of grades.

```
// pre (= initial₁): input == (anInt[1] anInt[2] ... anInt[n]) &&
//     n > 0 && for all i in {1,..., n}: anInt[i] in {0,..., 4}

// Step 1.  Obtain the input list of grades

// final₁ = initial₂: input == empty &&
//     Grades == (Grades[1] Grades[2] ... Grades[n]) &&
//     for all i in {1 ... n}: Grades[i] == anInt[i]
```

Note that we refer to the individual members of the list Grades through a subscript, e.g., Grades[i] refers to the ith element in the list. The value of each
element is the corresponding integer from input.

We now have an empty input and the requisite values in memory. The variable Grades has been identified to designate the list of input values. (Note
that we are using a different typeface like this to represent the values in the

computer's memory.) Given our goal, there are two possible next steps: obtain the number of grades in the list or sum the grades in the list. Since knowing the number of grades will be helpful in calculating their sum, we will obtain that number first.

```
// final₁ = initial₂: input == empty &&
//     Grades == (Grades[1] Grades[2] ... Grades[n]) &&
//     for all i in {1 ... n}: Grades[i] == anInt[i]

// Step 2.  Compute N = number of grades in the list

// final₂ = initial₃: input == empty &&
//     Grades == (Grades[1] Grades[2] ... Grades[n]) &&
//     for all i in {1 ... n}: Grades[i] == anInt[i] &&
//     N == n > 0
```

This establishes the need for a new variable N. Now we accomplish the summation.

```
// final₂ = initial₃: input == empty &&
//     Grades == (Grades[1] Grades[2] ... Grades[n]) &&
//     for all i in {1,..., n}: Grades[i] == anInt[i] &&
//     N == n > 0

// Step 3.  Compute Sum = sum of the grades in the list

// final₃ = initial₄: input == empty &&
//     Grades == (Grades[1] Grades[2] ... Grades[n]) &&
//     for all i in {1,..., n}: Grades[i] == anInt[i] &&
//     N == n > 0 &&
//     Sum == sum i in {1,..., N}: Grades[i]
```

Having both the sum of the grades and the number of grades, we can perform our last memory manipulation and calculate the GPA.

```
// final₃ = initial₄: input == empty &&
//     Grades == (Grades[1] Grades[2] ... Grades[n]) &&
//     for all i in {1,..., n}: Grades[i] == anInt[i] &&
//     N == n > 0 &&
//     Sum == Sum i in {1,..., N}: Grades[i]

// Step 4.  Compute GPA = Sum / N

// final₄ = initial₅: input == empty &&
//     Grades == (Grades[1] Grades[2] ... Grades[n]) &&
//     for all i in {1, ..., n}: Grades[i] == anInt[i] &&
//     N == n > 0 &&
//     Sum == Sum i in {1, ..., N}: Grades[i] &&
//     GPA == Sum / N
```

We have accomplished most of the requirements specified in the postcondition: input is empty and the GPA is correctly calculated. The last requirement is that the GPA be displayed in output.

```
// final₄ = initial₅: input == empty &&
//      Grades == (anInt[1] anInt[2] ... anInt[n]) &&
//      for all i in {1,..., n}: Grades[i] == anInt[i] and
//      N == n > 0 &&
//      Sum == sum i in {1,..., N}: anInt[i] &&
//      GPA == Sum / N

// Step 5.  Display GPA

// final₅ = post: input == empty &&
//      N == n > 0 && output == (sum i in {1,..., N}: anInt[i]) / n
```

Our breakdown is finished. Note that we no longer care about the values in memory, such as Grades or Sum. In fact, these variables are meaningless outside of the program. The only values visible outside of the program are input and output.

Many students find this process cumbersome—writing out so many pre- and postconditions seems like a lot of unnecessary work when the five steps are so simple. In fact, professionals often do not write out the pre- and postconditions for every step for just this reason. However, checking the pre- and postconditions at every step, even if done intuitively, does significantly enhance the quality of the software. Of course, for larger projects designing the individual steps and pre- and postconditions is essential. Thus for now we will be quite explicit about the pre- and postconditions—at least until the habit of thinking in terms of them becomes natural for you. Later we will drop back to just stating the pre- and postconditions for the major steps.

We still have more work to do in turning the above algorithm into a computer solution, since several of the steps are not expressed in terms of the functional capabilities of the computer. Following our breakdown strategy, we now look at each of the above steps as individual problems to be solved. (Note that we delete extraneous information from the various pre- and postconditions to emphasize that they represent separate problems at each step.)

Problem 1. Obtain the input list of grades   In general, this step will require a further breakdown because inputting an entire list of grades, or other data, is not within the functional capabilities of the computer. However, we have developed software to enhance the functional capabilities of the computer to include input of an entire list; this is the read function. We will assume this capability here, thus completing step 1 as follows:

```
// pre: input == (anInt[1] anInt[2] ... anInt[n]) && n > 0 &&
//      for all i in {1,..., n}: anInt[i] in {0,..., 4}

Step 1.  Grades.read() ;

// input == empty && n > 0 &&
```

```
//      Grades == (Grades[1] Grades[2] ... Grades[n]) &&
//      for all i in {1,..., n} : Grades[i] == anInt[i]
```

Problem 2. Compute N = number of grades in the list

Similarly, the function `length` will compute the desired length directly.

```
// Grades == (Grades[1] Grades[2] ... Grades[n])
```

Step 2.   N = Grades.length() ;

```
// N == n > 0
```

Here, we have chosen not to repeat the specification of `Grades`, since it does not change in this step.

Problem 3. Compute Sum = sum of the grades in the list

This problem does require further breakdown.

```
// Grades == (Grades[1] Grades[2] ... Grades[n])
```

```
// Sum == sum i in {1,..., N}: Grades[i]
```

Note that the `Sum` quantifier suggests moving through the list of grades while adding the individual values together. This implies that we will need to control the flow of our steps in order to repeat the summation process over and over for all elements in the list. This leads us to choose an iterative structure for this breakdown step.

```
// Grades == (Grades[1] Grades[2] ... Grades[n])
```

Step 3.   for all Grades[i] with i in the range 1 to N inclusive
            add Grades[i] to the running total, Sum.

```
// Sum == sum i in {1,..., N}: Grades[i]
```

However, this is not quite correct. Before using the value of the variable `Sum` (which we have done when adding to the running sum), we must initialize that value at 0. Thus we rework Step 3 as follows:

```
// Grades == (Grades[1] Grades[2] ... Grades[n])
```

Step 3.1.   Sum = 0 ;

```
// Grades == (Grades[1] Grades[2] ... Grades[n]) && Sum == 0
```

Step 3.2.   for all Grades[i] with i in the range 1 to N inclusive
              add Grades[i] to the running total, Sum.

```
// Sum == sum i in {1,..., N}: Grades[i]
```

Now we have a correct breakdown for this step according to the specification.

Problem 4. Compute `GPA = sum / N`   This can be accomplished directly.

```
// N > 0 && Sum == sum i in {1,..., N}: Grades[i]

Step 4.  GPA = Sum / N ;

// GPA == (sum i in {1,..., N}: Grades[i]) / N
```

Problem 5. Display GPA   This too can be accomplished directly.

```
// GPA == (sum i in {1,..., N}: Grades[i]) / N

Step 5.  cout << GPA << '\n' ;

// post: output == (sum i in {1,..., N}: AnInt[i]) / N
```

Thus we can summarize the breakdown in the following series of steps. Note that all the intermediate assertions have been removed from these combined steps; only the original problem's precondition and postcondition remain.

```
// pre: input == (anInt[1] anInt[2] … anInt[n]) && n > 0 &&
//        for all i in {1,..., n}: anInt[i] in {0,..., 4}

Step 1.    Grades.read() ;
Step 2.    N = Grades.length() ;
Step 3.1.  Sum = 0 ;
Step 3.2.  for all Grades[i] with i in the range 1 to N inclusive
              add Grades[i] to the running total, Sum.
Step 4.    GPA = Sum / N ;
Step 5.    cout << GPA ;

// post: output == (sum i in {1,..., N}: AnInt[i]) / N
```

Note also that at this point we have still not developed a complete match between our steps and the capabilities of computers. While C++ provides the capability to handle repetition statements such as the "for all" in step 3, the C++ repetition statements themselves are somewhat more structured. You have already seen examples of C++ loops in Chapter 3 and in the laboratory manual. The next section develops this concept of loops more carefully.

Iteration and Loops

As you have already seen, choosing an appropriate mechanism for controlling the sequence of operations in the computer is key to developing an effective algorithmic solution for a given problem. Frequently, this choice is suggested by the particular structure of the problem specification itself. For instance, a disjunction (||) appearing in a specification (precondition or postcondition) implies that a *selection* (if statement) must be made, while a *conjunction* (&& operator) suggests the use of a sequence of independent computations. A quantifier (for all, there is, Sum, etc.) calls for an *iterative* (for or while loop) statement; and a recurrence definition of a function calls for either a loop or a recursive solution. As we explore various problems and their solutions, we will try to demonstrate how the specifications are useful to help determine the control structures.

In this section, we focus on the design of iterative and recursive control forms which allow a series of statements to be repeated. It is often difficult to be confident that our design generates a correct solution. In this section, we look at two alternative formulations, using a loop and using recursion, and discuss how their corresponding specifications ensure correctness.

The loop allows us to write a sequence of statements that will be repeated several times.

Definition   A *loop* is a sequence of statements that can be executed 0, 1, or any finite number of times n.

The loop is one of the most fundamental and important of all the algorithm design concepts. Why do programs need loops? There are two major reasons:

1.   Economy of expression

2.   Unpredictability of input size

Both of these reasons for loops can be illustrated in the following scenario: Suppose we need to design an algorithm that computes Sum as the sum of six grades, given by the variables g1 through g6, respectively. One way to accomplish this would be through the following declaration and sequence of C++ statements:

```
float Sum, g1, g2, g3, g4, g5, g6 ;
...
Sum = 0.0;
Sum = Sum + g1;
Sum = Sum + g2;
Sum = Sum + g3;
Sum = Sum + g4;
Sum = Sum + g5;
Sum = Sum + g6;
```

This approach is, of course, both awkward and inflexible. If we had to extend this problem slightly and require Sum to be the sum of, say, 100 grades, this approach would become unsatisfactory.

Still more difficult, and bordering on impossible, would be an extension of the problem so that Sum must be computed as the sum of an *unpredictable* (yet finite) number of grades n. That is, the value of n cannot be predetermined at the time the program is written, so the program must be equipped to compute the sum Sum for any particular value of n whenever it is executed, or, as computer people say, *run*. That is to say, in one run of the program n might be 6, while in another run of the same program n might be 100 and in another, perhaps 1000.

What we need here are language facilities that permit the ability to write a statement or group of statements that can be repeatedly executed, but with a different interpretation for each repetition. This ability is provided by the C++ for and while statements, either of which allows any statement or group of statements to be repeatedly executed, but with a different interpretation upon each repetition. This is what we need to simplify the awkward construction for computing the sum of n values.

Let's illustrate these abilities separately. Suppose first that we declare a single variable g of type list in place of the six variables g1 through g6. Then we can rewrite those declarations and statements as follows, without changing their meaning:

```
float Sum ;
list g ;
...
Sum = 0 ;
Sum = Sum + g.element(1) ;
Sum = Sum + g.element(2) ;
Sum = Sum + g.element(3) ;
Sum = Sum + g.element(4) ;
Sum = Sum + g.element(5) ;
Sum = Sum + g.element(6) ;
```

That is, the postcondition for this sequence is still

```
// Sum == sum i in {1,..., 6}: g.element(i)
```

and we now have two variable declarations instead of six.

Now, the last six statements in this list are identical with each other, except for the index i within the list reference g.element(i); that is, i varies from 1 to 6 among these statements. In order to generalize these six statements so that they are identical, we need to introduce the variable (say i) which yields the sequence shown in Figure 4–2: It might seem as if we are regressing at this point, since we now have twice as many statements to type, but there is method to our madness. That is, every pair of statements after the first two statements in Figure 4–2 is identically the following:

```
Sum = Sum + g.element(i) ;
i = i + 1 ;
```

```
Sum = 0 ;
i = 1 ;
Sum = Sum + g.element(i) ;
i = i + 1 ;
Sum = Sum + g.element(i) ;
i = i + 1 ;
Sum = Sum + g.element(i) ;
i = i + 1 ;
Sum = Sum + g.element(i) ;
i = i + 1 ;
Sum = Sum + g.element(i) ;
i = i + 1 ;
Sum = Sum + g.element(i) ;
i = i + 1 ;
```

FIGURE 4–2   Summing a six-element list: A step toward the generalization.

The while statement allows any repeated group of statements, such as this pair, to be written just once. Its general form is shown in Figure 4–3; more detailed descriptions and examples of the while statement may be found in the laboratory manual.

When the while statement is executed, the conditional expression b is first evaluated. If the result is 1 (true), the sequence s; s; ... ; s is executed once. Then the conditional expression is evaluated again; if it is 1 (true), the sequence is repeated. This pair of actions is repeated over and over until the test reveals the conditional b to be 0 (false), at which time the repetition is finished and the statement following the while statement is finally reached.

When we use the while statement in a loop, however, we must take certain *initial steps* so that the loop will remain under control. That is, execution of the loop should always terminate after a finite number of steps, and upon termination the loop should satisfy its postcondition. For this reason, loops are often called *controlled loops*. The general structure of a controlled loop, which includes both the initialization statements and the while statement, is shown in Figure 4–4.

```
while ( b )
{
    s ;
    s ;
    . . .
    s ;
}
```

FIGURE 4–3   General form of the while statement: b is any conditional expression; s; s; ... ; s ; is any sequence of C++ statements.

```
initialization statements ;
while (b)
{
    s ;
    s ;
    ...
    s ;
}
```

FIGURE 4–4   General structure of a controlled loop in C++.

The requirements for a controlled loop are therefore that the initialization statements, conditional expression b, and statements s; s; ... ; s are written in such a way that (1) proper termination of the loop is guaranteed and (2) the loop's postcondition is satisfied.

In our example, the initialization statements are Sum = 0; and i = 1;, the conditional expression is i <= 6, and the statements being repeated are Sum = Sum + g.element(i); and i = i + 1;. That is, our example can be rewritten as the controlled loop shown in Figure 4–5.

```
Sum = 0;
i = 1;
while (i <= 6)
{
    Sum = Sum + g.element(i);
    i = i + 1;
}
```

FIGURE 4–5   Summing a six-element list: The generalization.

The for statement is a restricted form of the while statement which can be used in all situations where the number of repetitions in the loop is counted. We have seen many examples of the for loop in earlier sections. The present example can just as well be adapted to a for loop, which would have the form shown in Figure 4–6.

```
Sum = 0 ;
for (i=1; i<=6; i++)
    Sum = Sum + g.element(i) ;
```

FIGURE 4–6   Summing a six-element list: Abbreviated representation using a for loop.

Note in Figures 4–5 and 4–6 that the expression `i<=6` describes exactly the condition under which the loop should continue its repetition in order to achieve the equivalent of six identical pairs of statements like those that appear in Figure 4–2. These loops are thus equivalent to the original code shown in Figure 4–2.

Using the device of the controlled loop, we have achieved an economy and generality of expression that otherwise would have been difficult or impossible to achieve. Let's take another look at the iterative step in the GPA problem that was discussed in the foregoing section:

```
Step 3.1.   Sum = 0 ;
Step 3.2.   for all Grades[i] with i in the range 1 to N inclusive
               add Grades[i] to the running total, Sum.
```

Following this discussion of `while` loops, we can rewrite this as the C++ loop that appears in Figure 4–7.

```
Sum = 0;
i = 1;
while (i <= N)
{
   Sum = Sum + Grades.element(i);
   i = i + 1;
}
```

FIGURE 4–7   Summing in the GPA problem.

Note that step 3.2 in the GPA problem solution has the same meaning as the `while` loop in Figure 4–5 in the special case where N = 6. That is, the two loops differ only in the form of the conditional expression that governs the number of times the loop will be repeated and in the names of the variables. In Figure 4–5 the loop will be repeated six times, while in the GPA loop the number of iterations is determined by the variable N, the number of grades in the list `Grades`.

The kind of generality achieved by introducing the variable N allows us to solve the GPA problem. Without N, the solution would always be bound to computing the average of a fixed number of grades. This would be a far less satisfactory situation for this problem and for most problem-solving situations in general, since it would not satisfy the generality characteristic of an algorithm.

In order to develop a loop to solve a problem, we must keep in mind the goal of the loop (the postcondition), the initialization of the loop, the actions to be performed within the loop and how the loop will terminate. Of course the actions are directly responsible for ensuring the correct termination of the loop.

The necessity of dealing with these four elements is what makes loops seem more complicated than, say, conditional statements. Fortunately, we can use the pre- and postconditions and assertions which we have already developed to ease this task.

Designing a loop   It is probably clear that loops are intimately related to quantifiers that appear in assertions. For example, $\forall i \in \{1,\ldots,n\} : \cdots$ tells us that we must use a loop to accomplish the state in which this condition is true because we must ensure that it is true for *all* of the cases described. Similarly, $\exists i \in \{1,\ldots,n\} : \cdots$ tells us that we must use a loop to find *some* value of i for which the condition is true. The connection between loops and quantifiers is also obvious for quantifiers such as **Sum**, which tell us we must add together a series of elements.

Thus, our first hint in developing a loop is to examine the postcondition for each step and see whether or not it contains a quantifier. A second hint comes implicitly from such states as

```
// pre:  input == (c[1] c[2] ... c[n])
```

and

```
// post: input == empty
```

which tell us that we must accomplish some task for *all* elements in the input. Thus, a loop to cycle through all elements in input is implied.

Given that we recognize the need for a loop, how do we go about designing it? Fundamental to our design process is to recognize the goal for the loop. As is always the case in our designs, this goal is given by the postcondition for the algorithm step which contains the loop. That is, when our loop terminates our program must be in a state described by the postcondition. Thus the first step in loop design is the development of the postcondition, but this is the approach that we have been taking throughout.

For each loop we must develop three parts which, when combined, will satisfy the goal and guarantee progress toward termination. These parts are:

- The initialization statement(s)

- The termination condition

- The action(s) performed inside the loop

The purpose of the initialization statement(s) is to set up either, or both, of the termination condition and the actions. Typical examples are found in the necessity of initializing a counter or summation variable to 0 before beginning the loop, reading the first value from an input stream, etc. We could write formal pre- and postconditions for loop initialization, but it is usually sufficient to consider the entire loop as one structure in which the initialization statement is the first part.

The second element of the loop is the termination condition. In the `while` loop, iteration of the loop actions continues until the conditional expression b becomes false (although this implies that we should call it the "continuation condition," that's not standard terminology). This implies that we should choose our termination condition to ensure that all data is processed in accordance with the postcondition. Indeed, because we know that the termination condition is false at loop exit, the negation of the termination condition (this negation will be true since the condition is false) should be part of our postcondition. For example, in the GPA problem we have

```
// post: Sum == sum j in {1,..., N}: Grades[j]
```

which suggests that the loop run from 1 to N. Thus, our termination condition in the `while` statement is

```
while (i <= N) ...
```

Similarly when part of our postcondition in the word list problem states that input is empty, our termination condition looks like

```
while ( still words ) ...
```

and we exit the loop when there are no more words (input is empty).

The action(s) that are repeated inside a loop have a dual purpose; they must make progress toward accomplishing the goal specified by the loop's postcondition, and they must ensure progress toward meeting the loop's termination condition. Thus, in the `while` loop for the GPA problem, we have two actions:

```
Sum = Sum + Grades[i] ;
i = i + 1 ;
```

The first action makes progress toward the goal and the second ensures that the loop eventually terminates (while simultaneously moving the index on to the next element in the list). Similarly, in the word list problem we have

```
NWords = NWords + 1;
FindWord
```

Loop Invariance   This approach to designing loops can be placed on a more formal basis through the use of an important kind of assertion, called a *loop invariant* (or simply an *invariant*).

Informally, we think of an invariant as an assertion about the state of the computation which will remain true (i.e., which will not vary) before and after

each iteration of the loop. We tend to distinguish invariants from other kinds
of assertions in a program because they have a special relationship to that part
of the program where they are embedded. The following assertion is an invariant of the loop in the GPA program:

```
// inv: Sum == sum j in {1,..., i-1}: Grades[j] && 1 <= i <= N+1
```

To show that this is indeed an invariant of the loop, we can check that for
each value of i during execution of the loop,

1. sum is the sum of the first i-1 grades in the list Grades, and

2. The value of i is always inside the range from 1 to that value which will
    cause the loop to terminate.

Consider the example where Grades == (3 2 1 3), so that N == 4. The state
before each of the four iterations of this loop, and the accompanying corrobora-
tion of the invariant, can be summarized as follows:

Before iteration	State	Invariant corroboration
1	Sum==0 && i==1 && N=4	Sum == sum j in {1,..., 0}: Grades[j] && 1 <= 1 <= 5
2	Sum==3 && i==2 && N=4	Sum == sum j in {1,..., 1}: Grades[j] && 1 <= 2 <= 5
3	Sum==5 && i==3 && N=4	Sum == sum j in {1,..., 2}: Grades[j] && 1 <= 3 <= 5
4	Sum==6 && i==4 && N=4	Sum == sum j in {1,..., 3}: Grades[j] && 1 <= 4 <= 5
5	Sum==9 && i==5 && N=4	Sum == sum j in {1,..., 4}: Grades[j] && 1 <= 5 <= 5

Because iteration 5 does not take place [exit from the while statement occurs
because i <= N becomes 0 (false)], the invariant resolves into a statement of
the loop's postcondition upon exit from the loop. That is,

```
Sum == sum j in {1,..., i-1}: Grades[j] && 1 <= i <= N+1
```

resolves itself to

```
Sum == sum j in {1,..., N}: Grades[j]
```

since the value of i reaches N+1. Note that this is equivalent to the simultaneous events in which the invariant is true and the condition in the while

statement is false (because the `while` terminates when its continuation condition becomes false). That is,

```
(Sum == sum j in {1,..., i-1}: Grades[j]) && 1 <= i <= N+1
    && !(i <= N)
```

Because we are incrementing i by 1, at termination we know that i == N + 1, so that

```
Sum == sum j in {1,..., N}: Grades[j]
```

which is the postcondition for this step of the algorithm.

What is the relationship between the loop invariant and the sequence of statements s; s; ...; s that comprise the loop's body? In our example, we want to know how the statements

```
Sum = Sum + Grades.element(i) ;
i = i + 1 ;
```

interrelate with the invariant

```
(Sum == sum j in {1,..., i-1}: Grades[j]) && 1 <= i <= N+1
```

The loop's body is intentionally designed with two objectives in mind:

1. The body keeps the invariant true.

2. The body makes progress toward termination of the loop.

In general, a loop should do no more and no less than these two things—all else is irrelevant.

Recursion

An alternative to the use of iteration is *recursion*, the use of the idea being defined inside the definition itself. Consider, for example, a definition of *descendant* in an ancestral relationship. Dictionary definitions are inherently circular; descendant is defined as "to come from an ancestor or ancestry," while *ancestor* is defined as "a person from whom one is descended." As an alternative definition, we give the following:

> **Definition**   The *descendants* of a person are either the person's children or the descendants of such children.

With this definition we have clearly defined the concept and, given two individuals, can determine if one individual A is a descendant of another B by the following:

1. If A and B are in the same generation, then conclude that A is not a descendant of B.

2. If A is a child of B, then conclude that A is a descendant of B.

3. Otherwise, the answer is whether or not one of A's parents is a descendant of B.

In step 3 we are reapplying the same algorithm with A's parents each taking the place of A.

This is a recursive definition because we use the term we are defining, *descendant*, in the definition itself. Yet it is not a circular definition because the process of checking descendents does not continue indefinitely. Eventually we will answer the question either with the case of a child of B, or with the case that no ancestor of A is a child of B.

With reference to the family tree shown in Figure 4–8, let's take a look at how this definition applies to the two questions asked in Examples 4.2 and 4.3:

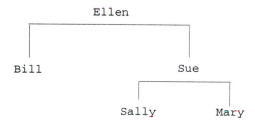

FIGURE 4–8   A sample family tree.

Example 4.2   Is Mary a descendant of Ellen?

1. Rules 1 and 2 do not apply, so we must apply Rule 3 to determine if Mary's parent, Sue, is a descendant of Ellen.

2. Rule 1 does not apply, but Rule 2 does so that we conclude that Sue is a descendant of Ellen.

3. Returning to our application of Rule 3 in Step 1, we are able to conclude that Mary is a descendant of Ellen.

Example 4.3   Is Mary a descendant of Bill?

1. Rules 1 and 2 do not match, so we must apply Rule 3 to determine if Mary's parent Sue is a descendant of Bill.

2.   Rule 1 applies to Sue and Bill so that we conclude that Sue is not a descendant of Bill.

3.   Returning to our application of Rule 3 in Step 1, we are able to conclude that Mary is not a descendant of Bill.

Recursion is frequently used in mathematics to define functions in terms of themselves. Just as in the example above, the definition must have a termination condition, a point at which we know the value directly.

Example 4.4   Suppose we define the function $f(n)$ as follows:

$$f(n) \quad = 1 \qquad \text{when } n == 0$$
$$= 3 + f(n-1) \qquad \text{when } n > 0$$

Such a formula is called a *recurrence relation*. This definition provides a starting value for computing the function f (namely, its value when $n == 0$). While we know how each value of f can be computed using the previous one, we don't have an explicit formula or rule for computing $f(n)$ directly. That is, the value of f for any particular value of n can be calculated by repeatedly applying the recurrence relation to increasingly larger values of n, beginning with $n == 0$. Thus, we first compute $f(0) = 1$, and then use it to compute $f(1) = 3 + f(0)$. This can be done repeatedly, giving the following table:

n	$f(n)$
0	1
1	4
2	7
3	10

...

Sometimes it is easy to infer a *non*recursive formula for computing $f(n)$ out of its recursive definition, and sometimes it is difficult. For Example 4.4, it is relatively easy, by looking at the pattern of values in the table, to infer the equivalent formula $f(n) = 3n + 1$. To verify this formula, we could prove it by a technique called *induction* (Chapter 7).

Example 4.5   Consider the recursive function:

$$f(n) \quad = 0 \qquad \text{when } n == 0$$
$$= 1 \qquad \text{when } n == 1$$
$$= f(n - 1) + f(n - 2) \qquad \text{when } n > 1$$

By repeatedly applying this recurrence relation, we can generate the following table:

n	$f(n)$
0	0
1	1
2	1
3	2
4	3
5	5
6	8
7	13
8	21
...	

This particular function is called the *Fibonacci function* and the sequence of values it produces is called the *Fibonacci sequence*. It is a useful function in many areas of applied mathematics. However, it is more difficult to find a non-recursive formula that would allow this function to be computed directly for any value of n than it is to use the foregoing recursive definition.

Throughout computer science and mathematics, recursive definitions are used because they can express key concepts clearly and succinctly. C++ provides for the direct implementation of recursive definitions. However, we will postpone this exploration of recursion as a means of control until we have discussed abstraction in the next chapter.

EXERCISES

4–1 Develop a `while` loop that satisfies the following specifications:

```
// pre:  L == (e[1] e[2] ... e[n]) && n > 0
// post: EvenSum == the sum of all elements in L with even
         subscripts && OddSum == the sum of all elements
         in L with odd subscripts
```

4–2 Develop a `while` loop that will input 25 integers and count the number of negative integers among them.

4–3 Develop a `for` loop that will read 100 integers and display those that are divisible by 5. Repeat the exercise using a `while` loop.

4–4 Write a program segment that will accomplish the following:

Set X to X + A   if X is negative.
Set X to X + A + B   if X is zero.
Set X to X + A + B + C   if X is positive.

4–5 Develop a `while` or `for` loop that will set all odd elements of a list which contain odd values to zero. That is, if the list is named `L`, your loop should examine `L[1]` and, if it contains an odd value, reset `L[1]` to 0. The same should be done for `L[3]`, `L[5]`, ..., while elements `L[2]`, `L[4]`, ... should be disregarded.

4–6 Tabulate a few values for each of the following recursively defined functions. Give an equivalent closed-form expression for each one.

    a. $f(n) = 3$ for $n = 0$
            $= f(n-1) + 5$ for $n > 0$

    b. $f(n) = 1$ for $n = 0$
            $= 2f(n-1)$ for $n > 0$

4–7 Develop a loop to display the first n Fibonacci numbers (1, 1, 2, 3, 5, 8, 13, ...), where the value of the variable n is known at the time the loop begins.

4–8 If you start with 1 yeast cell at the end of day 0 and each cell divides into 2 cells at the end of each subsequent day, how large is the colony after n days?

4–9 The *Ancestors* function takes an integer generation number and returns the number of ancestors a person had that many generations ago, assuming that every person in every generation has exactly two parents. That is, *Ancestors*(1) = 2, *Ancestors*(2) = 4, and so on. In particular, *Ancestors*(0) = 1, assuming that each person is an ancestor of herself or himself. Give a recursive definition of the *Ancestors* function.

BREAKING DOWN OTHER ALGORITHMIC PROBLEMS

This section explores the breakdown of two simple algorithmic problems that were introduced and specified in Chapter 3. Here, we concentrate on the identification of control structures and intermediate variables that evolve out of the breakdown.

Counting Words in a Text

Recall the pre- and postconditions:

```
// pre: input == a series of characters c[1] c[2] ... c[n] &&
//    n >= 0 && each c[i] is in the set ASCII
// post: input == empty && output == the word count
```

In this case, we have decided not to express the output in predicate logic because the latter notation would be more complicated than enlightening.

Considering this as an algorithmic problem, any solution must begin by obtaining the input string. Thus, step 1 has the following specifications:

```
// pre (= initial₁):
// input == a series of characters c[1] c[2] ... c[n] &&
//    n >= 0 && each c[i] is in the set ASCII

Step 1.   cin >> s ;
```

Before going any further, we must understand exactly what happens when we use the C++ operator >> with input stream `cin` and string variable `s` as its arguments. That is, does it input a single character, a single word, or the entire input text in one fell swoop? The rest of the design of our algorithm hinges critically upon the answer to this question.

In fact, the operator >> retrieves and stores in `s` the next contiguous sequence of *nonwhitespace* (i.e., neither blank, carriage return, nor tab) characters in the input stream, skipping over any leading whitespaces in the process. Knowing this fact simplifies the design of our algorithm greatly. A precise postcondition for Step 1 can be stated in the following fairly tedious form:

```
// final₁ = initial₂ =
// input == c[k+1] ... c[n] && n>=0 &&
//    s == c[j] ... c[k] && j<=k &&
//    for all i in {1,..., j-1}: c[i] is whitespace &&
//    for all i in {j,..., k}: c[i] is nonwhitespace &&
//    (c[k+1] is whitespace or k == n)
```

Let's take a more careful look at the postcondition: the result s will be a contiguous string of nonwhitespace characters from the beginning of the input stream, with all leading whitespace characters skipped (note the condition on the characters from 1 through j–1) and terminated by either a whitespace character (`c[k+1]` is whitespace) or the end of the input string (k is the index of the last character in s).

Before proceeding further, we should also agree on an operational definition of what a word is, from the program user's point of view. For convenience, we will select the definition that coincides with the operational characteristics of `cin`, as described above:

> **Definition** A *word* is defined as any contiguous string of non-blank, non-tab, and non-carriage return characters.

Having selected this definition, we can proceed with the breakdown of the problem.

Our first step may have either succeeded or failed, depending on whether or not there are *any* words whatsoever in the input. That is, an empty input should result in a resulting word count of 0, a case that must be accommodated by the program. In general, however, the second step should be a process that counts, one by one, each word in the input as soon as it is read. Thus, the simple statement:

```
Step 2.  Count the number of words in the input
```

actually will resolve itself into a loop that has the following form, preconditions, and postconditons:

```
// final₁ = initial₂ =
// input == c[k+1] ... c[n] && n>=0 &&
//     s == c[j] ... c[k] && j<=k &&
//     for all i in {1, ..., j-1}: c[i] is whitespace &&
//     for all i in {j, ..., k}: c[i] is non-whitespace &&
//     (c[k+1] is whitespace or k == n)

Step 2.1.  initialize NWords == the word count for input
Step 2.2.  while there are more words in the input
Step 2.2.1.   count the word just read
Step 2.2.2.   read another word from the input

// final₂ = initial₃ =
// NWords == word count for input c[1] c[2] ... c[n]
```

This loop should terminate when there are no more words in the input to be counted.

And now Step 3 can be specified and completed as follows:

```
// final₂ = initial₃ =
// NWords == word count for input c[1] c[2] ... c[n]

Step 3.  cout << "The number of words is " << Nwords << ".\n" ;

// (final₃ =) post:
// output == word count for input c[1] c[2] ... c[n]
```

And we are done! But not really, of course, because once again the requirements of Step 2 do not match the functional capabilities of a computer. But we have accomplished the first level of breakdown within a stepwise refinement—which means we have made significant progress toward a solution. We now take a closer look at step 2. The required loop requires that the word count must be initialized to zero, since there will have been zero words counted before we scan the first one. A completed C++ loop for this process is shown below, where Nwords represents the word count.

```
Step 2.1.  Nwords = 0 ;
Step 2.2.  while (cin >> s)
Step 2.2.1.  Nwords++ ;
```

Notice here that the expression cin >> s plays a dual role; it retrieves the next word from the input and it determines whether that operation was successful. That is, when the input runs out of words to supply the program (signaled by typing `ctrl-d` at the keyboard), this function returns the value 0 (**false**), which will terminate repetition of the `while` loop. For this reason, Step 2.2.2 is no longer needed. Step 3 therefore begins exactly when the number of words in the input has been calculated, one by one, and left in `Nwords` by Step 2.

We have now completed the breakdown for solving the "Count the words" problem.

Monitoring a Tic-Tac-Toe Game

Recall that in this problem we are monitoring a game; that is, we are simply displaying the results rather than having the computer play one side of the game. In this program, two players alternate moves. Each move is given by clicking the mouse in the square on the board where the players want to place an X or O. The first person to play is X. Control of the game and determination of the winner is entirely in the hands of the players. When a player clicks the mouse anywhere outside the 3x3 board, the program will end the game.

Graphics programs are particularly interesting in that they typically make use of a number of system provided routines to handle the actual graphics operations. There are a number of standard systems, such as GKS, GL and PHIGS; Turbo C++ and Think C++ provide their own routines. This text attempts to simplify and unify basic graphics concepts by providing a series of operations in the C++ class `Grids`. The functional capabilities of our computer thus includes the ability to initialize a grid and display either an X or an O in any given grid location using a mouse click.

One of the first steps in virtually every computer program, but particularly for programs dealing with graphical output, is to initialize the state of the display system:

```
// pre (= initial₁): input == a series of tic-tac-toe moves

Step 1.   Initialize the board and the game.

// final₁ = initial₂ =
// input == a series of tic-tac-toe moves &&
//     the board is initialized
```

The problem statement tells us that we will be repetitively obtaining moves and displaying them; this implies that our program will consist of a loop. Following our discussion as we solved "Count the words", we realize that we must start by obtaining the first move:

```
// final₁ = initial₂ =
// input == a series of tic-tac-toe moves &&
//     the board is initialized

Step 2.   Obtain the first move from input.
```

```
Step 3.      While there are still moves,
Step 3.1.      If it's X's turn
Step 3.1.1.      Display an X at the indicated grid location
                 else
Step 3.1.2.      Display an O at the indicated grid location
Step 3.2.      Obtain the next move from input

// (final₂ =) post: input == empty &&
//      output == a display of these moves on a tic-tac-toe board
```

This solution description is also not complete. Details of C++ and the `Grid` class that allow programs to obtain moves, to display the moves, etc., need to be filled in before we can further develop this solution. We postpone our discussion of these details until later in the chapter.

EXERCISE

4–10 Develop a breakdown for the problem of computing a^b which was introduced in Chapter 3. How many major steps are there? Does any step require a loop? Explain.

ABSTRACTION

We wish to recall two important points from our discussion in the preceding section:

- The absolute necessity of writing clear pre- and postconditions for breaking down the algorithm and intermediate steps.

- The importance of the breakdown process in controlling the complexity of the solution as we develop it.

The process of *abstraction*, introduced in this section, allows us to address the second of these two points. That is, it allows us to concentrate on the problem at hand, without worrying about details that do not influence the solution at this level.

As we developed breakdowns, we often first expressed portions of algorithms as steps that could not be directly executed by the computer. For instance, neither of the following steps can be encoded as a single C++ statement:

- Compute `Sum` = sum of the grades in the list

- Find a word

Later we went back and viewed each of these as a separate problem that submitted to its own breakdown. This process of ignoring details as we develop a solution is absolutely critical. Developing a solution to a complex problem would be extremely difficult if we had to keep track of all facets of the solution, to the lowest level of detail, all at once. Of course, eventually we have to worry about details because we must express our solution in terms of the functional capabilities of the computer.

The process of collecting details under a single name which summarizes their meaning is called *abstraction*. Basically, we assume that a required capability exists; for example, "find a word." We go on with our solution. Eventually we must return to *find a word*, but we do so by treating it as a separate problem. Thus while we are worrying about the original problem's solution, we don't bother with the details of "find a word"; and while worrying about a solution to "find a word," we don't bother with the details of the original problem. Our use of abstraction again emphasizes the use of pre- and postconditions as the glue which makes the pieces of the solution work together correctly.

As we develop solutions, our basic strategy is to develop algorithms that read well and are understandable without further explanation. Thus, in the solution to counting the number of words in a text, the details of finding a single word are unnecessary and cumbersome. It is clearer just to be able to write the phrase, "find a word."

Procedural Abstraction, Classes, and Objects

The ideal situation is when we can recognize that certain sub-problems are archetypical, such as *find a word*. It is easy to imagine a large number of problems which require the ability to find a single word; sometimes the word will be as we have previously defined it, sometimes the word may allow digits (as in C++ identifiers), etc. But the basic process is similar. Recognizing this universality in the *find a word* problem means that we have discovered an abstraction.

This form of abstraction goes under the general title of *procedural abstraction*, because we are abstracting a process. A procedural abstraction's full definition must include a title, parameters and pre- and postconditions. With this information we are able to use the abstraction even though we will have no idea of the actual steps needed to accomplish the process. In many respects this is ideal, because we can avoid getting bogged down in details.

The use of *parameters* arises as a means of generalizing an abstraction. For example, if we develop an abstraction named FindWord which will allow us to locate words in a text for use in the word counting problem, we would like to be able to reuse this abstraction in other text processing applications. Yet this particular FindWord is tied to the string variable named S. Generating a new version of FindWord tailored to the specific string would negate much of the value of the abstraction process. Parameters allow us to specify a generic string variable name as we develop the abstraction; later we specify the actual string variable to be processed when we use the abstraction. We explore this process in the next chapter.

In many situations we will also need to know the steps by which the abstraction is affected; in this case we will have a *complete procedural abstraction*.

> **Definition** The process of remembering a detailed series of steps, giving them a name, parameters, and pre- and postconditions, is called a *complete procedural abstraction*. This differs from *procedural abstraction*, which is simply the process of naming, parameterizing, and defining specifications (pre- and postconditions) for a C++ function that may or may not already be implemented as a series of steps. We identify a *routine* with the series of steps in a complete procedural abstraction.

That is, complete procedural abstraction suggests a strategy for implementing a well-specified function, while procedural abstraction does not. Both, however, give a name, parameters, and pre- and postconditions for the desired function.

An entirely different form of abstraction, which is also of great usefulness, is called a *class*.

> **Definition** A *class* is a data type, together with a specific collection of related procedural abstractions that application programs can use to manipulate the values of variables of that type. A variable *v* that has a particular class *t* as its type is called an *object* of that class.

Thus, a class is a kind of "data abstraction" that allows us to define special kinds of variables, called objects, without worrying about how their related functions and attributes are implemented in the computer. Just as in procedural abstraction, we eventually have to worry about implementation details, but this can be deferred until we are ready.

To illustrate these concepts, consider the realm of graphical programming, in which the key variables are the graphical objects themselves alongside the algorithms which manipulate them. The tic-tac-toe display program is a good example of this point. If we have access to a class that allows us to define a variable that represents the tic-tac-toe board, its individual cells, and some basic "moves" on the board, we have gone a long way toward solving the problem. Programming is in large part a combination of using procedural abstraction, classes, and objects to solve problems. Niklaus Wirth, developer of the Pascal and Modula programming languages, makes this point explicitly in the title and content of his text *Algorithms + Data Structures = Programs*. Programming styles that focus primarily on the objects in a problem are known as "object-oriented programming," or OOP for short. Programming styles that focus on procedural decomposition of a problem are called "procedural programming." In this text, we use a combination of these styles, which may in reality be an accurate reflection of what many software designers do today.

In this chapter, we focus on the use of procedural abstractions and classes that have been implemented by others. That is, we are not concerned with the sequence of steps that defines a function, but only the function's name, parameters, pre- and postconditions, and possible uses in problem solving. In the next chapter, we shall be concerned with the process of implementing our own procedural abstractions, to cover cases where existing libraries do not provide the functional capabilities that we require for the problem being solved.

USING CLASS LIBRARIES

C++ (and many other programming languages) incorporates built-in abstractions for such operations as reading integers or displaying integers (an integer must be converted into a succession of characters in order to be displayed on the screen). Similarly, we have also encountered the type `string`, which allows us to handle entire sequences of characters, a facility which is not native to the computer but is available in most programming languages.

Many of the abstractions that will assist us the most in problem-solving are either built into programming languages or have been developed by other programmers and are provided in libraries. An example of the first type are the C++ operators (+, *, −, etc.). They are abstractions because they hide the messy details of arithmetic and conversion between integers, real numbers, and so forth when arithmetic is performed. An example of the second type are the many mathematical functions such as `sqrt`, `sin`, or `log` which are available in C++ through its `math` library. Thus, a user need not worry about how to actually calculate the square root of a number, but may use the `sqrt` function and be assured that the correct result will be returned.

Manuals that accompany the particular language and/or compiler which you use will provide the specifications for the built-in routines. Other routines are provided by the operating system. In Turbo C++, for example, separate libraries are used to add enhanced capabilities. Some libraries are provided already, while other libraries can be created by the programmer for later use.

Recall the principle that the easiest way to solve a problem is to remember that you have (or someone else has) already solved parts of it, and then reuse those parts without reinventing them. Mastering the ability to find out what is already available for your use is an excellent example of this principle. In the case of libraries and language features, someone else has already solved the problem and packaged the solution for you.

The major abstractions used in this text are the `list` and `grid` classes, along with the *string* type. Strings are provided as part of the standard C++ library, while `lists` and `grids` have been developed by the authors in C++ and are provided with the laboratory materials. When considered as classes, each of these consists of a data type (e.g., `grid` or `list`) together with an associated collection of functions that apply specifically to objects and values of that type. For example, the function `strlen(s)` gives the length of the string s, while the analogous function `L.length()` gives the length of (num-

length of (number of elements in) the list L. Similarly, the reference s[i] selects the *i+1*st character in the string s, while L[i] selects the i+1st element in the array L and L.element(i) selects the ith element in the list L.

There are other subtle differences among these alternatives. For example, the application of arithmetic operators to string values should generally be avoided, since they will not yield an intuitively correct, or even useful, result. For instance,

```
s = s * "1.5" ;
```

(where s denotes a string variable) will not compute a product, even if the value of s is a string representation of a number.

We can read and store a collection of real numbers, when they are typed enclosed in parentheses, into a variable of type list, either from the keyboard or from an external file, using the operator read, but we cannot use the notion of a list to achieve the same end with a collection of strings. We can use arrays instead of lists to store a collection of strings, but we do not have the flexibility to read and store such a collection without inventing an entirely new operator for arrays that has the functional capability of read.

These various distinctions and restrictions are summarized in Figure 4–9, which shows the functional overlaps among arrays, ints, chars, floats, and lists. The message here is that neither the array nor the list offers all the advantages of the other without carrying some compensating disadvantage. This situation is typical of many situations in computing; professionals in the field often refer to this as the "tradeoffs and consequences" of making a choice

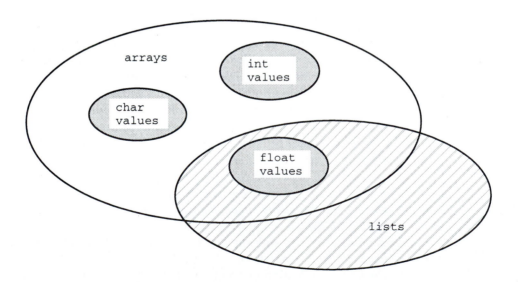

FIGURE 4–9 Distinctions among lists, arrays, strings, and numbers.

among suboptimal alternatives. Below we will look into these classes in some
detail.

Lists

The GPA program makes use of the class `list` and its related operators, which
are summarized in Figure 4–10. Programmers may use the type `list` and its
operators by simply placing the following statement at the top of the program.

```
#include "ListClass.h"
```

Any C++ program that includes the class `ListClass` is enabled to easily
input and display an entire list of numbers rather than one number at a time.
This is a helpful feature for many algorithmic problems, and we have used it
extensively in this text.

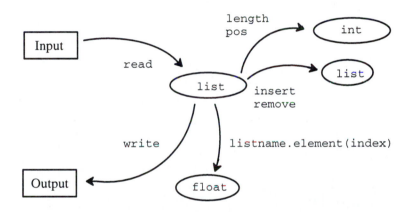

FIGURE 4–10   Summary of the `list` operators.

An object that is declared to be of class `list` will therefore have a complete
list of values, as does the object `grades` declared in the GPA program for the
purpose of storing a list of grades:

```
list grades ;
```

The expression `grades.read()` obtains from the input any list of numerical values, provided that they are enclosed within parentheses, and stores these
values as the value of `grades` and assigns the length of `grades` as the number
of values read. Thus, for example, if we type the input:

```
(3 2 1 3)
```

the function `grades.read()` will leave the variable `grades` in the state:

```
grades == (3 2 1 3)
```

and the length of `grades` assigned the value 4.

The function `grades.length()` returns the number of values that are currently stored in `grades`, while the expression `grades.element(i)` returns the value of the `i`th element in the list `grades`. The integer `i` itself is the *index* of the element returned. Thus, the call `grades.length()` returns the value 4 and `grades.element(3)` returns the `float` value 1.

Strings

For developing solutions to problems like counting the number of words in a text, we need to utilize the services of an entirely different type, called the *string*. Some of the functions that can be used to process and transform strings in C++ are summarized in Figure 4–11.

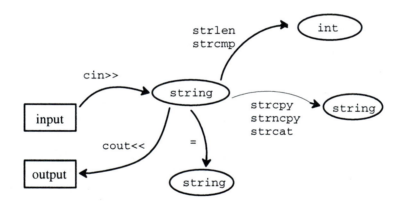

FIGURE 4–11 Summary of the `string` type and some related functions.

Programmers may use any of these character string functions by placing the following statements at the top of the program.

```
#include <iostream.h>
#include <string.h>
```

We give here a few brief examples that exemplify the use of strings in the solution of text-processing algorithmic problems. A more complete definition of these functions is given in the laboratory manual.

To declare a string variable, say `s`, to contain any string of 255 or fewer characters, we write a declaration in the following way:

```
char s[256] ;
```

The number 256 defines the memory size allocated for any value that is assigned to the string variable s (including the null character \0 that terminates
the value). We may assign a string value to this variable using either a strcpy
or a cin>> expression, and have the same effect as if we were assigning values
to int or float variables. Thus, we can write one of the statements

```
strcpy(s, "Hello World!") ;
cin >> s ;
```

to achieve the effect shown in the center of Figure 4–12. The cin function has
an interesting byproduct when it is invoked. That is, it returns the value 1
(**true**) as long as the input operation is successful, and returns the value 0
(**false**) otherwise (that is, when the end of the input is reached). Thus, it is not
unusual to see a statement like

```
while (cin >> s) ...
```

specifying the continuation of a loop as long as there is input remaining to be
processed.

Figure 4–12 also shows the effect of using various other string functions.

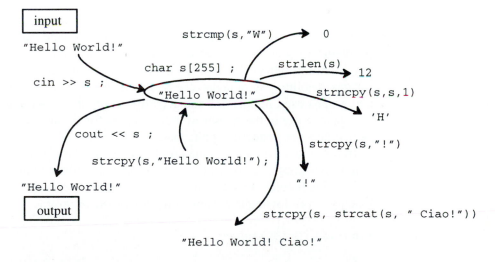

FIGURE 4–12   Using some of the string functions.

The function strlen computes the length of a string (the number of characters in it, including blanks, punctuation marks, and other special characters in
the ASCII set).

The `strcmp` function compares two strings, and returns 1 or 0 if they are identical (in length and content) or not, respectively. Thus, when we write `strcmp(s,"W")` we are asking to compare the current value of string s with the (constant) string `"W"`. If the value of s is anything but the 1–character string `"W"`, the function `strcmp` returns the value 0.

The function `strncpy` is also used to copy a string value into a string variable. It differs from `strcpy` by enabling a numeric length to be specified to limit the number of characters copied. Thus, `strncpy(s,s,1)` says to copy into s that substring of s which begins in position 0 and has length 1.

Finally, the function `strcat` concatenates, or joins, two strings end-to-end, to form a single string. It creates a larger string by inserting, or embedding, an additional string at a given starting position. Thus, if s = `"Hello World!"`, then `strcat(s, " Ciao!")` creates the new string

```
"Hello World! Ciao!"
```

of length 18. Combining this with the `strcpy` function, we can alter the string s to have this new value as follows:

```
strcpy(s, strcat(s, " Ciao!"))
```

The Grid Class

Although the numeric and string data types cover a wide variety of algorithmic problems, they do not help us solve problems that require the representation of graphic information. Such problems include the display and analysis of x-ray images, satellite photographs, chess and other board games, and various charts and graphs used in business and scientific computing. Although we are looking specifically at the graphical requirements for tic-tac-toe, the principles revealed here are generally applicable.

In order to solve board game problems, we need a new class, called a `grid`, that allows programs to display and perform transformations on a square array of individual cells. Programmers may use any of the grid functions by simply placing the following statement at the top of the program.

```
#include "GridClass.h"
```

This class assumes that each cell in an n×n grid is identified by its row and column number, `i` and `j`. The cell can be filled by a graphical representation of any one of the 256 ASCII characters, using either of the following functions:

```
set_cell (i, j, value) ;
set_cell_display (i, j, value) ;
```

The only difference between these two is that the first assigns a new character value to the cell without altering the display of the grid on the screen, while the second makes the change and updates the display of the grid accordingly.

A sample 3×3 grid whose cells have various settings is shown in Figure 4–13. This figure also shows how the rows and columns of a grid are conventionally numbered. The cell in row 1, column 2 is filled with x; the cell in row 2, column 1 is gray filled: the cell in row 3, column 3 is filled with o, and the remaining six cells are blank filled.

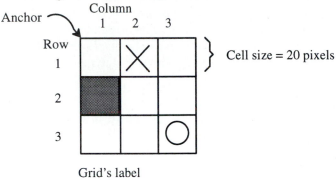

FIGURE 4–13 A 3x3 grid and its cell settings.

The number of rows and columns, as well as the size of each cell in a grid variable, are determined at the time that variable is declared in the program. The *cell size* is measured in *pixels*, which are fixed-sized tiny graphical display units on the screen that cannot be more finely divided. Each cell in the grid of Figure 4–13 is 20 pixels high and 20 pixels wide. The *anchor* for a grid is the location of its upper left-hand corner when the grid is actually displayed on the screen. This location is given as a pair of *xy* coordinates, where the upper left corner of the screen has coordinate values (0,0) and the lower righthand corner has coordinate values (200, 200). To declare an object of class grid, the following declaration is needed:

```
grid variablename(gridsize, cellsize, anchor-x, anchor-y, label);
```

For instance, the grid in Figure 4–13 is declared as follows if it has the name board and is placed on the screen as shown in Figure 4–14:

```
grid board (3, 20, 10, 10, "my grid") ;
```

Unlike lists and strings, we must always begin any program that uses objects in the grid class with the following statements:

```
open_text () ;
open_graphics () ;
```

and end any such program with the statements:

```
close_graphics() ;
close_text() ;
```

The first of these two pairs clears the screen and creates two *windows*, a graphics window on the left and a text window on the right. All grids that are created by the program appear in the graphics window, while all text input and output will appear in the text window. The details of these and other graphics functions are more fully explained in the laboratory manual. The second pair of statements returns the screen to its original state.

Once declared, a grid object can be displayed on the screen any time during program execution using the following statement:

```
board.display_grid () ;
```

This statement creates the display shown in Figure 4–14, for the grid board that was declared above.

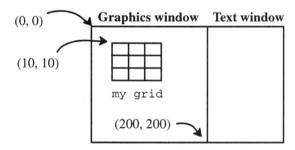

FIGURE 4–14   Layout of the screen for graphics output.

If we want to set a cell of our grid board to a different pattern, we use one of the functions set_cell or set_cell_display. For example, the statement

```
board.set_cell(1,2,'x') ;
```

places an X in the cell in row 1, column 2 of the board. The result of this action will appear immediately in the graphics window only if we use the statement

```
board.set_cell_display(1,2,'x') ;
```

Otherwise, only the internal value in row 1, column 2 of board will be changed (while the version of board that appears on the screen will be unchanged).

Following a series of such changes to individual cells, the program may wish to redraw the grid on the screen in its entirety. This can be done using the following statement.

```
board.display_grid () ;
```

To retrieve the current value stored a cell in row i and column j of a grid, the function cell(i,j) can be used. For instance, if we want to test whether the cell in row 1, column 2 of board has the letter x in it, we write:

```
if (board.cell(1,2) == 'x') ...
```

Finally, to retrieve the row and column number of a cell where the mouse was clicked last, the functions get_click(i,j) and locate_cell(i,j) can be used. For example, we could write:

```
board.get_click(i,j);
if (board.locate_cell(i,j)) ...
```

to retrieve the coordinates i and j of a cell on the board where the mouse is clicked. The function get_click retrieves the pixel coordinates of the next mouse click to occur in the graphics window. The function locate_cell converts these coordinates to row and column numbers in the grid where the mouse was clicked. If the mouse click was outside the grid, locate_cell returns 0 and leaves the values of i and j unchanged; otherwise it returns 1. Thus, the normal place to use the function locate_cell is inside an if or while statement, which serves to ask the question "was the mouse clicked inside the grid?"

Readers may notice that this discussion has focused on the nature of graphics objects themselves, rather than on the functions for manipulating them. This style of design is characteristic of *object-oriented programming*, which is more extensively developed in Volume II of this series.

Using grids in programs: Tic-tac-toe   The fully developed program for tic-tac-toe is shown in Figure 4–15. Even though the development of this program hasn't yet been fully discussed, it is instructive here to point out in the text of this program where the uses of the grid class and its related functions actually appear inside a program. These uses are circled in Figure 4–15.

EXERCISE

4–11 Consider the problem of monitoring a customer's session at an automatic teller machine (ATM). Specifically, suppose we wanted to develop a program that, for an individual customer, accepts deposits,

```
// This program monitors a game of tic-tac-toe with
// two players.

#include <iostream.h>
#include "GridClass.h"

void main ()
{
// pre: input == a series of mouse clicks by alternate players.

    const int anchor_x = 45;    // x and y coordinates of the
    const int anchor_y = 45;    // board in the graphics window
    int move_number = 1;
    int row, col;
    char current_player;

// Step 1.  Initialize the board and the game.
    open_graphics ();
    grid board (3, 40, anchor_x,anchor_y, "Tic Tac Toe Board");
    open_text ();
    cout << "Welcome to Tic-Tac-Toe!\n\n" ;
    cout << "Click on a cell for the next move, or else\n"
       << "click outside the board to end the game.\n";

// Step 2.  Obtain the first move from input.
    board.get_click(row, col);

// Step 3.  While there are still moves, alternate turns
//          between 'x' and 'o'.
    while (board.locate_cell(row, col))
    {
       if (move_number % 2 == 1)  // determine turn: 'x' or 'o'
          current_player = 'x';
       else
          current_player = 'o';
       board.set_cell_display (row, col, current_player);
       move_number++;
       board.get_click(row, col);
    }

// Step 3.  Close graphics windows.
    close_graphics ();
    close_text ();

// post: input == empty &&
//    output == a display of the moves on a tic-tac-toe board.
}
```

References to the Grid type and related functions

FIGURE 4–15   Uses of the Grids abstraction in the tic-tac-toe program.

withrdrawals, and balance inquiries. Each of these transactions is keyed by a mouse click in a labeled 1×1 grid, as illustrated in Figure 4–16. In that figure, a customer has made four transactions—one deposit, two withdrawals, and one balance inquiry—before clicking on the grid "No More Transactions."

a. Given the following specifications, along with the illustration in Figure 4–16, suggest a breakdown of this problem into a series of steps that satisfies those specifications.

```
// pre: input == an initial account balance of 0 and
//   a series of mouse clicks in the grids labeled
//   'Deposit,' 'Withdrawal,' and 'Balance Check,'
//   followed by a final click in the grid labeled
//   'No More Transactions.'  Each mouse click in
//   'Deposit' or 'Withdrawal' is accompanied by an
//   amount typed in the text window.

// post: output == a series of changes to the account
//   balance that reflect each deposit or withdrawal,
//   interspersed with a display of the balance whenever
//   it is requested, and followed by a display of the
//   balance after the last transaction is processed.
```

b. What specific variables and objects are needed to solve this problem?

c. What `grid` functions appear to be useful for solving this problem?

Graphics window	Text window
□ Deposit □ Withdrawal □ Balance Check □ No More Transactions	Welcome to First City Bank Click mouse for next transaction Enter the amount of your deposit: 200 Click mouse for next transaction Enter the amont of your withdrawal: 50 Click mouse for next transaction Your balance is $ 125.00 Click mouse for next transaction Enter the amount of your withdrawal 25 Click mouse for next transaction Your final balance is: $ 125.00 Have a nice day!

FIGURE 4–16   Simulating a customer's transactions at an ATM.

IMPORTANT DOMAIN KNOWLEDGE FROM MATHEMATICS

Throughout our discussion of algorithmic problem solving, we have taken for granted a certain level of knowledge about the domain in which the problem lies. In simple problems like the ones presented so far, the only domain knowledge that we need is an elementary familiarity with algebra and logic. For more advanced problems, we may need some higher-level knowledge in mathematics, computer science, the physical sciences, the social sciences, linguistics, economics, or business in order to fully develop the solution.

Key mathematical functions One area of domain knowledge that is fundamental to all of computing is the notion of a function, a notion that we first introduced in Chapter 2. There are a number of additional special functions that arise frequently enough in computing to warrant a brief introduction here.

Example 4.6 A class of functions that arises frequently in computing is the class of polynomial functions, such as x^2, $2x^3 + 1$, $x^5 - 5x$, and so forth. The general form for a polynomial function is:

$$p(x) = a_n x^n + a_{n-1}x^{n-1} + ... + a_1 x + a_0$$

Thus if $n = 3$, $a_3 = 2$, $a_2 = a_1 = 0$, and $a_0 = 1$, then $p(x) = 2x^3 + 1$.

Exponential and logarithmic functions are two classes of functions of such importance in computing that we need to devote some time to develop them carefully. We start with the exponential function.

Definition Let $X == Y == \mathbf{R}$, and let $f(x) = 2^x$. Then $f(x)$ is called the *exponential* function with base 2.

Since $2^0 = 1$ and $2^{-x} = \dfrac{1}{2^x}$ we can tabulate some values for the exponential function and sketch its graph, as shown in Figure 4–17.

The principal property of the exponential function is its rapid rate of growth. If x is increased by 1, $f(x)$ doubles since $2^{x+1} = 2 \times 2^x$. The following ancient puzzles illustrate this property; the first is from France and the second is from Persia.

Example 4.7 Suppose you have a pond on your property. There are lily pads growing in the pond and you notice that the surface area of the pond that they cover is doubling each day. At first this makes little difference, since the area they cover is quite small. However, you are aware that if they ever cover the pond completely, they will choke out all other life in the pond. After 29 days you observe that the pond is half covered. How many days do you have left to save your pond? (The answer, of course, is 1 day.)

Example 4.8   A certain individual offered to give a beautiful chessboard to the king if the king would give her one grain of rice on the first square, two grains of rice on the second square, four grains on the third, and so on until all squares on the chessboard were covered. Thinking little about what was being asked of him, the king readily agreed. It was not long before the king was bankrupt.

We can estimate how much rice the king actually owed to this individual. But first we need to recall some algebraic properties of the exponential function. The four properties we will need are:

(4.1)   *a.* $2^m 2^n = 2^{m+n}$
    b. $2^m / 2^n = 2^{m-n}$
    c. $(2^m)^n = 2^{mn}$
    d. $2^{m/n} = \sqrt[n]{2^m}$

where m and n are natural numbers. (These properties hold even if m and n are real numbers, but our applications will usually require only the simpler case.)

It is not hard to verify these properties. In Equation 4.1a, the left-hand side is the product of m 2s followed by a product n 2s. The result is a product of $m + n$ 2s. Verification of Equation 4.1b follows from a similar observation. The left-hand side of Equation 4.1c is the product of n copies of 2^m. That is, it is the product of n copies of a product of m 2s. Thus there are mn 2s multiplied together. To verify Equation 4.1d, we use the fact that Equation 4.1c can be extended to the case in which m and n are rational numbers. That is, $2^{m/n}$ can be written as $(2^m)^{1/n}$, so that Equation 4.1d follows directly using the fact that $2^{1/n} = \sqrt[n]{2}$.

We can now estimate the amount of rice the giver of the chessboard would have received had the king been able to meet his commitment. Let's consider

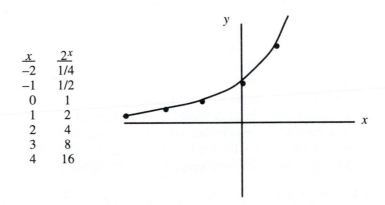

x	2^x
-2	1/4
-1	1/2
0	1
1	2
2	4
3	8
4	16

FIGURE 4–17   The exponential function and its xy graph.

the first few squares' commitment. On square 1, 1 (= 2^0) grain was to be given; on square 2, 2 (= 2^1) grains; on square 3, 4 (= 2^2) grains; and so on. Thus on day 64, the individual would have received 2^{63} grains of rice from the king. Now we have:

$$2^{63} = 2^{60} \times 2^3 = (2^{10})^6 \times 2^3$$
$$2^{10} = 1024 \approx 1000 = 10^3$$

Hence $2^{63} \approx (10^3)^6 \times 8$ $= 8 \times 10^{18}$. If we use an estimate of 50 grains of rice per gram, this is roughly equal to 1.6×10^{11} metric tons of rice, which substantially exceeds the entire world's production of rice.

The exponential function is one-to-one: thus, if $x_1 \neq x_2$ then $2^{x_1} \neq 2^{x_2}$. Its range is the nonnegative real numbers. Hence if we restrict its domain to be $\{x \in \mathbf{R} \mid x > 0\}$, then the exponential function's domain will be identical with its range (see Figure 4–17 again). Thus this function is invertible. The inverse of the exponential function is called the *logarithmic function*.

Definition   Let $X == \mathbf{R}$ and $Y == \{x \in \mathbf{R} \mid x > 0\}$. Let $f(x) = 2^x$. Then f^{-1} is called the *logarithmic function with base 2* and is denoted $log_2 (x)$.

Recall that for any function and its inverse, $f(f^{-1}(x)) = x$ and $f^{-1}(f(x)) = x$. These relationships give us the following equations, which relate the exponential and logarithmic functions to each other:

(4.2) $2^{\log_2 x} = x$

(4.3) $\log_2 (2^x) = x$

Example 4.9   Since $2^3 = 8$, $\log_2 8 = 3$. That is, $2^3 = 8$ answers the question "What do we get when we raise the number 2 to the third power?" $\log_2 8 = 3$ answers the question "To what power do we have to raise 2 in order to get 8?" Thus we have $\log_2 16 = 4$ and $\log_2 1024 = 10$.

The graph of the logarithmic function is given in Figure 4–18. We saw that the most important property of the exponential function is the rapidity of its growth. The most important property of the logarithmic function is the *slowness* of its growth. Note that $\log_2 8 = 3$, and $\log_2 16 = 4$. That is, adding 1 to x doubles 2^x, but doubling x only adds 1 to $\log_2 x$.

Another way to compare the logarithmic and exponential functions is this: $y = 2^x$ means that 1 must be doubled x times to get y. If x is a power of 2, $y = \log_2 x$ means that x must be halved y times to get 1. For example, $4 = \log_2 16$ means that 16 must be divided by 2 four times to get 1. Equations 4.4 through 4.8 describe some additional properties of the logarithmic function:

(4.4) $\log_2 1 = 0$

(4.5) $\log_2 2 = 1$

(4.6) $\log_2 mn = \log_2 m + \log_2 n$

(4.7) $\log_2 (m/n) = \log_2 m - \log_2 n$

(4.8) $\log_2 (m^n) = n \log_2 m$

Verification of these properties depends on the fact that the logarithmic function is the inverse of the exponential function. Below we verify Equations 4.4 through 4.6, and leave verification of the others to the reader.

To verify Equation 4.4, let $\log_2 1 = x$. Then $2^x = 1$, so that $x = 0$. To verify Equation 4.5, let $\log_2 2 = x$. Then $2^x = 2$, giving $x = 1$. To verify Equation 4.6, let $x = \log_2 m$ and $y = \log_2 n$. Then $m = 2^x$ and $n = 2^y$. Hence $mn = 2^{x+y}$ and hence $x+y = \log_2 (mn)$. Combining these, we get $\log_2 mn = \log_2 m + \log_2 n$.

Example 4.10 $\log_2 3 = 1.585$ and $\log_2 5 = 2.322$. We can use this information to compute each of the following:

a. $\log_2 6 = \log_2 (2 \times 3) = \log_2 2 + \log_2 3 = 1 + 1.585 = 2.585$
b. $\log_2 1.6 = \log_2 (8/5) = \log_2 8 - \log_2 5 = 3 - 2.322 = 0.678$
c. $\log_2 0.5 = \log_2 (1/2) = \log_2 1 - 1 = -1$

In C++, the exponential and logarithmic functions are supported, but in base e rather than in base 2. These are called `exp` and `log`, respectively, in the library `<math.h>`. Thus, to compute e^x given x, we write the C++ expression `exp(x)`. To compute $\log_e x$ given x, we write the expression `log(x)`.

Finite Series and Iteration Cumulative processes arise frequently in computing. For example, a program might repeat some particular calculation.

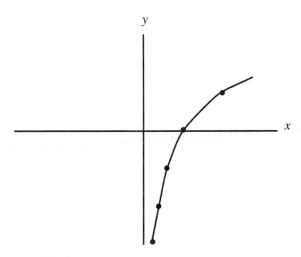

FIGURE 4–18 The logarithmic function.

Each repetition consumes a certain amount of time and memory. The programmer would like to be able to estimate the amount of time and space the program will take without actually running it.

Such calculations frequently require addition of fairly long lists of numbers or expressions. To facilitate these and related calculations, a special shorthand notation called *sigma notation* has been developed. It uses the Greek letter Σ (sigma) to stand for *sum*, an index that defines the range of values over which the sum is to occur, and the function to be summed. (Note the connection with the quantifier **Sum** introduced in Chapter 3). Suppose we want to write the sum of the first 20 integers, or $1 + 2 + 3 + \dots + 20$, in sigma notation. We write this as

$$\sum_{i=1}^{20} i$$

This is read, "Compute the sum of all integers i between 1 and 20, inclusive." The number 20 is the *upper limit*, the number 1 is the *lower limit*, and the variable i is the *index variable* for the sum.

Example 4.11 Here are some more examples of sigma notation:

a. $\displaystyle\sum_{i=1}^{n} i = 1 + 2 + 3 + \dots + (n-1) + n$

b. $\displaystyle\sum_{i=0}^{n} 3i = 0 + 3 + 6 + 9 + \dots + 3(n-1) + 3n$

c. $\displaystyle\sum_{i=1}^{n} (3i + 2) = 5 + 8 + 11 + \dots + (3n - 1) + (3n + 2)$

d. $\displaystyle\sum_{i=1}^{n-1} i = 1 + 2 + 3 + \dots + (n - 2) + (n - 1)$

e. $\displaystyle\sum_{i=2}^{n} i = 2 + 3 + 4 + \dots + (n - 1) + n$

f. $\displaystyle\sum_{i=1}^{n} i(3i + 2) = 5 + 16 + 33 + \dots + (n - 1)(3n - 1) + n(3n + 2)$

In fact, any function of an index variable i can be summed in this way. Consider the following general relationships:

$$(4.9) \quad \sum_{i=m}^{n} f(i) = f(m) + f(m+1) + \ldots + f(n)$$

$$(4.10) \quad \sum_{i=1}^{n} a_i = a_1 + a_2 + \ldots + a_n$$

Note the use of the *subscripts* in Equation 4.10. These are often used to distinguish elements of a list, a_1 being the first element in the list, a_2 the second, and so forth. We shall use this idea of a list often in dealing with program design.

Properties of Finite Series   Equations 4.11 through 4.14 give some basic properties of sums under sigma notation.

$$(4.11) \quad \sum_{i=1}^{1} a_i = a_1$$

$$(4.12) \quad \sum_{i=1}^{n} a_i = a_1 + \sum_{i=2}^{n} a_i$$

$$(4.13) \quad \sum_{i=1}^{n} a_i = a_n + \sum_{i=1}^{n-1} a_i$$

$$(4.14) \quad \sum_{i=1}^{n} a_i = \sum_{i=1}^{m} a_i + \sum_{i=m+1}^{n} a_i \qquad \text{if } 1 \leq m < n$$

We can justify these as follows: In Equation 4.11, the upper and lower limits are the same, so there can only be one term, the one corresponding to the common value of the limits. In Equation 4.12, the right-hand side is simply the left with the first term separated out. The right-hand side of Equation 4.13 is simply the left with the last term separated out. In Equation 4.14, the right-hand side is the left separated into two sums—one up to m, and one from $m + 1$ to n.

Equations 4.15 through 4.19 summarize some important additional properties of finite series.

$$(4.15) \quad \sum_{i=1}^{n} c = cn \qquad \text{where } c \text{ is any constant}$$

$$(4.16) \quad \sum_{i=1}^{n} cf(i) = c \sum_{i=1}^{n} f(i)$$

$$(4.17) \quad \sum_{i=1}^{n} (f(i) + g(i)) = \sum_{i=1}^{n} f(i) + \sum_{i=1}^{n} g(i)$$

$$(4.18) \quad \sum_{i=1}^{n} (f(i) - g(i)) = \sum_{i=1}^{n} f(i) - \sum_{i=1}^{n} g(i)$$

$$(4.19) \quad \sum_{i=1}^{n} (f(i + 1) - f(i)) = f(n + 1) - f(1)$$

We can justify these properties by the following observations: In Equation 4.15, the left-hand side is c added to itself n times. In Equation 4.16, the right-hand side is the same as the left with c factored out of the sum. In Equation 4.17, the right-hand side is the left with the terms rearranged. Equation 4.18 is left as an exercise, while Equation 4.19 is known as the *telescoping series*. The left-hand side can be written as

$$[f(2) - f(1)] + [f(3) - f(2)] + \ ... \ + [f(n + 1) - f(n)]$$

Now we can see that all terms besides $f(n + 1)$ and $f(1)$ cancel out, leaving $f(n + 1) - f(1)$.

Some important series in computing It's not usually enough to be able to model a cumulative process as a finite sum using sigma notation. Usually we would like a formula for the sum in terms of the upper and lower limits. A number of common series have well-established formulas and are worth committing to memory.

One such series that arises quite often in computing is the *arithmetic series* (also called the *arithmetic progression*):

$$1 + 2 + 3 + ... + (n - 1) + n$$

There is an interesting anecdote about this series. Carl Friedrich Gauss (1777–1855) was one of the great mathematicians of the nineteenth century. As a boy he was sent to a boarding school known more for its strict discipline than its academic quality. As a punishment, he and his classmates were given the exercise of adding up all of the integers from 1 to 100. The teacher had barely assigned the problem when Gauss raised his hand with the correct answer. Gauss had discovered a clever way to sum the arithmetic series with $n = 100$. He wrote the sum down horizontally, wrote it down again horizontally in reverse order, and then added the two sums term by term:

```
      1  +    2  +    3  +   ...  +   99  + 100
 +  100  +   99  +   98  +   ...  +    2  +   1
    101  +  101  +  101  +   ...  +  101  + 101
```

Gauss could see that the answer was half of 101×100, or 5050. Gauss's teacher recognized that the boy possessed an unusual talent for mathematics and recommended to his father that Gauss attend a school that would be better suited for a student of his ability. In fact, we can use Gauss's shortcut method to sum a more general series:

$$
\begin{array}{cccccccccc}
1 & + & 2 & + & 3 & + \ldots + & (n-1) & + & n \\
+ n & + & (n-1) & + & (n-2) & + \ldots + & 2 & + & 1 \\
\hline
(n+1) & + & (n+1) & + & (n+1) & + \ldots + & (n+1) & + & (n+1)
\end{array}
$$

Since there are n terms in this sum, it can be written simply as $n(n+1)$. Hence, the sum of the original arithmetic series is $n(n+1)/2$, since we had added it to itself to obtain the last line. The *closed form* sum of this series and the closed form sum for three similar series are given in Equations 4.20 through 4.23.

$$(4.20) \quad \sum_{i=1}^{n} i = \frac{n(n+1)}{2}$$

$$(4.21) \quad \sum_{i=1}^{n} i^2 = \frac{n(n+1)(2n+1)}{6}$$

$$(4.22) \quad \sum_{i=1}^{n} i^3 = \frac{n^2(n+1)^2}{4}$$

$$(4.23) \quad \sum_{i=0}^{n} 2^i = 2^{n+1} - 1$$

Equations 4.20 through 4.22 are called *p-series* since they are all of the form

$$\sum_{i=1}^{n} i^p$$

for some power p. Equation 4.23 is an instance of what is called the *geometric series* or *geometric progression*.

Example 4.12   Here are two examples that illustrate how these properties can be used to find closed form solutions for series.

$$\sum_{i=1}^{15} i = \frac{15(15+1)}{2} = 120$$

$$\sum_{i=7}^{20} i = \sum_{i=1}^{20} i - \sum_{i=1}^{6} i = \frac{20(21)}{2} - \frac{6(7)}{2} = 210 - 21 = 189$$

Example 4.13   Consider the problem discussed in Example 4.8. We can use Equation 4.23 to compute the total number of grains of rice that would be accumulated in 64 days, as follows:

$$\sum_{i=1}^{64} 2^{i-1} = \sum_{i=0}^{63} 2^i = 2^{64} - 1$$

Note that $2^{64} = 2 \times 2^{63} = 2^{63} + 2^{63}$, so $2^{64} - 1 = 2^{63} + 2^{63} - 1$. Recall that the number of grains of rice received on day 64 was 2^{63}. Hence, the amount of rice received on day 64 is 1 more than the number of grains received on all previous days added together! In general, geometric sums follow this pattern. That is,

$1 + 2 + 4 = 7$, which is 1 less than 8
$1 + 2 + 4 + 8 = 15$, which is 1 less than 16

and so on. This provides an alternative view of the rapid growth of exponential functions.

EXERCISES

4–12 Simplify the following:

a. $3^a \times 3^{-a}$
b. $(2^2)^3$
c. $27^{n/3}$
d. $2^3 / 2^4$

e. $\log_2 4$
f. $\log_3 (1/27)$
g. $\log_2 2^n$
h. $3^{\log_3 (x+1)}$

4–13 Expand each of the following sums:

a. $\displaystyle\sum_{i=1}^{10} 2^{i-1}$

b. $\displaystyle\sum_{i=1}^{n} \frac{i}{i+1}$

c. $\displaystyle\sum_{j=m}^{n} a_j$

d. $\displaystyle\sum_{i=0}^{0} a_i$

4-14 Express each of the following using sigma notation:

    a. $17 + 21 + 25 + ... + 65$
    b. $2 + 5 + 10 + 17 + ... + 101$
    c.   The sum of the odd numbers from 0 to 1000, inclusive
    d.   The sum of the positive integers under 300 that are divisible by 3
    e.   The sum of the square roots of all positive integers under 1000

4-15 Compute the sum of each expression developed in Exercise 4-14.

4-16 In Nepal, rice paddies are often built on terraced hillsides. A bird's-eye view of one such collection of paddies is given in Figure 4-19. The inner quarter-circle at the summit is not cultivated. Moving out from the summit, paddies alternate with steep, uncultivated slopes. Assume that on a particular hill, the radius of the summit circle is 75 meters and each successive concentric ring from there on out has a width of 50 meters. Suppose also there are 10 rings containing paddies, not just the three that are shown in Figure 4-19.

    a.   Use sigma notation to write an expression for the total area covered by rice paddies.

    b.   Find the total area covered by the rice paddies.

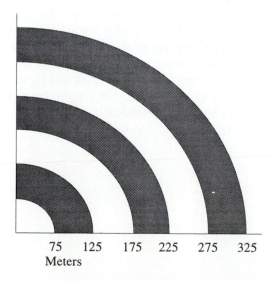

75   125   175   225   275   325
Meters

FIGURE 4-19   Bird's-eye view of rice paddies in Nepal.

4-17 Compute the following sums:

a. $\displaystyle\sum_{i=1}^{25} i$

b. $\displaystyle\sum_{i=0}^{13} 2i(i+1)$

c. $\displaystyle\sum_{i=6}^{12} 3i^2$

d. $\displaystyle\sum_{k=5}^{10} 2^k$

e. $\displaystyle\sum_{i=1}^{n} 2$

f. $\displaystyle\sum_{i=0}^{5} (2i+1)$

g. $\displaystyle\sum_{i=2}^{5} i^2$

h. $\displaystyle\sum_{i=1}^{0} a_i$

4-18 *a.* Justify Equation 4.18.

b. Show that the sum of the first n odd integers is n^2.

SUMMARY

In this chapter, we have focused our attention on two key activities in the problem solving process. First, we have explored how the pre- and postconditions, together with an understanding of state, may be used to design a solution to an algorithmic problem. Second, a key component of this design process is the intelligent usage of abstraction.

Abstraction has three complementary aspects. First, we use abstraction when we ignore, or postpone, the details of a particular step in breaking down an algorithm out of its initial specifications. Second, we use procedural abstraction to mean the development of a function that will be the basis for future algorithms. A third dimension of abstraction is the use of classes to create and manipulate objects with new types, as we did in the tic-tac-toe design. We then explored two of the many predefined classes that are available in the C++ libraries for your use: lists and grids. We emphasize that the MAPS methodology, and the design techniques presented therein, requires both experience and creativity for its effective use in problem solving.

CODING AND PRESENTATION

We have come a long way in our study of algorithmic problem solving. In fact, we have come most of the way, using MAPS, from interpreting the original problem statement to developing a running computer program. The process of understanding the nature of the problem, specifying the nature of the solution and designing a solution are considerably more difficult than coding the final program. This point is often difficult for beginning students to believe.

Coding a program seems awkward at first because it is such an unnatural process. Computer languages are not very flexible and the rules of expression are often tedious. But once the syntactic and semantic conventions become familiar and experience is gained, implementing a design becomes a reasonably straightforward activity. In fact, if an implementation is not easily accomplished, that is usually a sign that the design, rather than the program code, is at fault.

A common mistake in program development is to modify a program to meet new requirements without backing up to modify the specification, design, and abstractions that led to the program code. The result of taking such a shortcut is a program that is increasingly difficult to understand, to modify, or to correct. We have emphasized the MAPS methodology because it provides an effective method for solving a wide range of problems, from small to large, in many different application areas, from numeric to text to graphics. It should therefore be clear that MAPS is not usually a serial, one-pass process; it is an iterative one in which various stages are repeated as the problem statement changes and/or errors are detected in the design or implementation.

TECHNIQUES FOR CREATING NEW ABSTRACTIONS

Once the abstraction stage of program development is completed, our first activity within the coding stage is to identify existing abstractions, within the language or a library, that can be reused within the current problem design. This was the focus of discussion in Chapter 4, where we illustrated how to find, within C++ function libraries (e.g., strings, arithmetic functions) and class libraries (e.g., `ListClass.h` and `GridClass.h`), those types, classes, and related functions that are directly useful for the problem being discussed.

Now inevitably there will be gaps. That is, while we will be able to "one-stop shop" for solutions to all of the abstractions we have identified for our problem, others will not be available in this manner, and we will have to implement them ourselves. The process of implementing our own abstractions (functions) and completing the coding of problems in C++ is the main subject of this chapter. We begin by looking at some examples.

Developing a Procedural Abstraction: Finding Words in a String

In the previous chapter, we developed an algorithm for finding a word as a sub-step process within the "Count the words" problem. The necessity to find words in a text is a problem that arises very frequently in computing (e.g., creating an index, searching a database for information about a particular author, etc.). Since finding a word is a common problem, it makes sense to solve it once and for all, and then just recall the solution when we need to.

Recall from the previous chapter that complete procedural abstraction suggests a strategy for implementing a well-specified function, while procedural abstraction does not. Both, however, give a name, parameters, and pre- and postconditions for the desired function.

Abstraction is one of the most powerful ideas of computer science and is one of our major tools in dealing with complex problems. Let's take a look at how complete procedural abstraction can help us solve the problem of counting words in a text. In the following example, we assume that S is a character string variable containing *zero or more words*, each word being a string of non-blank (nonwhitespace) characters. Note that this problem differs from, and in fact generalizes, the word counting problem discussed in the previous chapter, since there we took advantage of the fact that the statement

```
cin >> S ;
```

skips past leading blanks, automatically finds the next contiguous sequence of nonblanks, and stores it in S.

Example 5.1 The complete procedural abstraction `FindWord` places the first word that appears in an input string S into the string `Result` and sets k to mark the position of the end of that word in S.

```
FindWord (S, Result, k)
// pre: S == "aChar[1] ... aChar[n]" && n >= 0
Step FW.1.   While at a whitespace
        Step FW.1.1.  Move to next character
Step FW.2.   Initialize Result to the empty string
Step FW.3.   While at a nonwhitespace and there are characters
        Step FW.3.1.  Add (concatenate) it to Result
```

```
          Step FW.3.2.  Move to the next character
// post: (Result == "aChar[j] ... aChar[k]" &&
//           for all i in {1,..., j-1}: aChar[i] is whitespace &&
//           for all i in {j,..., k}: aChar[i] is nonwhitespace &&
//           (aChar[k+1] is blank || k == n)
```

The key point is that we have given this abstraction a name, so that we may use that name later to solve problems and we may use its constituent steps later to implement the abstraction itself. In the "Count the words" problem, this means that we could start with weaker assumptions about the power of `cin >>` and assume that the input is just a sequence of characters (not words). That is, we now have a procedural abstraction that can find whole words (by invoking our abstraction `FindWord`). Thus, an alternative version of the "Count the words" problem becomes:

```
// pre: input == "aChar[1] aChar[2] ... aChar[n]" && n >= 0
Step 1.   Set S = the entire input string
Step 2.   Set NWords = 0
Step 3.   FindWord (S, Result, k)
Step 4.   While (Result != "")
          {
Step 4.1. Set S = "aChar[k+1] ... aChar[n]"
Step 4.2. NWords = NWords + 1 ;
Step 4.3. FindWord (S, Result, k) ;
          }
Step 5.   Display the resulting value of NWords
// post: output == NWords
```

Of even greater importance here is that we may use the `FindWord` abstraction whenever we have a programming problem that requires finding a word in a text. For instance, recall the first example in Chapter 4 where we were required to input a number of names. By using this new `FindWord` abstraction (with a suitable definition of "word"), we can more easily solve that problem. Essentially, this new abstraction adds a new operation to the functional capabilities of the computer; by implementing `FindWord`, we have created a more powerful computer!

Parameters: the Key to Abstraction

The need to reuse an abstraction requires that the variables mentioned in its pre- and postconditions become "parameterized." That is, consider the function `FindWord`. If we want to use it in a program that has a different name for the string `S`, then `S` itself becomes sort of a placeholder for whatever that name might eventually be. If, on the other hand, we had to generate a new version of FindWord for *every* application that uses these steps to find a word in a different string from `S`, we would lose most of the value of the abstraction process itself. Thus, the role of the name `S` must change from that of a variable in the process to that of a placeholder for a variable. When such a role change occurs, this is called *parameterization*, and the name S itself becomes a *parameter* rather than a variable.

The process of parameterization in a procedural abstraction involves the following steps:

- Locate within the specifications all variables that either provide values to or deliver results from the abstraction (these become the *parameters* for the abstraction).

- Rename those variables with more generic names. Identify all references to these variables within the steps of the complete procedural abstraction, and systematically rename each of those references accordingly.

- In an application program, use the abstraction by giving its name along with the names of the actual variables that correspond with the parameters, and that will supply values to, or hold results from, that particular use (these variables are the *arguments* for that particular use of the abstraction in an application program, and this particular use is known as an *invocation* or a *call*).

As an example, let's reconsider the abstraction FindWord. First, we look at the specifications:

```
// pre: S == "aChar[1] ... aChar[n]" && n >= 0
// post: (Result == "aChar[j] ... aChar[k]" &&
//        for all i in {1,..., j-1}: aChar[i] is whitespace &&
//        for all i in {j,..., k}: aChar[i] is nonwhitespace &&
//        (aChar[k+1] is blank || k == n)
```

and see that three variables S, Result, and k require parameterization. It is important to recognize just those variables which need parameterization. For instance, k is required to modify the original string S in preparation for the next iteration of the loop, and we choose not to treat n as a parameter because it can be computed immediately from the parameter S using the standard string function length. Finally, we systematically replace these variables with more generically named ones: InputString, Result, and EndWord.

Then we rewrite the complete procedural abstraction for FindWord in terms of these newly-discovered parameters.

Definition   FindWord places the next word in an input string Input-String into a string Result. It also places the index of the next character, after the word found, in EndWord.

```
FindWord (InputString, Result, EndWord)
// pre: InputString == "aChar[1] ... aChar[n]" && n >= 0
```

```
Step FW.1.  While at a whitespace
      Step FW.1.1.  Move to next character
Step FW.2.  Initialize Result to the empty string
Step FW.3.  While at a nonwhitespace && there are characters
      Step FW.3.1.  Add (concatenate) it to Result
      Step FW.3.2.  Move to the next character
// post: (Result == "aChar[j] ... aChar[EndWord]" &&
//     for all i in {1,..., j-1}: aChar[i] is whitespace &&
//     for all i in {j,..., EndWord}: aChar[i] is nonwhitespace
//          && (aChar[EndWord+1] is blank || EndWord == n)
```

Note that we have renamed two of the three variables that we identified as parameters (Result was already generic, so we didn't rename it) in the heading of this abstraction, as well as throughout the steps that reference them.

Identifying New Abstractions

An important skill in algorithmic problem-solving is to develop a knack for recognizing common abstractions as they reappear in different problem-solving contexts. Once it is recognized, an abstraction can be rather easily packaged for reuse in the form of a function—the trick is to recognize the abstraction in the first place! Some commonly used abstractions are evident in the example problems that we have been exploring and in the program segments that used various quantified predicate logic expressions.

We have been studying algorithms for solving the GPA problem, for computing a^b, for counting the words in a text string, and for displaying graphical information. When we look for abstractions that appear in these problems, several repeated patterns occur. Some even jump out at us! For example, the calculation of the sum S for an arbitrary list of integers was embedded inside the algorithm for computing the GPA. Summing the numbers in a list is surely an abstraction, since it is useful in a wide variety of other algorithms, such as balancing a checkbook or totaling the gate receipts at a sporting event.

What would an abstraction for the summation process look like? Suppose we name it sum, and identify its parameters and specifications for an arbitrary input list L as the procedural abstraction shown in Figure 5–1.

Because we have been looking at instances of this abstraction already, we know that its complete procedural abstraction will look something like Figure 5–2. Notice here that we have written out the individual steps for this abstrac-

```
sum(L, result)
// pre: L == (e[1] e[2] ... e[n]) && n >= 0 &&
//     for all i in {1,..., n}: e[i] is a number
// post: result == Sum i in {1,..., n}: e[i]
```

FIGURE 5–1   A procedural abstraction to sum the elements of a list L.

```
sum(L, Result) ;
// pre: L == (e[1] e[2] ... e[n]) && n >= 0 &&
//    for all i in {1,..., n}: e[i] is a number
  Result = 0;
  i = 1 ;
  while (i <= n)
  {
    Result = Result + L.element(i) ;
    i = i + 1 ;
  }
// post: Result == Sum i in {1,..., n}: e[i]
```

FIGURE 5–2   A complete procedural abstraction sum.

tion in C++ style syntax, anticipating that these steps will eventually be encoded as the body of a C++ function.

In order to complete the transformation of this abstraction into C++ syntax, we must decide whether to encode it as a void function, in which the results are passed back through reference parameters, or as a nonvoid function, in which the result is returned immediately. A completed C++ void function for the sum abstraction is shown in Figure 5–3. Notice that the parameter result, designating the value to be returned to the calling program, is marked (with &) as a reference parameter since it designates a value returned by the function to the calling program. The parameter L is not so marked, since it is a value passed to the function from the calling program.

The equivalent nonvoid function for this abstraction is shown in Figure 5–4. Note here that the role of result is now as a local variable rather than a parameter, and the value returned to the calling program is flagged by an explicit

```
void sum(list L, float & Result)
{
// pre: L == (e[1] e[2] ... e[n]) && n >= 0 &&
//    for all i in {1,..., n}: e[i] is a number
  int i = 1 ;
  int n = L.length() ;
  Result = 0 ;
  while (i <= n)
  {
    Result = Result + L.element(i);
    i = i + 1 ;
  }
// post: Result == Sum i in {1,..., n}: e[i]
}
```

FIGURE 5–3   A C++ implementation of sum as a void function.

```
float sum(list L)
{
// pre: L == (e[1] e[2] ... e[n]) && n >= 0 &&
//    for all i in {1,..., n}: e[i] is a number
  int i = 1 ;
  int n = L.length() ;
  float Result = 0 ;

  while (i <= n)
  {
    Result = Result + L.element(i) ;
    i = i + 1 ;
  }
  return Result ;
// post: Result == Sum i in {1,..., n}: e[i]
end;
```

FIGURE 5–4   Implementation of `sum` as a nonvoid function.

`return` statement. These changes are dictated by the peculiarities of C++ syntax, and have no effective impact on the nature of the abstraction itself.

The `Power` program is another candidate for procedural abstraction and implementation. From the specifications given in Chapter 3, a procedural abstraction for `Power` can be defined as in Figure 5–5.

```
Power(a, b)
// pre: a and b are integers && (a != 0 ||
// (a==0 && b>0)) && MinInt <= a^b <= MaxInt
// post: Result == a^b
```

FIGURE 5–5   Procedural abstraction for the `Power` function.

Our design discussion at the end of that chapter concluded that the **Prod** quantifier was the key that led to the loop shown in Figure 5–6. The implementation of this complete procedural abstraction as a C++ function is shown in Figure 5–7.

We have already discussed the `FindWord` abstraction in considerable detail. We could abstract the *entire* word-counting program into a function in the manner suggested in Figure 5–8.

Many other program segments have such widespread usefulness that they can be abstracted as routines for reuse. Consider the following four simple abstractions that can be used in a variety of list-processing algorithmic problems:

- Find the index of the largest value among the first `m` values of a list `L` (Figure 5–9).

```
Power(a, b)
// pre: a and b are integers &&
//   (a != 0 || (a==0 && b>0)) &&
//   MinInt <= a^b <= MaxInt
  Result = 1 ;
  i = 1 ;
  while (i <= b)
  {
    Result = Result * a ;
    i = i + 1 ;
  }
// post: Result == a^b
```

FIGURE 5–6 Complete procedural abstraction for the Power function.

```
int Power(int a, int b)
{
// pre: a and b are integers &&
//   (a != 0 || (a==0 && b>0)) &&
//   MinInt <= a^b <= MaxInt
  int i = 1 ;
  int Result = 1 ;

  while (i <= b)
  {
    Result = Result * a ;
    i++;
  }
  return Result ;
// post: Result == a^b
}
```

FIGURE 5–7 Implementation of the Power function.

```
WordCount(s)
// Pre: s == a series of characters c[1] c[2] ... c[n]
//      && n >= 0 && each c[i] is an ASCII character
// Post: Result == the number of words in s
```

FIGURE 5–8 The procedural abstraction WordCount.

- Find the index of the smallest value among the first m elements of a list L (Figure 5–9 again).

- Interchange, or *swap*, two elements in a list L (Figure 5–10).

- Search a list L to determine whether or not a particular number $\dot{x}$ appears within it and return its *pos*ition (if any) in L (Figure 5–10 again).

The specifications for `max` and `min` are remarkably similar. In fact, they only differ in the choice of relational operator (>= vs <=) that appears in the post-condition. This similarity should lead to efficient coding when we implement these abstractions. We return to that question later in this chapter, when we discuss techniques for combining code fragments from existing abstractions.

```
max(L, m)
// pre: L == (e[1] e[2] ... e[m] ... e[n]) && n >= 0 &&
//      each e[i] is a number
// post: n > 0 && for all i in {1,..., m}: e[j] >= e[i] &&
//          Result == j ||
//          n == 0 && Result == 0

min(L, m)
// pre: L == (e[1] e[2] ... e[m] ... e[n]) && n >= 0 &&
//      each e[i] is a number
// post: n > 0 && for all i in {1,..., m}: e[j] <= e[i] &&
//          Result == j ||
//          n == 0 && Result == 0
```

FIGURE 5–9 The procedural abstractions `max` and `min`.

The specification for `pos` (Figure 5–10) is especially interesting in the disjunction that is used to define its postcondition. Recall that a postcondition states what must be true for any correct implementation of the abstraction. When there is a disjunction in the postcondition, at least one of the disjuncts (alternatives) must be true. Look at the first predicate in the first disjunct which states that, for some index i, there is an element e[i] in the list which matches the parameter x (i.e., x==e[i]). The first predicate in the second dis-

```
swap(L, j, k)
// pre: L == (e[1] ... e[j]...e[k] ... e[n]) && 1 <= j,k <= n
// post: L == (e[1] ... e[k]...e[j] ... e[n])

pos(x, L)
// pre: L == (e[1] e[2] ... e[n]) && x is a number && n >= 0
// post: there is i in {1,...,n}: x == e[i] && result == i ||
//      for all i in {1,..., n}: x != e[i] && result == 0
```

FIGURE 5–10 The abstractions `swap` and `pos`.

junct states that there is no i for which this match occurs. Thus, these two disjuncts are mutually exclusive and all-encompassing. If x is to be found in the list, then we will be in the state described by the first disjunct; if x is not to be found in the list, then we will be in the state described by the second disjunct. The postcondition therefore covers all possible outcomes for any particular input list L and search argument x.

An example that illustrates these abstractions is shown in Figure 5–11 for a particular list L. Here, we see that L contains 12 numbers. Each number might represent, for instance, a monthly rainfall total in inches, so that `L.element(1)` represents a 2.5-inch rainfall for the month of January, `L.element(2)` represents a 4.4-inch rainfall for February, and so on.

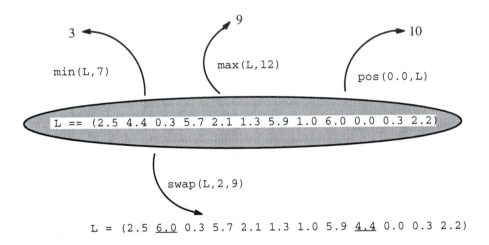

FIGURE 5–11   Illustration of the `max`, `min`, `swap`, and `pos` routines.

From the `min` abstraction, we conclude that an invocation of the form `min(L,7)` is asking for the index in L of the smallest rainfall level that occurred in the first 7 months, and would receive the result 3 as an answer. Similarly, the routine `max(L,12)` asks for the index of the largest rainfall level among all 12 readings in L, and therefore would receive the result 9. `pos(0.0,L)` searches L for an occurrence of the specific value 0.0 and returns 10, its position in the list. Finally, the routine `swap(L,2,9)` swaps, or interchanges, the second and ninth elements of L, as shown by the underlined entries in L at the bottom of Figure 5–11.

Implementing the list abstractions   One of our motivations for presenting procedural abstractions separately from their implementations is to remind you that, during program design, only the specifications of an abstracted routine are necessary and relevant. That is, you do not need to understand the particular steps of, e.g., max when you want to invoke it in your own program. It is only necessary to know the specifications. Of course, you will often be responsible for implementing the abstractions and must become familiar with the process. Figures 5–12, 5–13, and 5–14 show complete procedural abstractions, including implementation details, of the four list processing abstractions discussed above.

```
max(L, m)
// pre: L == (e[1] e[2] ... e[m] ... e[n]) && n >= 0 &&
//       each e[i] is a number
  if (m > 0)
  {
    Result = 1 ;
    i = 2 ;
    while (i <= m)
    {
      if (L.element(i) > L.element(Result))
        Result = i ;
      i = i + 1 ;
    }
  }
  else
    Result = 0 ;
// post: n > 0 && for all i in {1,..., m}:e[j] >= e[i] &&
//               Result == j ||
//       n == 0 && Result == 0
```

FIGURE 5–12 Complete procedural abstraction for max.

Particularly intriguing among these is pos, which must handle the case when the searched-for item x does not appear in the list. Consider what would happen if we used a simpler routine:

```
i = 1 ;
while (L.element(i) != x && i <= n)
  i = i + 1 ;
```

Then, as we reach i == n, the assertion

```
(L.element(n) != x) && (n <= n)
```

is (still) true, so that we would continue to execute the loop, resetting

```
i = i + 1 (== n + 1)
```

Now as we check the boolean condition we have

```
min(L, m)
// pre: L == (e[1] e[2] ... e[m] ... e[n]) && n >= 0 &&
//    each e[i] is a number
  if (m > 0)
  {
    Result = 1 ;
    i = 2 ;
    while (i <= m)
    {
      if (L.element(i) < L.element(Result))
        Result = i ;
      i = i + 1 ;
    }
  }
  else
    Result = 0 ;
// post: n > 0 && for all i in {1,..., m}:e[j] <= e[i] &&
//       Result == j ||
//       n == 0 && Result == 0
```

FIGURE 5–13 Complete procedural abstraction for min.

```
swap(L, j, k)
// pre: L == (e[1] ... e[j]...e[k] ... e[n]) && 1 <= j,k <= n
  hold = L[j] ;
  L[j] = k ;
  L[k] = hold ;
// post: L == (e[1] ... e[k]...e[j] ... e[n])

pos(x, L)
// pre: L == (e[1] e[2] ... e[n]) && x is a number && n >= 0
  i = 1 ;
  found = 0 ;
  while (i <= L.length() && !found)
    if (L.element(i) == x)
      found = 1 ;
    else i = i + 1 ;
  if (found)
    Result = i ;
  else Result = 0 ;
// post: there is i in {1,...,n}: x == e[i] && result == i ||
//    for all i in {1,..., n}:x != e[i] && result == 0
```

FIGURE 5–14 Complete procedural abstractions for swap and pos.

```
(L.element(n+1) != x) && (n+1 <= n)
```

which would specify an attempt to access the value L.element(n+1), which
does not exist in L (since the size of L is n). This implementation would there-

fore lead to a programming error that would in turn cause program termination. Rearranging the two conjuncts above, so that the check on the size of i occurs first, will not necessarily solve this problem (some compilers simultaeously check all conjuncts in a conditional, while others check them in reverse order). The only safe approach to an implementation is therefore the one shown in Figure 5–14.

As you study the various implementations, pay particular attention to our choice of C++ for vs. while structures. We use the for when we know how many iterations will be required and the while when we don't.

Recursive Implementations

As an alternative to the iterative loop implementations discussed above, we can select recursive ones instead. Often the use of recursion presents a simpler, more elegant control structure for implementing abstractions.

Figure 5–15 gives a definition of max in terms of a recurrence relation, as introduced in a previous section. Note that the three branches of the definition cover all possible cases, and there is one branch with a known (non-recursive) result.

$$
\begin{aligned}
\text{max}(L,k) \ &= \ 1 && \text{if } k \ == \ 1 \\
&= \ k && \text{if } k \ > \ 1 \ \&\& \ e_k \ > \ e_{\text{max}(L, \ k\text{-}1)} \\
&= \ \text{max}(L,k\text{-}1) && \text{if } k \ > \ 1 \ \&\& \ e_k \ <= \ e_{\text{max}(L, \ k\text{-}1)}
\end{aligned}
$$

FIGURE 5–15   Recursive definition of max(L,k).

Let's take a closer look at this definition in order to understand it better. We start with an arbitrary list L for which we wish to find a value of k that indexes the maximum value of e_k within the range $1 \leq k \leq m$

$$L \ == \ (e_1 \ e_2 \ \dots \ e_m \ \dots \ e_n)$$

and increasingly larger values of the index k between 1 and m. For a sublist of length 1, L's maximum value can only be the element e_1. If k == 2 then max(L,2) is the index of the larger of e_1 and e_2, and if k == 3 max(L,3) is the index of the larger of e_3 and $e_{\text{max}(L,2)}$—that is, the index of the larger of e_3 and (the larger of e_1 and e_2). This reasoning continues until finally max(L,m) is the index of the largest of e_m and e_{m-1}, ..., e_1, and hence of the entire list e_m, e_{m-1}, ..., e_2, and e_1.

Let's take a closer look at the max recursive function implementation (Figure 5–16) in order to see how it works. We see that the 3-line recurrence relation originally conceived for max in Figure 5–15 is directly encoded into C++ as a nested series of if statements. The recursive aspects of the function are underlined. There, max invokes itself recursively with the arguments L and m-1. Thus, an entire series of invocations for max is activated in order to determine the index of the largest element in a sublist of L.

To illustrate the operation of this recursive implementation, let's trace the invocation max(L,4) with the list L = (2 5 4 3 8 6). The series of events that takes place in the process of computing the result, 2, is shown in Table 5–1; recall that the function returns the index of the maximum element, not the element itself.

Each successive invocation of max, beginning with the first, performs a comparison of e_m with the maximum value of a sublist with one less element, until an invocation is reached where the length of the sublist is 1. (In this example, that occurs at invocation 4.) At that moment, the result 1 is returned, which confirms that e_1 is always the maximum value in a list of length 1. This result is returned to invocation 3, so now max compares e_2 and e_1. Since e_2 is larger, invocation 3 returns the index 2 to invocation 2. Invocation 2 performs the comparison between e_3 and e_2, determines that e_2 is greater, and passes the index 2 on to invocation 1. There, the comparison $e_4 > e_2$ is finally made, and the result 2 is returned to the calling program.

A more graphical way to view recursion is to use a treelike structure showing the paths between invocations, arguments passed, and results returned. Such a structure is illustrated in Figure 5–17.

This recursive version of max can be compared with the iterative version in Figure 5–14. It is important to note that it is always possible to design either a recursive or loop solution to a problem; your choice is usually based on factors such as ease of implementation, clarity, and efficiency.

```
int max(list L, int m)
{
// pre:   L == (e[1] e[2] ... e[m] ... e[n]) && n >= 0 &&
//      each e[i] is a number
  if (0<m && m <= L.list_length())
    if (m == 1)
       return 1 ;
    else if L.element(m)>L.element(max(L,m-1))
            return m  ;
         else return max(L,m-1) :
  else
    return 0 ;
// post: n > 0 && (for all i in {1,...,m}: e[j]>=e[i]) &&
//          result == j ||
//        n == 0 && result == 0
)
```

FIGURE 5–16   Recursive implementation of max.

TABLE 5–1 COMPUTING max(L,4)

Invocation of `max`	m	Sublist of `L`	Activates invocation	Comparison e_m>`max(L,m-1)`	Return result
1	4	(2 5 4 3)	2	3>`max(L,3)`	2
2	3	(2 5 4)	3	4>`max(L,2)`	2
3	2	(2 5)	4	5>`max(L,1)`	2
4	1	(2)	none	none	1

Another example of a recursive design that matches the mathematical definition closely is shown in Figure 5–18 for the `Power` function. This design directly reflects the specifications, along with and the original recurrence relation that defined `Power`. It is this close match of recursive design and implementation that encourages frequent use of recursion in the implementation of functions.

Using Domain Knowledge: Newton's Method

The C++ function `pow`, in the library `<math.h>`, is designed to compute a^b, where a and b are any appropriate `float` values. Thus, we really didn't need `Power`, or even a special function to compute square roots.

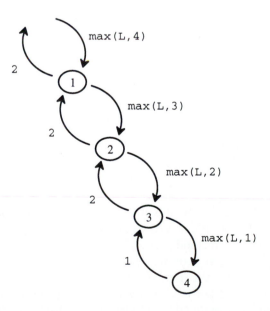

FIGURE 5–17 The structure of recursive invocations for `max(L,4)`. Invocation numbers are circled; descending arrows, arguments; ascending arrows, results.

```
int Power(int a, int b)
{
// pre: a and b are integers &&
//  (a != 0 || (a == 0 && b >  0)) &&
//  MinInt <= a^b <= MaxInt
if (a == 0)
  return 0 ;
else if (b == 0)
  return 1 ;
else return a * Power(a, b-1) ;
// post: Result == a^b
}
```

FIGURE 5–18   The recursive `Power` function.

But suppose we didn't have this very useful function `pow`, and suppose we needed a square root function. For example, we might want to compute the standard deviation for a series of numbers, in addition to their average. Such a computation requires a routine that calculates the square root of x for any non-negative real value x. The development of such a function, say `Sqrt(x)`, can proceed from the following specifications.

```
Sqrt (x)
// pre: x >= 0
// post: Result == y && abs(y*y - x) < epsilon
```

FIGURE 5–19   Specifications for the `Sqrt` abstraction.

Here, the use of `epsilon`, which represents a very small number (e.g., 10^{-4}), emphasizes the fact that the square root of many numbers can only be approximated. For example, the square root of 2 is approximated to four-digit accuracy as 1.414; in this case `epsilon == 0.001`.

A well-known technique in the domain of mathematics for approximating square roots is known as "Newton's method." In fact, Newton's method is a general technique for finding roots of equations, of which the equation $y^2 = x$ is a special case. Newton's method proceeds iteratively as follows. We start with an initial guess at the square root of x, say $y = 1$. The particular choice for this initial guess impacts only the number of iterations required to approximate a root for the equation, but not the accuracy of the approximation. We then repeatedly recompute an improved "next guess," y', from the present one using the following formula:

$$y' = \frac{y + x/y}{2}$$

The repeated application of this formula creates a series of guesses that very quickly converges toward the desired square root of x. For example, if $x = 2$ and the initial guess $y = 1$, the calculations shown in Table 5–2 occur.

Thus, through our domain knowledge of Newton's method, we can develop a program to approximate the square root of any nonnegative real number by writing a simple loop that will halt when two successive approximations y and y' are sufficiently close (say, within 0.0001) to each other in absolute value.

TABLE 5–2   FIRST STEPS IN NEWTON'S METHOD FOR APPROXIMATING $\sqrt{2}$.

Guess (y)	x/y	Calculation of y'
1	2/1 = 2	(1+2)/2 = 1.5
1.5	2/1.5 = 1.33333	(1.5+1.33333)/2 = 1.41667
1.41667	2/1.41667 = 1.41176	(1.41176+1.41667)/2 = 1.41422
1.41422	...	...

There is an alternative way to calculate square roots, however, that allows a much simpler level of mathematical domain knowledge than the one in which Newton's method resides. That alternative requires us instead to creatively apply two functions that are available in the C++ standard library. In particular, C++ provides the functions `exp(x)` and `log(x)` which compute the mathematical function e^x and the natural logarithm of x, $ln\ (x)$, respectively. Combining this with our domain knowledge of how these functions are related,

$ln\ a^b = b\ ln\ a$
$e^{ln\ a} = a$

we have an alternative simplified method for calculating the square root y of x. Recall that we can write the square root of x as $x^{1/2}$. Taking logarithms, we have

$ln\ x^{1/2} = 1/2\ ln\ x$

Now, when we exponentiate this, we obtain:

$e^{\ 1/2\ ln\ x}$

which is:

$x^{1/2}$

which can be written simply in C++ as:

```
y = exp(0.5*log(x)) ;
```

Of course, this can be done most simply in the following way:

```
y = pow(x, 0.5) ;
```

Thus, the approach we choose in implementing an algorithmic problem can be strongly influenced by the domain knowledge that we bring to the problem from related disciplines as well as the C++ function libraries themselves.

Adapting Code for Solving New Problems

We started with a discussion of how to use previously created abstractions and routines and moved to a discussion of how to discover new abstractions and create associated new routines. Now we turn to explore methods for combining and adapting preexisting routines for reuse in solving new problems.

The simplest method of code reuse is to insert the needed function verbatim just before the text of the program that needs it, and then invoke that function from within that program. For the grade averaging program, this method is illustrated in Figure 5–20. There, steps 3 and 4 are combined because the function sum is used instead of a loop to sum the elements of the list of grades.

```
//  This program computes the GPA for a series
//  of one or more numeric grades, each in the
//  range 0.0 .. 4.0, entered from the keyboard
//  or a file as a list.  Brian Davies -- 7/2/93

#include <iostream.h>
#include "ListClass.h"

int sum(list L)
{
// here we insert the body of the function sum
}

void main ()
{
    list grades;
    int number_of_grades;
    float sum=0.0, gpa;

// pre: input == (grades[1] grades[2] ... grades[n]) &&
//      n > 0 &&
//      for all i in {1 ... n}: grades[i] in {0.0 ... 4.0}
```

```
// Step 1.  Obtain the input list of grades.
   cout << "Please enter a list of grades: ";
   grades.read();


// Step 2.  Compute the number of grades in the list.
   number_of_grades = grades.length();
   if (number_of_grades > 0)
   {

// Steps 3 and 4.  Compute the GPA.
      gpa = sum(L) / number_of_grades;

// Step 5.  Display the GPA.
      cout << "\n\nThe GPA of these grades is " << gpa << ".\n";
   }

// post: (n == 0 && output == empty) || (n > 0 &&
//    output == (sum i in {1,...,n}: grades[i]) / n)
}
```

FIGURE 5–20   Revision of the GPA program using the function sum.

A variation of this method is to have the function saved in a separately-compiled file, and then reference that file in a #include statement at the top of the application program that needs it. For example, we would need a

```
#include "ListClass.h"
```

statement at the top of a program that uses any of the list functions, and a

```
#include "GridClass.h"
```

statement at the top of any program that reuses any of the functions in the grid class.

There are four basic methods we can apply to effectively adapt existing code for new purposes. These are called *abutment*, *nesting*, *tailoring*, and *merging*.[2] These methods are described and illustrated in the following paragraphs.

Abutment   This is the simplest method of combining two routines. If R1 and R2 are existing routines, then the act of *abutment* creates a new routine R that is composed of R1 sequentially followed by R2. An illustration of abutment is shown in Figure 5–21 for a portion of the GPA problem. There, the process of calculating the GPA is sequentially abutted to the process of dis-

---

2.   E. Soloway, "Learning to Program = Learning to Construct Mechanisms and Explanations," *Communications of the ACM* (September 1986) 29(9): 850.

playing the GPA, since the latter must follow the former in order of execution.

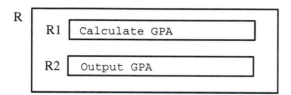

FIGURE 5–21 Creating a new routine R by abutting routines R1 and R2.

Nesting A new routine R can be formed by *nesting* an existing routine R1 inside another existing routine R2. Nesting occurs when we use a routine as an argument in a function call, for example, or when we place it inside a conditional or looping control structure. This is illustrated in Figure 5–22, where the input of a word is nested inside the loop which controls the reading of an entire text.

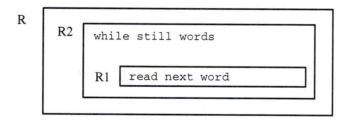

FIGURE 5–22 Creating a new routine R by nesting routines R1 and R2.

Tailoring A new routine R can be formed by *tailoring* an existing routine R1. That is, the original purpose of R1 can be slightly modified, generalized, or narrowed so that it performs the function that is required for R. Suppose we tailor the routine max (which finds the index of the maximum value in a list) in order to create a min routine (which finds the index of the minimum value in a list). What do we need to modify in the routine max so that it fulfills the specifications for min? It turns out that very little needs to be done, and the resulting code is far more easily obtained by tailoring existing code than by developing the function `min` completely from scratch. The necessary modifications of `max` that are required to achieve `min` are summarized in Figure 5–23.

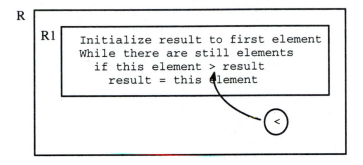

FIGURE 5–23   Creating a new routine R by tailoring routine R1.

Merging   A new routine R can be formed by *merging,* or interleaving, the individual steps of two existing routines R1 and R2. This is illustrated abstractly in Figure 5–24, where we have merged the steps of the `min` routine with the steps of the `max` routine to form a new routine that computes both the maximum and the minimum in a single loop through the list rather than requiring two separate loops.

```
R
   R1   |  Initialize maxList to first element
        |  Initialize minList to first element   R2
        |  While there are still elements
   R1   |  {
        |     if this element > maxList
        |        maxList = this element
        |     if this element < minList            R2
        |        minList = this element
        |  }
```

FIGURE 5–24   Creating a new routine R by merging routines R1 and R2.

Note that in Figure 5–24 the statement `while there are still elements` is the same whether it comes from `max` or `min`. That is, the overall logic required for implementing either of these two routines, or both together, is identical.

EXERCISES

5–1 Develop a function `max_factor` that will compute the largest factor of a given integer *n* that is still less than *n* itself (e.g., `max_factor(100)=50`, `max_factor(15)=5`, and `max_factor(13)=1`). Give preconditions and postconditions that show its complete design specifications.

5–2 Assume that A, B, and C represent the lengths of the sides of a triangle. Write preconditions and postconditions for a function that will return 1 (**true**) if A, B, and C are the sides of a right triangle and 0 (**false**) otherwise. Implement this specification as a C++ function.

5–3 Under what conditions can a void function be converted to an equivalent nonvoid function? Under what conditions can the reverse be done? Explain.

5–4 Illustrate the dynamics of the recursive implementation of `max(L,m)` from Figure 5–16 by showing the sequence of invocations and results returned when

```
L == (6 5 4 3 2 1)
```

and `m == 6`. Are there any economies, in terms of the number of invocations required, when the maximum value happens to occur first in the list? Explain.

5–5 Rewrite the following function by replacing the `for` loop with a `while` loop that accomplishes the same result. Develop pre- and postconditions for this function. To what extent is this function similar to the function `min` (Figure 5–13)?

```
typedef float arrayList[255] ;
int indexOfMin (arrayList anyArray, int n)
{
// Returns the index of a minimum element in an array
  int i, indexOfMinSoFar ;
    indexOfMinSoFar = 0;
    for (i=1; i<n; i++)
       if (anyArray[i] < anyArray[indexOfMinSoFar])
          indexOfMinSoFar = i;
    return indexOfMinSoFar ;
}
```

5–6 Develop specifications for a recursive function `sum(L,n)` that returns the sum of the first n elements in the List `L`. Implement that function.

5–7

   a.   Develop specifications and a recursive function `Fib(n)` that computes, for the integer n, the nth Fibonacci number, according to the following definition:

$$
\begin{aligned}
\text{Fib}(n) \quad &= 0 & &\text{for } n == 0 \\
&= 1 & &\text{for } n == 1 \\
&= \text{Fib}(n{-}1) + \text{Fib}(n{-}2) & &\text{for } n > 1
\end{aligned}
$$

   b.   Show the graphical representation of this function's execution when it is invoked to compute `Fib(4)`.

   c.   Now rewrite this function without using recursion; that is, use a loop instead of a recursive invocation.

5–8

   a.   Describe in English the nature of the following function.

```
int myFun (int n)
{
    if (n == 0)
      return 0 ;
    else if (n % 2 == 0)
      return n + myFun(n-1) ;
    else
      return myFun(n-1) ;
}
```

   b.   Develop pre- and postcondtions for the function `myFun`.

5–9 Create a version of `pos(x,L)`, including pre- and postconditions, which returns the first occurrence of x in L (recall that our version does not specify which occurrence is returned if there is more than one).

5–10 Complete the implementations of `max(l,m)` from its complete procedural abstraction given in Figure 5–12. Do the same for `min(l,m)`.

5–11 Implement `pos(x,L)` by developing a nonrecursive C++ function from its complete procedural abstraction.

5–12 The routine `pos(x,L)` is useful when we want to determine whether or not a list contains duplicates. Develop a complete C++ program that, for an arbitrary list of numbers L, uses pos to help discover and display all numbers that appear more than once. For example, the list

```
L == (1 2 3 5 4 1 5 1)
```

would cause the program to display the following duplicates:

```
1
5
```

Can you think of an actual application in which a program that discovers duplicates would serve a useful purpose?

5–13 Develop a recursive implementation of the pos function.

5–14 Develop specifications for, and then implement, the function relativelyPrime. This function should take two integer parameters m and n, return the result 1 (**true**) if m and n have no common factor other than 1, and return 0 (**false**) otherwise. For example,

```
relativelyPrime(8,9) == 1
relativelyPrime(8,10) == 0
```

since 8 and 10 have the common factor 2.

5–15 Specify and then implement a function that will return 1 if the first element of a list is greater than all the others, and 0 otherwise. Your function should be named isBigger and should have a single parameter designating the name of the list. Write a driver program that will call your function in order to establish that it is working correctly.

5–16 Design and implement a Boolean function in C++ that will examine the first n elements of a list L, return 1 if these elements are in decreasing order, and return 0 otherwise. Note that the following predicate can be used to describe this property of L being in decreasing order:

```
for all i in {1,..., n-1}: L.element[i] > L.element[i+1]
```

Your function should be named CheckOrder and should have parameters for both the list L itself and the number of elements n to be examined. Write a driver program that will call your function in order to establish that it is working correctly.

PROGRAM PRESENTATION

The program in Figure 5–25, which is our final version of the GPA program, contains a composite of three levels of language: the C++ code; the process description, which states in English what is happening at each step of the process that the program describes; and the assertions that describe the state of the computation before and after various steps in the process are executed.

```
//  This program computes the GPA for a series
//  of one or more numeric grades, each in the
//  range 0.0 .. 4.0, entered from the keyboard
//  or a file as a list.  Brian Davies -- 7/2/93

#include <iostream.h>
#include "ListClass.h"

void main ()
{
    list grades;
    int number_of_grades;
    float sum = 0.0, gpa;
// pre: input == (grades[1] grades[2] ... grades[n]) &&
//      (n > 0) &&
//      for all i in {1,..., n}: grades[i] in {0.0 ... 4.0})

// Step 1.  Obtain the input list of grades.
    cout << "Please enter a list of grades: ";
    grades.read();
// input == empty && grades == (grades[1] grades[2]... grades[n])

// Step 2.  Compute the number of grades in the list.
    number_of_grades = grades.length();
//  n > 0
    if (number_of_grades > 0)
    {

// Step 3.  Compute the sum of the grades in the list.
        for (int i = 1; i <= number_of_grades; i++)
            sum = sum + grades.element(i);
// sum == Sum i in {1,...,n}: grades[i]

// Step 4.  Compute the GPA.
        gpa = sum / number_of_grades;
//  GPA == sum / n

// Step 5.  Display the GPA.
        cout << "\n\nThe GPA of these grades is " << gpa << ".\n";
    }

// post: ((n == 0) && (output == empty)) || ((n > 0) &&
//      output == (sum i in {1,...,n}: grades[i]) / n)
}
```

FIGURE 5–25 A heavily over-annotated version of the GPA problem.

Together, these three levels contain a lot of redundancy; that is, they express the same ideas in three different styles—formal algorithmic (C++), informal algorithmic (English), and formal declarative (specifications). This redundancy emphasizes the fact that a programmed solution to an algorithmic problem is written to serve the interests of three very different audiences:

1. The *computer*, which executes the program

2. The *authors*, who design and implement the program

3. The *readers*, who maintain and verify the program's correctness

The computer is interested only in the C++ code; it will follow the code precisely as it carries out the steps of the process. The authors are interested in the C++ code, the annotated English commentary, and the pre- and postconditions, so that they can correctly develop, understand, and later modify or improve the program. The readers are interested in the C++ code and the accompanying preconditions, postconditions, and even sometimes the embedded assertions, so that they can develop a rigorous demonstration (verification) of the program's correctness.

Not all views need to be represented in the final presentation of the program itself. In this section, we discuss the issue of program presentation in light of each of these three views, using the solution to the GPA problem for illustration.

The Computer's View

Consider the computer's view of the GPA solution. The computer is interested only in the actual C++ code, which is isolated all by itself in Figure 5–26. Although we have shown this program listing with indentation, that indentation has no value to the computer either. The listing could equivalently have been written in the form shown in Figure 5–27, and still be executed with the same results as the execution of the program in Figure 5–26! That is, these two programs are equivalent from the computer's point of view, even though neither one is adequate from the developer's or the reader's point of view.

```
#include <iostream.h>
#include "ListClass.h"

void main ()
{
    list grades;
    int number_of_grades;
    float sum=0.0, gpa;

    cout << "Please enter a list of grades: ";
    grades.read();
    number_of_grades = grades.length();
    if (number_of_grades > 0)
    {
        for (int i = 1; i <= number_of_grades; i++)
            sum = sum + grades.element(i);
        gpa = sum / number_of_grades;
        cout << "\n\nThe GPA of these grades is " << gpa << ".\n";
    }
}
```

FIGURE 5–26   The GPA program from the computer's point of view.

```
#include <iostream.h>
#include "ListClass.h"
void main () { list grades; int number_of_grades; float sum=0.0,
gpa;
cout << "Please enter a list of grades: ";grades.read();
number_of_grades = grades.length(); if (number_of_grades > 0) {
for (int i = 1; i <= number_of_grades; i++) sum = sum +
grades.element(i);
gpa = sum / number_of_grades; cout << "\n\nThe GPA of these
grades is " <<
gpa << ".\n"; } }
```

FIGURE 5–27   An equivalent version of the GPA program from the computer's point of view.

The Developer's View

Beginning programmers sometimes confuse the computer's view of a program with that of the reader (the developer or the human verifier). That is, beginners are tempted to present the program by itself, without commentary documentation or specifications as the solution to an algorithmic problem. However, such a presentation does not support well the goals of designing, implementing, and presenting reliable programs.

When we rigorously follow the process of algorithmic problem solving, our aim is to develop a fully annotated program, in which the annotation identifies the original problem definition and the major steps that are required to achieve the solution. For the GPA problem, a completed "reader-friendly" program should look something like the version shown in Figure 5–28, complete with descriptive commentary at the top, pre- and postconditions, and a short description of each major step in the solution.

```
//  This program computes the GPA for a series of one or more
//  numeric grades, each in the range 0.0 .. 4.0, entered from
//  the keyboard or a file as a list.  Brian Davies -- 7/2/93

#include <iostream.h>
#include "ListClass.h"

void main ()
{
    list grades;
    int number_of_grades;
    float sum=0.0, gpa;

// pre: input == (grades[1] grades[2] ... grades[n])
//      && n > 0 &&
//      for all i in {1,..., n}: grades[i] in {0,...,4.0}

// Step 1.  Obtain the input list of grades.
    cout << "Please enter a list of grades: ";
    grades.read();

// Step 2.  Compute the number of grades in the list.
    number_of_grades = grades.length();
    if (number_of_grades > 0)
    {

// Step 3.  Compute the sum of the grades in the list.
        for (int i = 1; i <= number_of_grades; i++)
          sum = sum + grades.element(i);

// Step 4.  Compute the GPA.
        gpa = sum / number_of_grades;

// Step 5.  Display the GPA.
        cout << "\n\nThe GPA of these grades is " << gpa << ".\n";
    }

// post: (n == 0 && output == 0) || (n > 0 &&
//      output == (sum i in {1,..., n}: grades[i]) / n)
}
```

FIGURE 5–28   The same program from the developer's point of view.

The version in Figure 5–28 differs from the version in Figure 5–25 because it excludes intermediate assertions. Those assertions are most useful when the program is being actively tested or verified. Program testing and verification are introduced separately in Chapters 6 and 7.

The Reader's View

Often the person who reads a program is someone different from the person who develops it. For instance, if the requirements for a program change and the original developer of the program is no longer available to implement the changes, then someone else must make the changes. Moreover, in a large software project that involves several persons, it is not uncommon for someone other than the author of a program module to read it, check it for correctness, or even run it through a set of diagnostic testing experiments to make sure that it is correct (see Chapters 6 and 7 for more discussion of testing, correctness, and robustness).

In short, *a program* is not only an executable piece of code, it *is* simultaneously *a complete set of technical documentation for the software system that it represents*. Thus, the text of a program should meet very high standards for readability as well as performance.

By the time the solution to an algorithmic problem has been fully developed and tested, the C++ code should be reasonably self-documenting when it is read by someone unfamiliar with the problem but familiar with the methodology and the application domain from which the problem is taken. That is, the text of the program—with its documentation, stepwise structure and pre- and postconditions—should be as easy to read for a professional colleague as an article in the *New York Times* would be for any well-educated person.

A complete presentation of the solution for an algorithmic problem should include, in addition to the program text itself, the following items:

1. An introduction, written in English, identifying the author(s) and describing the problem, the solution and any unusual or innovative aspects of the solution

2. A sample of the input and output from one or more runs of the program

3. A summary of the results of testing and/or verifying (see next chapter) the programs steps, as appropriate

In short, the presentation should complete the solution of a problem so that it can be understood by any interested reader. The reader may be your instructor for now, but generally the reader can be any other professional problem solver (programmer or software engineer) who has the task of revising or extending the given problem and its solution.

Style Considerations for Human Readers While computers are oblivious to the style in which a program is presented, as we saw above, human readers are most assuredly not. Therefore, such conventions as indentation, variable name choice, etc., are of fundamental importance when designing a solution that must be understandable to humans.

A major element of style is the proper choice of abstraction level. Recall that a motivating factor in our MAPS methodology is that the correctness of the solution should be apparent with minimal study. The best way to achieve this is through consistent use of abstraction and hiding the details for these abstractions until they are needed. Thus, if we are designing a program to count the number of words in a text, the main logic in our program design might look like this:

```
initialize;
readWord;
while wordFound
  add 1 to the number of words read
  readWord
```

Here, the details of initialization, how to read a word, how to tell if a word was found, etc., are hidden so that the reader can easily see the overall control structure of the program. We assume that such details can be handled correctly during the development of the solution. If we had included all the details at this level from the outset, the program would have been much longer and the design much less clear. As we have discussed in a previous chapter, each of these abstractions can be "wrapped" in its own C++ container (i.e., function). Thus our main C++ program can be read like the algorithm discussed above.

Two other features which are important to humans, but not to computers, are the choice of variable names and the use of a consistent indentation style. In our GPA program, we used variable names such as `grades`, `sum` and `GPA` so that their meaning will be intuitive for human readers. These names have no particular meaning to the computer, of course, because the machine does not share our general level of experiential knowledge. Note also that we carefully indent certain portions of this program, in order to show clearly what statements are repeated in the `while` loop. This indentation pattern is entirely for the human, who will use it to clearly understand our intent, and not for the computer, whose first operation on the program is actually to eliminate extraneous blanks. (This clarifies why the braces { and } are required to delineate many C++ constructs.)

CODING AND PRESENTATION OF OTHER ALGORITHMIC PROBLEMS

It is time to finish the implementation of the three problems that were begun in previous chapters. We now look at their inherent abstractions and implementation details.

The idea of data abstraction is also of great utility. Data abstraction allows us to work in terms of familiar objects, such as lists and grids, without worrying about how they are implemented in the computer. Just as in procedural abstraction, we eventually have to worry about details, but only when we are ready. In graphics-oriented problems, the key abstractions are often the graphical objects themselves, rather than the algorithms which manipulate the output. The tic-tac-toe display program is a good example of this point. If we have an abstraction for the board and its individual cells which allows for easy use, then we have gone a long way to solving the problem. Niklaus Wirth makes this point explicitly in his book entitled *Algorithms + Data Structures = Programs*.

Computing a^b

The main feature of the algorithm is in Step 2 where we compute a^b. The design of this loop is aided by thinking about some of the simple cases, where the value of the variable b is small and the resulting variable `result` $==$ a^b is computed as shown in Table 5–3.

TABLE 5–3   INTERMEDIATE RESULTS FOR THE POWER PROGRAM

Value of b	Calculation of a^b	Postcondition
1	result = a;	result == a
2	result = a;	
	result = result*a;	result == a*a
3	result = a;	
	result = result*a;	
	result = result*a;	result == a*a*a
4	result = a;	
	result = result*a;	
	result = result*a;	
	result = result*a;	result == a*a*a*a

From the cases in Table 5–3, we can make the following observations:

1. The number of iterations of the loop is b.

2. The loop's initialization is given by the assignment `result = 1`.

3. The statement to be repeated b times is the assignment
    `result = result*a`.

These simple cases also provide some insight into the nature of the loop's invariant. That is, *before* the ith iteration of the loop, where $1 \le i \le b$, the value of `result` is given by:

```
// result == a^(i-1) && 1 <= i <= b
```

Exit from the loop will occur after the bth iteration at which point `i == b+1`. Thus our invariant must be

```
// inv: result == a^(i-1) && 1 <= i <= b+1
```

which is true before and after every loop. At termination we have

```
// inv: result == a^(i-1) && 1 <= i <= b+1 && i == b+1
```

which resolves into `result == a^b`, which is very close to the postcondition for the problem.

So if we use the variable `i` to control the number of iterations in the loop, it should run through the range of integers from 1 to b in order for the correct result for `result` to be computed. These considerations lead to the annotated C++ program shown in Figure 5–29. (As noted earlier, this program should *never* be written in practice, due to the availability of the `pow` function in the C++ library `<math.h>`. The program is included here only for illustration.)

```
#include <iostream.h>
void main ()
{
// This program computes the bth power of a.
// Pre: input == a b && (a != 0 || (a == 0 && b > 0))
// && minInt <= a^b <= maxInt
   float result ;
   int a, b, i ;

// Step 1.  Obtain the values of a and b.
   cout << "Enter two integers a and b:" ;
   cin >> a >> b ;

// Step 2.  Compute a^b
// Step 2.1  Set result = 1.
   result = 1 ;
// Step 2.2  For b times
   i = 1 ;
   while (i<=b)
   {
// inv: P == a^(i-1) && 1 <= i <= b+1
   result = result * a ;
   i++;
   }
   cout << "Power(a,b) = " << result << "\n" ;
// post: input == empty && output == a^b
}
```

FIGURE 5–29   A program to compute a^b.

Counting Words in a Text

Our solution to the word counting problem itself is given in Figure 5–30. It is simplified by the power of the C++ stream input function >>, which essentially allows the program to read input text one word at a time. Were it not for this functionality, the word counting process would be significantly more complex, as discussed earlier in this chapter.

```cpp
// This program counts the number of words in a text and
// displays the resulting count. A word is defined as any
// sequence of nonblank characters preceded by the
// beginning of the text or a blank, and followed by either
// a blank, tab, or carriage return (called "whitespace" in
// C++).  End of the input is signaled by typing ctrl-d.
// Brian Davies -- 7/93

#include <iostream.h>
#include <string.h>

void main ()
{
    int Nwords = 0;
    char s[25];     // a word of text; at most 24 characters

// pre: input == a series of characters c[1] c[2] ... c[n] &&
//      n >= 0 && each c[i] is in the set ASCII

// Step 1.  Prompt for input and obtain an input word.
    cout << "Enter any text, followed by ctrl-d:\n\n";
    while (cin >> s)

// Step 2.  Account for the word
        Nwords++;


// Step 3.  Display the resulting word count.
    cout << "The number of words is " << Nwords << ".\n";

// post: input == empty && output == the word count
}
```

FIGURE 5–30   The complete word counting program.

Monitoring a Tic-Tac-Toe Game

The grid class was introduced in the previous chapter; we suggest that you review this material before proceeding. With these new methods, the program shown in Figure 5–32 monitors a game of tic-tac-toe by calling for an alternating sequence of moves from two players and redisplaying the outcome of each move in the graphics area of the screen.

In this program, two players alternate moves. Each move is given by clicking the mouse in the square where the players want to place an x or o. The first person to play is x. Control of the game and determination of the winner is entirely in the hands of the players. When a player clicks the mouse outside the grid, the program will end the game. A sample sequence of three moves and the resulting board are shown in Figure 5–31.

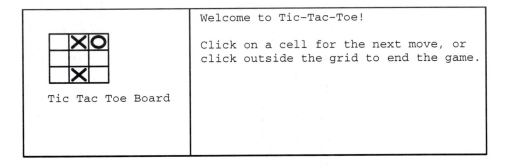

FIGURE 5–31   Series of three moves in tic–tac–toe.

While this program is not an entirely satisfactory implementation of a realistic tic-tac-toe game, it does illustrate somewhat the use of basic methods that accompany the class `grid` as an aid for visualizing the output of certain kinds of algorithmic problems.

There are several reasons why this program is not a fully satisfactory simulation of tic-tac-toe. First, note that the program allows a player to "erase" the other player's move by simply specifying the same row and column number used in a previous move. Second, the program has no idea of the status of the game. That is, it is unequipped to recognize a move in which X wins, O wins, or the game is a "cat's game" (that's tic-tac-toe vernacular for a tie). Third, the program is unprepared to *be* one of the players, making intelligent moves in response to moves by the person playing the opposing piece.

The first and second of these weaknesses are fairly easy to eliminate from this program. The third and fourth require more sophisticated kinds of additions, which would fall within the area of computing called *artificial intelligence* (AI). That is, they would enable the program to simulate intelligent human behavior, albeit in a very limited way.

We have investigated quite a number of algorithms, along with the C++ language tools which can be used in their implementation. We have used several

```cpp
// This program monitors a game of tic-tac-toe with
// two players.  Brian Davies -- 7/93

#include <iostream.h>
#include "GridClass.h"

void main ()
{
// pre: input == a series of mouse clicks by alternate players.

    const int anchor_x = 45;    // x and y coordinates of the
    const int anchor_y = 45;    // board in the graphics window
    int move_number = 1;
    int row, col;
    char current_player;

// Step 1.  Initialize the board and the game.

    open_graphics ();
    grid board (3, 40, anchor_x, anchor_y, "Tic Tac Toe Board");
    open_text ();
    cout << "Welcome to Tic-Tac-Toe!\n\n" ;
    cout << "Click on a cell for the next move, or\n"
       << "click outside the grid to end the game.\n";

// Step 2.  Obtain the first move from input.

    board.get_click(row, col);

// Step 3.  While there are still moves, alternate turns
//          between 'x' and 'o'.

    while (board.locate_cell(row, col))
    {
      if (move_number % 2 == 1)  // determine turn: 'x' or 'o'
        current_player = 'x';
      else
        current_player = 'o';
      board.set_cell_display (row, col, current_player);
      move_number++;
      board.get_click(row, col);
    }

// Step 3.  Close graphics windows.

    close_graphics ();
    close_text ();

// post: input == empty &&
//    output == a display of the moves on a tic-tac-toe board.
}
```

FIGURE 5–32 Program to monitor a game of tic-tac-toe.

data types, including integers, reals, strings, lists and grids; and several statement types, including assignments, conditionals, loops, and I/O. Having studied these tools and examples and worked with the laboratory manual, you are gaining some facility in designing and writing small programs in C++. The exercises in this section provide more practice. Remember, learning to design programs, like learning to play a musical instrument, requires not only study but practice. When running the exercises on your computer, remember that few programs run the first time, so be patient and keep trying. Your success will improve if you keep at it!

EXERCISES

5–17 Write C++ statements that will display YES if the variable K is an odd positive integer (such as 1, 3, 5, ...) and display NO otherwise.

5–18 Write C++ statements to set m equal to the absolute value of n without using the absolute value function.

5–19 Write a loop that will display a doubling sequence of n numbers, where n is given as input. (That is, each number is twice the previous number displayed.) Rewrite this loop as a recursive function.

5–20 Design and implement a program that will read 25 integers and count the number of negative integers it finds among them.

5–21 Design and implement a program that will read 100 integers and display those which are divisible by 5.

5–22 Write a program segment that will do one of the following:

Set X to X + A	if X is negative,
Set X to X + A + B	if X is zero, or
Set X to X + A + B + C	if X is positive.

5–23 What do the following program segments do? That is, if you were to run these programs, exactly what would the output be?

```
a.   int k, j, m ;
     float n ;
     k = 4 ;
     j = 8 ;
     m = 9 ;
     n = m / j + k * 1.0 - m / j ;
     cout << "n = " << n ;
```

```
b.  int m, j ;
    m = 4 ;
    j = 1 ;
    while (j < m)
    {
        j = j + 2 ;
        m = m + 1 ;
    }
    cout << "m = " << m << "j = " << j ;
```

```
c.  int k, j  ;
    for (k=1; k<=10; k++)
    {
        j = 10 - k ;
        if (j <= 4)
            j = j - 1 ;
    }
    cout << "j = " << j << "k = " << k ;
```

```
d.  int n, m  ;
    n = 0 ;
    m = 1 ;
    while (m <= 101)
    {
        n = n + 1 ;
        m = m + 5 ;
    }
    cout << "n = " << n ;
```

```
e.  int j, k, m  ;
    k = 0 ;
    for (j=1; j<=3; j++)
        for (m=1; m<=4; m++)
            k = k + 1 ;
    cout << "k = " << k ;
```

```
f.  int j ;
    list k ;
    k.element[1] = 1 ;
    for (j=2; j<=4; j++)
        k.element(j) = k.element(j - 1) + j ;
    k.write() ;
```

```
g.  int j ;
    list m ;
    j = 1 ;
    while (j <= 2) do
    {
        m.element(j + 2) = j ;
        m.element(3 - j) = j ;
        j = j + 1 ;
    }
    m.write() ;
```

5–24 Trace execution of the program `Power` for the particular input 5 and – 4, by showing all values of the variables a, b, P, and i before each step is executed.

5–25 Write specifications and then implement a program to display the first 11 Fibonacci numbers. The Fibonacci numbers are 1, 1, 2, 3, 5, 8, 13, 21, 34, …

5–26 Write specifications and implement a program to compute the factorial of an integer n (denoted $n!$). Recall that the definition of $n!$ is:

$$0! = 1$$
$$n! = n \times (n-1)!$$

5–27 Design specifications and write a C++ program which will read some text and calculate and display a count of the number of instances of the substring "and".

5–28 Trace execution of the word counting program by showing all the values of the variables i and nwords during its execution with the following input text.

"Able was I ere I saw Elba."

5–29 Corroborate that the loop invariant in the word counting program is valid for the input in Exercise 5–28 by interpreting it for each value of i that causes nwords to change its value. For example, the first interpretation of the invariant would occur when i=6 and would read as follows:

```
// nwords == 1 for "Able " && 1 <= 6 <= 26
```

5–30 Design and write a program in C++ which will read in some text and then reverse and display that text. That is, if the input to your program is
"may 1994"

then your program's output should be

"4991 yam"

5–31 Refine the tic-tac-toe program of Figure 5–32 so that it will prevent a player from placing an x or an o on a space that is already occupied. When such an attempt is made, the program should politely advise the player to make an alternative move and then record that move.

5–32 Design and write a complete C++ program to compute the total cost of a mail order for a series of items. It should contain a loop that reads the quantity and price of each item and keeps track of the running total. After the last item is entered, the program should display the total cost of the order and the total number of items ordered. The total cost should reflect a 5% sales tax. Be sure to include pre- and postconditions for this problem, in addition to the program itself.

CHOOSING A PROGRAMMING LANGUAGE

As we have discussed in this chapter and earlier ones, the individual steps that combine to form a complete, implementable process description, or algorithm, must be written in a very exact linguistic style. The English language, by its nature, is an inadequate medium for reaching this level of precision. For instance, the five-step algorithm for computing grade point averages, which is shown in Chapter 2, is too vague to be useful.

The kinds of languages that are useful for describing algorithms at a level of precision that computers can understand and execute are called *algorithmic languages*, or *programming languages*. As you well know, C++ is a very versatile and useful programming language. In general, programming languages differ from English in three fundamental ways:

1. Programming languages have a limited vocabulary and syntax. Thus, programs can describe only algorithms and are not useful for writing most other (nonalgorithmic) kinds of prose.

2. The vocabulary of a programming language contains only those basic kinds of actions that a computer can understand and carry out, and no others. For example, a programming language supports all of the usual arithmetic actions (addition, subtraction, multiplication, division, comparison); text-processing actions; graphical display actions; and input/output actions. Actions that the computer cannot carry out are many and varied—jogging, throwing, catching, feeling, making quiche, and creating oil paintings are just a few. Thus, these sorts of actions are also outside the vocabularies of programming languages.

3. The syntax of a programming language is quite rigid, and does not allow for much variation in style. For example, the calculation of the quotient of `sum` and `n` is expressed as `sum/n` and no other way.

The description of a process, or algorithm, in a programming language is called a *program*. Programs are executable by computers, whereas English-language descriptions of algorithmic processes are not. (Some programming languages are English-like by design, so that their programs will look something like English. COBOL is one such language. However, the freedom of expressive style that we normally associate with English prose is missing from even these programming languages.)

There are many different programming languages to choose from when describing algorithms. Some are particularly well-suited for teaching and learning about computers and algorithmic problem solving. C++ is such a language, and we have used it in all our examples throughout this text. Other popular programming languages are C, Pascal, Modula-2, Ada, FORTRAN, COBOL, LISP, Scheme, and machine-level assembly languages. We introduce the notion of assembly language in Chapter 8. Some of the other languages in this list are well-suited for professional programming (e.g., C and Ada) but are not as useful for teaching and learning about the algorithmic problem-solving process.

By now, we are familiar with the general syntax of C++. Thus, it is easy to see that the C++ program shown in Figure 5–26 is a realization of the GPA problem we have described informally in English. (But the program in Figure 5–27 is much less revealing in this regard!)

Note in Figure 5–25 that the original specifications and five steps of the process description are inserted following *comment delimiters* //, so that the correspondence between those steps and groups of statements in the C++ program can easily be identified. Because these are written as C++ comments, the entire program can be directly executed on a computer without further modification.

Features, Performance, and Portability Issues

The C++ statements in Figure 5–26 represent an implementation of the GPA problem in a particular programming language. The meaning of each statement is strictly defined, and tends to make precise the looser style of the English language descriptions of each step in the process. For example, the words

```
Obtain the input list of grades
```

in Step 1 of the algorithm are made precise in the two C++ statements in Figure 5–25:

```
cout << "Enter a list of grades: " ;
grades.read() ;
```

The cout << input function provides a prompt to the user of this program, describing the kind of input that the program expects to receive, and the read function accomplishes the act of obtaining the entire input list of integers.

Limitations of the ASCII Character Set   When we incorporate assertions and other comments into the text of a program, we need to accommodate the limitations of the ASCII character set, which is the standard set of characters and their computer encodings used by all major computer manufacturers. (ASCII is an acronym for *A*merican *S*tandard *C*ode for *I*nformation *I*nterchange.) Using a standard character set, we can transfer information between different computers (like Macintoshes and IBM PC's, for example). The full list of ASCII characters and their computer encodings appears in Appendix A.

Scientists normally use Greek letters and other special symbols, subscripts, and superscripts when writing the mathematical and logical expressions of assertions. In the GPA problem, for example, we use expressions like grades$_i$, $\emptyset$, and $\leq$ when writing assertions in conventional mathematical style, following the notation introduced in Chapter 2. Unfortunately, we had to abandon the use of these symbols early on, since they are not included in the ASCII character set, and programs can have only ASCII characters in order to run correctly. Therefore, when writing an algorithm as a C++ program, we have used the ASCII substitute conventions that were developed in Chapter 3.

Syntax and Semantics

While a language's syntax defines the grammar for all programs that can be written, ultimately we are concerned with the meanings of the different statements in our programs. The actions performed by the computer in executing each statement is given by that statement's semantics. Some C++ statements, such as declarations of variables, cause an action to be taken during program compilation. Others, such as assignment, arithmetic and control statements, result in actions during program execution. Still others, such as a declaration that also assigns an initial value to the variable, cause both compile-time and run-time actions to occur. Therefore, it is necessary to master both the syntax and the semantics of each statement in order to ensure that the statement accurately reflects the meaning that we want to express from the solution design.

As we have seen, the semantics of most C++ statements are fairly straightforward. Yet, their style can be a bit bizarre at times (e.g., using the ++ operator to increment the value of an operator). Confusion can arise from some of these idiosyncrasies, such as the designation of = for assignment and == for equality testing. For instance, if we write the following statement:

```
a = 1 ;
if (a = 2)
    a = a + 1 ;
```

the value of a will be assigned three times, with a final value of 3. That is, the value of a will be reassigned to 2 when the condition inside the if statement is evaluated. However, if we had written the following,

```
a = 1 ;
if (a == 2)
    a = a + 1 ;
```

the resulting value of a would have been 1, since no reassignment would occur in the second or third line.

This sort of error is common in C++, since mathematically the sign = usually means equality rather than assignment. In general, the semantics of a programming language should be clearly understood, and assumptions about the correspondence between programming languages and other scientific and mathematical styles should be made cautiously.

The GPA Program in Another Language: Pascal

Throughout the development of our problem-solving methodology, we have tried to place an emphasis on the more abstract elements of the process rather than the concrete syntax of the C++ solution. Only in this chapter have we really focussed on the program code that completes the solution to a problem.

The particular choice of programming language, in this setting, is relatively immaterial. That is, one can use any one of several alternative programming languages and still develop an effective solution to each of the problems discussed in this text, as well as a wide range of others. To illustrate this point, consider the familiar GPA problem solution recoded in the Pascal programming language, which is shown below.

```
program ComputeGPA;
{ This program computes the GPA for a series of one or
  more numeric grades, each in the range 0..4, entered
  at the keyboard as a list.  }
 uses
  lists;
 var
  grades : list;
  i, n : integer;
  sum, GPA : real;
begin
{ pre: input == (grades[1] grades[2] ... grades[n]) && n > 0
  && for all i in {1,..., n}: grades[i] in {0,..., 4} }

{ Step 1.  Obtain the input list of grades }
 writeLn ('Enter a list of grades:');
 readList (grades);

{ Step 2.  Compute n = the number of grades in the list }
 n := lengthList(grades);

{ Step 3.  Compute sum = the sum of the grades in the list }
 sum := 0;
 i := 1;
 while i <= n do
 begin
   sum := sum + grades[i];
   i := i + 1
 end;
```

```
{ Step 4.  Compute GPA = sum/n }
   GPA := sum / n;

{ Step 5.  Display GPA }
   writeLn('The GPA of these grades = ', GPA : 5 : 2)

{ post: input == empty &&
   output == (Sum i in {1,...,n}: grades[i]) / n }
end. {ComputeGPA}
```

A careful examination reveals that this solution has many of the earmarks of our earlier C++ solution. The comments convey the pre- and postconditions, as well as the individual steps of the breakdown. Only the syntactic details, like how one writes an assignment statement, differ between C++ and Pascal. Effectively, either language could have been chosen without materially affecting the quality of the solution whatsoever.

Later in your study of computer science, you will have an opportunity to learn and master the features of other programming languages and styles. Computer scientists are surprisingly multilingual in this sense.

SUMMARY

We have now discussed almost the entire MAPS methodology. We have developed abilities in predicate logic in order to precisely state *what* our solutions are to accomplish in precise specifications. We have used those specifications to design solutions. During our design step, we have employed the power of abstraction to allow us to temporarily ignore the details of problem solution while concentrating on the abstractions. In some cases, the details have already been implemented by others, so that we can reuse built-in functions or library routines to simplify our coding process. In other cases, we must develop our own routines to ensure an effective implementation of the problem.

In Chapters 6 and 7, we shall finish our development of the MAPS methodology by looking at *Stage 6: Testing and Verification*. It is a simple fact that more time is spent testing, verifying, and maintaining software programs than in all the other stages of developing them. This fact alone should impress upon you the importance of the discussions in the next two chapters.

PROGRAM ROBUSTNESS AND TESTING

At this point, we have almost completed our study of the MAPS methodology. The two stages left are (1) testing and verification and (2) presentation. In this chapter we will explore testing in detail and then develop several examples which illustrate how to put the entire MAPS methodology together. In the context of these examples, we cover presentation as well. Testing itself depends heavily on the thought paradigm we have called *abstraction*, since testing involves making observations and testing hypotheses. But in putting the whole MAPS process together we use all modes of thought: theory (in forming specifications), abstraction (in the dialogue, breakdown, and testing), and design (throughout). We begin by introducing three properties a completed program needs to have—correctness, robustness, and user-friendliness.

WHEN IS A PROGRAM CORRECT? ROBUST? USER-FRIENDLY?

What does it mean for a program to be correct?

> **Definition** A program is *correct* if, for all possible inputs that satisfy its preconditions, it terminates with an output that satisfies its postconditions. Similarly, a function is correct if, for all possible values of its input parameters that satisfy its preconditions, it terminates and its output parameters (results) satisfy its postconditions.

For example, the grade point averaging program is correct in this sense. That is, for all inputs of the form (Grades[1] Grades[2] ... Grades[n]) and $n > 0$ and each Grade[i] is in the range $\{0, \dots, 4\}$, the program computes and displays the average of the grades and then stops. Table 6–1 shows sample inputs and outputs for different runs of the program.

A careful look at the program in Figure 6–1, however, raises some questions about what happens when the input does *not* conform to the specifications given in its preconditions.

TABLE 6–1 RESULTS FOR SEVERAL RUNS OF THE GPA PROGRAM

Input	Output
(3 1 2 4)	2.50
(2)	2.00
(2 3 3 3 3 3 3 2)	2.75

For example, what if the input is the empty list ( )? What if the input contains a list of numbers that are not all in the range {0, ..., 4}, like the list of revenues used in Figure 6–7*b* that is intended for an entirely different problem? What if the input list contains something besides numbers, like the list of 12 month names in Figure 6–7*a*?

```
#include <assert.h>
#include <iostream.h>
#include "ListClass.h"

void main ()
{
    list grades;
    int number_of_grades;
    float sum=0.0, gpa;

// pre: input == (grades[1] grades[2] ... grades[n]) && n > 0 &&
//      for all i in {1,..., n}: (grades[i] in {0.0,..., 4.0}

// Step 1.  Obtain the input list of grades.
    cout << "Please enter a list of grades: ";
    grades.read();

// Step 2.  Compute the number of grades in the list.
    number_of_grades = grades.length();
    assert(number_of_grades > 0);

// Step 3.  Compute the sum of the grades in the list.
    for (int i = 1; i <= number_of_grades; i++)
        sum = sum + grades.element(i);

// Step 4.  Compute the GPA.
    gpa = sum / number_of_grades;

// Step 5.  Display the GPA.
    cout << "\n\nThe GPA of these grades is " << gpa << ".\n";

// post: (n == 0 && output = empty) || (n > 0 &&
//       output == (sum i in {1,..., n}: grades[i]) / n)
}
```

FIGURE 6–1 Body of the GPA program.

One way to answer these questions is simply to run the program with several alternative inputs that fail to meet the problem's preconditions and observe what happens in each case. Let's look at the body of this program and analyze how it would handle each of these cases (see Figure 6–1).

This is such a simple program that a straightforward analysis is convenient. In the case where the input is empty, the condition n > 0 is not satisfied, so the program halts with a message to the effect that the assertion in Step 2 has failed. However, in the case where the input numbers are not all in the range {0, ..., 4}, the program dutifully produces their average and (mis)labels the result as a GPA, even though not all the input numbers may be valid grades (according to the problem specification).

Finally, consider a case where the input is not completely numeric:

```
(3 1 hello 2)
```

How the program handles this depends upon how the read function handles a non-numeric value. That is, the values returned by grades.read() for i = 1, 2, and 4 are the numbers 3, 1, and 2 respectively. But what about the value returned by grades.read() for i = 3 (in which grades[3] == hello) ? Does the program register an error? Does it return some sort of default numerical value, such as 0, whenever a nonnumber is entered as input? Note that an examination of the pre- and postconditions for read does not necessarily answer this question, since they only deal with cases where the input is correct. However, by running the program, we discover that the reference grades[3] returns the result 0 for this particular list, and the resulting "average" displayed by the program is therefore 1.50.

Despite these problems, we emphasize that the grade averaging program is still technically correct, in the sense of the above definition. However, it is not robust.

> **Definition**   A program is said to be *robust* if it meets both of the following requirements:
>   1. It is correct.
>   2. For all inputs that do not satisfy the problem's preconditions, it terminates and produces an output that reflects the fact that an input error has occurred.

The grade averaging program is surely not robust, even though it is correct. In general, the creation of robust software is a far more complex exercise than the creation of correct software. Yet robustness is a highly desirable characteristic for computer software that is used by people who are not familiar with the details of the program's design or who are likely to make occasional errors while typing the input.

How can the program in Figure 6–1 be made robust? We need to make two basic changes. First, we need to review (and perhaps revise) the read function to ensure that it sets the error flag within the list class whenever a nonnumber is entered in the input list. Step 1 in the program will then ensure that each grade is explicitly examined for correctness (that is, for being numeric and for being in the range {0, ..., 4}). Second, we should augment the conditional statement that tests for n > 0 with an else part, so that the program will display an appropriate error message when the empty list is presented as input. We can revise step 1 as follows:

```
// Step 1. Obtain the input list of grades.
    cout << "Please enter a list of grades: \n" ;
    grades.read();
    n = grades.length();
    if (grades.has_error() || n == 0)
     validinput = 0 ;
    else
    { validinput = 1;
      for (i=1; i<=n; i++)
        if (grades.element(i)<0 || grades.element(i)>4)
          validinput = 0;
    }
    if (! validinput)
     cout << "Input is not valid; program terminates.\n"
    else
    {
    ...
```

Here, the new variable validinput indicates whether or not the list conforms to the requirement given in the precondition. The rest of the program in its original form will follow this new code, except that the test for n>0 can be dropped from the original version (since it has been incorporated into this revised version of step 1).

A third valuable attribute of programs is *user-friendliness*. User-friendliness suggests a number of characteristics of programs: readability of displays, pleasing graphics, easy access to help messages, logical flow, and constructive advice in the case of invalid input. How can our GPA program be made user-friendly in the latter sense? We can revise step 1 as shown below.

```
// Step 1. Obtain the input list of grades.
    do
    {
      cout << "Enter a list of grades: \n" ;
      grades.read();
      n = grades.length();
      if (grades.has_error() || n == 0)
       validinput = 0 ;
      else
      { validinput = 1;
        for (i=1; i<=n; i++)
          if (grades.element(i)<0 || grades.element(i)>4)
            validinput = 0;
      }
    } while (! validinput) ;
```

This revision is more constructive than the previous one, since it gives the user multiple opportunities to reenter the input list of grades. That is, the program continues to loop in step 1 until a correct list of grades is entered, after which steps 2 through 5 can be executed as before.

EXERCISES

6–1 Is the tic-tac-toe program a correct program? Is it robust? Explain.

6–2 Show how the tic-tac-toe program can be altered so that it is more user-friendly.

6–3 Consider the tic-tac-toe program discussed in earlier chapters.

  a. Revise the precondition so that the exact nature of an individual legal move is accurately described.

  b. Considering this revision, what additional changes could be made to make the program more robust?

6–4 Is the word counting program correct? Is it robust? Explain.

6–5 Show how the word counting program can be altered so that it is more user-friendly.

ENSURING ROBUSTNESS: TEST CASE DESIGN

Whatever can go wrong will go wrong.
—Murphy

Solving algorithmic problems can be a cruel discipline. First of all the designer must worry about the program performing correctly for all inputs that are provided in the problem's specifications; secondly, he or she must also be concerned about how the program will respond when it encounters incorrect or unanticipated input. Thus, the problem solver quickly learns to become a healthy skeptic about the infallibility of any program that purports to be a solution for a particular algorithmic problem. Invariably we hear the call "I've found the last bug!" from the computer lab, only to learn later that it was really the next-to-last bug, or the next-to the next-to-last bug, or ...

How can we solve complex problems and design software with a high degree of reliability? That is, how can we ensure that our programs will perform predictably and correctly both for expected and unexpected input combinations? The MAPS problem-solving methodology provides a framework which, if carefully followed, can lead to the development of robust programs—programs that not only perform correctly for correct input, but also perform "gracefully" for a wide range of incorrect input.

A fundamental stage in the MAPS methodology is stage 6, testing and verification. It is this stage which, in the long run, may be the most critical in the entire development process. If a program is not correct, as determined by the systematic application of testing and/or verification methods, then all the other stages in the MAPS method are useless.

A classic set of techniques for ensuring program correctness, robustness, and user-friendliness falls under the simple rubric *testing*. Testing techniques have been developed by software designers and engineers over the past several decades.

> **Definition**   *Program testing* is the systematic application of test cases to a program or function for the purpose of exposing and correcting errors (or "bugs") in the program. These test cases consist of different selections of input data values, chosen intentionally to exercise the program under a wide range of conditions that may or may not have been anticipated by the program's designer. Collectively, the data that makes up these test cases is called a *test suite*.

The use of the word *bug* to describe a program error has an interesting history. In the early 1940's, a Mark I computer used at Harvard was built with relays—electromechanical switches. One day, after a program had failed, the operator found a dead moth in one of the relays. That is, there was a bug in the system.

To be sure, the result of testing is weaker than the result of verification. That is, testing cannot, by its limited nature, ensure the absense of errors—it can only show that errors are present.

There are many ways of designing a test suite and applying it to a particular function or program. More complex testing strategies are required for programs that represent larger software systems than those we are studying. We will concentrate here on the design and application of rigorous testing methods for relatively small programming problems, leaving the issue of large software testing to Volume II in this series.

Example: Testing a Complete Function

When we develop a procedural abstraction for a well-defined subproblem, or for a routine, it is necessary to test it by repeatedly exercising the function using a wide variety of values for its input parameters, making sure in each case that it produces results that are consistent with its postconditions.

Test suites can become large rather quickly. Consider the total number of possible valid input lists for the function max that we could construct, using 0 or more elements and assuming that each element is an integer in the range

-2^{15} to $2^{15}-1$. There are $2^{16}=65{,}536$ different one-element lists of this kind alone, and there are an astronomical number of n-element lists (where $n > 1$) of this kind—surely too many to include in a test suite. Thus we need a strategy for selecting a reasonably sized suite of test data.

We proceed by selecting a small but meaningful subset of the possible parameter values, exercising the function using each member of the subset, and displaying the result. A convenient means for doing this is to write a program called a *driver*, one that literally "drives" the function with each of the selected test parameter values and displays the results for visual checking.

Let's illustrate these ideas by considering the construction of a test suite for max. There are two classes of strategies for testing functions: *white-box testing* and *black-box testing*. Black-box testing checks to see if data which satisfies the preconditions also satisfies the postconditions but doesn't look inside the function. White-box testing uses knowledge of the code to design test data. Our focus here will be on white-box testing. There are many approaches to white-box testing, but a useful way is to employ the following six principles:

1. Be sure every statement in the function is executed at least once in running the test data.

2. Test every conditional for both the True and False values of every simple predicate in its condition. (For example, a condition of the form A>B && C>D would require four sets of test data—to test both the true and the false values for both the conditions A>B and C>D.)

3. Loops are most likely to be in error at their beginning and end. Thus if a loop is supposed to execute a maximum of m times, test it for data sets of size 0, 1, 2, k, m−1, m, and m+1 where k is some value between 2 and m−1.

4. Test every switch statement for each individual case.

5. Remember that "bugs lurk in corners and hide at boundaries." Thus test data sets should include extreme cases like empty lists, lists with one member, and lists of the maximum size allowed in a setting if there is such a maximum.

6. Although it is impossible to anticipate every combination of invalid data a user might enter, some likely possibilities should be tried.

Table 6–2 contains a suite of test data that could be used to test max. The first few test cases deal with the extreme cases of empty lists and one element lists (Principle 5). The selection of the values of m in those cases is guided by Principle 2 applied to the first conditional.

The remaining cases were selected to satisfy Principle 3 for a larger list. Note that the data in the list is ordered in such a way that the innermost conditional is tested on both sides when m is 3 or 4.

TABLE 6–2   SAMPLE TEST DATA FOR THE max FUNCTION

| Input parameters | | Expected |
L	m	result
( )	0	0
( )	1	0
(2)	0	0
(2)	1	1
(2)	2	0
(3 1 8 2)	0	0
(3 1 8 2)	1	1
(3 1 8 2)	2	1
(3 1 8 2)	3	3
(3 1 8 2)	4	3
(3 1 8 2)	5	0

It is also convenient to store our test suite on a separate disk file, so that we do not need to retype it every time we want to test the function. Figure 6–2 shows the general structure of a driver. The notation <f(x,y)> stands for any void function f with input parameters <x> and output parameters <y>; <test suite file> denotes the name of the file from which the test suite of data can be retrieved. This structure is easily adapted for the purpose of testing a nonvoid function f(x) rather than a void function f(x,y): the variable y is identified with the result of the function, the statement <f(x,y)> is replaced by the assignment y = f(x) in the driver shown in Figure 6–2, and the documentary comments are altered in obvious ways to reflect that a nonvoid function is being tested.

A driver for max is shown in Figure 6–3. The output for this driver, when applied to the file with external name maxtests, is shown in Figure 6–4. Note that the read function is used to read a series of lists from this file, rather than just one. The processing of the last input list from this file is detected by calling the list function end_of_input, which is similar to the function eof for ordinary files.

As we can see, the creation and exercising of a driver is a fairly mechanical process. When carefully used, however, drivers not only help us to uncover errors in the program but also suggest ways for making a function more robust and user-friendly than it otherwise would have been. Exercising the function with a suite of unknown input data values can lead to some surprising results! However, it is preferable to make these discoveries at the time of testing rather

```
void <f(x,y)>
{
...
}

void main ()
{
  // This driver tests the function <f(x,y)>
  // using a test suite of input data
  // from the file <test suite file>

  declarations for variables <x> and <y>
  corresponding to parameters x and y> ;

  istream <test suite file> ;
  char file_name[20] ;

  cout << "Begin test for function <f(x,y)>\n" ;
  cout << "Enter name of the test suite file: ";
 <test suite file>.open(file_name, ios::in) ;
  <test suite file> >> <x> ;
  while ( ! <test suite file>.eof() )
  {
   cout << "Input paramaters = " << <x> ;
   <f(x,y)>;
   cout << "Result of f(x,y) = " << <y> ;
   <test suite file> >> <x> ;
  }
  <test suite file>.close() ;
  cout << "End test for function <f(x,y)>" ;
}
```

FIGURE 6–2   General structure of a driver.

than later, when the function has been turned over to an unsuspecting person for general use.

We should test a complete program "from the bottom up." That is, we should test all functions before testing the whole program that uses them. Such testing is called *unit testing*. After this is done, we can proceed with the testing of the entire program in a way that is analogous to the testing of a function. This latter type of testing is called *integration testing*.

We convert the program into a sort of *autodriver* for itself by adding an outer loop that systematically reads alternative input data from an external file containing a test suite and then proceeds through its normal sequence of steps, producing output for all data in the test suite rather than just one input set.

```
#include "ListClass.h"
#include <iostream.h>

int max (list L, int m)
```

```
{
// pre: L == (e[1] e[2] ... e[n]) && n>=0 &&
//         each e[i] is a number

  int Result = 1;
  if (0 < m && m <= L.length())
  {
    for (int i=2; i<=m; i++)
      if (L.element(i) >= L.element(Result))
        Result = i;
  }
  else
    Result = 0;
  return Result;
// post: n > 0 && for all i in {1,..., m}: e[j] >= e[i] &&
//               Result == j, or
//         n == 0 && Result == 0
}

void main()
// This driver tests the function max(L,m) using a test suite
// of input data from the file 'maxtests' -- see text chapter 6
{
    list L;
    int m;
    cout << "Begin test for functions max(L,m) \n";
    cout << "Enter the test file name as 'maxtests': ";
    L.read();
    while (! L.end_of_input())
    {
        cout << "\nInput list L = ";
        L.write();
      cout << "\nEnter m: " ;
      cin >> m ;
      int j = max(L, m) ;
      cout << "Result of max(L,m) = " << j << "\n" ;
      L.read() ;
    }
    cout << "\n\nEnd test for function max(L,m) \n";
}
```

FIGURE 6–3   A driver for max.

Example: Testing a Complete Program

Consider the GPA program which was modified to be more user-friendly. To test this modified program, we convert it into an autodriver as shown in Figure 6–5, and then run it against a file containing several alternative input lists of grades, rather than just one. The autodriver code consists simply of an additional do loop that surrounds the executable text of the program. This modifi-

```
Begin test for function max(L,m)
Enter the file name as 'maxtests':
maxtestsuite
Input list L =
()
Enter m: 0
Result of max(L,m) = 0
Input list L =
()
Enter m: 1
Result of max(L,m) = 0
  .

  .

  .

Input list L =
(3 1 8 2)
Enter m: 5
Result of max(L,m) = 0
End test for function max(L,m)
```

FIGURE 6–4   Results of running the max driver with input from the file maxtests.

cation causes the program to read and process several different input lists until
end_of_input occurs, signaling the end of the test run.

EXERCISES

6–6 Consider the tic-tac-toe program discussed in earlier chapters. Create an
appropriate suite of test data for this program.

6–7 Create an autodriver for the tic-tac-toe program.

PROGRAM TESTING AND DEBUGGING METHODS

A successful test is one that finds errors. It's always easy to write test data that
results in a program running until it completes; the challenge is to write test
data that will discover bugs, no matter how subtle they might be. But discovering errors is not enough; they still have to be corrected. That process is called
debugging. It is one of the most challenging aspects of software development
and, in commercial settings, is often one of the most expensive—it has been
known to consume as much as 40% of the cost of developing a piece of software. For students, debugging is often time-consuming and frustrating. Thus
it is worth our while spending some time learning how to debug effectively.

```
void main ()
{
  do {
  // pre: input == (grades[1] grades[2] ... grades[n]) &&
  //      n > 0 &&
  //      for all i in {1,..., n}: grades[i] in {0.0 ... 4.0}
    list grades;
    int number_of_grades;
    float sum = 0.0, gpa;
    int validinput ;
    do
    {
      cout << "Enter a list of grades: \n" ;
      grades.read();
      n = grades.length();
      if (grades.has_error() || n==0)
        validinput = 0 ;
      else
      {
        validinput = 1 ;
        for (i=1; i<=n; i++)
          if (grades.element(i)<0 || grades.element(i)>4)
            validinput = 0;
      }
    } while (! validinput) ;
    for (int i = 1; i <= number_of_grades; i++)
      sum = sum + grades.element(i);
    gpa = sum / number_of_grades;
    cout << "\n\nThe GPA of these grades is " << gpa << ".\n";
  // post: (n == 0 && output == 0) || (n > 0 &&
  //      output == sum i in {1,..., n}: grades[i])
  } while (! L.end_of_input()) ;
}
```

FIGURE 6–5   An autodriver for the user-friendly version of the GPA program.

Programs typically encounter three different types of errors. They are:

- *Compile-time* (or *syntax*) errors

- *Run-time* errors

- *Logical* errors

Syntax errors are the easiest to find and to correct—in fact, the compiler finds
these errors for you. Correcting them is simply a matter of correcting one's
syntax. Thus we won't spend time on them here. Run-time errors are errors
that show up during program execution and cause a program to halt. A typical
example is a divide-by-zero error; another is attempting to read character data
into an integer variable. In most cases, these errors are accompanied by a diag-

nostic that tells what error occurred and where it occurred. Thus these are usually not difficult to correct either, although sometimes it can be difficult to figure out why conditions that caused such an error arose. In the case of logical errors, however, the program compiles successfully and runs to completion with no errors being reported. The only way to know that a logical error has occurred is to run the program with test data and observe that the results are not as expected. Thus we will focus on logical errors for the rest of this section.

Finding logical errors may be difficult. There is no algorithm for finding them; in fact at the present time, debugging is more an art than a formalized process. It is much like a physician trying to diagnose a disease. The physician sees the symptom(s) and based on these has to determine a cause. Three debugging strategies often used are:

- *Brute force*   This typically means loading a program with `cout` statements in an attempt to determine where the anticipated values of the variables are going awry. In its worst form, brute force degenerates to changing lines until something is found that works.

- *Backtracking*   Starting from the point where the error occurs, backtracking is reading the code backwards until the error is found.

- *Cause elimination*   This strategy is like the scientific method. Faulty test results are taken as data, hypotheses are formed as to what could have caused such a result, further tests may be run to check the hypotheses, adjustments in the hypotheses are made if necessary, and when the cause is identified, its source is located in the code and corrected.

One can see from the physician analogy why brute force is a poor strategy—imagine yourself the patient of a physician who tries to diagnose your illness by giving you multitudinous medical tests without carefully thinking first about which ones are relevant for your symptoms. Even worse, imagine a physician who tries to cure you by trying treatments one after another in hopes of finding one that might work. Backtracking is better, but still inadequate—much time can be wasted reading code that doesn't need to be read and often the cause of the problem is read right past because the reader doesn't know what he or she is looking for. Pursuing the physician analogy a little further, we can see why cause elimination is the best strategy—it is like the physician observing the symptoms and forming a hypothesis about their cause. Some additional tests may be required. But eventually, the cause is (tentatively) identified and only then is a treatment attempted.

Like medical treatments, however, changes made in an attempt to debug a program can have unwanted side effects. Thus after an error has been corrected, it is necessary to go back and rerun all of the test data to be sure that even tests which succeeded earlier still succeed.

Following is a simple debugging example. Realistic programs are normally much longer than this and hence much harder to debug. But we believe that this example illustrates some important points about debugging. So, even though you can probably find the error simply by reading the code, we are going to apply cause elimination to debug it.

Example 6.1

```
float sum(int n, list L)
{
// Pre: L is a list of real numbers of length n or more.
    float total = 0.0;
    int i ;

    for (i=1; i<n; i++)
       total = total + L.element(i) ;
    return total ;
// Post: sum is the total of the first n numbers in L.
}
```

```
Test data:
    n    L                  sum
    0    ()                 0
    1    (2.1)              0
    3    (2.1 3.5 1.8)      5.6
```

Note that this program works correctly on the empty list, but is in error on the two non-empty lists. We can't tell much from the second test, but the result of the third test suggests that sum is omitting the nth item in the list from the sum but is adding the first $n-1$ items correctly. (Note that this hypothesis is consistent with the result of the second test.)

This is an example of what's sometimes called an OBOB ("off-by-one bug"). It typically results from incorrect initialization of a loop variable or an incorrect terminating condition in a loop. Thus our cause elimination analysis has led us to two possibilities for the error, the initialization $i = 1$ and the terminating condition $i < n$. To correct the error, however, we have to think more carefully about what is causing it. Since the nth item in each list is being omitted from `total`, the function needs to be modified so that the loop iterates one more time. There are two ways to accomplish this: initialize i to 0 rather than 1 or modify the condition to $i <= n$. Suppose we initialize i to 0 rather than 1. The program then reads:

```
float sum(int n, list L)
{
// Pre: L is a list of real numbers of length n or more.
    float total = 0.0;

    for (int i=0; i<n; i++)
       total = total + L.element(i) ;
    return total ;
```

```
// Post: sum is the total of the first n numbers in L.
}
```

Test data:

n	L	sum
0	()	0
1	(2.1)	0.0
3	(2.1 3.5 1.8)	5.6

Note that the test data yields the *same* incorrect results when n = 1 and n = 3; in fact, the error is even more obscure than it was before we made the change! The problem is that the revised function calculates L[0] + L[1] + ... L[n–1] instead of L[1] + L[2] + ... L[n] and our implementation of the list class does not guarantee anything about the value of L[0]—in fact, the value of L[0] is 0, which explains the answers shown above. This illustrates the point that attempting to correct a bug, even after its cause has been identified, can introduce new errors. Thus, before attempting to correct a bug, it is essential to understand both what the program is doing before the change is made and what it will do after the change.

When debugging long programs, it is often necessary to apply cause elimination in the context of a technique called *binary partitioning*. If we are unable to form a reasonable hypothesis as to the cause of the error, we examine the erroneous result and see which variables in the program could have contributed to it. We then restrict our attention to just those functions which modify those variables. We introduce cout statements (or use a debugging tool) to allow us to see the values of the relevant variables immediately before and immediately after execution of those functions. In this way we can identify which function(s) are in error. We then try again to form a reasonable hypothesis as to the cause of error. If we are still unable, we can examine the relevant variables at the midpoint of the function thus determining which half of the function is in error. We can continue this process (of binary partitioning) until we have a reasonable hypothesis as to the cause of the error.

Debugging is difficult. There are many reasons for this, some intrinsic to the nature of software, some psychological. Four reasons intrinsic to software are: (1) a computer language is a very pliable medium—it provides many ways to make errors; (2) the sources and symptoms of errors are often widely separated; (3) errors may have multiple causes; and (4) errors may be intermittent. Two psychological reasons are: (1) debugging if often done under the pressure of time deadlines—this adds greatly to its frustration; (2) every time we discover a bug, it tells us that we made a mistake—this can be hard to take, especially if we encounter a lot of bugs in a program we wrote. Thus it's not hard to see why commercial software vendors typically insist that all software they market be tested by persons other than its authors.

Ultimately the best debugging tool is writing the program correctly in the first place. Although this is an ideal that is hard to realize, aiming for it will yield software that is much easier to debug. The best "preventive medicine" for bugs is carefully following the MAPS process. Furthermore, programs written in this way are normally easier to debug than programs which are not—the logical, understandable structure makes it easier to hypothesize likely causes of errors and the hierarchical design makes it easier to locate likely causes. In the next chapter, we will discuss another important means of preventing bugs—software verification.

A few miscellaneous points remain to conclude our discussion of debugging. There are a number of software tools which can assist in debugging. These include debugging compilers, tracers, memory dumps, and cross reference maps. But, although these help, they are not a substitute for careful analysis of the cause of erroneous results. Also, programmers are sometimes tempted to add "kludges," which are patches to the program that enable it to process the test data correctly, even though the cause of the error has not been found. This is a dangerous and undesirable practice since it is almost certain that for some sets of data the error will reappear and the kludge will not catch it; thus, because it makes the error seem intermittent, it doesn't solve the problem but only makes the program harder to debug. Lastly, one of the most valuable debugging resources available to the programmer is other people. It's astonishing to spend hours searching for a bug, only in desperation to show it to a friend or colleague who glances at it and says, "Oh, here it is!" A fresh perspective can often see things missed by someone too close to the problem. One implementation of the latter observation is the growing use of *walkthroughs* as a quality assurance aid in the software industry. Walkthroughs are an organized presentation of a piece of software by an author to knowledgeable colleagues. Such presentations have proven to be the most effective means discovered to date for catching bugs. Walkthroughs will be discussed in more depth in Volume II of this series.

EXERCISE

6–8 At this point in your computing experience, you have had the opportunity to debug several programs you have written. Which of the three debugging techniques most clearly approximates the methods you have used? Give a specific example of a program you debugged and a debugging strategy you could have used which would have been more effective than the one you actually used.

A MAPS MATHEMATICAL CASE STUDY: MOVIE REVENUES

We are now ready to put our entire algorithmic problem-solving method (MAPS) together and solve a problem from beginning to end. In the course of this activity, we will emphasize the importance of identifying and reusing routines in a creative way. One of the strengths of the MAPS method is that it not only serves as a guide for solving a particular problem—it also leaves the problem solver with a set of new routines that can be used in solving more complex problems later.

The Dialogue

The problem we shall solve is this: develop an algorithm that will take a list of gross monthly revenues and display all months whose revenues are below the average revenue for the list, the highest and lowest revenues, and the month that had the highest revenue.

Our first reaction to this problem statement is that it is vague. That is, there are a lot of missing details. We need more information before we can proceed to the next step in solving the problem. This is typically the case in problemsolving; it is not odd behavior to admit incomplete understanding and ask a series of questions that will unravel those details. Intelligent problem solvers begin by asking questions and getting clarification before they begin to think about solutions. Thus, we conduct a *dialogue* with the person who poses the problem so that a clear understanding of the problem can be reached. For this problem we should ask the following questions:

1. How will the input be presented? Chronologically by month? Randomly? In order by revenue? Will the input be in one or two lists? Will the names be explicitly presented with the revenues, or will the revenues be presented alone?

2. What is a valid revenue anyway? That is, will a revenue be any nonnegative real number? Is there a maximum valid revenue? Are the numbers presented in dollars and cents or in larger units?

3. In the output, should we display the months with below-average revenues in alphabetical order, in order by increasing size of revenue, or simply in chronological order? Should we display the average revenue itself?

4. Might more than one month have the highest revenue reading, and if so, should the algorithm display the names of all such months?

In pursuing these questions, it is usually appropriate to give a sample input and corresponding output for the problem; a picture is worth a thousand words! Examples serve to visually resolve many of these questions, as well as give some clues about how to go about solving the problem as a whole. In Figure 6–6, the input is presented in a single list (with revenue amounts given in thousands of dollars), and the program must distinguish between month names (list entries with *odd* indices 1, 3, 5, ...) and revenues (list entries with *even* indices 2, 4, 6, ...).

However, the input and output for this problem can just as well be presented in other ways. Two reasonable alternative input configurations are shown in Figure 6–7. In one alternative, the input appears as two lists rather than one; in the other, the input appears without the month names. In this case, the program must explicitly generate the 12 month names and assume that the 12 input revenues are given in chronological order by month.

The Specifications

Suppose that Figure 6–7*b* shows the input presentation expected by the program and Figure 6–6 shows the output presentation. Now we can construct

INPUT

```
(January 150.5
February  228.6
March 132.7
April 140.0
May   115.5
June  109.0
July 129.5
August 115.6
September 168.0
October 193.5
November 112.0
December 141.6)
```

OUTPUT

```
REVENUE STATISTICS
average = 144.7
highest = 228.6
lowest = 109.0
months below average:
     March
     April
     May
     June
     July
     August
     November
     December
Highest month(s):
   February
```

FIGURE 6–6   Sample input and output for the revenue problem.

```
January
February
March
April
May
June
July
August
September
October
November
December

(150.5 228.6
132.7 140.0
115.5 109.0
129.5 115.6
168.0 193.5
112.0 141.6)
```

```
(150.5 228.6
132.7 140.0
115.5 109.0
129.5 115.6
168.0 193.5
112.0 141.6)
```

(*a*)   (*b*)

FIGURE 6–7   Two alternative input presentations for the revenue problem. (*a*) Input as two lists; (*b*) input as revenues only.

specifications—a set of preconditions and postconditions—that define the problem more precisely. These specifications will clarify the details of the problem solution as we develop them in subsequent steps.

The precondition for the revenue problem can be given in the following way:

```
// pre: input == (e[1] e[2] ... e[12]) &&
// for all i in {1,...,12} e[i] is the revenue for the ith month
```

Thus, if the program were given the particular input shown in Figure 6–7*b*, this precondition would be satisfied; the program will interpret the value of e[2] as 228.6 (the revenue for February), and so on. However, readers should note that if the input were presented in one of the other alternative configurations, this precondition would *not* be satisfied.

The postcondition for the revenue problem can be defined in the following way:

```
// post: input == empty && output ==
//       REVENUE STATISTICS
//          average = (Sum i in {1, ... ,12}: e[i]) / 12
//          highest = Max i in {1, ..., 12}: e[i]
//          lowest = Min i in {1, ..., 12}: e[i]
//          months below average:
```

```
//              {m[j]: e[j] < (Sum i in {1, ... ,12}: e[i]) / 12}
//          Highest month(s): {m[j]:
//           e[j] == Max i in {1, ..., 12}: e[i] && 1 <= j <= 12}
```

Here, the input specification describes the general form and substance of the input, and the output specification summarizes the required relationship between the input and the output. In particular, we see that *two* lists are needed—a list $(m_1\ m_2\ ...\ m_{12})$ of 12 month names and a list of 12 input revenue levels. These are treated in *parallel correspondence* with each other. (Note that since the list of month names is not provided as input, it must be somehow generated by the program in the form of a 12-entry array.) That is, the facts that `m[2] ==` `February` and `e[2] == 228.6` mean that the amount of revenue for February was 228.6 million.

Thus, the solution for this problem can be described in terms of those months whose corresponding revenue levels have certain relationships to the highest, lowest, and average revenue levels. The notation of logic is particularly helpful here because we can simultaneously express the specifications briefly and accurately. An English-language description of the input and output requirements could not have been written with the same precision and brevity.

The Breakdown

Many independent goals, or steps, become evident as we begin to think about this problem and its specifications. Initially, our solution must generate the list of month names and obtain from the input the list of revenue readings. Also, our solution will need to determine the average, highest, and lowest revenue readings. It will need to display the names of those months whose revenue readings were below this average, as well as the month(s) that had the highest revenue reading.

The solution for this process therefore can be initially broken down into the four routines and five data elements that are shown in Figure 6–8. We have accomplished two important things in this initial stage of the breakdown; we have identified the principal routines that will be needed in the solution and we have identified and assigned names to the principal lists (`month_names` and `revenues`) and the principal variables (`avg_revenue`, `max_revenue`, and `min_revenue`) that the solution requires.

Let's think about two new elements of the problem solution—the sequential relationships between the routines, and the extent to which we can use known routines to help construct a solution to this problem. We can determine the sequence of events described in Figure 6–8 informally (just by thinking about what must occur first, second, etc.) or formally (by describing pre- and post-conditions for the individual routines that we have identified and then ordering them logically and in the context of the original problem's specifications). An informal analysis leads to the initial ordering described in Figure 6–9, along with the original problem specifications in their proper places.

We see that the four routines must be placed in this order so that the problem's postcondition will be completely satisfied. In particular, the reading of revenue data (step 1) must precede all other steps. By itself, step 1 leads to satisfaction of the specification `input == empty` in the postcondition. Similarly, the calculation and display of the average must take place next (step 2), for two reasons. First, the average is needed as input to (i.e., a precondition for) step 3, where we need to determine and display the months whose revenues are below average, and step 4, where we find and display the month(s) with the highest revenue. Second, the problem's postcondition specifies that the average, maximum, and minimum revenue levels be displayed before the output from steps 3 and 4 is displayed. Finally, step 3 must precede step 4 because that is the order in which their respective outputs are required by the problem's postcondition.

Defining Abstractions

We now have the revenue problem solution defined to a point where we can step back and evaluate the effort that is needed to solve each of its parts. That is, for each step in the solution, we need to decide first whether it should be broken into substeps. In this example, steps 1 and 2 can individually be broken into substeps to further clarify their individual goals.

This further breakout is shown in Figure 6–10. Here we see that step 1 has two constituent parts—step 1.1 and step 1.2—which initialize the list of month

Routines

Initialize lists of months and revenues

Display months that are below average

Display average, maximum, and minimum revenue.

Display month(s) with highest revenue

Data Elements

month_names	An array of 12 month names
revenues	A list of 12 revenue readings
avg_revenue	The average of these readings
max_revenue	The maximum revenue among all 12 readings
min_revenue	The minimum revenue among all 12 readings

FIGURE 6–8   Breakdown of routines and data elements for the revenue problem.

```
// pre: input == (e[1] e[2] ... e[12]) && for all i in
//    {1,..., 12}: e[i] is the revenue for the ith month
```

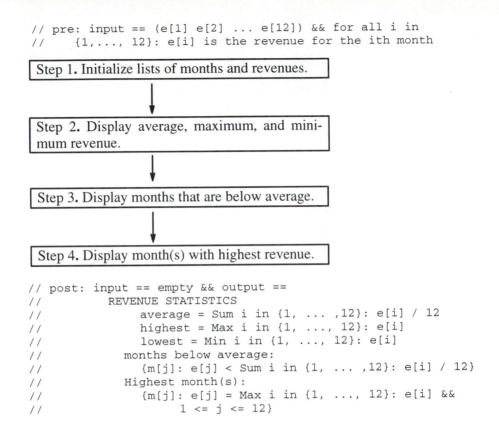

Step 1. Initialize lists of months and revenues.

Step 2. Display average, maximum, and minimum revenue.

Step 3. Display months that are below average.

Step 4. Display month(s) with highest revenue.

```
// post: input == empty && output ==
//          REVENUE STATISTICS
//              average = Sum i in {1, ... ,12}: e[i] / 12
//              highest = Max i in {1, ..., 12}: e[i]
//              lowest = Min i in {1, ..., 12}: e[i]
//          months below average:
//              {m[j]: e[j] < Sum i in {1, ... ,12}: e[i] / 12}
//          Highest month(s):
//              {m[j]: e[j] = Max i in {1, ..., 12}: e[i] &&
//                  1 <= j <= 12}
```

FIGURE 6–9 Initial ordering and specifications for the steps in the revenue problem.

names and read the list of revenues, respectively. Step 2 has three constituent parts; step 2.1 computes and displays the average revenue, step 2.2 computes and displays the maximum revenue, and step 2.3 computes and displays the minimum revenue. Note that the individual substeps in this further breakout are sequenced carefully to reflect the order in which the postcondition specifies that the output should be displayed. This level of attention to detail, though perhaps seeming unnecessary in such a simple example as the present one, becomes increasingly important as the complexity of algorithmic problems increases.

Subdividing and sequencing the individual steps should continue until each substep is clearly recognizable as an instance of a routine, can be solved directly by combining existing (known) routines together, or can be solved directly by developing an entirely new routine. In our example, we see that we need to develop a new routine for step 1.1, whereas step 1.2 is an instance of the routine `read`. Step 2.1, on the other hand, can be solved by combining two old routines, `average` and `<<`. That is, the computation of the average and the display

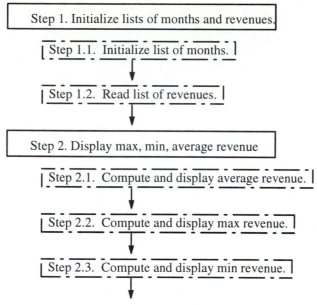

FIGURE 6–10   Further breakout of steps 1 and 2 of the revenue problem.

of the result are two separate actions and each has an associated routine that describes it. Similarly, step 2.2 combines the two routines max and <<, and step 2.3 combines the two routines min and <<.

Neither of steps 3 and 4, however, lends itself to such straightforward combining of routines. We haven't yet seen any routine that will directly solve problems like these, and we will have to create a new solution in each of these cases. That is, we need routines which will display all the months whose revenue is below average and display the month(s) whose revenue is the maximum, respectively.

Both of these steps seem to require the same sort of strategy—a search of the list of revenue values to find those values which have a certain property. For each one that does have that property, its index in the list revenues can be used to identify the corresponding month name in the array month_names. Look at the example input that was shown at the beginning of this section. The average of the revenue readings given there is 144.7 million. The revenue for March is 132.7 million, which is below average. Therefore, the name March should be displayed as one of the outputs of step 3. To find all such months, we need to examine all 12 revenue readings in the same way. This leads to the following loop:

```
// Step 3. Display months that are below average.
       cout << "   Months below average:\n";
       for (int i = 1; i <= revenues.length(); i++)
        if (revenues.element(i) < avg_revenue)
          cout << "      " << month_names[i][0] << endl;
```

It is worth noting here that, even though we used creativity to construct a solution for step 3 in the revenue problem, the solution still requires us to combine some familiar routines together by the processes of *abutment* and *nesting* discussed in the previous chapter. For example, note that the routine << is nested within the routine if, which is nested within the looping routine for. The looping routine itself is abutted to the routine <<, to complete the solution to step 3.

Having completed step 3, we can reuse this strategy to complete step 4. Note here that the maximum revenue reading may in fact be reached in more than one month. In the worst case, all 12 months might have the same revenue reading, in which case they all should be displayed as output by step 4!

```
// Step 4. Display month(s) with the highest revenue.
        cout << " Highest month(s):\n";
        for (i = 1; i <= revenues.length(); i++)
         if (revenues.element(i) == max_revenue)
           cout << "     " << month_names[i][0] << endl;
```

Notice that the solution to step 4 has been achieved by *tailoring* the solution to step 3. This is a common practice in algorithmic problem solving, and should be used whenever two steps seem intuitively to require the same kind of process.

Can steps 3 and 4 be *merged* together into a single for loop and still solve the problem? Not in this case. Readers should think about what would happen if a single for loop had both the if statements from steps 3 and 4 nested within it.

Coding

Simply put, *coding* is the translation of an algorithmic problem's solution into a program, complete with documentation. In solving an algorithmic problem, much of the coding emerges during the breakdown and abstraction stages. For example, we have completely coded steps 3 and 4 of the revenue problem in the process of discovering new routines that are appropriate for them. We also have steps 1 and 2 fairly well in hand; we know that we can implement them by reusing and combining existing routines used for other problems.

The coding process largely involves gathering together all the parts of the problem solution and making sure that the entire result is coherent, understandable, and faithful to the original problem's pre- and postconditions. It is usually helpful to employ a skeleton like that shown in Figure 6–11 when the coding is done in C++.

We can code this particular program that we have been developing using the skeleton in Figure 6–11 as a guide. Here, note that the routines average, max, and min are assumed to be stored separately in the library called List-Tools.h, and the various other operators on lists of reals are assumed to be stored in the library called ListClass.h. Once the skeleton of the program is

```
#include libraries from which routines will be retrieved

void main ()
{
// comment briefly describing the problem,
//   the overall structure of the solution,
//   the author, and the date

declarations of the variables in the breakdown
// pre: the problem's preconditions

// Step 1. description of step 1 in the breakdown

// Step 2. description of step 2 in the breakdown
 .
 .
 .
// post: the problem's postconditions
}
```

FIGURE 6–11   Skeleton for coding the steps of a C++ program.

thus completed, the C++ code for the individual steps can be completed and inserted in the proper places.

Completing the code for the input steps requires that appropriate prompts be supplied to the user so that the input will be entered in a well-informed way. This leads to the following outline of step 1:

```
// Step 1. Initialize lists of months and revenues.
   init_months(month_names);
   cout << "Enter a list of 12 revenue readings: \n";
   revenues.read();
```

Here, we will need to design a routine `init_months` so that the array `month_names` can be properly initialized with the names of the 12 months. We can also add guard-type input screening (for cases where adherence to the preconditions must be explicitly enforced by the program). For example, rather than fulfilling part of step 1 simply by writing

```
cout << "Enter a list of 12 revenue readings: \n";
revenues.read();
```

we could have made an explicit, continuous check for a 12-element input list, using a loop in the following way:

```
do
{
  cout << "Enter a list of 12 revenue readings: \n";
  revenues.read();
} while (revenues.length() != 12) ;
```

We complete the C++ code for steps 2 through 4 for the complete program shown in Figure 6–12.   Note that the body of the function `init_months` has been omitted, since it is left as an exercise.

Testing

The goal of program testing and verification is to ensure to the greatest extent possible that the solution designed is correct and complete in all respects. That is, we want to ensure that the program's execution, using any input that is allowed by the precondition, will deliver a result that is consistent with the post-condition. Because verification and testing are so fundamental to the process of algorithmic problem solving, we shall discuss them further in Chapter 7.

Presentation

When the solution to an algorithmic problem has been fully developed and tested, the C++ code should be reasonably self-documenting when it is read by someone unfamiliar with the problem but familiar with the problem-solving methodology and the domain from which the problem is taken. That is, the text of the program—with its documentation, stepwise structure, and pre- and post-conditions—should be as easy for a professional colleague to read as an article in the *New York Times* would be for any well-educated person.

A complete presentation of the solution for an algorithmic problem should include, in addition to the program text itself, the following items:

1. An introduction, written in English, identifying the author(s) and describing the problem, the solution, and any unusual or innovative aspects of the solution;

2. A sample of the input and output from one or more runs of the program;

3. A summary of the results of verifying and/or testing the program's steps, as appropriate.

In short, the presentation should complete the solution of a problem so that it can be understood by any interested reader. The reader may be your instructor for now, but in the future could be any other professional problem solver (programmer or software engineer) who has the task of revising or extending the given problem and its solution.

EXERCISES

6–9 Develop an appropriate suite of test data for the revenues program. In light of the six principles of test case design, explain why this is an appropriate suite.

```
// This program computes certain revenue statistics on
// revenue from given month data.  Brian Davies -- 7/2/93
#include <iostream.h>
#include "ListTools.h"      //note: ListTools #includes ListClass
typedef char *(name_list[13][20]);
void init_months (name_list month_names)
... // details of this function are omitted

void main ()
{    name_list month_names;   // The 12 month names
     list revenues;           // The 12 revenue readings
     float avg_revenue;       // The average of these readings
     float max_revenue;       // The maximum of these readings
     float min_revenue;       // The minimum of these readings
// pre: input == (e[1] e[2]...e[12]) &&
// for all i in {1,...,12}: e[i] is revenue for the ith month

// Step 1. Initialize lists of months and revenues.
        init_months(month_names);
        cout << "Enter a list of 12 revenue readings: \n";
        revenues.read();
// Step 2. Display max, min, and average revenues.
        cout << "\n\nREVENUE STATISTICS\n";
        avg_revenue = average(revenues);
        cout << "  Average: " << avg_revenue << endl;
        max_revenue =
         revenues.element(max(revenues, revenues.length()));
        cout << "  Highest: " << max_revenue << endl;
        min_revenue =
         revenues.element(min(revenues, revenues.length()));
        cout << "  Lowest:  " << min_revenue << endl;
// Step 3. Display months that are below average.
        cout << "  Months below average:\n";
        for (int i = 1; i <= revenues.length(); i++)
         if (revenues.element(i) < avg_revenue)
           cout << "     " << month_names[i][0] << endl;
// Step 4. Display month(s) with the highest revenue.
        cout << "  Highest month(s):\n";
        for (i = 1; i <= revenues.length(); i++)
         if (revenues.element(i) == max_revenue)
           cout << "     " << month_names[i][0] << endl;

// Post: input == empty and output ==
//   REVENUE STATISTICS
//      average = (Sum i in {1,...,12}: e[i]) / 12
//      highest = Max i in {1,...,12}: e[i]
//      lowest = Min i in {1,...,12}: e[i]
//      months below average:
//       m[j]: e[j] < (Sum i in {1...12}: e[i]) / 12
//      highest month(s):
//       m[j]: e[j] = Max i in {1...12}: e[i]
}
```

FIGURE 6–12   The complete C++ revenues program.

6–10 Suppose you are using MAPS to design a program that will read a number expressed in roman numerals and display its value in arabic numerals. In the dialog and specifications stages, you have decided that the input string will be all capital letters from the set {I, V, X, L, C, D, M}. Recall that the values of these roman "digits" are 1, 5, 10, 50, 100, 500, and 1000, respectively. You have also decided that the digits in the input string will be in nonincreasing order by value; thus the arabic number 4 will be written as the roman numeral IIII (rather than IV). Under these assumptions, work through the details of the specifications and breakdown stages of MAPS for this problem.

6–11 Give the output that would appear if we merge the two `for` loops in steps 3 and 4 of the revenue problem into a single `for` loop that contains both of their individual `if` statements, given the sample input shown in Figure 6–7. That is, assume we merge steps 3 and 4 as follows:

```
cout << "  months below average:";
cout << "  Highest month(s):";
for (int i = 1; i <= revenues.length(); i++)
{
  if (revenues.element(i) < avg_revenue)
    cout << " " << month_names[i][0];
  if (revenues.element(i) == max_revenue)
    cout << " " << month_names[i][0];
}
```

6–12 Give an invariant for the loop in step 3 of the revenue problem.

6–13 Complete the body of the function `init_months` in the revenue program.

6–14 Continue the MAPS design of the roman numerals problem introduced in Exercise 6–10, by defining abstractions and then coding the complete program. Can you employ abstractions that you have seen before? What new abstractions need to be implemented, and what sort of creativity or domain knowledge will you use to complete them?

6–15 Modify the pre- and postconditions for the Revenues program and the code so that it: (1) can handle input of the form given in Figure 6–7*a* and, (2) can handle not just 12 months and revenues but any length list. Note that in this form Revenues becomes quite general—with minor changes of names and labels, it could generate statistical reports on many situations—e.g., a company's income by quarter, by month, or even over a number of years.

6–16 Design and implement a **management information** system for a small company. Your program **should read a** personnel file that has an employee number and an annual salary for each employee. Design the program to display a report. Design the layout of your report carefully; each item should be labeled. In order to test your program, design a simple personnel file consisting of an employee number and annual salary for each employee. In your report, display the following:

a. The total annual payroll, the maximum, minimum, and average annual salaries.

b. A breakdown of similar information for each of the following salary ranges:

```
         salary <  15,000
15,000 < salary <  20,000
20,000 < salary <  30,000
30,000 < salary <  45,000
45,000 < salary
```

(that is, the number of employees in each range, along with the maximum, minimum, and average salaries in each range).

6–17 Develop a MAPS-style design for a pari-mutuel horse race betting system. Before the race, the user will enter each bet as it is made, giving the number of the horse and the amount of the bet. After the "last bet" bell has rung, the program should compute and display the payoff for each horse, which is computed by dividing the total amount bet on all horses by the amount bet on that horse. For example, in a race with three horses where $100 was bet on horse 1, $150 was bet on horse 2, and $250 was bet on horse 3, the payoffs would be 5 to 1, 3.33 to 1, and 2 to 1, respectively. You don't necessarily have to implement the entire program; just do the design (MAPS stages 1 through 4).

A MAPS TEXT PROCESSING CASE STUDY PROBLEM: CRYPTOGRAPHY

Computers have been used since World War II to assist in solving cryptographic problems that require discovering the coding scheme, or cipher, that underlies an encoded message. Here is an example of the well-known Caesar cipher, which turns the message

```
SERGEANT PEPPERS LONELY HEARTS CLUB BAND
```

into the encoded message

```
VHUJHDQW SHSSHUV ORQHOB KHDUWV FOXE EDQG
```

Here the underlying coding scheme is simply to replace each letter in the message by the one that follows it by three positions in the alphabetic sequence. Other, more elaborate coding schemes are used in practice, and sometimes the discovery of the cipher as well as the original message can be a very complicated task.

The problem here, however, is a simple one: Given a series of messages encoded in the Caesar cipher, decode each one and display the text of the decoded message on the screen. Thus, for the encoded message shown above, the output would be SERGEANT PEPPERS LONELY HEARTS CLUB BAND.

Stage 1: The dialogue There are few issues surrounding this problem, so we are tempted to go straight to the design. However, it is important to address and resolve certain questions of detail. For example, can the input text contain both upper- and lowercase letters of the alphabet or even other (non-alphabetic) characters? The answer is presumably yes, and all such characters should be rendered in the decoding exactly as they appeared in the original message. For example, the blank in the encoded message retains its original place in the decoding.

Stage 2: The specifications The specifications for this problem can be stated as follows:

```
// pre: input == a series of messages, each one a sequence of
//      characters c₁ ... cₙ representing an encoding in the
//      Caesar cipher
// post: output == a series of decoded texts of the form
//      d₁ ... dₙ, for which each dᵢ satisfies the relation
//      cᵢ == Caesar(dᵢ) && cᵢ is an alphabetic character ||
//      for all i in {1,...,n}: cᵢ == dᵢ
```

Here, Caesar(d_i) denotes the function that consists of the Caesar encoding of the ith character d_i in the output text. That encoding is defined in Table 6–3.

Stage 3: The breakdown The program will need to execute three main steps for every message that it decodes. An input step will retrieve an encoded message, a translation step will perform the actual decoding, and an output step will display the resulting decoded message. These steps can be summarized in the following way:

```
do
{
// Step 1.  Retrieve a message.

// Step 2.  Decode the message.

// Step 3.  Display the decoded message.

} while there are still messages to be decoded ;
```

If we agree that the maximum length of a message is limited by the maximum length of a C++ string (255 characters in most implementations), then there is little difficulty in realizing the input and output steps for this program. If we allow more generality, some more careful considerations for the storage of the message and its decoding need to be made. We shall stick to the simpler version in this solution.

Thus, the program can have two major string variables, say `message` and `decode`, both of type `string`. The decoding itself can be done in either of two ways. One way is to store the letters of the alphabet in an array, say `Caesar`, so that the decoding of any particular letter `Caesar[i]` can be directly retrieved as `Caesar[i-3]`. If we use this strategy, we must take care to deal properly with the first three letters at the beginning of the alphabet. (Why?)

TABLE 6–3 THE CAESAR CIPHER

Letter l	Caesar(l)	Letter l	Caesar(l)
a	d	A	D
b	e	B	E
...			
x	a	X	A
y	b	Y	B
z	c	Z	C

Another way to decode a letter in the alphabet is to perform arithmetic on the ordinal number that corresponds to its ASCII representation. For example, the ordinal value of the letter A is 65, which is three less than the ordinal value of the letter D, 68. Thus, if c is a letter of the input message, then the C++ function `char(int(c)-3)` delivers the decoded letter, provided again that c is not one of the first three letters of the alphabet. (Why?)

Stage 4: Defining abstractions   Step 2 in this program, the decoding of the message, can be viewed as the nesting of two routines. That is, a function that computes the inverse of the Caesar cipher function (see Table 6–3) for a single letter of the alphabet can be nested inside a routine that scans each one of the individual letters of the encoded message. The latter can be realized as a simple `for` loop, while the former can be realized as a C++ function, say `CaesarInverse(c)`, that takes a single character c as a parameter and returns the corresponding decoded character as a result. The nesting takes place because this same decoding operation takes place for every letter in the original message. We can define specifications for these two routines in the following way:

```
Decode(message)
// pre: message == c1c2...cn
// post: result == d1d2...dn &&
//      for all i in {1,..., n}: di == CaesarInverse(ci)}
```

```
CaesarInverse(c)
// pre: c is a character
// post: result == d, && either
//      d is alphabetic && Caesar(d) == c ||
//      d is not alphabetic && d == c
```

Stage 5: Coding These two specifications can be coded as C++ functions in the following way:

```
char *Decode (char *message)
{
// pre: message == c1c2...cn
  int i ;
  char *decoded = message ;
   for (i=0; i<strlen(message); i++)
      decoded[i] = CaesarInverse(message[i]);
    return decoded ;
// post: result == d1d2...dn &&
//      for all i in {1,...,n}: di == CaesarInverse(ci)
}
```

```
char CaesarInverse (char c)
{
// pre: c is a character

  char d ;
  int j ;
  char *alpha = strcat("abcdefghijklmnopqrstuvwxyz",
                       "ABCDEFGHIJKLMNOPQRSTUVWXYZ") ;
  j = strpos(c, alpha);    // look for c in the alphabet
  if (j == 0)
     d = c;               // c is not alphabetic
  else if (j <= 3)
     d = alpha[23 + j];   // decode a, b, c
  else if (j <= 26)
     d = alpha[j - 3];    // decode d, e, ..., z
  else if (j <= 29)
     d = alpha[23 + j];   // decode A, B, C
  else
     d = alpha[j - 3];    // decode D, E, ..., Z
  return d ;

// post: result == d &&
//    (d is alphabetic && Caesar(d) == c ||
//     d is not alphabetic && d == c )
  }
```

Note that the function `CaesarInverse` uses a function `strpos`, which is as yet undefined. This function, when called should return the position of its first argument in the string given by its second argument. Hence, the call

```
strpos("i", "abcdefghijklmnopqrstuvwxyz")
```

should return the value 9. The complete specification and implementation of this function is left as an exercise.

Having these in hand, we can construct the balance of the program in the following way:

```
char CaesarInverse ...

char * Decode ...

void main ()
{
// This program decodes a series of messages and displays each
// decoding; it assumes that each message is encoded using the
// Caesar cipher.

// pre: input == a series of lines, each containing a message
  char message[256], decoded[256] ;
  char achar;

  do
  { // Step 1.  Obtain a message, character by character.
    cout << "Enter a coded message on a single line, and \n" ;
    cout << "enter <RET> to quit:\n" ;
    message = "" ;
    cin >> achar ;
    while (achar != '\n')
    {  strcat(message, achar);
       cin >> achar;
    }

// Step 2.  Decode the message.
    decoded = Decode(message);

// Step 3.  Display the decoded message.
    cout << "The decoded message is:\n" ;
    cout << decoded ;
  } while (message != "") ;

// post: input == empty && output == the corresponding messages
//   decoded
}
```

Stage 6: Testing It is helpful to test this sort of program using an input text stored in a separate file. That way, the input coded messages do not have to be tediously retyped each time the program runs. A modest alteration of the above program to accomplish this would have an additional file variable, and then the end of the program would be conditioned upon reaching the end of that input file. The discussion of testing and drivers earlier in the chapter should provide sufficient information for concretely accomplishing this step. One possible suite of test data to include in coded.txt is:

```
*
b
B
d
dD
Dd
abcdefghijklmnopqrstuvwxyz ABCDEFGHIJKLMNOPQRSTUVWXYZ
aaaaaaaaaaaaaaaaaaaaaaaaaaaaaaaaaaaaaaaaaaaaaaaaaaaaaaaaaaaaaaa
aaaaaaaaaaaaaaaaaaaaaaaaaaaaaaaaaaaaaaaaaaaaaaaaaaaaaaaaaaaaaaa
aaaaaaaaaaaaaaaaaaaaaaaaaaaaaaaaaaaaaaaaaaaaaaaaaaaaaaaaaaaaaaa
aaaaaaaaaaaaaaaaaaaaaaaaaaaaaaaaaaaaaaaaaaaaaaaaaaaaaaaaaaaaaaa
<RET>
```

This suite tests the empty string at the end since the empty string is used to terminate the program. It begins, then, by testing each of the five cases in the `switch` statement and simultaneously tests the behavior of strings of length 1. Next it tests six strings of length 2, exercising different combinations of the five cases. The third to last line presents the entire alphabet, upper and lower case, while also testing `Decode`'s ability to handle a moderately long string. The line of 255 a's is the extreme case of the longest string.

Stage 7: Presentation The presentation of this problem's solution would require several test runs of the program to be made and a printed copy of the output for each run obtained. Combining this output with a listing of the program itself, a brief written explanation of its purpose, and any unusual operating characteristics, would complete the presentation.

EXERCISES

6–18 The function CaesarInverse uses a function `strpos`, which, when called, should return the position of its first argument in the string given by its second argument. Hence, the call

```
strpos("i", "abcdefghijklmnopqrstuvwxyz")
```

should return the value 8 (not 9; recall that string indexing begins at 0). Give a complete specification and implementation for this function.

6–19 One variation of the Caesar cipher which is much more difficult to crack is the following. Take a sequence of digits (such as 345) and repeat it indefinitely (345345345 ...). The first letter of the message to be encoded is shifted 3 places in the alphabet, the second 4 spaces, etc. Write a function `Decode` which will accept an encoding sequence as input and then decode messages coded using this cipher.

6–20 Design an appropriate suite of test data for the program described in Exercise 6–19.

A MAPS GRAPHICAL CASE STUDY PROBLEM: THE GAME OF LIFE

The game of life was invented in 1970 by John H. Conway. Its purpose is to provide a simple graphic simulation of population change through a series of generations. The game is played on a rectangular grid, which represents the "world" for a particular species of living organisms (people, amoebas, chickens, or whatever). In the grid, each shaded cell represents a single living organism, and the entire collection of shaded cells on the grid represents the entire population that is alive in a particular generation. For example, Figure 6–13 shows a population of six live chickens in a world that can accommodate a total of 64 chickens in any single generation.

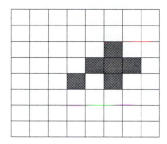

FIGURE 6–13   A generation of six chickens for the Game of Life.

Each new generation of chickens follows from the previous one in accordance with four simple rules that govern each individual chicken's survival, death, or birth. These rules are related only to the physical environment in which the chickens exist—that is, the conditions of overcrowding or low population density in which each chicken finds itself. The environment of a cell on the grid is defined as that collection of cells that immediately adjoin it. These four rules are:

1. Survival.   A chicken survives into the next generation if it has two or three living neighbors in the current generation.

2. Birth.   A chicken is born in the next generation if (*a*) it does not exist in the current generation and (*b*) it has exactly three living neighbors in the current generation.

3. Death by loneliness.   A chicken dies in the next generation if it has zero or one living neighbor in the current generation.

4. Death by overcrowding.   A chicken dies in the next generation if it has four or more living neighbors in the current generation.

Thus, if we extend the sample in Figure 6–13 to the next generation, our chicken population will become transformed as shown in Figure 6–14.

We see in Figure 6–14*b* that the chicken in the lower left has died of loneliness, while two chickens in the "cross" have died of overcrowding. The other three chickens in the cross have survived, since they had three neighbors in the previous generation. Finally, three new chickens were born in cells that were unoccupied and had exactly three neighbors in the previous generation. Figure 6–15 gives another example of the first two generations.

After some experimentation, we can see that the configuration of chickens in each new generation may look very different from the preceding generation. The Game of Life and related games with slightly different sets of rules have been studied with fascination by mathematicians and scientists alike. Scientists have studied ways to apply this kind of simulation, or modeling technique, to help them understand population change in real life.

The problem here, however, is simply to develop a program that, for any initial configuration of chickens in an 8×8 grid of cells, displays the sequence of generations that follows from the four rules of survival, birth, and death.

Stage 1: The dialogue   Our program should provide the user with a convenient means for describing the initial configuration of chickens in the grid. While it would not be difficult to generalize the program so that it can handle a grid of any reasonable size, that is not particularly important to the principal goal of the program, so we shall ignore it. However, we shall incorporate a facility by which the user controls the passage of time from one generation to the next and ultimately decides to stop the process.

We can envision the input as having two parts. First, the user enters the row and column numbers of the individual cells that are occupied by chickens in the first generation. Second, the user enters a series of commands that designate that the program should either progress to the next generation and display it, or terminate the game.

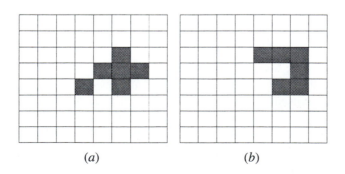

(*a*)   (*b*)

FIGURE 6–14   First two generations in the Game of Life. (*a*) Six chickens in the first generation; (*b*) six in the second.

The output is simply a series of displays, as shown in Figure 6–13. The initial display shows the first generation; the next display, in response to a user command, shows the second generation; the third display, if called for, shows the third generation, and so on. At any stage in the process, the user may also ask to review the previous generation, so that any two-generation sequence can be viewed back and forth by the user (in the spirit of Figure 6–14 or 6–15).

Stage 2: The specifications   After the dialogue, we can write a definition of the specifications for this problem as follows:

```
// pre: input == a series of mouse clicks in cells (x[i],y[i])
// of the lefthand grid, followed by a click outside the grid,
// followed by a series of "n" keystrokes, followed finally by
// by "q", && n>0 && for all i in {1,...,n}: 1<=x[i],y[i]<=8

// post: output == a series of displays of the game of life,
// in which the first display is given by the cells originally
// clicked, and each successive display (in response to "n")
// is the next generation that follows from the previous one,
// under the rules of survival, birth, and death.
```

Here, the sequence of one-character keystrokes "n" is used to give the user control over the transition from one generation to the next. That is, the typing of character "n" signals the program to compute the next generation from the previous one, and then to display it. At any instant in time the user will be able to view the two most recent generations computed, but no earlier ones. The initial generation, entered by the user through a series of mouse clicks, is designated as generation 0 in this sequence.

Stage 3: The breakdown   Several ideas come immediately to mind when we think about solving this problem. First, it will be useful to employ the facilities of the `grid` class. Second, since there will be two grids on the screen at any one time during a run of the program, it will be useful to declare two vari-

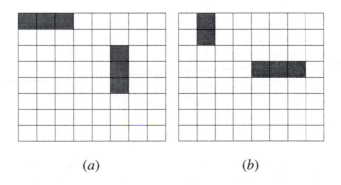

(a)   (b)

FIGURE 6–15   Another example for the Game of Life. (a) First generation; (b) second generation.

ables of type `grid`, say `last_gen` (the grid on the left) and `current_gen` (the grid on the right).

The program will need to implement three general steps in order to simulate the Game of Life. The first step will initialize the two grids `last_gen` and `current_gen`, retrieving the input mouse clicks and filling the appropriate cells in `last_gen`. Step 2 will compute and display the next generation. Step 3 will actually manage the computation of the next generation from the current one and display the result.

Furthermore, the sequencing of these three steps can be governed by the overall looping structure shown below. There, a `while` statement controls the loop, and each repetition of the loop results in a new generation being computed and displayed.

```
// Step 1. Initialize and display the 0th generation.

while (control != 'q')
{
// Step 2. Compute and display the next generation.

// Step 3. Enter the control code.
}
```

The variable `control` is used to record each keyboard character that the user types to command whether or not the next generation will be computed and displayed, and `done` is a switch that becomes true when the user enters "q" as the control code. For this reason, steps 2 and 3 are repeated; that is, a separate command is needed to govern each successive repetition of the loop.

Step 1 is accomplished by first setting up `current_gen` and `last_gen` as 8 × 8 grids with a cell size of, say, 15 pixels, with appropriate coordinates and labels to make them appear side by side on the screen. Step 1 needs to receive input mouse clicks in different cells of the lefthand grid to identify the live cells in the first generation. It terminates when the user clicks outside this grid.

```
// Step 1.  Initialize and display the 0th generation.
    open_text ();
    cout << "The game of life.\n" << endl;
    open_graphics ();
    grid last_gen (life_grid_size, 15, 15, 30,
                "Generations 0, 2, ...");
    grid current_gen (life_grid_size, 15, 150, 30,
                "Generations 1, 3, ...");
    cout << "Click the cells to be alive in generation 0, \n"
       << "then click outside the grid to start the game.\n" ;
    last_gen.get_click(row, col);
    while (last_gen.locate_cell(row, col))
    {
      last_gen.set_cell_display (row, col, '*');
      last_gen.get_click(row, col);
    }
    cout << "\nEnter 'n' to see the next generation, \n"
```

```
            << "or enter 'q' to quit. \n" ;
    cin >> control ;
```

Step 2 is the most complex part of the problem and therefore ought to be subdivided into parts. That is, for any computation and display of the next generation, we need to identify the roles of `current_gen` and `last_gen` (their roles reverse from one generation to the next), and then recompute whichever grid represents the current generation using the four rules of survival. Determining the configuration for the next generation is abstracted as the function `next_generation`. Similarly, the display of the next generation is controlled by the user typing "n", so either one of these two grids may be displayed inside this step. The generation number, `gen_number`, is incremented in either case. The oddness or evenness of this variable determines the roles of the two grids for each repetition. Here is the code for the basic logic of step 2.

```
// Step 2.  Compute and display the next generation.
      gen_number++;
      cout << "\nGeneration " << gen_number << ".\n" ;
      if (gen_number % 2 == 1)              // odd generations
      {   next_generation(last_gen, current_gen);
          current_gen.display_grid ();
      }
      else
      {
          next_generation(current_gen, last_gen);
          last_gen.display_grid ();
      }
```

Step 3 is straightforward, since it is realized by a single function call following a user prompt.

```
// Step 3.  Enter the control code.
      cout << "\nEnter 'n' to see the next generation, \n"
          << "or enter 'q' to quit. \n" ;
      cin >> control ;
```

The `next_generation` function can be further subdivided into parts, since for each cell the number of living neighbors must be counted. We'll abstract that task as the function `neighbors`. The `next_generation` function can thus be constructed by embedding the neighbors function inside a loop that examines each cell in the current generation separately. A `switch` statement can be used to discriminate the four rules of birth, death, and survival from each other. The `next_generation` function has the general control structure shown in Figure 6–16 when applied to the computation of `current_gen` from `last_gen`:

```
void next_generation (grid & input_grid, grid & output_grid)
{
// pre: input_grid contains the current generation
```

```
        for (int i = 1; i <= input_grid.grid_size (); i++)
          for (int j = 1; j <= input_grid.grid_size (); j++)
            switch (neighbors(input_grid, i, j))
              { case 2:      // Rule 1.  Survival
                  if (input_grid.cell(i, j) == '*')
                    output_grid.set_cell(i, j, '*');
                  break;

                case 3:      // Rule 2.  Birth
                  output_grid.set_cell(i, j, '*');
                  break;

                case 0:      // Rule 3.  Death by loneliness
                case 1:
                  output_grid.set_cell(i, j, ' ');
                  break;

                case 4:      // Rule 4.  Death by overcrowding
                case 5:
                case 6:
                case 7:
                case 8:
                  output_grid.set_cell(i, j, ' ');
              }
  // post: output_grid == the next generation of cells, computed
  //    from the four rules and input_grid.
  }
```

FIGURE 6–16   The `next_generation` function.

Stage 4:   Defining abstractions   The major new abstractions that are needed for this program are summarized as follows:

```
int neighbors (grid & the_grid, int x, int y)
// post: result == the number of living neighbors of
//    cell (x, y) in the_grid
grid next_generation (grid & input_grid, grid & output_grid)
// post: result == the next generation of cells, computed
//    from the four rules and input_grid.
```

The remaining abstractions can be implemented directly from the functions that are available for the `grid` class.

Stage 5:   Coding   The code for this program is shown in several parts, many of which have already been presented. What remains to be shown is the function `neighbors`, which appears in Figure 6–17, and the remainder of the main program, complete with declarations.

The `neighbors` function, shown in Figure 6–17, counts the number of living neighbors for the `x,y`th cell in grid `the_grid`. Note that a *neighbor* is any

```
int neighbors (grid & the_grid, int x, int y)
{
    int count = 0;
    for (int i = x - 1; i <= x + 1; i++)
       for (int j = y - 1; j <= y + 1; j++)
          if (((i != x) || (j != y)) &&
             (the_grid.cell(i, j) == '*'))
             count++;
    return count;

// post: result == the number of living neighbors of
//    cell (x, y) in the_grid
}
```

FIGURE 6–17 The `neighbors` function.

living cell that directly abuts cell x, y on any of its four sides or four corners. Thus, every cell can have at most eight neighbors. However, cells that are on an edge of grid `the_grid` have fewer than eight neighbors. For example, cell 1, 1 can have no more than three neighbors and cell 1, 2 can have no more than five.

The main body of the program is shown in Figure 6–18. It shows the declarations and remaining details that are needed to complete the C++ coding task. For instance, the variable `gen_number` is needed to keep track of the current generation being computed and displayed. The rest of this program is self-explanatory, since it follows from the earlier stages of our MAPS process.

```
// This program implements John H. Conway's game of life.  This
// game simulates the development of a population on an 8 x 8
// grid.   Brian Davies 7/3/93

#include <iostream.h>
#include "GridClass.h"
const int life_grid_size = 8;

int neighbors(grid & the_grid, int x, int y) ...

void next_generation (grid & input_grid, grid & output_grid) ...

void main ()
{
// pre: input == a series of mouse clicks in cells (x[i],y[i])
// of the lefthand grid, followed by a click outside the grid,
// followed by a series of "n" keystrokes, followed finally by
// by "q", && n>0 && for all i in {1,...,n}: 1<=x[i],y[i]<=8

    char control;
    int gen_number = 0;
    int row, col;
    int done = 0;
```

```
// Step 1.  Initialize and display the 0th generation.
...
   while (! done)
   {

// Step 2.  Compute and display the next generation.
...

// Step 3.  Enter a control code.
...
   }
   close_graphics ();
   close_text ();

// post: output == a series of displays of the game of life,
// in which the first display is given by the cells originally
// clicked, and each successive display (in response to "n")
// is the next generation that follows from the previous one,
// under the rules of survival, birth, and death.
}
```

FIGURE 6–18   Main body of the Game of Life program.

Stage 6: Testing   We will not present all the details of the testing process for the Game of Life here, but rather, will summarize it and leave the details for the lab exercises.

The first step is to design drivers for the functions `next_generation` and `neighbors`. The individual steps of the program itself can be tested in sequence, beginning with step 1, which initializes the grids when `gen_number` is 0, including the retrieval of mouse clicks and shading the selected cells. Test data therefore needs to be designed so that we can check the following initial input situations:

1. The most likely places errors will occur—mouse clicks at the corners and edges of the grid,

2. Clicks in some ordinary cells in the interior of the grid,

3. Multiple clicks in the same cell,

4. At least one fairly large initial generation, for which we have hand-calculated the next gneration.

Once the initialization step is tested and debugged, each successive step in the remainder of the program can be tested in turn. The same test data suite can be used to test the `neighbors` and `next_generation` functions.

Once the individual functions have been tested, the next step is to perform an integration test by converting the main program into an autodriver as was done earlier. Although it is tempting to use the same test data as was used above, it would be better to cover the four cases mentioned above with different data.

Stage 7: Presentation   Presentation of this program is complete when a write-up of its general purpose is prepared, together with a listing of the program itself and some sample outputs. The write-up should present not only a summary of what the program does but how it handles exceptional situations and any other limitations that the user may encounter.

EXERCISES

6–21   Devise a "terminal state" for the game of life, that is, an initial configuration which remains the same in each succeeding generation.

6–22   Devise a "steady state" for the game of life, an initial configuration which changes in the next generation but is returned to after two or more generations.

6–23   Determine by hand what each of the following initial generations in the Game of Life will produce in generations 2 and 3.

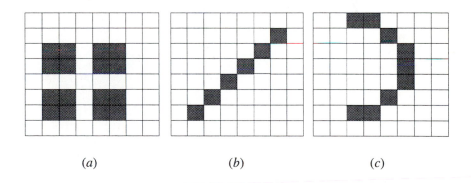

(a)   (b)   (c)

SUMMARY

This chapter completes the introduction to problem solving and programming using MAPS. We have expanded our understanding of what it means for a program to be completed by examining the notions of correctness, robustness, and user-friendliness. We have developed a systematic method for testing programs and presented an approach to debugging that is called cause elimination. And we have carried through the entire MAPS process—the dialogue, specifications, breakdown, defining of abstractions, coding, testing, and presentation—for several examples.

The next chapter introduces an alternative methodology for ensuring program correctness: formal verification. Because the discipline of formal verification is an emerging one and because it is ambitious to introduce it in a first course in computing, many instructors will choose to skip most or all of that chapter in this course. You are encouraged, nevertheless, to browse Chapter 7, since it provides more insights into the connections between logic, proof, and computer science. Because we believe that the discipline of formal program verification is an important and rapidly-evolving one, we provide this material optionally for those instructors who want to introduce it in the first course.

LOGIC AND PROGRAM CORRECTNESS

The use of logic in computing is ubiquitous. We have already seen its central role in problem solving and programming. In this optional chapter, we explore the impact of logic on the process of determining formally whether a program is correct. Testing, which we studied in the previous chapter, is a useful tool for finding errors in programs. But it can never show that a program is correct, only that it is incorrect. Showing that a program is correct requires more powerful reasoning tools than we have studied so far.

In terms of the three modes of thinking in computing which we have identified, the material in this chapter is clearly in the area of theory. Specifically, we begin by developing some skills in formal reasoning with logic, using equivalence laws and rules of inference. Along the way, you can expect to gain experience with the notion of proof, and several different proof strategies. This experience will stand you in good stead in many other areas of computer science if that becomes your major field of study. After laying a foundation in logic, we then turn our attention to methods of proving programs correct. These methods have proved to be controversial among computer scientists, however. Thus we conclude with a brief survey of the debate over formal methods of proving programs correct.

REASONING WITH PROPOSITIONS

In Chapter 3, we defined a proposition as a statement which is unambiguously true or false. We also defined a predicate as a statement which involves variables and which is unambiguously true or false under any legitimate assignment of values to its variables. In this section, we explore some fundamental aspects of reasoning with propositions. When used in this context, *reasoning* means the systematic development of new information from given information, as expressed in the form of propositions and predicates.

We need to develop means by which we can determine whether any two arbitrarily selected propositions are equivalent, so that one can be substituted for the other. We also need to find an alternative to the truth table for determining whether or not an arbitrary proposition is a tautology since truth tables for more than a few variables become so large that they are unwieldy. Finally, we need to explore how reasoning methods can be helpful in solving logic problems that are stated in English. We follow the typical mathematical pattern of defining terms formally and precisely and use symbols to denote abstractions. This will give our work a generality not possible otherwise. Ordinarily, the price we pay by doing this is that we lose some applicability. That is, the real world is very complex, and it is often difficult to match real world situations to our formal abstractions. But this method serves us well in computing, because computers, unlike the real world, are so unambiguous. Thus formal logic turns out to be a very valuable intellectual tool for the discipline of computing, for example, in the analysis and design of computer programs or the design of computer circuits.

Equivalence

Consider the proposition $(p \wedge q) \vee (p \wedge \sim q)$, whose truth table appears below.

p	q	$(p \wedge q) \vee (p \wedge \sim q)$
true	true	true
true	false	true
false	true	false
false	false	false

The truth values in the last column of this table are the same as the values in the column for p, so we can say that $(p \wedge q) \vee (p \wedge \sim q)$ is in a sense equivalent to p. Thus, if we encounter $(p \wedge q) \vee (p \wedge \sim q)$ in a situation, we can simply replace it by p.

As we begin to think about reasoning with propositions, we see that one concern is the need to simplify complex propositions. Our approach to this concern will be to define precisely what it means for two propositions to be equivalent, and then to see how we can use equivalent propositions to simplify complex expressions.

Definition Two propositions p and q are *equivalent* if they have the same truth value in every state.

In other words, p and q are equivalent if they have identical truth tables. Thus, one way to test for equivalence of two propositions is to write out their truth tables. There is another way that will often prove helpful, however, which is given in the following theorem. Recall that a tautology is a statement that is true for every assignment of values to its variables.

Theorem   Two propositions p and q are *equivalent*, denoted $p \equiv q$, if and only if $p \Leftrightarrow q$ is a tautology.

This theorem is not difficult to prove. First, assume that p and q are equivalent. Then, in any state, either both are **true** or both are **false**. Therefore, in any state $p \Leftrightarrow q$ is either (**true**$\Leftrightarrow$**true**) or (**false**$\Leftrightarrow$**false**), making $p \Leftrightarrow q$ a tautology. Now suppose, on the other hand, that $p \Leftrightarrow q$ is a tautology, and that S is a state in which p is **false**. Since $p \Leftrightarrow q$ is a tautology, q must be **false** also. Similarly, if S is a state in which p is **true**, q must be **true** in that state also.

The usefulness of this theorem is that it enables us to show that p and q are equivalent without truth tables—by deductively showing that $p \Leftrightarrow q$ is a tautology. We see how to do this below.

TABLE 7–1   EQUIVALENCE LAWS

Commutativity	Associativity
$p \wedge q \equiv q \wedge p$	$p \wedge (q \wedge r) \equiv (p \wedge q) \wedge r$
$p \vee q \equiv q \vee p$	$p \vee (q \vee r) \equiv (p \vee q) \vee r$
Distributivity	DeMorgan's laws
$p \wedge (q \vee r) \equiv (p \wedge q) \vee (p \wedge r)$	$\sim (p \vee q) \equiv \sim p \wedge \sim q$
$p \vee (q \wedge r) \equiv (p \vee q) \wedge (p \vee r)$	$\sim (p \wedge q) \equiv \sim p \vee \sim q$
Law of implication	Law of the biconditional
$p \Rightarrow q \equiv \sim p \vee q$	$p \Leftrightarrow q \equiv (p \Rightarrow q) \wedge (q \Rightarrow p)$
Property of negation	Identity
$\sim (\sim p) \equiv p$	$p \equiv p$
Law of the excluded middle	Law of contradiction
$p \vee \sim p \equiv \textbf{true}$	$p \wedge \sim p \equiv \textbf{false}$
$\vee$–simplification	$\wedge$–simplification
$p \vee p \equiv p$	$p \wedge p \equiv p$
$p \vee \textbf{true} \equiv \textbf{true}$	$p \wedge \textbf{true} \equiv p$
$p \vee \textbf{false} \equiv p$	$p \wedge \textbf{false} \equiv \textbf{false}$
$p \vee (p \wedge q) \equiv p$	$p \wedge (p \vee q) \equiv p$

Properties of Equivalence

There are several equivalence laws that are useful in various applications of logic. Table 7–1 summarizes the most common ones. Notice that many of these properties parallel a similar collection of laws that was introduced in Chapter 2 for sets (see Table 2–2). Furthermore, many of these properties have natural analogies in arithmetic. For instance, the commutative, associative, and distributive laws of arithmetic allow us to simplify arithmetic expressions, and in a similar fashion, the commutative, associative, and distributive laws identified in Table 7–2 allow us to simplify logical propositions.

We use these properties in various ways. Commutativity, for example, allows us to reorder propositions for further simplification. Associativity allows us to drop parentheses. For example, since $p \wedge (q \wedge r) \equiv (p \wedge q) \wedge r$, we can equivalently write $p \wedge q \wedge r$. The distributive law allows for factoring of propositions. This law is directly analogous to the arithmetic law that allows us to write $3 \times 5 + 3 \times 7 = 3 \times (5 + 7)$. De Morgan's laws are often very helpful in dealing with expressions involving negation. The law of implication allows us to equivalently write an implication using only the operators $\vee$, $\wedge$, and $\sim$.

Before using these equivalence laws, we should convince ourselves that they *are* actually correct. To do this, we need only to construct a truth table for each side of the equivalence and verify that the two truth tables are identical. Thus we use truth tables to build up a set of logical tools which will later allow us to work without truth tables. We illustrate this construction for the law of implication and leave the rest of the constructions as exercises.

Example 7.1 To show that $(p \Rightarrow q) \equiv (\sim p \vee q)$, we can construct a truth table as follows:

p	q	$p \Rightarrow q$	$\sim p \vee q$	$(p \Rightarrow q) \Leftrightarrow (\sim p \vee q)$
true	true	true	true	true
true	false	false	false	true
false	true	true	true	true
false	false	true	true	true

Simplifying Propositions Using the Properties of Equivalence We now turn our attention to simplifying propositions. *Simplifying* here means putting a proposition in a different form that is more useful for some purpose, usually a form that has fewer variables and/or operators than the original proposition.

To simplify a proposition, we write out a series of numbered steps. Each step contains a proposition on the left and a reference to a particular property of equivalence on the right. The proposition on the left is always equivalent to the one in the step directly preceding it, by virtue of the property stated on the right. For example, suppose we want to simplify the proposition $(p \Rightarrow q) \wedge (p \Rightarrow r)$. Step 1 lists that proposition, and steps 2 through 4 contain equivalent propositions:

1.	$(p \Rightarrow q) \wedge (p \Rightarrow r)$	
2.	$(\sim p \vee q) \wedge (\sim p \vee r)$	Law of implication
3.	$\sim p \vee (q \wedge r)$	Distributivity
4.	$p \Rightarrow (q \wedge r)$	Law of implication

Here, we see that step 2 results from step 1 by the law of implication, step 3 results from step 2 by distributivity, and step 4 results from step 3 by the law of implication.

Example 7.2 A truth table can be used to show that $((p \Rightarrow q) \wedge p) \Rightarrow q$ is a tautology. We can also use the equivalence laws to show that this is a tautology; that is, we show that it is equivalent to the simple proposition **true**.

1.	$((p \Rightarrow q) \wedge p) \Rightarrow q$	
2.	$((\sim p \vee q) \wedge p) \Rightarrow q$	Law of implication
3.	$((\sim p \wedge p) \vee (q \wedge p)) \Rightarrow q$	Distributivity
4.	$(\mathbf{false} \vee (q \wedge p)) \Rightarrow q$	Contradiction
5.	$(q \wedge p) \Rightarrow q$	$\vee$–simplification
6.	$\sim ((q \wedge p) \wedge \sim q)$	Law of implication
7.	$\sim ((p \wedge q) \wedge \sim q)$	Commutativity
8.	$\sim (p \wedge (q \wedge \sim q))$	Associativity
9.	$\sim (p \wedge \mathbf{false})$	Law of contradiction
10.	$\sim \mathbf{false}$	$\wedge$–simplification
11.	**true**	Negation

Example 7.2 supplies quite a bit of detail; every application of a property of equivalence is treated as a separate step. As we become more familiar with these properties, we can often abbreviate our work. In fact, there is an analogy with algebra, where our familiarity and facility with manipulating complex expressions allows us to simplify them by combining several algebraic properties in each step. Contrast, for example, the following two simplifications of the equation $5x + 1 = 3x + 2$:

1. $5x + 1 = 3x + 2$	1. $5x + 1 = 3x + 2$
2. $2x = 1$	2. $(5x + 1) - 1 = (3x + 2) - 1$
3. $x = \dfrac{1}{2}$	3. $5x + (1 - 1) = 3x + (2 - 1)$
	4. $5x + 0 = 3x + 1$
	5. $5x = 3x + 1$
	6. $5x - 3x = (3x + 1) - 3x$

7. $(5 - 3)x = (1 + 3x) - 3x$
8. $2x = 1 + (3x - 3x)$
9. $2x = 1 + (3 - 3)x$
10. $2x = 1 + 0x$
11. $2x = 1$
12. $(\frac{1}{2})2x = \frac{1}{2}$
13. $((\frac{1}{2})2)x = \frac{1}{2}$
14. $1x = \frac{1}{2}$
15. $x = \frac{1}{2}$

The 3-step simplification on the left is more akin to what we do if we are experienced with the properties of arithmetic, while the 15-step simplification would be typical of a novice effort. In this text, we will work toward developing a level of familiarity with logic that will let us more nearly approximate arguments like that shown on the left, often combining several properties in each step. However, knowing the underlying properties upon which such arguments are based is essential to a clear understanding of the process.

Example 7.3 contains a shorter series of steps in simplifying the proposition $(p \Rightarrow (q \wedge r)) \wedge (\sim p \Rightarrow (q \wedge s))$. This particular simplification is typical of many simplifications in which the object is to separate the role of one variable (in this case, q) from the other variables.

Example 7.3   Simplify $(p \Rightarrow (q \wedge r)) \wedge (\sim p \Rightarrow (q \wedge s))$:

1. $(p \Rightarrow (q \wedge r)) \wedge (\sim p \Rightarrow (q \wedge s))$
2. $(\sim p \vee (q \wedge r)) \wedge (p \vee (q \wedge s))$
    Law of implication, negation
3. $(\sim p \vee q) \wedge (\sim p \vee r) \wedge (p \vee q) \wedge (p \vee s)$
    Distributivity, associativity
4. $((\sim p \wedge p) \vee q) \wedge (\sim p \vee r) \wedge (p \vee s)$
    Commutativity, distributivity
5. $q \wedge (\sim p \vee r) \wedge (p \vee s)$ Law of contradiction, $\vee$-simplification
6. $q \wedge (p \Rightarrow r) \wedge (\sim p \Rightarrow s)$ Law of implication

Rules of Inference: The Idea of Proof

In the study of logic, we are primarily interested in forms or patterns of reasoning. We would like to find a methodology that allows us to be able to say whether or not a particular conclusion is a *valid* one—that is, whether its conclusions must be true whenever its premises are true. We know that truth tables work well for simple propositions, but they become tedious when there are more than a small number of variables or operators.

So, we seek an alternative methodology that allows us, in some legitimate way, to arrive at conclusions about propositions. In such a methodology, called a proof, the pattern of reasoning involves a series of steps that are a series of logical inferences, each one leading to the next in a formally justifiable way. The proof process is an extension of the methodology developed for simplifying propositions. However, proofs include an important additional ingredient: making an *inference* from an *assumption*. Inferences in proofs are allowed by virtue of a small collection of *rules of inference*. That is, a rule of inference allows certain kinds of propositions to follow from certain others that are already known to be true or assumed to be true. These rules are summarized in Table 7–2.

Definition   A *proof* in propositional calculus is a sequence of steps designed to show that a certain proposition is a tautology. Each step in the proof is either (1) a proposition already proven, (2) a proposition that follows from an earlier step by a rule of inference, or (3) a proposition introduced as an assumption in preparation for a subsequent step. Each step that is an assumption is so designated by being enclosed in brackets, [and]; all other steps are accompanied by a justification. Each introduction of an assumption must be accompanied by a subsequent application of the ⇒-introduction law or the ~-introduction law, and the last step in the proof must be the proposition itself.

The simple proof in Example 7.4 shows that the proposition $p \Rightarrow p$ is a tautology. We could easily show this using a truth table, but this provides a good opportunity for introducing the notation and style of proofs.

Example 7.4   To prove $p \Rightarrow p$:

1. $[p]$
2. p 1
3. $p \Rightarrow p$ ⇒-introduction, 1, 2

The first line contains the assumption $[p]$. At the outset of a proof, we can assume anything we think will lead us eventually to the conclusion as long as we subsequently apply the ⇒-introduction law or the ~-introduction law to it.

Assumptions, along with any subsequent steps that follow from them, are conventionally indented, so that the logic of subsequences of steps can be easily distinguished from the rest of the proof. Since p is assumed true, it surely follows that p is true; thus step 2 follows from step 1 directly. We make the note "1" in the right-hand column to show from which previous step this step follows. We then use the ⇒-introduction rule of inference (substituting p for q into the general form given in Table 7–2) to conclude in step 3 that $p \Rightarrow p$ is a tautology. Note that step 3 no longer depends on the assumption of p. The absence of indentation calls attention to this fact.

TABLE 7–2 RULES OF INFERENCE

$\Rightarrow$-introduction

$$[p]$$

$$\frac{q}{p \Rightarrow q}$$

$\Rightarrow$-elimination

(*modus ponens*)

$$p \Rightarrow q$$
$$\frac{p}{q}$$

(*modus tollens*)

$$p \Rightarrow q$$
$$\frac{\sim q}{\sim p}$$

$\wedge$-introduction

$$p$$
$$\frac{q}{p \wedge q}$$

$\wedge$-elimination

$$\frac{p \wedge q}{p} \qquad \frac{p \wedge q}{q}$$

$\Leftrightarrow$-introduction

$$p \Rightarrow q$$
$$\frac{q \Rightarrow p}{p \Leftrightarrow q}$$

$\Leftrightarrow$-elimination

$$\frac{p \Leftrightarrow q}{p \Rightarrow q} \qquad \frac{p \Leftrightarrow q}{q \Rightarrow p}$$

$\sim$-introduction

$$[p]$$

$$\frac{\textbf{false}}{\sim p}$$

$\sim$-elimination

$$p$$
$$\frac{\sim p}{\textbf{false}} \qquad \frac{\textbf{false}}{p}$$

$\vee$-introduction

$$\frac{p}{p \vee q} \qquad \frac{q}{p \vee q}$$

$\vee$-elimination

$$\begin{array}{cc} & [p] \ [q] \\ \frac{p \vee q \quad r \quad r}{r} \end{array}$$

The placing of two propositions on the same line separated by commas (as for example, $p \Rightarrow q$, $q \Rightarrow p$) denotes the fact that both $p \Rightarrow q$ and $q \Rightarrow p$ are known to be true. (Presumably these two propositions have already been proven.) The $p \Leftrightarrow q$ under the line indicates that $p \Leftrightarrow q$ can be validly inferred as the next step in a proof. Table 7–2 is based on a similar table developed by the German mathematician Gerhard Gentzen; it reflects the rules of inference that are used in normal discourse and that form the foundation for most studies and applications of formal logic.

When one proposition appears above another as in

[p]
q
___
$p \Rightarrow q$

the notation means that if assuming p enables us to follow a process of reasoning that concludes with q, then $p \Rightarrow q$ may validly be inferred. This rule may require some justification. Recall the truth table for $p \Rightarrow q$; if p is true and if it necessarily follows from that that q must be true, then it must be the case that the entire implication $p \Rightarrow q$ must be true. (***True*** $\Rightarrow$ ***True*** is ***True***.)

A careful comparison between these rules and some of the properties of equivalence that appear in Table 7–1 reveals some interesting parallels. For instance, the law of the biconditional given in that table leads directly to the two rules of inference called $\Leftrightarrow$-introduction and $\Leftrightarrow$-elimination in Table 7–2. Similarly, the law of contradiction leads directly to the ~-elimination rule of inference. However, many of the rules of inference have no corresponding precedent among the properties of equivalence.

As an alternative to truth tables, rules of inference can be used to justify the individual steps that appear in a proof that a given proposition is a tautology. Furthermore, as we shall see, proofs are far more versatile than truth tables, since truth tables become unwieldy when there are more than three or four variables and do not provide any basis for reasoning deductively with propositions.

We can convince ourselves fairly easily that these rules of inference make sense in an intuitive way. For instance, the rule of $\wedge$-introduction simply says that if we have proved that p and q are tautologies in two separate earlier steps in the proof, then we can conclude that $p \wedge q$ is a tautology in the current step. Similarly, the $\Rightarrow$-elimination rule (familiarly known as *modus ponens*) says that if we have already proved $p \Rightarrow q$ and p to be tautologies in previous steps, then we can conclude that q is a tautology in the current step.

In our proofs, we will work from step to step to find, in each step, a new tautology that draws us closer to the goal—the last proposition of the proof. We will justify each step either on the basis of an equivalence rule (that is, the step will be the result of substituting the right-hand side of an equivalence from Table 7–1 for the left-hand side, or vice-versa) or on the basis of a rule of inference. In addition to using these sources, we need to develop proof strategies, specific ways of approaching a proof that can be helpful in a variety of different situations. These situations arise not only in the study of logic but also in its various applications in computing, mathematics, and the sciences in general.

Proof Strategies

In this section we present some basic strategies for developing a proof that a given proposition is a tautology using the equivalence laws and the rules of inference. Examples 7.5 through 7.11 provide several illustrations of using rules of inference to deduce conclusions involving abstract propositions. We apply these ideas to propositions involving ordinary English in the next section.

Example 7.5   To prove $p \Rightarrow (q \Rightarrow p)$:

1.	$[p]$	Assumption
2.	$[q]$	Assumption
3.	p	1
4.	$q \Rightarrow p$	$\Rightarrow$-introduction, 2, 3
5.	$p \Rightarrow (q \Rightarrow p)$	$\Rightarrow$-introduction, 1, 4

If we are trying to prove that any proposition of the form $p \Rightarrow q$ is a tautology, it is fair to begin by assuming p in step 1 of the proof, then see if a series of steps can lead to q. If so, the last step in the proof is $p \Rightarrow q$ itself. We used this strategy twice in Example 7.5 and once earlier in Example 7.4. Note that the lack of indentation shows that step 5 is true without making any assumptions.

Using modus ponens   Suppose someone says, "If you open that cage, the tiger will escape," and now assume that I open the cage. Surely the conclusion, by modus ponens, is that the tiger will escape. Similarly, if you hear Joyce say, "If *Our Town* is being performed, I will get tickets," and you subsequently discover that *Our Town* is being performed, you can conclude that Joyce will get tickets (if Joyce is a truthful person). Example 7.6 gives one more illustration of modus ponens in a deductive proof.

Example 7.6   To prove $((p \Rightarrow q) \wedge (r \Rightarrow p) \wedge r) \Rightarrow q$:

1.	$[(p \Rightarrow q) \wedge (r \Rightarrow p) \wedge r]$	Assumption
2.	$r \Rightarrow p$	$\wedge$-elimination, 1
3.	r	$\wedge$-elimination, 1
4.	p	Modus ponens, 2, 3
5.	$p \Rightarrow q$	$\wedge$-elimination, 1
6.	q	Modus ponens, 4, 5
7.	$((p \Rightarrow q) \wedge (r \Rightarrow p) \wedge r) \Rightarrow q$	$\Rightarrow$-introduction, 1, 6

Using $\wedge$-Elimination and Modus Tollens   Another deductive proof is shown in Example 7.7, in which we use both modus ponens and the $\wedge$-elimination rule of inference. As before, we begin the proof with a carefully chosen assumption and work deductively from there.

Example 7.7   To prove $((p \Rightarrow q) \wedge \sim q) \Rightarrow \sim p$:

1.	$[(p \Rightarrow q) \wedge \sim q]$	Assumption
2.	$p \Rightarrow q$	$\wedge$-elimination, 1

3.	$\sim q$	$\wedge$-elimination, 1
4.	$\sim p$	Modus tollens, 2, 3
5.	$((p \Rightarrow q) \wedge \sim q) \Rightarrow \sim p$	$\Rightarrow$-introduction, 1, 4

Using ~-Elimination and ~-Introduction   The second ~-elimination rule says that when we start with a **false** assumption, any conclusion p is a tautology. Thus, we can have a very sophisticated logical argument in which one invalid premise (no matter how minor that premise might seem) makes all of our conclusions uncertain. Many such arguments may be valid, as long as they don't depend on use of the **false** premise.

Example 7.8   To prove $((p \Rightarrow q) \wedge \sim q) \Rightarrow \sim p$ without using modus tollens:

1.	$[(p \Rightarrow q) \wedge \sim q]$	Assumption
2.	$p \Rightarrow q$	$\wedge$-elimination, 1
3.	$\sim q$	$\wedge$-elimination, 1
4.	$[p]$	Assumption
5.	q	Modus ponens, 2
6.	$\sim q$	3
7.	**false**	~-elimination, 5, 6
8.	$\sim p$	~-introduction, 4
9.	$((p \Rightarrow q) \wedge \sim q) \Rightarrow \sim p$	$\Rightarrow$-introduction, 1, 8

Example 7.9 is more complicated.

Example 7.9   To prove $(p \Rightarrow (q \Rightarrow r)) \Rightarrow ((p \Rightarrow q) \Rightarrow (p \Rightarrow r))$:

1.	$[\,p \Rightarrow (q \Rightarrow r)\,]$
2.	$[p \Rightarrow q]$
3.	$[\,p\,]$
4.	q
5	$q \Rightarrow r$
6.	r
7.	$p \Rightarrow r$
8.	$(p \Rightarrow q) \Rightarrow (p \Rightarrow r)$
9.	$(p \Rightarrow (q \Rightarrow r)) \Rightarrow ((p \Rightarrow q) \Rightarrow (p \Rightarrow r))$

(Justifications for the steps in this proof are left to the reader.)

Using the Biconditional in a Proof   For proofs of the form $p \Leftrightarrow q$, an effective strategy is to prove $p \Rightarrow q$ and $q \Rightarrow p$ separately, and then use the rule of $\Leftrightarrow$-introduction as the last step in the proof.

Example 7.10   To prove $(p \Rightarrow q) \Leftrightarrow (\sim p \vee q)$, we must first show that $(\sim p \vee q) \Rightarrow (p \Rightarrow q)$ is a tautology (steps 1–13 below), and then we must show that $(p \Rightarrow q) \Rightarrow (\sim p \vee q)$ is a tautology (steps 14–22). We then apply the rule for $\Leftrightarrow$-introduction as the last step in the proof. The strategy of steps 1–11 is to show that $p \Rightarrow q$ can follow from either of the assumptions $\sim p$ (step 2) or q (step 8).

1.	$[\sim p \vee q]$	Assumption
2.	$[\sim p]$	Assumption
3.	$[p]$	Assumption
4.	$p \wedge \sim p$	$\wedge$-introduction, 2, 3
5.	**false**	$\sim$-elimination, 4
6.	q	$\sim$-elimination, 5
7.	$p \Rightarrow q$	$\Rightarrow$-introduction, 3, 6
8.	$[q]$	Assumption
9.	$[p]$	Assumption
10.	q	8
11.	$p \Rightarrow q$	$\Rightarrow$-introduction, 9, 10
12.	$p \Rightarrow q$	$\vee$-elimination, 1, 2, 7, 8, 11
13.	$(\sim p \vee q) \Rightarrow (p \Rightarrow q)$	$\Rightarrow$-introduction, 1, 12

14.	$[p \Rightarrow q]$	Assumption
15.	$p \vee \sim p$	Law of excluded middle
16.	$[p]$	Assumption
17.	q	Modus ponens, 14, 16
18.	$\sim p \vee q$	$\vee$-introduction, 17
19.	$[\sim p]$	Assumption
20.	$\sim p \vee q$	$\vee$-introduction, 19
21.	$\sim p \vee q$	$\vee$-elimination, 16, 18, 19, 20
22.	$(p \Rightarrow q) \Rightarrow (\sim p \vee q)$	$\Rightarrow$-introduction, 14, 21
23.	$(p \Rightarrow q) \Leftrightarrow (\sim p \vee q)$	$\Leftrightarrow$-introduction, 13, 22

Proof by Contradiction The $\sim$-introduction rule of inference is the basis for an important proof technique known as *proof by contradiction*. A typical application of this technique in mathematics would go as follows: Let T be a triangle with sides 2, 3, and 4. Suppose we want to prove that T is not a right triangle. If we assume the contrary, that T *is* a right triangle, we conclude by the Pythagorean theorem that the square of the length of its hypotenuse is equal to the sum of the squares of the other two sides, that is, $2^2 + 3^2 = 4^2$. But we know that $4 + 9 \neq 16$. This leads, using $\sim$-elimination, to the value **false**. Thus, by $\sim$-introduction, our original assumption—T is a right triangle—is also **false**.

Suppose we want to prove that $((p \Rightarrow q) \wedge p) \Rightarrow q$ is a tautology. Then let us assume that it is **false** in all cases—that is, assume its negation is a tautology—and see if that assumption leads to a contradiction. This is the strategy used in Example 7.11.

Example 7.11   To prove $((p \Rightarrow q) \wedge p) \Rightarrow q$:

1. $[\sim (((p \Rightarrow q) \wedge p) \Rightarrow q)]$ Assumption
2. $\sim (\sim ((p \Rightarrow q) \wedge p) \vee q)$ $\Rightarrow$-elimination, 1
3. $\sim q$ De Morgan's laws, $\wedge$-elimination, 2
4. $((p \Rightarrow q) \wedge p)$ $\wedge$-elimination, 2
5. $(p \Rightarrow q)$ $\wedge$-elimination, 4
6. p $\wedge$-elimination, 4
7. q Modus ponens, 5, 6
8. **false** $\sim$-elimination, 3, 7
9. $((p \Rightarrow q) \wedge p) \Rightarrow q$ $\sim$-introduction, 1, 8

Solving Word Problems

Logic and proof methods can also be used to solve a wide variety of *logic problems*, or *word problems*, in which new information can be deduced from a modest amount of given information. Examples 7.12 and 7.13 use the properties of equivalence, the rules of inference, and the techniques of proof:

Example 7.12   Wishes are horses provided that horses cannot fly. Also, beggars do not ride provided that wishes are not horses. If it is not the case that both beggars ride and wishes are nonequine, then horses can fly. If the inability of horses to fly and the inability of beggars to ride are not alternatives, then beggars are not rich. But beggars do ride. Are beggars rich?

The first step in solving problems like this is to introduce a variable to represent each of the basic propositions that are mentioned. As is typical of word problems like this (and real-life problems as well, for that matter) the phrasing is usually a little tricky to decipher. Nevertheless, suppose we introduce the following variables:

W = wishes are horses
HF = horses can fly
BRD = beggars can ride
$BRCH$ = beggars are rich

We can then represent the five individual statements in the original problem by the following five propositions, respectively:

1. $\sim HF \Rightarrow W$
2. $\sim W \Rightarrow \sim BRD$
3. $\sim (BRD \wedge \sim W) \Rightarrow HF$
4. $\sim (\sim HF \vee \sim BRD) \Rightarrow \sim BRCH$
5. BRD

Using these as we would use assumptions in an ordinary proof, we can draw the following series of inferences, the last being a statement about the variable of interest, BRCH, itself:

6.	W	Modus tollens, 2, 5
7.	$\sim BRD \lor W \Rightarrow HF$	De Morgan's laws, 3
8.	$\sim BRD \lor W$	$\lor$-introduction, 6
9.	HF	Modus ponens, 7, 8
10.	$BRD \land HF$	$\land$-introduction, 5, 9
11.	$(HF \land BRD) \Rightarrow \sim BRCH$	De Morgan's laws, 4
12.	$\sim BRCH$	Modus ponens, 10, 11

We have therefore proved that beggars are not rich.

Example 7.13   On Tuesdays, either Timson is in the churchyard or Agnes is in the church office. Timson is never found in the churchyard without Stanley. Stanley leaves the churchyard on Tuesday only when he goes for a walk with Agnes. If Hutchinson committed the burglary, Stanley was not in the churchyard. The burglary occurred on Tuesday. Could Hutchinson have been the burglar?

We will use the following variables:

p = Timson was in the churchyard
q = Agnes was in the office
s = Stanley was in the churchyard
h = Hutchinson was the burglar
u = The burglary occurred on Tuesday

We can now symbolize the original problem statement as follows:

1.	$u \Rightarrow (p \lor q)$
2.	$p \Rightarrow s$
3.	$\sim s \Rightarrow \sim q$
4.	$h \Rightarrow \sim s$
5.	u

To deduce something about the variable of interest, h, we can reason as follows:

6.	$p \lor q$	Modus ponens, 1, 5
7.	$[q]$	Assumption
8.	s	Modus tollens, 3, 7
9.	$q \Rightarrow s$	$\Rightarrow$-introduction, 7, 8
10.	s	$\lor$-elimination, 2, 6, 9

11. $\sim h$ Modus tollens, 4, 10

Thus, Hutchinson was not the burglar.

EXERCISES

7–1 Use truth tables to show that the following are equivalences:

a. $p \vee (q \wedge r) \equiv (p \vee q) \wedge (p \vee r)$
b. $\sim (p \vee q) \equiv \sim p \wedge \sim q$
c. $p \Rightarrow q \equiv \sim (p \wedge \sim q)$
d. $p \vee \mathbf{false} \equiv p$
e. $p \wedge \mathbf{true} \equiv p$
f. $p \wedge (p \vee q) \equiv p$

7–2 Simplify the following propositions by finding an equivalent proposition with fewer operators and/or variables:

a. $(p \vee q) \wedge (\sim p \vee \sim q)$
b. $(p \wedge q) \vee (p \wedge \sim q) \vee (\sim p \wedge q) \vee (\sim p \wedge \sim q)$
c. $p \vee (\sim p \wedge q)$
d. $\sim p \Rightarrow p$
e. $p \Rightarrow \sim p$
f. $((p \wedge q) \Rightarrow p) \Rightarrow (p \vee q)$
g. $(p \Rightarrow (q \wedge \sim q)) \Rightarrow \sim p$

7–3 Give a proof for each of the following tautologies, using the rules of inference.

a. $((p \Rightarrow r) \wedge (r \Rightarrow q)) \Rightarrow (p \Rightarrow q)$
b. $((p \vee q) \wedge (p \Rightarrow s) \wedge (q \Rightarrow s)) \Rightarrow s$

7–4 Justify the steps in each of the following two proofs:

a. $((p \Rightarrow q) \wedge (q \Rightarrow r)) \Rightarrow (p \Rightarrow r)$
   $((\sim p \vee q) \wedge (\sim q \vee r)) \Rightarrow (\sim p \vee r)$
   $\sim ((\sim p \vee q) \wedge (\sim q \vee r)) \vee (\sim p \vee r)$
   $(\sim (\sim p \vee q) \vee \sim (\sim q \vee r)) \vee (\sim p \vee r)$
   $(p \wedge \sim q) \vee (q \wedge \sim r) \vee (\sim p \vee r)$
   $((p \wedge \sim q) \vee \sim p) \vee ((q \wedge \sim r) \vee r)$
   $(\sim p \vee (p \wedge \sim q)) \vee (r \vee (q \wedge \sim r))$

$$((\sim p \vee p) \wedge (\sim p \vee \sim q)) \vee ((r \vee q) \wedge (r \vee \sim r))$$
$$\textbf{\textit{true}} \wedge (\sim p \vee \sim q) \vee (r \vee q) \wedge \textbf{\textit{true}}$$
$$(\sim p \vee \sim q) \vee (r \vee q)$$
$$\sim p \vee (q \vee \sim q) \vee r$$
$$\sim p \vee \textbf{\textit{true}} \vee r$$
$$\textbf{\textit{true}}$$

b. $(p \Rightarrow (q \wedge \sim q)) \Rightarrow \sim p$
$$(p \Rightarrow \textbf{\textit{false}}) \Rightarrow \sim p$$
$$\sim (p \wedge \sim \textbf{\textit{false}}) \Rightarrow \sim p$$
$$\sim (p \wedge \textbf{\textit{true}}) \Rightarrow \sim p$$
$$\sim p \Rightarrow \sim p$$
$$\sim p \vee p$$
$$\textbf{\textit{true}}$$

7–5   The **nand** function is defined as follows:

p	q	p **nand** q
true	true	false
true	false	true
false	true	true
false	false	true

Show that the operators $\sim$, $\wedge$, $\vee$, and $\Rightarrow$ can all be defined in terms of **nand**. That is, find propositions made up of only p's, q's, and **nand**'s whose truth tables match those for $\sim p$, $p \vee q$, $p \wedge q$, and $p \Rightarrow q$, respectively.

7–6   Demonstrate that each of the following propositions is a tautology by using a series of rules of equivalence that makes them equivalent to **true**:

a. $(\sim p \vee q) \Rightarrow (q \vee \sim p)$
b. $(p \Rightarrow q) \Leftrightarrow (\sim q \Rightarrow \sim p)$
c. $(p \Rightarrow \sim p) \Rightarrow \sim p$
d. $((p \vee q) \wedge \sim p) \Rightarrow q$
e. $((p \vee q) \wedge (p \Rightarrow s) \wedge (q \Rightarrow s)) \Rightarrow s$
f. $((p \Rightarrow q) \wedge (p \Rightarrow r)) \Rightarrow (p \Rightarrow q \wedge r)$
g. $((p \Rightarrow q) \wedge (r \Rightarrow s)) \Rightarrow ((p \vee r) \Rightarrow (q \vee s))$
h. $((p \Rightarrow q) \wedge (r \Rightarrow s) \wedge (\sim q \vee \sim s)) \Rightarrow \sim p \vee \sim r$

7–7   Using the rules of inference, give a proof for each of the tautologies listed in Exercise 7–6.

7–8 Consider the proposition $((p \vee q) \wedge \sim p) \Rightarrow q$.

    a.   Show that it is a tautology, using a truth table.

    b.   Show that it is equivalent to the following statement by assigning appropriate variables to each of the phrases.

        "Either the Red Sox are better than the A's or the Pirates are better than the Reds. The Red Sox are not better than the A's. Therefore, the Pirates are better than the Reds."

    c.   Prove that this proposition is a tautology by using appropriate equivalences and rules of inference. Hint: Let step 1 in your proof be the assumption that the left-hand side of this implication is true, and then conclude using $\Rightarrow$-introduction.

7–9 On Paradox Island, residents belong to one of two clans. One clan always tells the truth and the other clan always lies. A visitor to Paradox Island encounters three residents, Einstein, Planck, and Bohr. Einstein says "Either I or Bohr belongs to a different clan from the other two." To which clan does Bohr belong?[3]

7–10 Abigail, Bridget, and Claudia often eat dinner together. Each orders either coffee or tea after dinner. If Abigail orders coffee, then Bridget orders the drink that Claudia orders. If Bridget orders coffee, then Abigail orders the drink that Claudia doesn't order. If Claudia orders tea, then Abigail orders the drink that Bridget orders. Which one (if any) of the three always orders the same drink after dinner?

PREDICATES AND PROOF BY INDUCTION

Reasoning with predicates is similar to reasoning with propositions because there are rules of inference that regulate which steps are allowed. Frequently, we take representative values for the variables in a predicate (so that it becomes a proposition) and use the rules of inference for propositions. However, reasoning with predicates involves some additional rules of inference, which are summarized in Table 7–3.

As Table 7–3 suggests, the $\exists$-introduction and $\exists$-elimination rules are reminiscent of De Morgan's laws. The $\forall$-introduction and $\forall$-elimination rules are also widely used in proofs. The first says that if we can establish that $R \Rightarrow P$ is valid, then we can assert, in a later step of the proof, that $\forall R(i) : P(i)$ is also valid. The second says that if $\forall R(i) : P(i)$ is valid, then for any particular value i_0 of i, $R(i_0) \Rightarrow P(i_0)$ is also valid.

---

3.   Adapted from *The Great Book of Mind Teasers and Mind Puzzles* by George J. Summers, New York, Sterling Publishing Co., 1986.

Suppose we want to establish that every even integer greater than 2 is not prime. In this case R is the predicate

i is an integer $\wedge$ $(i > 2)$ $\wedge$ i is even

and P is the predicate

i is not prime

We need to show that $R \Rightarrow P$ is valid. This is typically done by taking a representative i_0 that satisfies R and showing that i_0 must satisfy P also. Thus our proof might begin with:

Let i_0 be any even integer for which $i_0 > 2$.

From this assumption, we conclude that i is not prime (since i's evenness requires that 2 be a factor of i). Therefore, we conclude that all even integers i which are greater than 2 cannot be prime.

TABLE 7–3   RULES OF INFERENCE FOR QUANTIFIED PREDICATES

$\forall$-introduction	$\forall$-elimination
$\dfrac{R \Rightarrow P}{\forall\ R(i) : P(i)}$	$\dfrac{\forall\ R(i) : P(i)}{R(i_0) \Rightarrow P(i_0)}$
$\exists$-introduction	$\exists$-elimination
$\dfrac{\forall\ R(i) : P(i)}{\sim \exists\ R(i) :\sim P(i)}$	$\dfrac{\exists\ R(i) : P(i)}{\sim \forall\ R(i) :\sim P(i)}$

Proof by Induction   The validity of predicates with quantifiers can often be established by a method of proof known as *mathematical induction* (or *induction*). This is a very important concept in programming as well as in mathematics. That is, inductive methods are used both in the design of programs and in their formal verification. Induction also has strong connections with the mathematical notions of recursive functions and their applications in problem solving and programming.

To prove the validity of the predicate $\forall\ R(n) : P(n)$ in the special case where $R(n)$ has the form $n \in \{1, 2, \ldots\}$, we consider two cases separately:

Base case: Prove $P(1)$.

Induction step: Prove $P(i) \Rightarrow P(i+1)$ for any $i \geq 1$.

The base case simply establishes the validity of P for the starting value, $i = 1$. The induction step says that, if we can show that $P(i) \Rightarrow P(i+1)$ for any i, then this establishes the validity of $P(1) \Rightarrow P(2) \Rightarrow \ldots$. Now, since $P(1)$ is valid, surely $P(2)$ is valid [since $P(1) \Rightarrow P(2)$], and thus so is $P(3)$ [since $P(2) \Rightarrow P(3)$], and so on.

The idea of induction can be illustrated by an analogy. Suppose someone wants to climb a flight of stairs. Only two skills are needed to complete this process—the skill to get to the first stair and the skill to walk from each stair to the next one. With these two skills, one can climb the stairs without having to be immediately concerned with how to get to any one particular stair. Furthermore, these two skills make the length of the staircase irrelevant to completing the process by induction. That is, the skill of getting to the first stair is analogous with proving the base case $P(1)$. The skill of walking from the ith stair to the $i+1$st stair is analogous with proving the induction step $P(i) \Rightarrow P(i+1)$ for any $i \geq 1$. The statement $\forall n \in \{1, 2, \ldots\} : P(n)$ is the statement that $P(n)$ is true for every n and is therefore analogous to being able to climb the stairs.

While we cannot use a truth table to justify the process of induction, we can justify it by modus ponens and our knowledge of the properties of the natural numbers. That is, if we know that $P(1)$ is true and that $\forall i \in \{1, 2, \ldots\} : P(i) \Rightarrow P(i + 1)$, we can write the following statements by substituting different integers for i:

$P(1)$

$P(1) \Rightarrow P(2)$

$P(2) \Rightarrow P(3)$

...

Combining the first two lines, we can conclude by modus ponens that $P(2)$ is valid. Combining the truth of $P(2)$ with the third line, we can conclude again by modus ponens that $P(3)$ is true. We can continue in this fashion indefinitely, so that $\forall n \in \{1, 2, \ldots\} : P(n)$ is valid.

Example 7.14   Suppose we want to prove by induction that

$$\forall n > 0: \sum_{j=1}^{n} j = \frac{n(n + 1)}{2}.$$ Consider the two cases:

Base case:

Prove that $\displaystyle\sum_{j=1}^{1} j = \frac{1(1 + 1)}{2}$.

Induction step:

Prove that $\displaystyle\sum_{j=1}^{i} j = \frac{i(i+1)}{2} \Rightarrow \sum_{j=1}^{i+1} j = \frac{(i+1)((i+1)+1)}{2}$.

The base case is apparent by arithmetic. That is, $1 = \frac{2}{2}$. The induction step is not too difficult to prove either, using the properties of finite sums.

$$
\begin{aligned}
\sum_{j=1}^{i+1} j &= \sum_{j=1}^{i} j + (i+1) & \text{Property of } \Sigma \\
&= \frac{i(i+1)}{2} + (i+1) & \text{Assuming } \sum_{j=1}^{i} j = \frac{i(i+1)}{2} \\
&= \frac{i(i+1)}{2} + \frac{2(i+1)}{2} & \text{Algebra} \\
&= \frac{(i+1)[(i+1)+1]}{2} & \text{Algebra}
\end{aligned}
$$

At first it may appear that mathematical induction is circular reasoning. What is actually happening, however, is some "hypothetical thinking." We are saying, "Suppose $P(n)$ is true. Can we get from there to $P(n+1)$?" This does not prove $P(n+1)$ but only that $P(n)$ implies $P(n+1)$. Consider again the analogy of walking up stairs. We are saying, in essence, "Suppose I am on the nth step. Can I get from there to the next one?" This does not say that we can get to the nth step, only that we can go from there to the $n+1$st. It is the combination of the ability to go from each step to the next one and the ability to get to the first one [i.e., to prove $P(1)$] that makes it possible to get to the nth.

Example 7.15   Prove that if $0 < r < 1$ then

$$\sum_{i=0}^{n} r^i = \frac{1 - r^{n+1}}{1 - r}$$

First let $n = 0$. The left- and right-hand sides (LHS and RHS) of the above equation become:

$$\text{LHS} = \sum_{i=0}^{0} r^i = r^0 = 1, \text{ since } r \neq 0$$

$$\text{RHS} = \frac{1-r}{1-r} = 1, \text{ since } r \neq 1$$

This completes the base case. Now assume $P(n)$, that is assume that

$$(7.1) \quad \sum_{i=0}^{n} r^i = \frac{1 - r^{n+1}}{1 - r}$$

We will show that this implies

$$\sum_{i=0}^{n+1} r^i = \frac{1 - r^{n+2}}{1 - r}$$

Adding r^{n+1} to both sides of Equation 7.1, we get

$$\text{LHS} = \sum_{i=0}^{n} r^i + r^{n+1} = \sum_{i=0}^{n+1} r^i$$

$$\text{RHS} = \frac{1 - r^{n+1}}{1 - r} + r^{n+1}$$

$$= \frac{1 - r^{n+2}}{1 - r}$$

Example 7.16   Let S be any finite set and suppose S has n members. Show by induction that S has 2^n subsets.

Solution   We let $P(S)$ denote the collection of all of the subsets of S. Suppose $n = 0$. Then $S = \phi$. Hence $P(S) = \{\phi\}$, and hence S has 1 ($= 2^0$) subset. This is the base case for the inductive proof.

Now suppose any set S with n members has 2^n subsets. To prove the induction step, let T be an arbitrary set with $n+1$ members and denote T by

$$T = \{t_1, t_2, ..., t_n, t_{n+1}\}$$

The subsets of T can be split into two distinct collections—those that include t_{n+1} and those that do not. Every subset of $\{t_1, t_2, ..., t_n\}$ is also a subset of T. Hence there are, by the induction hypothesis, 2^n subsets of T which do not include t_{n+1}. Each set which includes t_{n+1} can be looked upon as the union of a subset of $\{t_1, t_2, ..., t_n\}$ and $\{t_{n+1}\}$. Hence there are also 2^n sets that include t_{n+1}. Thus T has $2^n + 2^n = 2 \times 2^n = 2^{n+1}$ subsets.

One way to visualize this proof is to list the subsets as follows:

Not including t_{n+1}	Including t_{n+1}
ϕ	$\{t_{n+1}\}$
$\{t_1\}$	$\{t_1, t_{n+1}\}$
$\{t_2\}$	$\{t_2, t_{n+1}\}$
$\{t_1, t_2\}$	$\{t_1, t_2, t_{n+1}\}$
.	.
.	.
.	.
$\{t_1, t_2, ..., t_n\}$	$\{t_1, t_2, ..., t_n, t_{n+1}\}$

The left-hand list is all the subsets of $\{t_1, t_2, ..., t_n\}$. The right-hand list is set up so that each set is the union of $\{t_{n+1}\}$ with the corresponding set from the left-hand list. Thus, there are 2^n subsets in each list.

Note that, in spite of its name, proof by induction actually involves a form of deductive reasoning, not a form of inductive reasoning. Inductive reasoning refers to the technique found in science that is sometimes called the *scientific method*; it involves inferring general principles from specific cases. For instance, the astronomer Kepler used inductive reasoning in inferring laws for planetary motion from the voluminous data he had collected. Mathematical induction, however, follows the typical deductive process—working from axioms, previously proven theorems, and definitions to new theorems by using rules of inference.

EXERCISES

7–11 Assume that the function *Factorial: N → N* is defined recursively as follows:

Factorial (1) = 1
Factorial (n) = n × *Factorial* (n–1)   for n > 1

Prove by induction on n that this definition is equivalent to the nonrecursive definition:

Factorial (n) = 1 × 2 × ... × (n − 1) × n

7–12 Suppose that a function *f*(n) is defined by the following rule:

f(0) = 1
f(n+1) = 2*f*(n) for all n > 0

Show by induction that *f*(n) = 2^n .

7–13 Show that the sum of the first n odd numbers is n^2.

7–14 Prove the following generalizations of De Morgan's laws:

a. $(\bigcup_{i=0}^{n} A_i)' = \bigcap_{i=0}^{n} A_i'$

    (Note: $\bigcup_{i=0}^{n} A_i$ means $A_0 \cup A_1 \cup \cdots \cup A_n$)

b. $(\bigcap_{i=0}^{n} A_i)' = \bigcup_{i=0}^{n} A_i'$

    (Note: $\bigcap_{i=0}^{n} A_i$ means $A_0 \cap A_1 \cap \cdots \cap A_n$)

7–15 Verify the following relationships by mathematical induction:

a. $\displaystyle\sum_{i=0}^{n} (i(i+1)) = \frac{n(n+1)(n+2)}{3}$

b. $\displaystyle\sum_{i=0}^{n} i^2 = \frac{n(n+1)(2n+1)}{6}$

c. $\displaystyle\sum_{i=0}^{n} i^3 = \frac{n^2(n+1)^2}{4}$

ENSURING CORRECTNESS: PROGRAM VERIFICATION

As a general methodology, program verification has as its goal the rigorous application of mathematical logic to formally prove that the program appearing between its precondition and postcondition actually corroborates those specifications under all possible circumstances of execution. Formal verification, in this sense, is a fairly new development in the software field. We believe that a basic understanding of the methods, goals, and limitations of formal verification is important. This subject is truly on the "cutting edge" of research in the discipline of computing. Program verification also provides readers with an alternative view of program correctness that attempts to address the major weakness of conventional software testing techniques: that they can never *guarantee* corrrectness.

The style of verification used here is informal, emphasizing principles rather than belaboring the proof process with a great deal of detail. We start by assuming that the familiar properties of numbers and arithmetic that we know from mathematics are generally upheld when arithmetic is used in programs. This is a strong assumption. We already know, for example, that the numbers

```
{
  // preconditions
  //
   s₁;
  //
   s₂;
  //
    .
    .
    .
  //
   sₙ;
  //
  // postconditions
}
```

FIGURE 7–1   Initial layout for a proof tableau: the empty tableau.

in mathematics—integers and reals—do not all have exact representations in C++ programming. We also know that real and integer arithmetic in mathematics always yields exact results, while in computation an error is introduced in many cases. For the purposes of this introduction, we ignore these details in order to simplify the presentation and develop an appreciation for its principles and general methodology.

The Proof Tableau

To verify a program, we develop a *proof tableau*. An initial proof tableau, or "empty tableau," is just a listing of the body of the program with its preconditions, postconditions, and an empty comment placed before and after each statement, as shown in Figure 7–1. The goal of verification is to fill this empty tableau with valid assertions. Each statement in the program must precede and follow an assertion we can justify by a systematic line of reasoning that leads from other assertions whose validity has already been established. Thus, program verification is the process of developing a series of assertions (and accompanying reasons) in a way that parallels the development of a proof in logic. The result of this process is called a *proof of the program's correctness*, or simply a *proof*.

Definition   A *proof* is a set of assertions P_1, P_2, ..., P_{n+1} which, when inserted successively between the statements s_1, s_2, ..., s_n in an empty tableau, produces the following completed proof tableau:

```
{
// preconditions
//  P₁
   s₁ ;
//  P₂
   s₂ ;
   ...
//  Pₙ
   sₙ ;
//  Pₙ₊₁
// postconditions
}
```

In this, the following assertions are valid (i.e., are tautologies):

1. $preconditions \Rightarrow P_1$
2. `// Pᵢ sᵢ ; // Pᵢ₊₁` for all i in $\{1, \ldots, n\}$
3. $P_{n+1} \Rightarrow postconditions$

The notation `// Pᵢ sᵢ; // Pᵢ₊₁` means that, relative to the ith statement `sᵢ;` in the program, if the assertion P_i is valid before `sᵢ;` executes, then the assertion P_{i+1} will be valid after `sᵢ;` executes. In other words, P_i and P_{i+1} are respectively preconditions and postconditions for the statement `sᵢ;`.

Suppose we have the program and empty tableau shown in Figure 7–2. That is, we want to prove the correctness of that program, which is designed to compute and display the product of any two input numbers n1 and n2.

```
{
// pre: input == n1 n2 && output == empty

//
                          (s₁)
   cin >> x >> y ;  ←⟍___⟋
//
                          (s₂)
   z = x * y ;      ←⟍___⟋
//
                          (s₃)
   cout << z ;      ←⟍___⟋
//

// post: input == empty && output == n1 * n2
}
```

FIGURE 7–2   Empty tableau for a simple three-statement program.

To complete this proof, we need to discover and justify the tableau's assertions P_1 through P_4, one by one, until the tableau is complete. The result is shown in Figure 7–3.

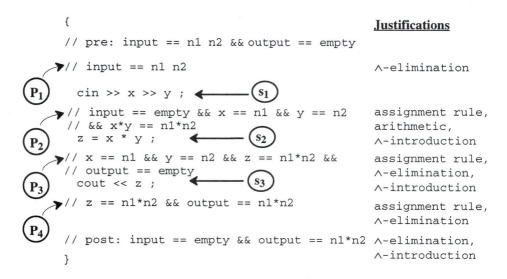

```
{                                                                    Justifications
    // pre: input == n1 n2 && output == empty

    // input == n1 n2                                        ∧-elimination
P₁      cin >> x >> y ;              ← s₁
    // input == empty && x == n1 && y == n2    assignment rule,
    // && x*y == n1*n2                         arithmetic,
P₂      z = x * y ;                  ← s₂       ∧-introduction
    // x == n1 && y == n2 && z == n1*n2 &&     assignment rule,
    // output == empty                         ∧-elimination,
P₃      cout << z ;                  ← s₃       ∧-introduction
    // z == n1*n2 && output == n1*n2           assignment rule,
                                               ∧-elimination
P₄
    // post: input == empty && output == n1*n2 ∧-elimination,
}                                              ∧-introduction
```

FIGURE 7–3   Completed proof tableau for a simple program.

The justifications shown in the right-hand column of Figure 7–3 are based on the application of logical equivalences and rules of inference to the sequence of C++ statements. Some of these justifications (e.g., arithmetic) are based on the normal assumptions we make about the properties of arithmetic. Others (e.g., ∧-introduction) are carried over from the rules of inference in logic. Still others (e.g., assignment rule) are rules of inference that reflect properties of individual C++ statements, and will be introduced below. The completed proof tableau thus mirrors the style of an ordinary proof in logic.

The Assignment Rule of Inference

Like other mathematical proof systems, program verification uses axioms and rules of inference. The rules of inference are generalizations about the behavior of specific kinds of program statements in C++ programs. These rules provide specific guidance for deriving new assertions from existing ones for particular types of statements.

In formal program verification, the inference system, and especially the rules of inference, are much more elaborate than what is presented here. We will consider four basic rules of inference for programs: the *assignment rule*, the *procedure rule*, the *conditional rule*, and the *loop rule*.

Definition   The assignment rule of inference.

a. `// P(e)   v = e ; //`
─────────────────────────────────
`// P(e)   v = e ; // P(v)`

b. `// input == n   cin >> v ; //`
───
`// input == n   cin >> v ; // input == empty && v == n`

c. `// output == empty && e == n   cout << e ; //`
───
`// output == empty && e == n   cout << e ; // output == e`

Part *a* of this rule says, in effect, that if a proposition P is valid for the state of expression e *before* the assignment v = e is executed, then we can infer the same proposition about the state of variable v *after* the assignment statement is executed.

Parts *b* and *c* of the assignment rule acknowledge the fact that the `cin` and `cout` statements also have the effect of assignment. In the `cin` statement, the source of a value for the assignment is the input stream and the target is the variable v. In the `cout` statement, the source of the assignment is the expression e and the target is the output stream itself. Part *b* of the assignment rule means, in effect, that `cin >> v` *removes* a value n from the input stream and assigns it to the variable v. Part *c* says that `cout << e` *appends a copy* of the current value n of expression e to the output stream. This is a straightforward formalization of what we already understand about the actions of `cin` and `cout` when we use them in our programs.

For example, in the program in Figure 7–2, suppose we know only that the values of x and y are some numbers n1 and n2 before execution of the assignment z = x*y. Then we also know that x*y == n1*n2 by the rules of arithmetic. We can use this knowledge in the following way:

```
// x*y == n1*n2
   z = x*y ;
// z == n1*n2                              assignment rule
```

All we have done in making this inference is to substitute z for all occurrences of the expression x*y in the known proposition P(x*y) to achieve the new proposition P(z). Note that we have marked this inference in the proof with a justification in the right-hand margin, so that the reason for the inference is clear. This is consistent with the style of proof that is generally used in logic.

It is also clear that this rule is easily extended to accommodate `cin` and `cout` statements having two or more variables. For simplicity, we will not encumber this rule by trying to formalize all these variations, but will use this rule in our proofs as if it had been generalized in these ways.

For another example, consider the first statement of the program in Figure 7–2, for which the following is true when we begin reasoning about it:

```
// input == n1 n2
   cin >> x >> y ;
//
```

Part *b* of the assignment rule allows us to draw the following inference:

```
// input == n1 n2
   cin >> x >> y ;
// input == empty && x == n1 && y == n2      assignment rule
```

This formally justifies that the values of x and y are assigned by a cin statement, and those values are simultaneously deleted from the input stream.

Similarly, part *c* of the assignment rule allows us to reason through the cout statement in Figure 7–2, beginning with

```
// z == n1*n2 && output == empty
   cout << z ;
//
```

The important inference here is that z must have the value n1*n2 in order for that value to appear in the output stream. Formally, we draw this conclusion by applying the assignment rule as follows:

```
// z == n1*n2 && output == empty
   cout << z ;
// output == n1*n2                           assignment rule
```

Reasoning about programs always requires that we actively use our knowledge about the properties of arithmetic, even though we do not usually need to explicitly write down all the details of that knowledge during the proof process itself. Here is another example. Suppose we know that the value of a variable i is nonnegative immediately before the assignment i = i+1 is executed in a program. How can the assignment rule help us to reason through this? Formally, we start with

```
// i >= 0
   i = i+1 ;
//
```

From this, using the assignment rule *and* the properties of inequalities in arithmetic, we infer the following:

```
// i >= 0
   i = i+1 ;
// i > 0                             assignment rule, arithmetic
```

If we analyze the exact details of this step, we discover that if `i >= 0` before the assignment, then `i+1 >= 1`. Thus, for the purposes of the assignment rule, we identify the variable `v` as `i`, the expression `e` as `i+1`, and the assertion `P(e)` as `i+1 >= 1`. From this, we can infer `P(v)`, or `i >= 1`. Applying properties of arithmetic again, we can rewrite this assertion in terms of the variable `i`, yielding `i > 0`.

Reusing the Rules of Inference from Logic

When we write a program proof, in addition to the rules that define program behavior and the properties of arithmetic, we use rules of inference. These rules allow assertions to "move" through a program, so that we can use them to draw new inferences at other locations. We can therefore achieve a coherent thread of reasoning that spans the program from beginning to end.

To illustrate, consider again the simple program whose proof appears in Figure 7–3. Note how we used the assignment rule to develop certain parts of the assertions P_1 through P_4. But what about their interconnections? For example, how do we justify a migration of the assertion `input == empty` from P_2, where it originates, through P_3 and P_4, and finally into the postcondition, where it is needed to complete the proof? Although the assignment rule doesn't allow us to justify this migration, the rules of inference from logic do.

The first step of the proof in Figure 7–3 contains the assertion P_1

```
// input == n1 n2
```

which is inferred, by ∧-elimination, from the precondition

```
// input == n1 n2 && output == empty
```

The derivation of P_2 results from combining three different steps: the assignment rule, the properties of arithmetic, and the ∧-introduction rule of inference. In particular, the proposition `x*y == n1*n2` appears in P_2 in preparation for deriving assertion P_3 from P_2 and s_2.

The rules of ∧-introduction and ∧-elimination are used throughout the proof. These rules of inference must be applied with special care, however, when the predicate to be added comes from a distant place in an earlier part of the program. For example, consider the reintroduction of the assertion `output == empty` into proposition P_3 after it had been missing from P_1 and P_2. We can do this only if no intervening statements in the program could have been executed that would invalidate this predicate: that is, no `cout` statements (or, equivalently, no applications of Part c of the assignment rule) intervene between the location where the predicate was last valid and the location where it is being reintroduced.

Rules for Conditionals

Programs contain other types of statements besides those that assign values to variables. In writing program proofs, therefore, we need to have access to axioms for reasoning about conditionals (if statements), procedure and function invocations, and loops. There are rules of inference that apply to these statement types.

Definition   The conditional rule of inference.

a.   // P && B s ; // Q
       P && !B $\Rightarrow$ Q
       _____
       // P if (B) s ; // Q

b.   // P && B s_1 ; // Q
       // P && !B s_2 ; // Q
       _____
       // P   if (B) s_1 ; else s_2 ; // Q

Part *a* allows us to infer the validity of Q through the conditional statement if we can infer it independently through either alternative—in one both P and B are **true** and we execute statement s, and in the other B is **false** and P $\Rightarrow$ Q is valid anyway. Part *b* is a simple extension in which the validity of Q is established independently through each of the two alternative paths—execution of s_1 (when B is **true**) or execution of s_2 (when B is **false**).

Consider the following assignment and conditional statements, which are designed to leave the value of variable z with the larger of the values of variables x and y.

```
z = x;
if (x <= y)
    z = y ;
```

To verify this, we want to establish the validity of assertion Q

```
Q: z == x && x > y || z == y && x <= y
```

which is a more formal way of describing the desired outcome for z. Both an assignment statement and a conditional statement appear in this sequence, so we will need to use both the assignment rule and the conditional rule of inference in verifying it. Thus, we can start with the following:

```
//
    z = x ;
// z == x
if (x <= y)
    z = y ;
// x > y && z == x || x <= y && z == y
```

In using the conditional rule, we identify P as z == x (P's validity follows from the line above it and the assignment rule) and B as x <= y. Thus, we must now justify the validity of assertion Q to complete the proof. Substituting for B, P, and Q in the conditional rule gives the following:

```
// z == x && x <= y
   z = y ;
// z == x && x > y || z == y && x <= y &&
// z == x && !(x <= y) ⇒ z == x && x > y || z == y && x <= y
```

To show the validity of this assertion, we consider the two cases x <= y and !(x <= y), which we know from arithmetic are the only possibilities.

When x <= y line 1 is valid, since the assignment z = y will be made and the assignment rule guarantees z==y as a consequent. The rule of ∧-introduction allows us to infer z==y && x<=y, and the rule of ∨-introduction allows us finally to infer z==x && x>y || z==y && x<=y. Line 2 is also valid, trivially, since !(x<=y) is **false** and **false** ⇒ p is valid for any proposition p.

In the second case, x>y, the second line of the above disjunction is valid. That is, both !(x<=y) (or equivalently, x>y) and z==x are valid, and therefore so is their conjunction, by ∧-introduction. But

```
z == x && !(x <= y)
```

is equivalent to

```
z == x && x > y
```

so that the entirety of line 2 has the form of an assertion p ⇒ p || q, which is valid by ∨-introduction. Line 1 is also valid, trivially, since x <= y is **false**. This completes the justification for assertion Q.

Consider the following alternative method for assigning the variable z the value of the larger of variables x and y.

```
if (x > y)
   z = x ;
else
   z = y ;
```

To verify this, we want to establish again the validity of assertion Q:

```
Q: z == x && x > y || z == y && x <= y
```

Again we use the conditional rule of inference along with other appropriate rules of inference, arithmetic, and identities. We begin with a partial proof tableau:

```
// true
if (x > y)
  z = x ;
else
  z = y ;
// z == x && x > y || z == y && x <= y
```

We identify B as $x > y$, s_1 as $z == x$, s_2 as $z == y$, and P as **true** (this latter means, in effect, that we don't care what the values of these variables are prior to execution of the conditional statement). Thus, part *b* of the conditional rule yields the following form, which we must show is valid in order to establish the validity of Q itself.

```
// true && x > y
  z = x ;
// z == x && x > y || z == y || x <= y
```

and

```
// true && !(x > y)
  z = y ;
// z == x && x > y || z == y && x <= y
```

Let's look at each line of this disjunction separately, as we did in the previous example. Line 1 corresponds to the case where $x > y$. Using the assignment rule, the identity property of the value **true**, and $\land$-introduction, we reach the following:

```
// x > y
  z = x ;
  // z == x && x > y
```

Now by $\lor$-introduction, we validate line 1 under the assumption $x>y$. Line 2 covers the alternative case, in which we assume $x <= y$. We can validate line 2 using arguments similar to those that were given for line 1.

Verifying Loops

To verify a loop in a program, it is necessary to take two independent steps: we must find and justify its associated assertions, and then we must verify its invariant by induction.

We can explain the meaning of a loop by "unraveling" it. That is, if we rewrite a loop as a sequence of occurrences of the loop body, we can see the exact nature of the generalization that the loop itself represents. Consider the while loop in Figure 7–4, which sums the integers from 1 to 5.

```
sum = 0 ;
i = 1 ;
while (i<=5)
{
    sum = sum+i ;
    i = i+1 ;
}
```

FIGURE 7–4   A simple while loop.

The five executions of the body of this loop can be unraveled in the following way:

```
sum = sum + i ;
i = i+1 ;
sum = sum + i ;
i = i+1 ;
sum = sum + i ;
i = i+1 ;
sum = sum + i ;
i = i+1 ;
sum = sum + i ;
i = i+1 ;
```

Recall the notion of a loop invariant, which is defined as follows:

Definition   A loop *invariant* is an assertion that is valid before and after every repetition of the loop, including the first repetition and the last.

An invariant for our above loop is

```
// inv: (sum == Sum j in {1,...,i-1}: j) && 1<=i<=6
```

We can see that this invariant is true, both before and after each repetition of the while loop. In particular, the invariant explains the following detailed expansion of the loop's individual steps:

```
// sum == 0 && i == 1
    sum = sum + i ;
    i = i+1 ;
// sum == 0+1 && i == 2
    sum = sum + i ;
    i = i+1 ;
// sum == 0+1+2 && i == 3
    sum = sum + i ;
    i = i+1 ;
// sum == 0+1+2+3 && i == 4
    sum = sum + i ;
    i = i+1 ;
// sum == 0+1+2+3+4 && i == 5
```

```
    sum = sum + i ;
    i = i+1 ;
// sum == 0+1+2+3+4+5 && i == 6
```

Another aspect of loops that is important for verification is that they terminate. That is, we are interested only in *controlled loops*, loops that will always terminate after a finite number of steps, no matter what the state of the variables at the time the loop begins execution. Different ways of describing this termination condition lead to three different types of loops, so we have three variations of the loop rule of inference. Each of these variations uses the invariant and the presumption of termination in a different way.

Definition   The loop rule of inference.

a.   `// inv && B  s ;  // inv`
  ──────────────────────────────────────
  `// inv  while (B) s ;  // inv && !B`

b.   `// inv s ;  // inv`
  ──────────────────────────────────────
  `// inv do { s ; } while (B) ;  // inv && B`

c.   `// inv && 1 ≤ i ≤ n s ;  // inv`
  ──────────────────────────────────────
  `// inv for (i=1; i<=n; i++) s ;  // inv && i == n+1`

Part *a* of this rule says, in effect, that if

`// inv && B  s ;  // inv`

is valid for a *single* execution of the loop's body `s`, then

`// inv  while (B) s ;  // inv && !B`

is valid for the entire loop. Note, in particular, that the condition for termination of the loop, `!B`, is explicit in this expression. Parts *b* and *c* of the loop rule are similar, though they are applicable to different kinds of C++ loops.

Reconsider the `while` loop in Figure 7–4. The loop rule allows us to infer the following assertions, in which `B` is the expression `i<=5`.

```
sum = 0 ;
i = 1 ;
while (i<=5)
// inv: (sum == Sum j in {1,...,i-1}: j) && 1<=i<=6
{
    sum = sum+i ;
    i = i+1 ;
}
// (sum == Sum j in {1,...,i-1}: j) && 1<=i<=6 && !(i<=5)
```

This last assertion simplifies to

```
// (sum == Sum j in {1,...,5}: j) && i == 6
```

by the application of elementary rules of arithmetic.

Considering forms *b* and *c* of the loop rule, we can see that the relationship between the invariant and the termination condition in each of these is slightly different, and yet each accurately reflects the meaning of the do and for statements. For example, if we rewrite the loop in Figure 7–4 as a do loop, the loop rule gives us the following:

```
sum = 0 ;
i = 1 ;
do
// inv: (sum == Sum j in {1,...,i-1}: j) && 1<=i<=6
{
  sum = sum+i ;
  i = i+1 ;
} while (i<=5) ;
// sum == Sum j ∈ {1,...,i-1}: j && 1<=i<=6 && i>5
```

The expression B is again i<=5, which specifies the condition under which the loop will continue. We can again simplify as follows, using the rules of arithmetic:

```
// (sum == Sum j in {1,...,5}: j) && i == 6
```

Finally, if we rewrite the simple loop in Figure 7–4 as a for loop, we see again that the loop rule generates the following assertion:

```
sum = 0 ;
for (i=1; i<=5; i++)
// inv: (sum == Sum j in {1,...,i-1}: j) && 1<=i<=6
  sum = sum+i ;
// (sum == Sum j in {1,...,i-1}: j) && 1<=i<=6 && i==6
```

Here, the last assertion again simplifies to

```
// (sum == Sum j in {1,...,5}: j) && i == 6
```

Using Induction to Verify the Invariant   So far, we have accepted the validity of the loop invariant informally. That is, we have assumed that the invariant is, indeed, valid for the loop that it describes. However, when we verify a program we must also scrutinize all of its loops' invariants for correctness.

How can we do this? Since each step of the loop is a discrete step that follows from the previous step, we can use the method of induction. Here, the basis for induction is the number i of the step in the loop that is about to be executed. Specifically, we need to show (1) that satisfaction of the invariant occurs before the first step, and (2) that satisfaction of the invariant after the first `i-1` steps (i.e., before the `i`th step) guarantees satisfaction of the invariant after the `i`th step (i.e., before the `i+1`st step). Consider again the following loop:

```
sum = 0 ;
for (i=1; i<=5; i++)
// inv: (sum == Sum j in {1,...,i-1}: j) && 1<=i<=6
   sum = sum+i ;
```

Before the first step in this loop, `i==1` and `sum==0`, so the invariant is easily seen to be satisfied for this case. Now, assume that the invariant is satisfied after the `i-1`st step, for some i = 2, 3, ..., 6. That is, assume:

```
(sum == Sum j in {1,...,i-1}: j) && 1<=i<=6
```

Now we must show by induction that a single execution of the entire body of the loop will guarantee that

```
(sum == Sum j in {1,...,i'-1}: j) && 1<=i'<=6
```

where `i'==i+1`.

We can do this by examining the effect of the two statements in the loop's body on the original invariant. That is, a single execution of the assignment `sum = sum+i` leaves

```
sum == i + Sum j in {1,...,i-1}: j
    == Sum j in {1,...,i}: j
    == Sum j in {1,...,(i+1)-1}: j
    == Sum j in {1,...,i'-1}: j
```

by simple algebra. The statement `i = i+1` leaves

```
1 <= i+1 <= 6   1 <= i' <= 6
```

since the limiting value of i = 5 in the `for` loop forces the limiting value of `i'` to be 6. Therefore, by induction, it follows that the loop invariant is valid, and this completes the verification of the loop itself.

Formal Versus Informal Verification

The techniques introduced here are sometimes called *formal verification techniques*. As we can imagine, the application of formal verification techniques to any reasonably large program can quickly become a difficult chore. Furthermore, there is a wide range of programming problems for which formal verification techniques have not yet been well developed. The process of formal program verification is now in its infancy—much needs to be done before it becomes an effective tool for ensuring program robustness.

There are, however, different levels of granularity at which we can apply program verification techniques. The process of *informal verification* seeks to provide a means for arguing convincingly that a given program is correct, but skipping much of the line-by-line detail that accompanies formal methods. This process is analogous to the ones we use in mathematics to prove a theorem or even simplify an algebraic expression. That is, when we simplify an algebraic expression we do not usually enumerate all the steps and their formal justifications in terms of basic algebraic properties (associativity, commutativity, etc.). Instead, we skip steps that are certain to be understood by the reader and list only the essential ones.

Such is the case for informal verification. Rather than verify a program by developing a complete proof tableau, we seek to focus on the most complex aspects of the program, and we argue by way of a brief English-language paragraph that these aspects satisfy their specifications. Thus, the notions of precondition, postcondition, and loop invariant still play an active role in the process, but the argument for the program's correctness is given more informally.

The Debate about Formal Verification

A number of eminent computer scientists have expressed doubts about the potential effectiveness of formal verification methods. In this subsection, we present a brief summary of some of their main objections.

- One objection is that programs can never be verified but algorithms potentially can be. That is, the correct execution of a program depends on a lot of things outside of the program itself—the compiler compiling it correctly, the hardware itself being designed correctly and being functional, and even things as mundane as whether or not a printer is turned on. Thus correctness must necessarily be a "relative correctness."

- There are practical difficulties with formal verification that have yet to be overcome. For instance, a formal verification requires that all input and output specifications be formally expressed. But we have already seen in this text how hard that can be and have often used informal specifications instead. Can we develop formal specification methods to the point where we not only can formulate such specifications correctly but, for large specifications, also understand them well enough to be helpful in verifying a program? At this point, the answer is uncertain. In fact, verification's success at this time has been primarily on small programs.

- Most errors in programs are specification errors, not logical errors. Thus verification, even if it is successful, still misses the more important problem.

- Even the best mathematicians make errors in proofs; thus it is not unreasonable to expect formal verification of programs to be in error as well.

In fact, some experimental evidence suggests that an alternative method called "walkthroughs" (which we discuss more in the next volume of this series) is at least as effective at finding errors in programs as formal verification.

- There exists more to thinking than formalism. Formalism can be helpful, but programming has a strong creative dimension which is not replaceable by formal methods. Thus we need to temper our hopes for formalism and recognize its limitations.

- Formalism can be daunting. Insistence on it can be counterproductive and can take the joy away from programming for many bright people who might then simply find something else to do.

It is conceivable that formal verification could be automated. For this to be possible, specification languages need to be developed that are precise and complete enough to formally and unambiguously describe the pre- and postconditions of any program. Also, programs would need to be written which can take another program as input and check whether it transforms initial states satisfying its preconditions into final states satisfying its postconditions. Such a development would certainly address some of the objections above. However, there are inherent theoretical limitations to such a project. For instance, one common programming error is the writing of infinite loops. It is impossible to write a program which could serve as a general purpose infinite loop detector. This impossibility is called the "halting problem" and will be discussed in some depth in Volume 4 of this series of texts.

One of the leading proponents of formal methods, Edsger Dijkstra, believes that fifty years from now formal methods will be the norm in computing and the discipline will thus look drastically different from today. Perhaps he is correct. There is much yet to be learned about these methods, their potential usefulness, and their limitations. For more information on this debate see *Program Verification: The Very Idea* by James H. Fetzer, CACM (31, 9) Sept. 1988 and *A Debate on Teaching Computer Science*, CACM (32, 12) Dec. 1989.

EXERCISES

7–16 Verify each of the following series of statements by filling in the missing precondition or postcondition, using the assignment rule of inference:

```
a.  //                        e.  //
        i = i+1 ;                     cout << x ;
    // i > 0                      // output == 12
```

```
b.  // i == 0                    f.  // i == 10
       i = i+1 ;                         j = 25 ;
    //                               //


c.  // i+j == 0                  g.  //
       i = i+1 ;                         s = s+t-1 ;
       j = j-1 ;                      // 0 <= s
    //


d.  // input == 4 7 5
       cin >> x ;
    //
```

7–17 Verify the following loop using the loop rule of inference, and include a proof (by induction) of its invariant.

```
// L == (e[1] e[2] ... e[m] ... e[n])
   j = 1 ;
   k = 2 ;
   while (k<=m)
   {
// inv: (for all i in {1,...,k-1}: e[j] <= e[i]) &&
//          2<=k<=m+1
      if (L[k]<L[j])
         j = k ;
      k = k+1 ;
   }
   Min = j ;
```

7–18 Write a controlled loop, using a `for` or `do` statement, that is equivalent to the loop in Exercise 7–17. Give an invariant and then verify your resulting loop.

7–19 Contrast the process of verification with the process of testing as competing styles for ensuring correctness, robustness, and user-friendliness for programs in general. What is an advantage of each? What is a disadvantage of each? For the game of life program that was developed in Chapter 6, which of these processes seems to be preferable, and why?

7–20 In each of the following, complete the missing assertion (using the conditional rule of inference) so that the given assertion will be valid:

```
a.  //
       if (a == 1) b = a ; else b = a + 1 ;
    // b == 1

b.  // i == n && j == m
       if (i == 0) j = 0 ; else j = 1 ;
    //
```

c. `// i == n && j == m`
        `if (i == 0) j = 0 ;`
   `//`

7–21 Verify the invariant for the loop in the program segment below, assuming that S == "R2D2". Write out the values of Loc and Count for each iteration of the loop.

```
Count = 0 ;
Loc = 0 ;
while (Loc < strlen(S)-1)
// inv: 0<=Loc<=Length(S)-1 &&
//       (Count == Num i in {1,..., Loc}: "0"<=S[i]<="9")
{
    if (S[Loc]>='0') && (S[Loc]<='9')
      Count = Count+1 ;
    Loc = Loc+1 ;
}
```

7–22 Find the invariant for the loop in the following function.

```
int IsSorted (list A)
{
  int i , result ;
  result = true ;
  for (i = 1; i <= A.length() - 1; i++)
    if (A.element(i) > A.element(i+1))
       result = false ;
  return result ;
}
```

7–23 For each of the objections to formal correctness mentioned in the last section, indicate (1) whether you believe it to be a valid objection and why and (2) explain what significance you see it as having, if any.

SUMMARY

This chapter introduced methods in mathematical logic that provide the foundation for program verification, an important topic in computing theory. Rules of equivalence and inference, deductive proof, inductive proof, and many examples were discussed. The idea of a program verification tableau was also presented, and the systematic verification of a simple C++ program was illustrated. The chapter concluded with a brief discussion of the differences between formal and informal verification and an outline of some of the objections that have been raised to formal verification.

LOGIC AND COMPUTERS

Up to this point we have focused primarily on algorithms—the use of a formal language to specify algorithms, the role of abstraction, MAPS, and methods for determining the correctness of algorithms. Our algorithms were written in C++; the resulting C++ programs were entered into a computer by means of an editor and then translated by a compiler into something the computer could execute. But we have only touched lightly on what happens after the program is compiled; we only briefly mentioned input-output, memory, operations, and control. Our purpose thus far has been to lay a foundation for some critical concepts in the organization of algorithms, not to examine the execution of programs at the machine level. Now that we have begun to understand algorithms, we are ready to delve into a discussion of their actual implementation on a computer, or, as some computer scientists describe it, to "look under the hood."

We begin by studying how information is represented in a computer. We then analyze the four principal components of a digital computer that manipulate this information: the memory, the arithmetic-logic unit, the control unit, and input/output. In this chapter, we describe the machine using logic and Boolean algebra, and design simple circuits representative of each major component of a computer, each time basing the construction on formal logic. In Chapter 9, we introduce assembly language and machine languages as intermediate levels between the hardware constructs of this chapter and the algorithmic (for example, C++) level of previous chapters. We will see how machine-level instructions are represented and executed and how machine language instructions are combined to realize computations, loops, procedure calls—indeed, programs. Finally, the lab manual contains an emulation model of a simple computer that demonstrates the functions and interconnectedness of these components. Our computer, known as `Marina`, allows you to witness the step-by-step execution of simple programs.

OVERVIEW OF COMPUTER ORGANIZATION

The term "computer" usually refers to a *digital* or *binary* computer, which is by far the most common form of computer today. This certainly includes the computer you use in your lab and all popular or familiar models. The distinguishing characteristic of *digital computers* is that they represent information in terms of discrete values. In contrast, *analog* computers represent information as continuous functions, relating numeric quantities by analogy; for example, voltage level to represent volume or length to represent temperature. That is the way a thermometer works: the volume of the mercury expands in proportion to the temperature. These are usually special-purpose machines designed for some particular application. The more common digital computers represent all information as discrete values or, more precisely, as sequences of digits. The word *binary* means that there are only two distinct digits available for this purpose. Although representation of information in a digital computer is often referred to as "numeric," digital computers are not limited to processing numeric data; indeed, digital machines can and do handle alphabetic and character data as well. A third category of computer, the hybrid machine, is a combination of the first two. Hybrid computers consist of analog and digital parts with connecting links. For the remainder of this chapter, we restrict our discussion to binary digital computers.

Digital computers are sometimes called *general-purpose computers* because we can program them to do a variety of things. That is, they can execute algorithms for many types of problems, depending on the software. For example, the same computer you use to run C++ programs also serves as a word processor for writing papers. Since computers can execute algorithms for many different types of problems, not just those involving numeric data, perhaps the older terms *data processing system* and *information processing system* are really more appropriate than "computer." Data or information processing can be defined as a series of planned operations on information to achieve a desired result. The computer is the agent that performs these operations. It accepts raw data as input, performs the operations, and generates output. Figure 8–1, an expansion of Figure 2–1, represents this relationship schematically. It also indicates that the computer itself seems to have two essential components: the *central processing unit* that performs the operations and *memory* for storing the information as it is processed. Each of these components of the computing model is described in the following sections.

Input and Output

Digital computers accept numbers, alphabetic letters, and symbols as input. Generally input comes from a logically separate device, such as a keyboard. We say it is logically separate because even though it may be physically part of the same machine, it is not involved in the actual computation process. Once the input device delivers the raw data to the computer, its task is complete. In

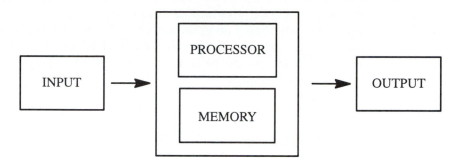

FIGURE 8–1   The input-process-output model of computation.

addition to the keyboard, other common input devices include a mouse, track-ball, joystick, and even a foot pedal. Information can also be entered from machine-readable media, such as magnetic tape or diskette, compact disk, or magnetic ink on paper. These media are useful for saving your work for future use or for reading data generated by another computer.

Results to be saved or returned to the computer user must be decoded from their internal representation and transferred to an external medium through an output device. The most common output device for desktop computers is the *cathode ray tube* (CRT) screen, or *monitor*. Other output media include printed hard copy, diskettes, and magnetic tape.

Input and output are generally classed together under the single title *input/output* or *I/O*. While the mechanisms for these operations are important, they are not central to the study of algorithms and are not discussed further here.

The Central Processing Unit

The heart of the computer is the *central processing unit* (*CPU* or just "processor"), which performs the actual "thinking." It has two major subsystems: the *arithmetic-logic unit* (ALU) and the *control unit*.

Arithmetic-logic unit   The ALU contains the circuitry for performing elementary operations, such as addition, subtraction, multiplication, division, and comparison. It can distinguish positive from negative values, perform calculations, make logical comparisons, and transfer information to other units of the computer.

Control unit   The control unit does just that: It controls or directs the operation of the various parts of the computing system. The general-purpose capability of the digital computer is the result of the programmability of the control unit. The computing machine, or *hardware*, can be made to perform any of a variety of processes (for example, C++ programs, word processing) simply by executing a program that characterizes that particular process. The control unit reads the instructions specified by the program and directs the arithmetic-logic unit to perform the appropriate steps. Its basic operation, called the *instruction cycle,* can be described as:

1. Locate and *fetch* the next instruction to be executed.

2. *Decode* the instruction to determine whether it is an add, move, etc.

3. *Manage* or direct the ALU to perform the operation specified by an instruction, including both internal data transfer and invocation of the specific arithmetic-logic unit.

Storage

The computer's *memory,* or data storage area, holds information or data while it is being processed. This includes the original input data, intermediate results, and output data. Information is stored electronically in the computer as a collection of digits, or "on-off" switches. Each item of information is stored in an individual location, or *cell,* which is specified by a unique address. Figure 8–2 illustrates the structure of the computer's memory. Notice that each location has both an address which identifies it as a unique location, and content or value, distinct from its address. In higher-level languages this distinction manifested itself as array indices and array content. The properties of this storage, such as *memory access time* (the length of time required to locate an item in

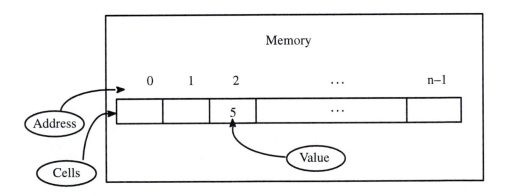

FIGURE 8–2 Computer memory.

storage, obtain it, and make it ready for use by other units of the computing system) and *memory size* (the number of distinct memory locations), determine much of the power of a given computer.

Stored Programs

Perhaps the single most important step in the evolution of computers was the realization that a program is data: information about the steps to be executed. As such it can be stored in a computer's memory rather than input each time it is needed. To understand the importance of this claim, consider the conditional statement of C++:

```
if ( <test> )
   action_1
else
   action_2
```

When a computer begins execution of this construct, it is unknown which of the possibilities, `action_1` or `action_2`, will be executed. If the instructions must be input as they are needed, some form of external intervention will be needed each time there is a choice for the next instruction. Perhaps a human operator must load the new instruction. With a stored program, the control unit may select the instruction to be executed after the test has been performed. Since both alternatives can be in memory, this selection proceeds at electronic speeds. John von Neumann is popularly credited with the invention of such a stored program computer (although others such as John Atanasoff, John Eckert and John Mauchly certainly contributed greatly to the idea). In his honor, the stored program computer is often called the *von Neumann computer.*

The internal representation for instructions is not the same as the human-oriented representation of a higher-level language such as C++. In fact, even the operations executable by the ALU—collectively called the machine language—are not the same as those available in C++. The description "higher-level" means that C++ is more readable by humans because its basic instructions are at a higher-level of abstraction or more complex than those of machine language. A problem solution, which has been formulated as an algorithm, must be transformed into detailed instructions the computer can understand—and *execute*. In previous chapters, you have translated the program into a higher-level language such as C++. A series of instructions, a *program*, can also be expressed in terms of a specific computer's *machine language*. The compiler translates the higher-level language *source program* into a machine language *object program*. An object program in memory is called a *stored program*.

Figure 8–4 expands Figure 8–2 to include this brief discussion of the structure of the digital computer. The remainder of this chapter describes the internal structure of computers and the representation of information in more detail.

FIGURE 8–3 The compilation process.

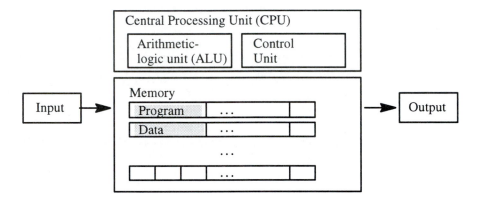

FIGURE 8–4 Major components of a computer.

All information is represented in a two-values (binary) system, and all operations are performed with a two-valued (Boolean) logic. Chapter 9 discusses the implementation of algorithms using this structure.

BINARY ARITHMETIC

As noted at the beginning of this chapter, computers are binary. That is, they use the binary number system. What is the binary system? How do computers use it? How is it different from the decimal system that we are used to using? And why do computers use it rather than the decimal system? We now attempt to answer these questions and investigate the implications that binary representation has on the design of computer systems.

Review of decimal notation

Binary arithmetic is conceptually identical to the decimal arithmetic you are used to. Most of us are so familiar with the decimal number system that we normally do not think about the meanings of the conventions inherent in the representations. Recall that the decimal representation is a *positional* number system; that is, the decimal representation of any number specifies the value as a sum of the individual digits times powers of ten. The number 4321 is actually

$$(8.1) \quad \begin{array}{lll} 4 \times 10^3 & = & 4000 \quad \text{plus} \\ 3 \times 10^2 & = & 300 \quad \text{plus} \\ 2 \times 10^1 & = & 20 \quad \text{plus} \\ 1 \times 10^0 & = & 1 \end{array}$$

In general, a number

$$d_n\, d_{n-1}\, d_{n-2} \ldots d_1\, d_0$$

represents the value

$$(8.2) \quad \sum_{i=0}^{n} d_i \times 10^i =$$
$$d_n \times 10^n + d_{n-1} \times 10^{n-1} + d_{n-2} \times 10^{n-2} + \ldots$$
$$+ d_1 \times 10^1 + d_0 \times 10^0$$

Informally, the positions are named according to the numbers that they represent: thousands, hundreds, tens, and ones (or units). Alternatively, we could name them after the corresponding power of ten that each represents: 3 (thousands), 2 (hundreds), 1 (tens), and 0 (units). Note that 10^0 is, in fact, 1 (more generally, by definition, any nonzero number raised to the 0 is 1). Because the powers are increasing from right to left, we number the positions accordingly. For similar reasons, the positions in the example are numbered from 0 to 3, rather than from 1 to 4. (Mathematicians and computer scientists have a tendency to count from zero rather than one—watch for more examples as we proceed.) By numbering the digits from right to left and beginning at 0, the number of each position is the same as the power of 10 that it represents. In Equation 8.1, the 1 in the zeroth position meant 1 times 10^0; the 2 in the first position meant 2 times 10^1, and so on. The positions at the left represent the largest powers of ten, and are therefore called *high-order* or *most significant* digits. The positions at the right represent the smallest (lowest) powers of ten and are therefore called the low-order or least significant digits.

The Arabic number system (the one commonly used today) also incorporates the important concept of zero. To represent a number as the sum of digits times powers of 10, you need to account for the case in which some specific power of 10 is not involved. For example, the number 102 represents the value

$$1 \times 10^2 + 0 \times 10^1 + 2 \times 10^0$$

This place-holding feature of the zero is a cornerstone of the Arabic number system. It enables us to multiply by 10 by simply adding a zero as a new last digit:

$$12,340 = 10 \times 1234$$

Adding the zero moves each digit one position to the left, so that it now occupies the position representing the next higher power of ten. Similarly, we can divide by ten by simply lopping off the last zero:

$$\frac{43210}{10} = 4321$$

If the last digit is not a zero, its removal has exactly the same result as does integer division in C++. Thus,

$$\frac{1234}{10} = 123$$

Other Radices

The Arabic system is not wedded to base ten. In fact, the above discussion can be generalized to any base. In such discussions, the base is more frequently referred to as the radix. A value represented in a given radix, R, is represented by a series of digits between 0 and $(R-1)$, inclusive. The number

$$d_n\, d_{n-1}\, d_{n-2}\, .\, .\, .\, d_1\, d_0$$

represents the value

(8.3) $$\sum_{i=0}^{n} d_i \times R^i =$$

$$d_n \times R^n + d_{n-1} \times R^{n-1} + d_{n-2} \times R^{n-2} + ,\ldots,$$

$$+ d_1 \times R^1 + d_0 \times R^0$$

Shifting a number to the left (i.e., adding a zero at the right) has the effect of multiplying by R; shifting to the right (removing a digit at the right) of dividing by R.

We can use Equation 8.3 to convert between bases as in Examples 8.1 and 8.2.

Example 8.1   Octal (base 8) to decimal:

$$\begin{aligned} 203_8 &= 2 \times 8^2 + 0 \times 8^1 + 3 \times 8^0 \\ &= 128 + 0 + 3 \\ &= 131_{10} \end{aligned}$$

Example 8.2   Binary to decimal:

$$1011_2 = 1 \times 2^3 + 0 \times 2^2 + 1 \times 2^1 + 1 \times 2^0$$
$$= 8 + 0 + 2 + 1$$
$$= 11_{10}$$

The parallelism extends further than just the representation. Operations on numbers are performed in exactly the same way, independent of the radix. For example, the algorithm for addition of two numbers can be described as shown in Figure 8–5.

```
Start at the rightmost digit.
While there are more digits:
     Add the current digit of each operand.
     If the sum is less than the radix
        then        record that sum,
        Otherwise   record the difference between the sum and the
                        radix,
                    add one to the next digit of operand 1.
```

FIGURE 8–5   Algorithm for integer addition.

Example 8.3   To find the sum of $16_{10} + 15_{10}$, start by adding 6 + 5. The sum is more than the radix (10), so record $11 - 10 = 1$ and carry 1 by adding it to the first digit of 16, giving 2. Now add the next digit from each operand giving $2+1 = 3$. The answer is 31.

Example 8.4   To find the sum of $16_8 + 15_8$, start by adding 6 + 5. The sum is more than the radix (8), so record $11 - 8 = 3$ and carry 1 by adding it to the first digit of 16, giving 2. Now add the next digit from each operand giving $2+1 = 3$. The answer is 33_8.

Table 8–1 shows the first 17 integers represented using four different radices: decimal, binary, octal, and hexadecimal. Notice that octal and binary systems simply inherited the symbols used in the decimal system. But the hexadecimal system needs 16 distinct digits and therefore used A, B, ..., F for the six digits following 9.

Binary Arithmetic

Humans almost always prefer to use decimal arithmetic. But there are significant technical problems in using decimal digits as the basic unit of information in a computer. Decimal representation would require a unique representation for each distinct decimal digit. To do this, we would have to design and build a device capable of distinguishing 10 separate states: one for 0, one for 1, and so on. We could imagine some electronic circuit designed to do just this, perhaps representing the 10 digits by 10 different voltage levels. However, it is obvious that in this scenario, a variation in voltage of just 10 percent could make a digit incorrect. In a positional number system, this error could be catastrophic, depending on the position of the incorrect digit. For example, in the representation of the number 4675, even a small error in the leftmost digit could result in an error of 1000, whereas an error in the rightmost digit would introduce an error of just 1. Such a machine would have to be built to very rigorous specifications.

TABLE 8–1   THE FIRST 17 INTEGERS, IN EACH OF FOUR NUMBER SYSTEMS

Decimal $(r = 10)$	Binary $(r = 2)$	Octal $(r = 8)$	Hexadecimal $(r = 16)$
0	0000	0	0
1	0001	1	1
2	0010	2	2
3	0011	3	3
4	0100	4	4
5	0101	5	5
6	0110	6	6
7	0111	7	7
8	1000	10	8
9	1001	11	9
10	1010	12	A
11	1011	13	B
12	1100	14	C
13	1101	15	D
14	1110	16	E
15	1111	17	F
16	10000	20	10

A binary system can represent numbers using only two distinguishable states. The representations for the digits 0 and 1 can be widely separated, reducing the possibility of error significantly. Consider a light switch: it is either on or off, never in-between. This practical consideration led computer designers to choose the binary system as the basis of the representation of information in computer hardware. Hence, all information internal to the computer is encoded as *binary digits*, or *bits*. These binary digits can be thought to represent any two-valued system of information: on-off, left-right, red-green, true-false, or one-zero. By combining blocks of bits, we can represent any data item we want using a binary system.

The general rules for radix arithmetic (see the previous section) apply to binary. Applying Equation 8.3 to base two we see that

$$d_n\, d_{n-1} d_{n-2}\ \cdots\ d_1 d_0$$

represents the value

$$(8.4)\quad \sum_{i=0}^{n} d_i \times 2^i\ =$$
$$d_n \times 2^n + d_{n-1} \times 2^{n-1} + \ \cdots\ + d_1 \times 2^1 + d_0 \times 2^0$$

Since humans use decimal numbers and computers use binary, we frequently need to translate between the two systems. Given a binary number, it is easy to find the decimal equivalent by simply applying Equation 8.4, as in Example 8.2. Translation in the other direction may not be quite as obvious. Given a decimal number, N_{10}, we want to find the unknown digits, d_i, for $0 \le i \le n$, in the expression

$$(8.5)\quad N_{10} = d_n 2^n + d_{n-1} 2^{n-1} + \ \cdots\ + d_1 2 + d_0$$

We can rewrite Equation 8.5 as

$$(8.6)\quad N_{10} = 2(d_n 2^{n-1} + d_{n-1} 2^{n-2} + \ \cdots\ + d_1) + d_0$$

This suggests that if we divide N_{10} by 2, the remainder is the binary digit d_0. This effectively tells us whether the number is even or odd; the remainder is the rightmost digit of the desired binary number. Repeating this step, we can factor out a 2 from the parenthesized part of Equation 8.6 and rewrite it as follows:

$$(8.7)\quad N_{10} = 2(2(d_n 2^{n-2} + d_{n-1} 2^{n-3} + \ \cdots\ + d_2) + d_1) + d_0$$

This factoring exposes d_1, which is the remainder of the parenthesized part of Equation 8.6 divided by 2, as the next digit of the binary number. Thus, we can find all the binary digits, from right to left, by successively dividing a decimal number by 2 and recording the sequence of remainders.

Example 8.5   Convert the decimal number $N = 29$ to binary.

$$(8.8)\qquad \begin{aligned} 29/2 &= 14 \ \ \text{rem } 1 \\ 14/2 &= 7 \ \ \text{rem } 0 \\ 7/2 &= 3 \ \ \text{rem } 1 \\ 3/2 &= 1 \ \ \text{rem } 1 \\ 1/2 &= 0 \ \ \text{rem } 1 \end{aligned}$$

Since the digits are generated right to left, the binary representation for 29_{10} is 11101.

*Hexadecimal Arithmetic

One additional radix of particular importance is base 16, or *hexadecimal*. While binary arithmetic is the true internal representation, it is very cumbersome for daily use because it requires so many digits to represent even relatively small values. Hexadecimal numbers provide an excellent compromise. A number in binary can easily be converted to "hex" by the following conversion. Consider an 8-digit binary number:

(8.9) $d_7 \ldots d_2 d_1 d_0$

which is actually

(8.10) $\displaystyle\sum_{i=0}^{7} d_i \times 2^i =$

$$d_7 \times 2^7 + d_6 + 2^6 + d_5 \times 2^5 + d_4 \times 2^4 + d_3 \times 2^3$$

$$+ d_2 \times 2^2 + d_1 \times 2^1 + d_0 \times 2^0$$

Factoring out 16 (which is also 2^4), we get

(8.11) $2^4 \times (d_7 \times 2^3 + d_6 \times 2^2 + d_5 \times 2^1 + d_4 \times 2^0) +$

$$2^0 \times (d_3 \times 2^3 + d_2 \times 2^2 + d_1 \times 2^1 + d_0 \times 2^0)$$

That is, it can be expressed as

(8.12) $2^4 \times D_1 + 2^0 \times D_0$

where each D_n is a number between 0 and 15. But, that is just the definition of a base-16 number. In fact any binary number can be rewritten as a sum

(8.13) $\displaystyle\sum_{i=0}^{n} (d_3 \times 2^3 + d_2 \times 2^2 + d_1 \times 2^1 + d_0 \times 2^0) \times 2^{4i} =$

$$\sum_{i=0}^{n} D_i \times 16^i$$

Every binary number can be converted to a hex number by grouping the digits into blocks of four digits each representing a power of 16. Each base-16 digit corresponds to four binary digits. Hexadecimal will thus provide an excellent abbreviation for base-2 numbers.

Example 8.6   The number 12_{16} is

$$1 \times 16^1 + 2 \times 16^0 = 1 \times 2^4 + 2 \times 2^0 =$$

$$1 \times 2^4 + 1 \times 2^1 = 10010_2$$

Example 8.7   The binary number

```
101001010011
```

can be converted to hexadecimal by first grouping it as

```
1010 0101 0011
```

and then converting each group individually.

```
1010 = A,    0101 = 5,    0011 = 3
```

so the hexadecimal value is A53.

Because it provides such a concise representation and because the conversion is so straightforward, hexadecimal is often used as a shorthand for binary.

EXERCISES

8–1 Convert the following from the base indicated into decimal:
  a. 177_8
  b. 1442_5
  c. 123_4
  d. AEC_{16}
  e. 11001010_2

8–2 Convert the following from decimal to the base indicated:
  a.   156 to base 8
  b.   756 to base 4
  c.   1000 to base 16
  d.   29 to base 2

8–3 Make the indicated conversions:
  a. 200_8 to base 16
  b. $1A2C_{16}$ to base 2
  c. ABC_{16} to base 8
  d. 577_8 to base 2

COMPUTER REPRESENTATION OF INFORMATION

Computers use binary arithmetic to represent numeric data. But that doesn't tell us how nonnumeric data is represented. Nor does it answer a less obvious—but equally important—question: How does a machine determine where one datum ends and another begins?

Storage cells

We have seen that the basic unit of information in the computer is the bit, or binary digit. A bit can be represented by a simple switch with "off" corresponding to 0 and "on" corresponding to 1. Further we have seen that by grouping bits together, we can represent more than two values. With a single bit, we can represent two distinct numbers, 0 and 1. With two bits, we can represent four numbers—00, 01, 10, and 11. In general, with m bits, we can represent 2^m distinct values. Alternatively stated, if we need n distinct values we will need at least $\log_2(n)$ bits. The perceptive reader may immediately ask, "What size groups does a computer allow?" Perhaps this would not be an issue if any size grouping were possible at any time. But a computer memory is constructed independently of the data which it will hold. This is analogous to an odometer: It has a fixed number of digits. You cannot represent a larger number than it will hold. While many sizes have been used, the most common are groups of 8, 16, or 32 bits. Figure 8–6 shows the relative sizes of these

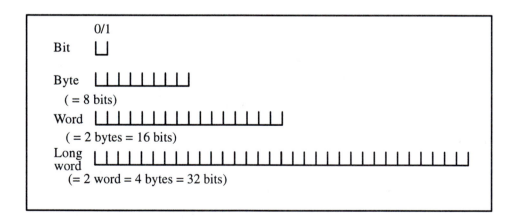

FIGURE 8–6 Bits, bytes, and words.

groups, calling them bytes, words, or long words; some systems call these same units bytes, half-words, and words. When the size of a unit is not important for discussion, we will use the term *cell* to refer to an arbitrary storage unit.

These particular sizes are chosen for several reasons: Sixteen bits allows 2^{16} possible values, usually

$$0 \leq i < 65536 = 2^{16}$$

which is a reasonable number of integers for many day-to-day purposes but not necessarily any better than 2^{17} or 2^{15}. You may have noticed that each of the common sizes is exactly a power of 2, and you will see later in this chapter additional reasons for this choice based on the common representations for character data. Incidentally,

$$2^{16} = 2^6 \times 2^{10} = 64 \times 1024 = 64K.$$

Unsigned Integers

The simplest computer representation of an integer is a right-adjusted binary integer. That is, the decimal number 5 could be represented as

(8.14)   0000 0000 0000 0101

and 29_{10} could be represented as

(8.15)   0000 0000 0001 1101

In general, using this "unsigned integer" technique, with m bits, we can represent the 2^m distinct values 0, 1, 2, …, 2^m-1. For $m=16$, this is 0 ... 65,535.

Signed Integers

Unfortunately, the unsigned representation above does not allow negative numbers. How can we represent the negative integers in binary? We need to add a sign bit or figure out some other way to divide the 2^m unique representations into positive and negative values.

Sign-magnitude notation   The most natural (and simplest) way to accomplish this is to assign the high-order (leftmost) bit to be a *sign bit*. Conventionally, the bit value 0 is used to represent positive values and 1 is used to represent negatives. In this notation, called *sign-magnitude notation*, the remaining $m-1$ bits represent the magnitude of the integer. Using this technique, $+29_{10}$ is represented as

(8.16)   0000 0000 0001 1101

exactly as before, but -29_{10} is represented as

(8.17)   1000 0000 0001 1101

Using sign-magnitude notation, one fewer bit is available for representing the magnitude. Therefore, the range of integer values i which can be represented with m-bit words is

(8.18) $- (2^{m-1} - 1) \le i \le + (2^{m-1} - 1)$

For m = 8, this is

(8.19) $- 127 = - (2^7 - 1) \le i \le (2^7 - 1) = 127$

The advantage to this approach is that it closely resembles the way humans habitually write numbers. But it also creates some problems. If the word size *m* is 4 bits, then 0000 represents the value 0. But then 1000 would represent –0! Is – 0 the same as 0? Although 0 and – 0 are the same mathematically, the sign-magnitude representation has two different representations for this entity. In addition to the mathematical problem that this representation creates, a computer using it would require additional circuitry in a number of places to recognize this "extra" representation for zero. For example, the conditional

```
if x = y
```

could not be implemented by simply comparing all the bits in the two cells to see if they were exactly the same. Even worse, this representation creates a problem for performing basic arithmetic operations. Consider the problem of adding 1 to 5, and to –5.

(8.20) $\quad$ 0101 (5_{10})
$\quad$ +   0001
$\quad\quad$ 0110 (6_{10})

which works fine, but addition of mixed-sign numbers by the straightforward algorithm (for example, Figure 8–5) yields an incorrect result:

(8.21) $\quad$ 1101 (-5_{10})
$\quad$ +   0001
$\quad\quad$ 1110 (-6_{10})

The correct addition would be

(8.22) $\quad$ 1101 (-5_{10})
$\quad$ +   0001
$\quad\quad$ 1100 (-4_{10})

That is, the addition of a positive and a negative number must be treated as a subtraction problem. That means that the control unit would have to check the signs of both operands before performing arithmetic. For these reasons, sign-magnitude representation is not usually used.

Two's complement notation   An alternative, though less obvious, approach to this problem is called *two's complement notation*. The basic idea is simple. Positive numbers are represented by counting upward from 0 and are therefore represented exactly like the unsigned binary numbers. Negative numbers, however, are represented by counting *downward* from 0. Notice however that this is exactly what you would get if you attempted to store 2^m in a cell of the size m. For example, if the word length m is 4, then $+5_{10}$ is represented as `0101`, and -3_{10} is represented as

$$2^4 - 3 = 16 - 3 = 13_{10} = 1101_2$$

In general, two's complement notation can be represented symbolically as

$$(8.23) \quad + i_{10} = i_2$$

$$(8.24) \quad - i_{10} = (2^m - i_{10})_2$$

On the surface, this method appears to have two immediate problems. First, if m (the word length) is 4, then what does a word like `1001` represent? Is it 9_{10}? Or is it -7_{10} $(16 - 9)$? We can fix this problem simply by agreeing to interpret those numbers which begin with 0 (i.e., those less than 2^{m-1}) as nonnegative and those which begin with 1 (i.e., those $\geq 2^{m-1}$) as negative.

Second, the values of negative numbers in this system are not immediately transparent to most people. Can we find an easy way to interpret a negative two's complement number such as 1001? The method can be found in the name two's complement. The complement of anything is that other thing which makes the first whole—in this case "whole" means a power of two, so the complement is the value needed to make a total of 2^n. But there is a simple trick that makes this much easier. Rewriting Equation 8.24 but adding and subtracting 1, we get

$$(8.25) \quad - i_{10} = (2^m - 1)_2 - i_2 + 1$$

The expression $(2^m - 1)_2$ is always a string of exactly m 1s. To see this, notice that 2^m is a 1 bit followed by m 0s. Subtracting 1 from that requires successive borrowing from each zero digit. For example, $(1000 - 1)_2$ is 0111_2 when $m = 3$. We could restate the two's complement calculation as: subtract the number from a string of all 1s and then add 1. Now, note that, in binary,

$$1 - 0 = 1 \text{ and } 1 - 1 = 0$$

Thus, subtracting a binary bit from 1 "reverses" that bit. Hence, the quantity

$$(8.26) \quad (2^m - 1)_2 - i_2$$

is found by simply *reversing* all the bits of i_2. The number found by changing all the 0s to 1s and 1s to 0s in a binary number is called the *ones' complement*. From Equations 8.25 and 8.26 we see that the two's complement of a number is found by adding 1 to the ones' complement, so the two's complement of 001101 is

(8.27)   001101
$\underline{\text{110010}}$ (ones' complement)
$\underline{+\qquad 1}$
110011

110011 is the two's complement of 13, or -13.

> **Example 8.8**   How would we represent -5 in a 6-bit system? Start with the binary representation for $+5 = 001101_2$. Then reverse the 0s and 1s to obtain the ones' complement 111010_2. Finally, add 1 ($+000001_2$) to 111010_2. The result, 111011_2, is -5 in two's complement notation.

The range of integer values i that can be represented in an m-bit two's complement system is

(8.28) $-(2^{m-1}) \le i \le +(2^{m-1}-1)$

For example, if $m = 16$ as in many computers, then the range of integer values is

(8.29) $-2^{15} \le i \le +2^{15}-1$ or

(8.30) $-32,768 \le i \le 32,767$

We return to the earlier question: How would -0 be represented in the two's complement system? Let's see what happens when we compute the two's complement of $+0$.

(8.31) $+0$ $=$ 0000 0000
$\qquad\qquad\quad\underline{\text{1111 1111}}$ (reverse the 0s and 1s)
$\qquad\qquad +\quad\underline{\text{0000 0001}}$ (add 1)
$\qquad\qquad = 1$ 0000 0000

Considering only the rightmost 8 bits of this result, we have 0000 0000 as the representation for -0, which is the same as that for $+0$. Since we allowed only 8 bits for the number, the sum overflows out of the cell and is lost. The result is therefore 0000 0000—exactly the same representation as 0. Thus, there is no problem resulting from two different representations for zero.

More importantly, in two's complement arithmetic, the addition of positive and negative numbers is performed in exactly the same way. Consider the earlier problem of adding 1 to $+5$ and to -5:

$$(8.32) \qquad \begin{array}{r} 0101 \\ + \ \underline{0001} \\ 0110 \end{array} \qquad \begin{array}{l} (= 5_{10}) \\ \\ (= 6_{10}) \end{array}$$

$$\begin{array}{r} 1011 \\ + \ \underline{0001} \\ 1100 \end{array} \qquad \begin{array}{l} (= -5_{10}) \\ \\ (= -4_{10}) \end{array}$$

That is, no special hardware is needed to handle the addition of negative or mixed-sign numbers. (Exercise 8–7 provides additional examples of arithmetic of two's complement numbers.) Alternately stated, at the bit level the result of a two's complement addition is the same as for unsigned numbers. Two's complement representation is therefore preferable because it allows both simplification and economy in circuit design.

There are other representations for integers, including the *binary coded decimal* (BCD) system. The computer representation of floating-point numbers (known in C++ as `float` numbers), such as 34.27 or 3.67×10^{12} is also important. These, as well as other conventions for representing information in a computer, are covered in more detail in Volume III of this series.

Representation of Characters

The representation of characters (alphabet, both upper- and lowercase; decimal digits; special characters, like "?" and "!"; and control characters, like <RET>) is related to but distinct from the representations of integers. The representation must be as complete a set as possible, and it must facilitate implementation of operations on characters (for example, successor) and strings (for example, concatenation). The complete set of integers is infinite, so a compromise is needed between the size of the set of integers to be accommodated and the number of bits to be allocated per integer. That compromise, as we know, typically results in a word length of 16 or 32 bits allowing 2^{16} or 2^{32} possible integers. On the other hand, a reasonably complete character set is much smaller. There are 26 uppercase and 26 lowercase alphabetic characters, 10 digits, and perhaps 32 printable special characters on a conventional keyboard. In addition, there are several control characters, such as carriage return, tab, line feed, bell, and delete. Assuming that there are about 30 of these, then the representation for characters must allow for about 125 distinct values. Seven bits would allow 2^7 possible characters—just sufficient. To allow greater flexibility, most systems allot 8 bits per character. This is, of course, exactly 1 byte—or one half the size of an integer. That is, a cell that holds 1 integer could also hold exactly two characters. And 1 byte is exactly 2 hex digits. This consistency is an additional reason for selecting cell length measures in powers of 2 bits.

We must still select the specific representation for each character, the specific pattern of bits that represents each character. We know that the coding scheme is designed to facilitate the operations to be implemented for character

THE ARITHMETIC-LOGIC UNIT

The arithmetic-logic unit (ALU) performs the individual steps of an algorithm. It is, in reality, a set of *operational units* with some accompanying storage cells called *registers*. The basic operational units are the electronic circuits which carry out the the various operations specified by the machine language instructions. (For better or worse, the basic operational units are themselves often called arithmetic-logic units.) Each operational unit performs a single machine-level operation: arithmetic (addition, multiplication, and so on), logical (**and**, **or**, **not**, logical shift, and so on), or other low-level operation.

Logic and Electronics

To examine the hardware realization of some of the basic machine operations, we will design and "build" some of these circuits—using the same Boolean logic that you have used for selection operations, proofs, and pre- and postconditions.

We tend to think of numbers and arithmetic as the most basic entities in computing. After all, numbers and addition are taught in elementary school, and numbers and arithmetic operations are always taught first in the elementary computer courses, whether in high school or college. However, addition and the other machine operations are actually defined in terms of Boolean logic. (You may want to review Chapter 3.) *Computers work in logic.* We have seen that the binary number system is used to represent numbers (or, in fact, all information) in the computer. But the integer operations can be described in terms of logic. Even the binary numbers themselves—ones and zeros—can also be thought of as a series of true and false values. Each digit has exactly two possible values. For example, 5_{10} is 101_2. But this is exactly the same as **true false true** if we replace 1 by **true** and 0 by **false**. More importantly, we can define *any* arithmetic operation (addition, multiplication, and so on) in terms of logical operations (such as **and** and **or**). Therefore, we will begin our construction project with a review of the elementary logical operations **and**, **or**, and **not**.[4]

The Boolean operations **and** and **or** are binary operations: They have two inputs or operands, and from these, each yields one result or output. Further, **and** yields a **true** output if and only if both its operands are **true**, as illustrated in Figure 8–7. The **or** operation yields a true result if either operand is true. We can construct the electronic analog of these and the other Boolean operations using semiconductor electronics. An **and** *gate*, shown in Figure 8–8, is a device which accepts two input signals, and produces a positive output signal if and only if both inputs are positive. If a positive signal indicates true, then the

---

4.   Recall that all C++ logical expressions use integers 1 (or nonzero) and 0 to denote the values **true** and **false**, along with &&, | |, and ! to denote the **and**, **or**, and **not** ($\wedge$, $\vee$, and $\sim$) logical operators. We shall use the latter representations of these values and operators, rather than the C++ representations, in this chapter.

a	b	a **and** b	a **or** b
true	true	true	true
true	false	false	true
false	true	false	true
false	false	false	false

FIGURE 8–7   Truth table for the **and** and **or** operations.

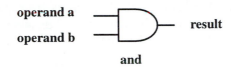

operand a

operand b

result

and

FIGURE 8–8   An **and** gate

and gate behaves exactly like the Boolean **and** operation. Similarly, we can construct electronic analogs for each of the other Boolean operations. Figure 8–9 shows the symbols representing the logic gates corresponding to the other

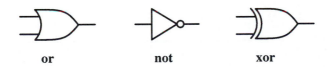

or

not

xor

FIGURE 8–9   The standard symbols for the logic gates or, not, and xor.

common Boolean operations as described in the truth tables of Chapter 3. One of these may not seem so common: The logical *exclusive or* operation, denoted **xor**, is defined as:

(8.33) a **xor** $b = (a \lor b) \land \sim (a \land b)$

Informally, this means "a or b, but not both." Actually, it is not necessary to have a separate operational unit for **xor;** that is, it can be constructed from the basic logical operations **not**, **and,** and **or.** Figure 8–10 shows a circuit for im-

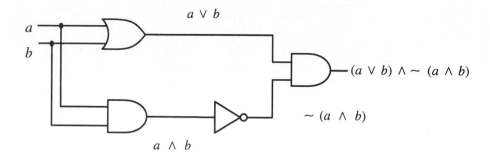

FIGURE 8–10   Creation of an **xor** from the basic Boolean operations.

plementing **xor** based on Equation 8.33. The output from the conjunction is negated. The outputs from the negation and the first disjunction are then both fed into the second disjunction to produce the result.

ALUs for the Logical Operations

It is easy to see how we might build ALUs to perform logical operations on the bits of a cell: Just use the corresponding gates on the individual bits of a cell. For example, we could build an *inverter* for calculating the ones' complement of a number by connecting every source bit to a **not** gate, as in Figure 8–11.

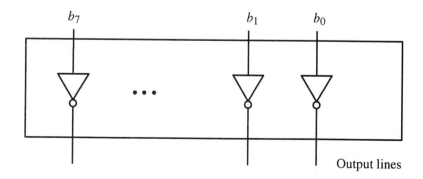

FIGURE 8–11   An 8-bit inverter.

Exercises 8–16 and 8–17 ask you to construct the similar bitwise **and** and **or** of two cells, connecting the two input cells together "bitwise": bit a_0 to b_0 to produce $a_0 \wedge b_0$, a_1 to b_1 to produce $a_1 \wedge b_1$ and so on.

An Adder ALU

Using the basic logical operations, we can design and build any of the operational units of a computer—including operations which are apparently not logical in nature. As an example, let's consider a unit that can add two binary integers. For example, such a circuit could perform the addition shown in Figure 8–12. Recall that the traditional addition process works from right to left, adding the digits in the rightmost column first. Binary computer addition uses exactly the same principle. For each position, we need to do two things: find the sum and check for a carry. First we calculate the sum. In the figure, we add the digits $9 + 1$ in (a); we add the bits $1 + 1$ in (b).

```
    9              001001
+  21          +  010101
   30             011110

   (a)              (b)
```

FIGURE 8–12 Binary integer addition. (a) Decimal notation; (b) binary notation.

The sum of two bits may be 0, 1, or 2—or, in binary, 0, 1 or 10. The table in Figure 8–13 shows these values represented as two separate binary values: the sum and the carry bits. The sum bit is 1 when the operands are different: when operand a is 1 and operand b is 0, or when operand a is 0 and operand b is 1. If both operands are the same, the sum bit is 0. Additionally, when both operands are 1, the sum is 2, so a 1 must be carried in the carry bit. We can rewrite these facts as logical propositions. We can represent the first case as

(8.34) $\quad a \wedge \sim b$

This proposition is equivalent to the circuit shown in Figure 8–14.

Operand a	b	Carry bit	Sum bit for $a + b$
1	1	1	0
1	0	0	1
0	1	0	1
0	0	0	0

FIGURE 8–13 A binary addition table.

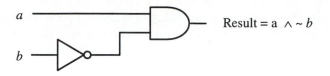

FIGURE 8–14   A diagram for the circuit corresponding to $a \wedge \sim b$.

Similarly, we can represent the second case as

(8.35) $\sim a \wedge b$

Since we want an output of 1 whenever either of these cases occurs, we can combine them with a logical **or**, giving the following proposition:

(8.36) $(a \wedge \sim b) \vee (\sim a \wedge b)$

We thus complete the sum bit circuit by combining the two circuits corresponding to the two parts of the operation, as shown in Figure 8–15a. If we test this circuit with all possible combinations for a and b, we see that this is exactly the definition of **xor** (see Exercise 8–10.) Figure 8–15a can be simplified by using an **xor** gate, as shown in Figure 8–15b.

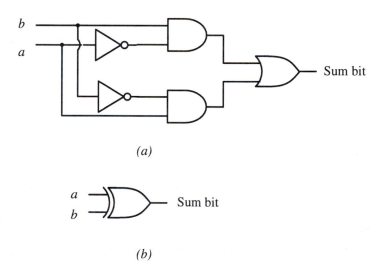

FIGURE 8–15   Constructing the sum. (a) The circuit; (b) the simplified circuit.

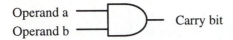

Operand a
Operand b

Carry bit

FIGURE 8–16   Use of an **and** gate to generate a carry bit.

Addition also requires carry operations. Hence, any electronic version of addition must also generate the carry value. We can see from Figure 8–13 that binary addition produces a carry only when the sum is 2, that is, if and only if the two bits being added are both 1s. Therefore, a circuit that generates a carry bit requires only a single **and** gate, as shown in Figure 8–16. Thus, the complete circuit for an adder requires two outputs—generation of the sum bit and generation of the carry bit—as well as its two inputs. Figure 8–17 shows the sum and carry combined into a single circuit.

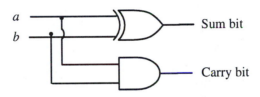

a

b

Sum bit

Carry bit

FIGURE 8–17   A half-adder: the combined schematic circuit diagram for generating the sum and carry bits.

However, we are not quite finished. Remember that as we continue the addition process, proceeding from right to left across a series of bits, we must also add in the carry bits that we generated. For each position, we must add three items: the two addends and the carry that was produced by the previous addition on the right. In Figure 8–12, the very first addition—that is, the rightmost digit pair—produced just such a carry, since $1 + 1 = 0$ with a carry of 1. This carry bit must be added into the addition for the next column. It seems that we have done only half a job! In fact, the device of Figure 8–17 is called a *half-adder*. How then can we make a *full–adder*?

A little reflection on this problem reveals that we really need to add three bits together, not two. Fortunately we can accomplish the addition of three bits using only the tools we have developed thus far. First, let's simplify our drawing of the half-adder of Figure 8–17 as a "black box," with only inputs and outputs showing, as illustrated in Figure 8–18.

Now using this "black box" version as a building block, we can design the circuitry for three inputs (a carry-in bit and the two operands a and b) and two outputs (a carry-out bit and a sum bit). Recall that addition is associative. That

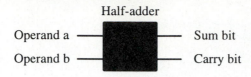

FIGURE 8–18 "Black box" representation of the half-adder of Figure 8–17.

is,

$$a + b + c = a + (b + c) = (a + b) + c$$

We can add any three bits by adding the first two, and then adding the third to that sum. We can do this with two half-adders and an **or** gate, as shown in Figure 8–19.

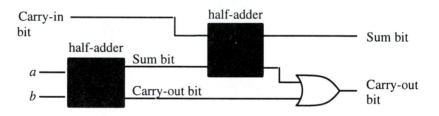

FIGURE 8–19 A full-adder constructed from two half-adders and an **or** gate.

The first half-adder produces the sum digit resulting from addition of operands a and b, which will always be zero or one. The second half-adder adds this sum and the carry bit from the previous full add operation (for bit zero this is just zero). The carry bit may be a little more difficult to understand. The full-adder should produce a carry if the sum of the two operands and the previous carry is two or more. Notice that the two outputs of the first half-adder cannot both be 1. If there is a carry out of the first half-adder, the sum from that half-adder must be 0. In that case, the sum of the second half-adder cannot be more than 1, and it will not produce a carry. Thus, at most one of the two half-adders will produce a positive carry. In terms of the diagram of Figure 8–19, a carry bit of 1 should be output whenever either half-adder produces a 1 carry bit. This is exactly the effect of the **or** gate.

In Figure 8–20, the 8-bit adder is built from eight independent 1-bit full-adders. The three inputs for each bit are at the top of its corresponding black box, and its two outputs are at the bottom; one operand is represented by the bits $a_7a_6a_5a_4a_3a_2a_1a_0$ and the other by the bits $b_7b_6b_5b_4b_3b_2b_1b_0$. The individual adders are chained together to simulate the way we do binary addition; the

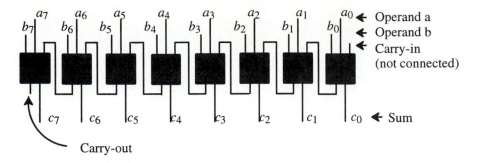

FIGURE 8–20   Eight-bit adder made from eight full-adders.

carry-out bit for each adder is attached to the carry-in bit for the adder on its left. This design is sometimes called a *ripple adder* because of the ripple effect that results as the the carry bit propagates to the left. Obviously we could create larger adders in exactly the same way: by chaining the appropriate number of full-adders together.

So far, we have shown that we can build an operational unit that correctly adds two positive integers of some predetermined length. But what about negative numbers? Will the adder we have designed allow us to compute such problems as −5 + 8, which we know should yield +3. Let's try it. First, convert the two numbers to (say) 8-bit binary representation. Recall that negative numbers are represented in two's complement form. Thus, −5 becomes 1111 1011 and 8 becomes 0000 1000. Figure 8–21 illustrates the addition of these two numbers. Ignoring the carry bit, we see that the answer is 00000011, or 3_{10}. The fact that we can add positive and negative numbers with a single circuit is actually a prime motivator for the use of two's complement notation. Try the adder for other combinations of positive and negative, negative and positive, and negative and negative, just to convince yourself that the adder works correctly in each case.

$$
\begin{array}{r}
1111\ 1011 \\
+\quad 0000\ 1000 \\
\hline
1\quad 0000\ 0011
\end{array}
$$

Carry-out

FIGURE 8–21   Addition of a negative number in two's complement form.

Overflow and carry-out Consider the sum of the decimal numbers 100 and 35, as shown in Figure 8–22. Figure 8–22*a* shows the decimal representation,

$$100_{10}$$
$$\underline{35_{10}}$$
$$135_{10}$$

(a)

$$0110\ 0100_2$$
$$\underline{0010\ 0011_2}$$
$$1000\ 0111_2$$

(b)

FIGURE 8–22   Overflow in addition. (*a*) In decimal; (*b*) in binary.

while Figure 8–22*b* is the corresponding 8-bit binary representation of the same calculation. Look at the binary addition carefully. Is $1000\ 0111_2$ actually the correct answer? Since the answer is a two's complement representation, the one in the leftmost bit of the result indicates that it is a negative number. The answer must therefore be incorrect. The reason is that this addition resulted in an *overflow*. From Equation 8.28, the range of numbers, i, representable in 8-bit two's complement form is

$$(8.37)\quad \begin{array}{c} -2^7 \le i \le 2^7 - 1, \quad \text{or} \\ -128_{10} \le i \le 127_{10} \end{array}$$

The result of this particular sum, 135_{10}, is too large and results in an *overflow*. Though we have not explicitly included this consideration in our adder design, such an overflow can be detected by a real computer's adder. If the sum of two positive numbers gives a negative result (as in Figure 8–22), we know an overflow has occurred. Similarly, if the addition of two negative numbers gives rise to a positive result, there has been an overflow. It is not possible to have an overflow when adding two numbers that have opposite signs (see Exercise 8–18).

Similarly, consider the sum of two negative numbers, −1 and −1 depicted in Figure 8–23. The carry into the sign bit simply keeps the values negative. But there is a 1 carried out of the cell. This bit, called a *carry bit,* or carry-out does not affect the addition, but it does provide some information about the operation just completed

When values overflow or carry out, this result is recorded in a special location called the *condition code register* (CC). In Chapter 9, we see how the ma-

$$1111\ 1111$$
$$\underline{1111\ 1111}$$
$$1\ 1111\ 1110$$

FIGURE 8–23   Carry out resulting from addition of negative numbers.

chine can take advantage of this simple result. Similarly, the carry-out result is always recorded.

EXERCISES

8–10 Write the logical expression corresponding to Figure 8–15. Show that this is really equivalent to the definition of exclusive or in Equation 8.33.

8–11 Draw the entire circuit for the full adder without using the black-box version of the half-adder or the exclusive or gate.

8–12 Add the following binary numbers by tracing their addition through the binary full-adder.

```
      1111 1111
 +    0000 0001
```

8–13 Add the following binary numbers by tracing their addition through the binary full-adder.

```
      0000 0111
 +    1111 1000
```

8–14 Treat Figure 8–20 as the internals of a black box 8-bit adder. Show how to link two 8-bit adders together to make a 16-bit adder. Be careful to deal explicitly with the carry-in and carry-out lines in your diagram.

8–15 Can the leftmost carry output from an addition be ignored in all cases? Explain.

8–16 Build an 8-bit **and** ALU, which combines two 8-bit input cells, a and b, bitwise so that the output bit i is $a_i \wedge b_i$.

8–17 Build an 8-bit **or** ALU, which combines two 8-bit cells, a and b, bitwise so that the output bit i is $a_i \vee b_i$.

8–18 Prove the claim that no overflow is possible when adding two numbers with opposite signs.

*Subtraction

We could build an entire subtraction unit from scratch. But there is a simpler way. Just as you would prefer to build software from existing modules, you can design hardware from existing constructs. Subtraction can be defined in terms of addition of signed numbers:

(8.38) $a - b = a + (-b)$

That is, since the addition unit works for negative numbers, we do not actually need a separate subtraction unit; we can simply use addition and negation:

1. Calculate $-b$, by finding its two's complement:
   a. Find the ones' complement.
   b. Add 1 to that.

2. Add this result to a.

The trick is recalling how we computed the two's complement. The two's complement is just the ones' complement plus 1. The groundwork is complete. The next step is to build the pieces, starting with a circuit to calculate the ones' complement (or just the *complement*). But we have already built a ones' complementer: it is the inverter that we created in Figure 8–11. So we could actually build a subtracter from two adders and an inverter, as shown in Figure 8–24.

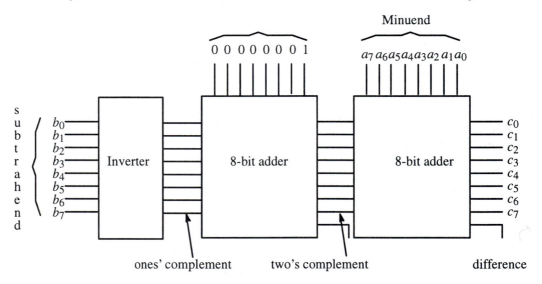

FIGURE 8–24   First attempt: simple subtracter constructed from existing components.

An alternative construction of the subtraction unit not only reuses the ideas but actually uses the adder ALU itself. However, we could use our knowledge of logic to improve the design of the inverter. Figure 8–25 shows that an **exclusive or** acts as a mask, letting some values through unchanged but inverting others. Any value **exclusive-or** 0 is just that value, but any value **exclusive-or** 1 is the negation of that value.

Trigger Signal	Input	Output
0	0	0
0	1	1
1	0	1
1	1	0

FIGURE 8–25   Results of using an **exclusive or** as a triggerable mask.

We can build a "switchable" complementer using **xor** gates rather than **not** gates. A single complement signal line, **xor**ed with every input line serves to "trigger" the entire function, as illustrated in Figure 8–26. That is, when the

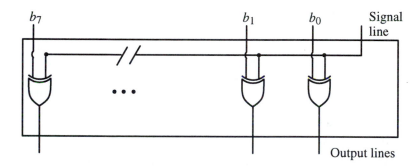

FIGURE 8–26   An 8-bit complementer.

signal line is 1, the unit passes the complements of all input digits to their output lines; otherwise, it transfers the original input digits directly to their output lines. This information can be written in propositional logic as

(8.39) $(\sim Signal \land Input) \lor (Signal \land \sim Input)$

which, in turn, simplifies to

(8.40)   Signal **xor** Input

The inverter of Figure 8–26 reverses all eight input digits in parallel (creates the ones' complement) whenever the signal line is 1 and passes all input digits through unchanged whenever the signal line is 0.

Using the complementer and trigger signal, we can design an 8-bit adder/subtracter by connecting the output lines from the complementer to the corresponding input lines for operand b of an 8-bit adder and activating the

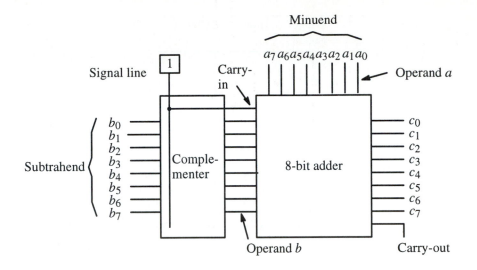

FIGURE 8–27   An 8-bit adder-subtracter.

complementer's signal line, as shown in Figure 8–27. If the combined unit receives a 1 in the carry-in line, the unit subtracts the subtrahend (sent through the eight input lines of the complementer) from the minuend (sent through the operand a lines) by adding what seems to be the ones' complement of the subtrahend. In reality, it adds the two's complement (which, you recall is the ones' complement plus 1) because the select signal itself (1) is also fed in as the carry bit to bit_0. It is zero when we are adding, so it makes no difference in that case.

Complement	Adder	Result
0	0	none
0	1	add
1	0	none
1	1	subtract

FIGURE 8–28   Use of two select signals to choose three actions.

Thus, the action performed by the adder/subtracter combination depends on the values in the two signal lines, the complementer signal and the adder signal, as shown in Figure 8–28. That is, we use two input signals to select three possibilities: two possible actions—add and subtract—and an inaction.

Notice that we have *reused* the 8-bit adder of Figure 8–20 and the complementer of Figure 8–26 as building blocks in the construction of the 8-bit subtracter. Reuse is a valuable principle for hardware design, just as it is for software design. Figure 8–29 shows a diagram for a more complete ALU, with a separate signal line for each operation. Many operations can be combined together in similar fashion.

EXERCISES

8–19 Write an algorithm in C++ to implement multiplication by combining the comparator, shifter, and adder. Consider defining a memory location as an `int  array[16]`, and use C++'s logical operators `&&`, `||`, and `!` to simulate their respective circuits.

8–20 Perform the subtraction problem

```
  0011 0000
– 0101 0101
```

by the usual algorithm. Then perform it again using the "invert and add" logic of this section.

8–21 Show what the circuit for the 8-bit complementer in Figure 8–26 would have looked like if we were unable to use the **xor** to simplify the one-bit complement function.

THE CONTROL UNIT

We originally set out to visualize and construct an entire ALU—the component of the computer that does both arithmetic and logic operations. So far, we have designed separate operational units for the logical operations **and**, **or**, and **not** and for integer addition and subtraction. Now we need to integrate these units into a single coherent ALU that will perform all of these operations.

We have already combined the operational units designed for addition and subtraction into a single unit. To accomplish this, we used two wires: a signal wire to invoke the adder/subtracter and a select wire to indicate whether the unit is to perform an addition or a subtraction. The value on the select wire determined whether the complementer is used (subtraction) or not used (addition). We can imagine that a plan for a more complete unit would look something like Figure 8–29.

Selection

The *control unit* must act as director, choosing which unit is to perform an operation and at what time. This suggests that it must have a way of selecting one

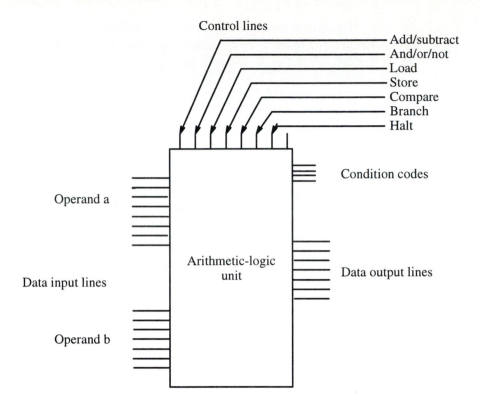

FIGURE 8–29   Block diagram of a complete ALU.

event out of the possible events and for signaling the time for that event. Once again, Boolean logic provides the answer, as suggested by our experience with the addition/subtraction unit. First, we did not need as many input lines as there are possible actions. In fact, we can specify eight operations with only three input lines (and, in general, we can select 2^n operations with n input lines). Second, recall that the operator **and** returns a true value only if both inputs are true. We can easily construct an **and** gate requiring three true inputs. If one input is **false, and** always returns a **false** value. Thus, we use a select signal to allow any specific value to be read, as in Figure 8–31.

FIGURE 8–30   Construction of a three-input **and** gate.

```
Select signal ────┐
                  ├──D──── Result = value if select
Value ────────────┘              is true,
                             = false otherwise
```

FIGURE 8–31   Use of an **and** gate to generate a selector.

We can extend this by combining multiple selectors to create a decoder circuit, which accepts a binary number as input and places a positive signal on exactly one of its output lines. This circuit, called a *decoder*, is shown in Figure 8–32. Each output line is the conjunction of four values, each either an input or the negation of an input. The 16 output lines represent all such combination of four inputs. For example if all inputs are 0, the top decoder element in the figure negates each of those 0s, thus sending all 1s to the **and** gate. All other elements have at least one unnegated input and thus do not produce a positive output if the input is all zeros. Similarly with any input other than all 0s, the first element will not produce a positive output. Such a decoder can be used to select one ALU, one register, or even one memory cell if it is large enough.

Clocks   A selector such as that in Figure 8–31 can also be used to select a point in time by combining it with a signal from a *system clock*. The clock is simply a pulse. Unless that pulse is positive, the selector does not choose the event.

EXERCISES

8–22   Design a complete 3-bit decoder.

8–23   A decoder could also be built using **and**s and **not**s. Build a 2-bit decoder that does not use **or** gates.

* Design Tradeoffs: CISC versus RISC

There are currently two competing philosophies for the design of the arithmetic-logic unit. The most obvious difference is in the number of instructions supported by the hardware. The traditional approach provides a great many instructions to facilitate efficient programming of the machine. The instruction sets for the IBM 4300 series mainframe computers, the DEC VAX minicomputer, the Motorola 680x0 (used in the Macintosh and the Sun workstation), and the Intel 80x86 (used in the IBM PS/2 and compatibles) all reflect this design philosophy. The Sun SparcStation and the RISC 1 on the other hand have a much smaller instruction set, as can be seen in Figure 8–33.

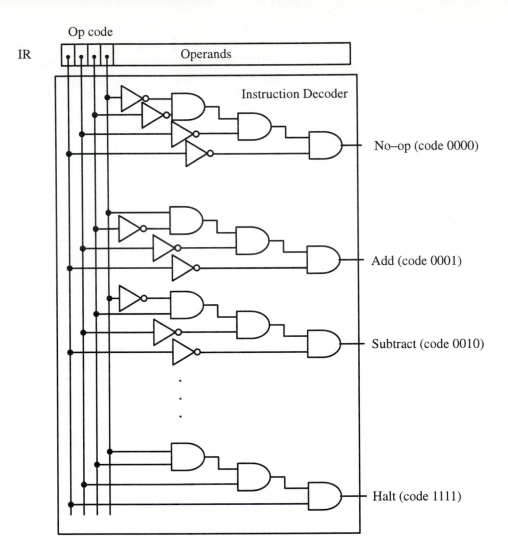

FIGURE 8–32   A simple decoder circuit

Neither approach includes a direct hardware implementation for the C++ statement types. For example, there is no `while` statement or `if` statement per se. These types of statements are implemented in software; that is, they are *translated* into groups of machine language statements which can then be executed by the computer. In any case, it is not always necessary to explicitly include an operational unit for each functional operation. For instance, it is unnecessary to include a separate subtracter unit because we can subtract by taking the two's complement of the subtrahend and adding. Thus, subtraction can be accomplished by using the complementer and adder units. As in Exercise 8–19, we can imagine doing multiplication by combining the shifter and adder.

A machine with a large number of operations is sometimes called a *CISC* (*Complex Instruction Set Computer*) machine. The large number of individual instructions and addressing modes are supported by a microcoded architecture.

DEC VAX	325
IBM 4300	187
Intel 80386	169
Motorola 68020	109
RISC 1	31
Sun SPARC	88

FIGURE 8–33 Instruction set sizes of some well-known computers.

A newer alternative, *RISC* (*Reduced Instruction Set Computer*), is designed to increase efficiency of operation by reducing the number of unique instructions and modes to be decoded and the number of operational units to be included in the system. The essence of the tradeoff is that CISC machines aim for efficiency by providing hardware-level support for every instruction that might be needed. In contrast, RISC machines provide only a limited number of instructions and modes. Their designers believe that you do best by making the most common instructions very efficient. They have fewer and simpler components. The arguments for each philosophy will be addressed in more detail in *Volume III* of this series.

MEMORY

As the processor performs the steps of the computation it must store the results of its work. It needs to store the input values as they are received, keep intermediate results as it progresses, and place the results until they are output. In addition, since the program itself is data, it must also be stored somewhere. Like the ALUs and the control mechanism, memory is constructed from logic gates.

Construction of a Memory Bit

The mechanism for holding a value over time goes by the unglamorous name of *flip-flop*. It is a bistable circuit, meaning that it can maintain either of two stable conditions. When the flip-flop is in one of the two states, we interpret it as a 1; if it is in the other state, we interpret it as a 0.   It also has two inputs

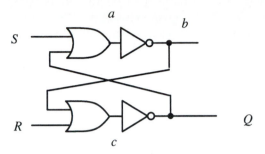

FIGURE 8–34   A basic flip-flop for holding one bit of data.

called S (set) and R (reset). When a signal arrives at either input, the flip-flop enters the corresponding stable state. The flip-flop stays in that state until it is reset by a second signal at the other input. As long as these signals are both zero, the basic flip-flop does not change state. When, and only when, a signal arrives, the circuit behaves differently. Thus, a flip-flop has exactly the properties we need to store a single bit of data. A value can be sent to the flip-flop, and that value remains until it is deliberately changed. To understand the transition, we will trace a signal through the circuit. At the start time, t_0, the flip-flop is in some state (that is, each labeled point in the flip-flop is either 0 or 1).

1. Assume that at time t_1 a set signal (1) arrives at S.

2. The disjunction therefore becomes **true** (at intermediate point a). The other input to the **or** gate does not matter—the result of the disjunction will be true.

3. The signal from a is negated, giving **false** at b.

4. By assumption, no signal is entering at the reset line R. Thus, both R and b are **false**, and the lower disjunction yields **false** at c.

5. That signal is negated, giving **true** at Q, which is fed back into the upper **or** gate. For the moment, it is irrelevant that this second true signal has arrived.

6. Eventually the transient signal S will cease (becomes 0 again). This will have no impact on the flip-flop, since Q is **true**. The disjunction of S and **true** is **true**. S has actually become irrelevant. The signal Q has taken over S's task.

7. With Q true, a is still **true**; b **false**, etc.

The output of the flip-flop is available at Q with no impact on the flip-flop. No matter what the initial state of a flip-flop, a set signal will cause the flip-flop to enter the set or 1 state and to stay in that state even after the set signal has ceased.

Note that the flip-flop is completely symmetrical. This symmetry provides the mechanism for terminating the set state. A signal at the reset line R will cause c to become **true** and Q to become **false**, thereby cutting off the support to the upper **or** gate. The signal will become **true** at b and **false** at Q. On the other hand, if a second set signal is received before a reset, no change will take place in the system. That is, placing a 1 where there is already a 1 causes no apparent change.

The obvious use for a flip-flop is as a bit of memory. Eight flip-flops together can represent a byte of memory.

EXERCISE

8–24 Describe the output states for each gate after reception of a reset signal.

*D-Flip-flops Unfortunately, the above configuration does not seem to be quite correct for use as a storage location. A signal arriving at a register (for example, as in Figure 8–34) is either a 1 or a 0. That value, whichever it was, should be kept by the register. However, setting or resetting a flip-flop requires a 1 signal on exactly one of the two lines. An incoming 0 signal is not distinguishable from a null (no change) signal. The solution to this problem requires two steps. **And**ing the incoming signal with a clock pulse can restrict set and reset to the appropriate times (Figure 8–35). Additionally, a single input value of 0 or 1 can be converted to a 1 at set or reset, as appropriate, by splitting the signal and inverting one of the two resulting signals. This will always produce

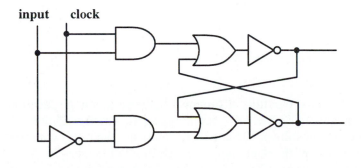

FIGURE 8–35 An improved flip-flop allowing transfer of data.

one true and one false signal. Normally the clock will be false and therefore both inputs will be 0. But when the clock signal is true, exactly one of the two lines delivers a 1 to the flip-flop. Such a flip-flop is called a *D-flip-flop*, since it takes a single data input. A register can thus be built using a set of D-flip-flops.

EXERCISE

8–25 Build a 4-bit storage cell using D-flip-flops as the basic building blocks.

Memory Organization

Memory can be envisioned as a series of slots or pigeonholes, each with a unique address to distinguish it from the others. Each cell has a size based on the size of the common data types. Every cell is the same size (typically 8, 16, or 32 bits)—independent of the type of the data it holds. Thus, some larger data will need more than one cell, and multiple items of some smaller data types may be packed into a single cell. These concepts are brought together as pictured in Figure 8–36. Note that the bits within each cell are numbered from right to left.

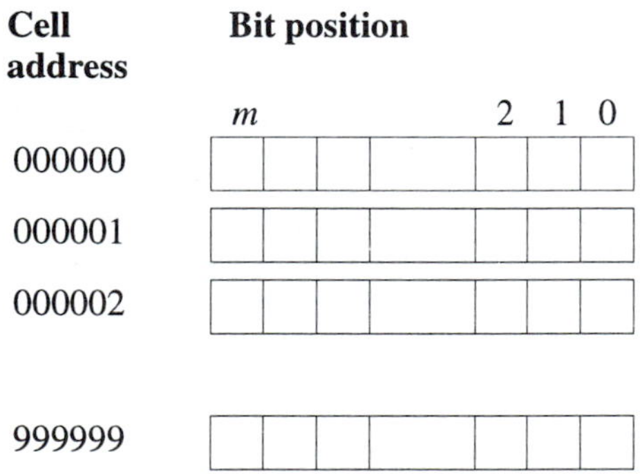

FIGURE 8–36 Memory organized into cells.

We must carefully distinguish between a storage location's address and its contents. In Figure 8–37, the storage cell, which might be called "A" in C++, is located at address 105 and its contents are the two's complement binary representation of the data value 17_{10}. High-level languages like C++ make this distinction *appear* less significant; the use of symbolic names and the other features of such languages makes address references and arithmetic seem almost automatic. At the functional machine level, where we deal with bits and

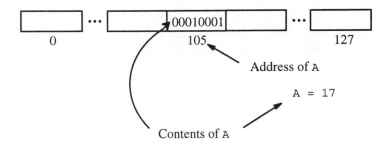

FIGURE 8–37   The distinction between address and content.

bytes and instructions, rather than data types and statements, nothing may be taken for granted.

The capacity of a particular computer's memory—that is, the number of bytes available—is called the memory size or *address space*. If we allow n bits to hold an (unsigned) binary address, then the memory capacity or address space is 2^n and the addresses range from 0 to 2^{n-1}.

Since address spaces are usually fairly large, they are often expressed in *kilobytes* (K bytes) or *megabytes* (M bytes). Here, 1 K byte is that number closest to 1000 that is also a power of 2, or 1024 (2^{10}). Similarly, 1 M byte is that number closest to 1,000,000 that is also a power of 2, or 1,048,576 (2^{20}). Hence, a computer with an address space of 256K bytes has $2^{18} = 262,144$ addressable locations, and one with 16 M bytes has $2^{24} = 16,777,216$ locations. Although these are the technically correct definitions of K bytes and M bytes, computer scientists often think about capacities more informally as if K = 1000 and M = 1,000,000, just because it is simpler. This is close enough as an approximation to the actual numbers to be useful.

Memory Access

We have now seen how memory is constructed and how it is organized. Now let's look at how it works. The memory system of the computer really needs to do two things. It must store an item of information in a particular location (and retain it there indefinitely), and it must allow a *fetch* of an item from a given byte or set of contiguous bytes.

To store a value in memory, the CPU must tell the memory both the value that is to be saved and the location where it will be saved. The memory unit locates a specific memory address in much the same manner as the CPU selects a specific ALU: It uses a decoder much the same as the ALU selects an instruction. Input to the decoder is the binary address of the desired location. As output the decoder sends a signal on exactly one selection line—the line that goes to the desired location in memory. The use of a decoder is perhaps most easily visualized by example. Assume, for the moment, that the address space is (a very limited) 128 bytes. This implies that the decoder must have 7 bits of input and 128 (2^7) output lines—one for each memory cell. The entire set of binary addresses ranges from 000 0000 to 111 1111—that is, address 0_{10} to address 127_{10}.

For a memory fetch, the selected cell returns its content. To accomplish this, the selection signal can be **and**ed with the content of the memory cells. Only the selected cell will generate any output. All others are ended with a **false** signal. A memory store requires the CPU simultaneously to send both the address and the content. The content is **and**ed with the output of the decoder. Only the selected cell receives any input.

Finally, the machine needs a way to initiate a read to or write from the store. It has additional read/write control lines, which specify `read` or `write` and initiate the operation. The selection lines are **and**ed with the decoder to create one signal which specifies, in effect, "read from (or write to) this cell now."

The Memory Hierarchy

Computer storage is divided into two general categories: *registers,* which are fast but expensive, and *random access memory* (*RAM,* also called *primary* or main memory), which is slower but cheaper. The distinction between the two types of memory is not one of logic but of technology. Simply put, speed costs. The faster registers are more expensive than the slower main memory. Therefore, machines have relatively few fast (but expensive) registers and much more of the slower (but cheaper) main memory.

The fast registers serve well as storage locations for storing small amounts of data for short periods of time. For example they may hold a loop counter or a temporary sum. The cheaper RAM on the other hand is useful for storing larger collections of data. For example, an array would normally be held in RAM.

One important use for data registers is to hold operands and results of arithmetic operations. If the adder can receive its operands from registers and place its result in a register, the whole operation will proceed much faster.

A data register must be large enough to hold one working unit of data. That is, if the ALU processes m bits at a time, a data register must also hold m bits. If the standard integer is 32 bits, the data register must be 32 bits wide ($m = 32$). As with main memory, an individual register can be selected using a decoder. But since there are far fewer, a much smaller decoder is needed.

In addition to the general-purpose data registers, special work registers hold status information, such as whether an overflow occurred. Some of these conditions are indicated by *condition codes*, which are kept in a *condition code register* (CC). Unlike data registers, work registers are not directly accessible by the computer program itself.

The number of general-purpose registers in a computer is another design decision. Largely this reflects a speed versus cost tradeoff. The more registers, the faster the computations. But it also reflects the CISC versus RISC choice discussed above. With a greater number of registers, it is possible to restrict all operations to use only register operands. It also facilitates subroutine calls (see Chapter 9). As you can see from Figure 8–38, RISC machines use a dramatically larger number of registers.

Secondary storage In addition to main memory and registers, the memory hierarchy has other levels. Most significant is *secondary storage*. You know secondary storage as disks and tapes. It is even slower than main memory but also cheaper. In addition it is nonvolatile and can be saved even when the machine is not running.

	Number	Size in Bits
DEC VAX	16	32
IBM 4300	16	32
Intel 8088	8	16
Intel 80386	8	32
Motorola 68000	16	32
Sun SPARC	128	32

FIGURE 8–38 General-purpose register configurations for several computers.

Cache A relatively new introduction to the memory hierarchy is *cache* memory. This level fits between main memory and registers and is typically used for storage of frequently accessed data or instructions.

* Parity

Even in the best of worlds, errors do occur. What happens when an error occurs in memory? We are actually lucky to have a binary machine—the result of an error in any specific bit is predictable: It is the inverse of the correct value. A *parity* check simply counts how many one or zero bits there are in the cell. It can be defined using either even or odd parity. In the case of even parity, all characters must have an even number of "on," or 1, bits. An extra bit is used to ensure this. For example, the letter B has ASCII code 42_{16}, which has the following 8-bit binary representation:

(8.41)   0100 0010

Since this representation already contains an even number of 1 bits, the parity bit is set to 0, giving the 9-bit representation

(8.42)   `0 0100 0010`

On the other hand, the letter C is represented as

(8.43)   `0100 0011`

In this case, the leftmost bit is set to 1 in order to retain an even number of 1s in an even-parity system. Thus, the character C is represented as

(8.44)   `1 1100 0011`

Parity checking allows a quick check (but not a correction) of each character as it is received by the computer from a peripheral device such as a disk or tape. Whenever a *parity error* occurs (there is an odd number of 1 bits in an even-parity system or vice versa), the system can request that the data be retransmitted. In more complicated parity schemes data can be self-correcting. Such schemes uniquely identify the bit in error. Once the error is identified, there is one possible correction for the bit: Invert it.

EXERCISE

8–26 Find which byte in the following message is in error, assuming an even-parity system.

`10010011 01001101 11001011 10100110`

* Historical Note: Magnetic Core

In the second and third generations of computers (1956–1975), a magnetic "core" was used to store each bit. The core was a small donut-shaped device made of ferric oxide, with wires running through its center, as shown in Figure 8–39. The core stores a 0 or 1 bit according to the direction of current flow through the selection wire that passes through it. Core memory had one advantage over modern memory: It was nonvolatile—it would maintain its setting even if the machine was shut down or lost power. However, as memory sizes grew and computers became ever faster, the core was replaced by solid-state devices, which were orders of magnitude faster and much smaller. However, because of the historic use of magnetic cores, RAM is still sometimes called "core memory."

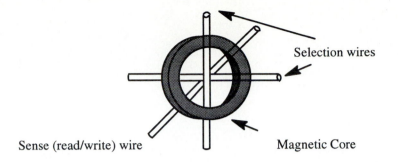

Selection wires

Sense (read/write) wire

Magnetic Core

FIGURE 8–39   Design of a pre-semiconductor magnetic core.

SUMMARY

Most computers are binary, or two-value, systems. As such their operation can be completely described using Boolean logic. Numbers are represented in binary. In fact all data—numeric and nonnumeric—is represented as collections of binary digits. The individual arithmetic operations are performed by arithmetic logic units, which are constructed of logic gates. Each of these logic gates corresponds to a logical operation: **and, or,** or **not**. In addition, decoders (the units that select a specific operation) and memory itself are built from logic circuits. Individual pieces of hardware are constructed from smaller constructs in a manner analogous to the creation of large programs from a collection of smaller subroutines.

PROGRAMS AND COMPUTERS

In Chapter 8, we described the construction of the various components of a computer from simple logical circuits. That description may seem far removed from the C++ Machine of the first seven chapters. C++ is a language involving powerful and flexible instructions, which are nicely tailored for writing algorithms. But Chapter 8 describes the computer itself in terms of arithmetic and logic units, each of which can perform only the simplest of operations. In this chapter we build a bridge between those two views of computing. The assembly language model or view of the internal structure of a machine is a more detailed version (lower level of abstraction) than that used by higher-level language programmers. Like the higher-level language model, the assembly language model is a variation on the general von Neumann Machine. On the other hand, it consists entirely of constructs supported directly by the machine-level model. The concepts described in this chapter are universal and can be applied generally to any assembly language running on any modern machine. However, for the sake of example, all concepts are illustrated using the language of a hypothetical machine called *Marina*. Through these examples, we explore all the basic computer organization concepts in a systematic manner.

ASSEMBLY LANGUAGE

As we saw in Chapter 8, the arithmetic logic unit (ALU) is capable of only very simple operations compared to those specifiable in C++. Assembly language and machine language both provide ways of describing algorithms, using those simple operations as the basic building blocks. Each machine language instruction corresponds to a single request for an ALU operation. Each assembly language instruction is basically a *symbolic form* of a machine language instruction. We discuss assembly language first because it is closer to the higher-level languages we have used. Yet, this language is capable of representing arbitrarily complex algorithms. In contrast, *higher-level languages,* which are more commonly used for describing algorithms, are relatively human-oriented and machine-independent. They allow arbitrarily complex operations. A C++ statement will usually correspond to *many* assembly or machine language statements, yet it provides no more power in terms of what can or cannot be computed.

Assembly language commands typically have the form

```
add item1, item2
```

meaning "add the value of `item1` to that of `item2`, leaving the result in `item2`." Similarly you could subtract one value from another, multiply two values, or negate a value. But you cannot add three values, perform more "complex" arithmetic operations such as exponentiation, or specify that a third location receive the result of the addition. Thus, the simple C++ statement

```
Sum = 17 + 5 ;
```

will require about three lines in a typical assembly language as shown in Figure 9–1.

```
load    17,R0    load the first operand into a data register
add     5,R0     add the second operand to the first
store   R0,Sum   store the result of the addition in Sum
```

FIGURE 9–1 Assembly commands equivalent to `Sum = 17 + 5;`

Odd as this short set of instructions may seem, each line plays an important role in the computation. The first statement, `load`, places the value 17 in a register where it can be manipulated efficiently (recall that a machine has a small set of fast registers and a much larger quantity of slower main memory). Because registers are so much faster, the operands for many instructions must be in registers. The second statement performs the actual addition, and the last statement performs the assignment—it copies the value to a location in main memory, where it can remain for an extended time.

The Assembly Language View of Memory

Every assembly language command requires memory access—at least one for fetching the instruction, and possibly additional accesses for the operands. The nature of this access plays a central role in understanding how the instructions actually work. So we begin our discussion of assembly language with a review of the memory concepts (as discussed in Chapter 8). In a stored program machine, the instructions themselves reside in memory. Every computer has two forms of internal memory: registers and main memory. The addressable unit of memory is the word or byte—in Marina's case, a 16-bit word. That is, pairs of adjacent bytes are grouped together to form a word. This allows integers to be in the range –32,768 to 32,767.

Main memory On any machine, RAM contains a relatively large number of contiguously addressed words. Marina's entire address space includes only

128 words, addressed from 0 to 127, or 000 0000$_2$ to 111 1111$_2$. That is a very small memory; many desktop computers today have several million bytes of RAM (and require more than 20 bits to address). But even Marina's small memory is large compared to its four registers.

Storage declarations   Individual storage locations can be given mnemonic names through the declare storage directive

```
<name>    ds
```

or the declare constant directive

```
<name>    dc      <value>
```

The ds directive is roughly equivalent to the variable declaration of C++. The dc can be thought of as comparable to the variable declaration with an initial value assigned at the same time.

Registers   Registers are much faster than main memory, but there are fewer of them. Marina has four data registers, called R0, R1, R2, and R3. The programmer cannot ask for additional registers nor change their names. Most Marina registers are 16 bits wide—the same as the cells of RAM storage. That's exactly enough to hold one integer, one instruction, or any other value that one cell of main memory can hold.

Assembly Language Syntax and Semantics

There are very few distinct statement types in assembly language. In fact, Figure 9–2 shows the complete set of instructions for the hypothetical language of Marina. The first four perform the obvious binary arithmetic operations. and, or, and not are logical operations corresponding to the Boolean operations **and, or**, and **not** of Chapter 3 and very similar to the logic gates or logical units described in Chapter 8. load and store are the two operations for moving data between RAM and the registers. The remaining operations are described in the next few sections.

Assembly languages also have a very simple—and uniform—syntax. Figure 9–3 shows the syntax used by our hypothetical machine Marina. A quick examination reveals that this is simply a generalization of the syntax used in Figure 9–1. Opcode (operation code) is the mnemonic name for the machine operation. Operand1 and Operand2 designate the operands. Generally assembly instructions specify that a value be combined (added, subtracted, etc.) with a second value, and the result left at the second location. We say that the first operand is the *source* operand and the second is the *destination* or *target* operand. Thus we can restate the description of Figure 9–1. The first line co-

<u>**Opcode Mnemonic Meaning**</u>

```
add        integer add
sub        integer subtract
mul        integer multiply
div        integer divide
and        logical conjunction (and)
or         logical disjunction (or)
not        logical negation (not)
rot        rotate bits of cell
bsr        branch to subroutine
ret        return from subroutine
load       load to a register
sto        store register to a memory word
cmp        compare
bra        branch unconditionally
blt        branch if less-than
beq        branch if equal
ble        branch if less-than or equal
berr       branch if arithmetic error
halt       halt execution
```

FIGURE 9–2   The Marina instruction set.

pies the source (the value, 17) to the target (register0); the second line adds a new source (the value, 5) to the same target (register0); the final line copies that result (as the source) to a new target (the variable, Sum). Operands may be registers (e.g., R0), main memory cells (e.g., Sum), or literals (e.g., 17). Label is an optional identifier, allowing us to reference the statement as part of a control structure. Finally, assembly language needs even more documentation than C++; any explanatory comments can be placed at the right of the operands to clarify the program for the reader.

This consistency makes it easier to understand new statements as they are encountered. For example, consider the following statements:

```
sub    a,b    ; How much larger is b than a?
mul    a,b    ; Multiply a times b
and    a,b    ; Calculate the logical conjunction of a and b
not    a      ; Calculate the logical negation of a
```

Notice the consistency of the syntax: Each operation is followed by its operands (even when there is only one, as in the case of not); the result of the operation always ends up in the second (destination register); and the comments

```
Label  opcode    Operand1,Operand2    ; Comments
```

FIGURE 9–3   Assembly language statement format.

describe the purpose of the statement. The syntactic structure provides a clear distinction between the operation and the operands. On the other hand, the simplicity implies that the content or meaning of a specific statement must be derived almost entirely from the meaning of the individual components. The structure of the statement provides little help.

C++ statements can manipulate variables, constants, literals, and expressions. These values may be of type `int`, `float`, `char`, or even user-defined. The types of assembly language operands, however, refer to their architectural properties. Operands can be in memory, or registers, or they may be immediate ("literal") operands. A memory operand is specified by the symbolic name of the memory location. A register operand is specified as Rn, where n is the register number (0, 1, 2, or 3 in Marina). Literal or immediate values are actually written as part of the instruction, like literals in a higher-level language. You can think of the term "immediate" as indicating that the value itself is written immediately after the instruction. In later sections, we will see a clearer distinction between immediate and RAM operands. Figure 9–4 shows three versions of `add`, each with a different form of operand.

Assembly language	Meaning
add X,R1	Add the content of RAM location X to register R1.
add 1,R1	Add the literal value 1 to R1.
add R1,R2	Add the contents of R1 to R2.

FIGURE 9–4   Assembly language operand configurations.

Although operands may be any of the three types, not all combinations are possible. Since you cannot place values into a constant, the destination may not be an immediate. Many machines (including Marina) also require that for some instructions no more than one of those operands may specify a RAM location. This apparently arbitrary rule reflects both the machine architecture—RAM to RAM operands may be physically impossible—and the mechanism for identifying operands. Recall that registers are much faster than RAM. Operations with RAM operands are slower—in direct proportion to the number of such operands. Since there are few registers, they are easy to specify. The number of distinct RAM locations, on the other hand, makes them more difficult to specify. Recall that you can specify n things with $\log(n)$ bits. Or, for an analogy, consider the difference between specifying a specific state within the United States (each has a unique name) and specifying a particular sea gull out of thousands on a beach. Hence, for the sake of efficiency, machines may restrict the number of RAM operands to one.

EXERCISES

9–1 Write Marina assembly language code to find the average of three numbers stored in locations called `first`, `second`, and `third`.

9–2 Write Marina assembly language code that calculates an exclusive or of the present contents of register 1 and register 2.

Algorithms in Assembly Language

Assembly language commands are much like simplified versions of C++ commands: Each operates on data items declared in the declaration section; each performs one step of an algorithm or function; and each can be grouped with others to form a function.

More complicated arithmetic In C++, the user can express arbitrarily complicated arithmetic expressions in a single statement by use of parentheses and default precedence rules. In assembly language however, each statement corresponds to a single arithmetic operation. To represent a more complicated arithmetic expression, the programmer must specify each step of the operation as a separate statement—in the precise order in which they are to be executed. Thus the C++ statement

```
a = b * (c + d) ;
```

can first be expanded into two statements

```
temp = (c + d) ;     // for some variable temp
a =  (b * temp) ;
```

which in turn is equivalent to the four Marina statements

```
load    c,R2
add     d,R2      ; R2 is now serving as temp
mul     b,R2      ; Now R2 = b*(c+d)
sto     R2,a      ; Final result goes into a.
```

And the C++ statement

```
a = (b*c) / (e*f) ;
```

should be thought of as the three C++ statements

```
num = (b * c) :
den = (e * f) ;
a = num / den ;
```

which in turn, might be accomplished in Marina as

```
load    c,R1
mul     b,R1        ; Leave num value in R1.
load    f,R2        ; And continue with calcs.
mul     e,R2        ; Reg2 is equivalent to den.
div     R2,R1
sto     R1,a
```

Here we begin to see how the programmer can take advantage of the relative properties of the two types of storage. R1 temporarily held the result of the first subcalculation until it was used three statements later. The operands for most operations are generally held in registers. That is, the items that you are currently working with should be in faster locations. If the value of num would not be used until many statements later, it would be better stored in RAM.

Example 9.1 We could perform subtraction in assembly language using the two's complement method of Chapter 8.

```
load    b,R0
load    a,R1
not     R1          ; Find ones' complement of A
add     1,R1        ; Now find two's complement
add     R1,R0       ; This is B - A
sto     R0,result
```

CONTROL STRUCTURES

As was the case with higher-level languages, the default order of execution of statements in assembly language is sequential: Each statement is executed after the syntactically preceding statement (usually the statement positioned above the current statement in a program listing). The control unit manages the execution of these commands. Normally it fetches a command, executes it, then fetches the next, and so on. Control operations alter this flow by selecting a different statement to be executed next. These statements do not alter data in the usual sense. They only instruct the machine not to execute the syntactically next statement but to branch or jump to some other statement instead. In C++, the control statements include:

- Conditionals   (if, switch)

- Iteration   (while, do, for)

- Procedural abstractions (function calls)

The set of assembly language control statements is much smaller—and seemingly much more primitive. Yet we can build structures corresponding to every C++ structure using this small set.

Branches

Consider the meaning of the C++ conditional

```
if ( <test> )
    <action>
```

The common interpretation is "if the test is true, then perform the action; otherwise skip over the action." When the test is false, we say that control is transferred to the instruction following the action. "Transfer of control" also describes the action of the only assembly language control statement: the *branch* or *jump* instruction. In Marina, the branch is specified as

```
    bra     <newloc>
```

where `<newloc>` is a label specifying some statement or location within the program. The destination of a branch statement must have a label. In the following example, the statement `next_one` is executed immediately after the branch:

```
            load    item1,R0
            bra     next_one
            load    item2,R0
next_one    add     R0,R0
```

The code copies `item1` into register 0, but the third instruction is skipped, resulting in register 0 ending with twice `item1`, not twice `item2`. Statement labels are actually very similar to the variable names created by C++ declarations: the label provides a way to refer to the statement. In this case, the label, `next_one`, provides a way for the branch statement to refer to its destination. Also note in passing that since the branch is always taken and there is no label on the following statement (`load item2,R0`), there is no way to get to the second copy statement; it is useless—but perfectly legal.

Conditional branches Unfortunately, the branch as described thus far is a relatively useless operation if used alone: It provides no choice. In contrast, all control structures in C++ entail a decision process: Perform this block of code or do not perform this block; repeat this block or do not. That is, useful control requires some mechanism for making decisions. To create useful control structures, assembly languages provide a restricted form of branch. The branch instruction we have seen thus far always branches and is therefore called an *absolute* or *unconditional branch*. A *conditional branch* may or may not be performed, depending on some logical condition. For example,

```
    beq    over_the_rainbow        ; example of "branch-on-equal"
```

is read, "If it is equal, branch to `over_the_rainbow`." Note that although the syntax says "branch if two things are equal," it does not specify which two things. Nothing in the above syntax indicates which two entities must be equal. In some very real sense, complete specification of a conditional branch requires four pieces of information or operands: the test to perform, two items to compare using that test, and a destination for the actual branch. To do this in a single statement would require a four-field instruction, something like

```
bra    equal, first, second, location    ; NOT CORRECT
```

which might be interpreted as branch to `location` if the two values `first` and `second` are equal. But assembly languages do not provide instructions this complex. Instead, most of them (including Marina) provide the *compare* statement

```
cmp    first,second
```

which compares `first` to `second` and determines if `first` is equal, greater than, or less than `second`. `cmp` does not change either the destination or the source operand; it only compares them. The general syntax of compare is

```
cmp    <source>,<destination>
```

The semantic rules are exactly the same as for the previous statements: Operands may be variables, constants, or literals; they can be in RAM or register. The result of the comparison is left in a special location called the *condition code register* (CC). A subsequent conditional branch uses that result to determine if it should branch (or not branch). In our early examination of Marina, we will always use the two statements in tandem:

```
     cmp    first,second
     beq    newloc
     another_statement
     ...
newloc
```

The above `cmp` compares the contents of `first` and `second` and branches to `newloc` if the two values are the same but falls through to the syntactically next statement, `another_statement`, if the values are not the same. You may think of compare and branch as a single statement, requiring two lines: The first specifies what items are to be compared and the second specifies what conditions are important and what to do if the condition is met. Marina provides three explicit conditional branches:

Statement	Meaning
beq	branch if equal
blt	branch if less than
ble	branch if less than or equal

A two-line pair—cmp and one of these three branches—can be used to create Marina structures equivalent to any of the C++ control structures.

Conditional Structures

The examples thus far are similar to the C++ conditional statement, whose general form is

```
if ( <test> )
    <action>
```

The <test> is usually a comparison between two values (for example, a == b or c < 2). The <action> is a block of code that is executed only if the test yields a true result. The conditional can thus be thought of as

```
if <test> is true
    then perform <actions>
    otherwise proceed immediately to the next statement.
```

The Marina compare statement corresponds roughly to the <test> and a conditional branch enables the program to bypass the <actions> when the test is false. Thus, the C++ code

```
if ( first != second )
    <action>
<following statement> ;
```

is equivalent to the Marina segment

```
    load    second,R0
    cmp     first,R0
    beq     following_statement
     <action>
following_statement
```

Notice that the test seems to be reversed. That is because the branch command specifies the conditions under which the action is skipped. The C++ conditional specifies the conditions under which the action is performed (not skipped).

You will recognize the three conditional branch tests in Marina (beq, blt, ble) as identical to three of the tests available in C++ (=, <, and <=) To create the other three logic tests, we can construct the test using logical negation. For example,

```
greater than or equal
```

is really the logical equivalent of

```
not (less than)
```

So the command "branch on greater than or equal" can be constructed as

```
blt  following_statement ; skip (negate) the test
bra  target              ; if get here it wasn't less-than
following_statement...
```

The remaining tests > and != can be constructed in analogous manners (see Exercise 9–3).

Else statements Conditionals with an else statement require two paths through the code, one that includes the <then action> and one that executes the <else action>. The general form in C++ is

```
if ( <test> )
    <then_action>
else <else action> ;
```

The corresponding Marina code is

```
            cmp     value1,value2
            bxx     second_part   ; where xx depends on
                                  ; the desired test
                <then_action>
                bra     after_all
        second_part
                <else action>
        after_all
```

Notice the unconditional branch at the end of the <then_action>. It is needed to avoid accidental execution of the else clause. It is unconditional since control will never get to that statement unless the then clause was executed. Also notice that indentation helps show the structure of the segment.

EXERCISES

9–3 Create Marina segments equivalent to the C++ conditional constructs.

```
if (a > b)
   <action>
```

```
if (a != b)
   <action>
```

9–4 Write Marina assembly language code that finds the larger of two numbers. Try the largest of three numbers.

9–5 Write Marina assembly language code to find the roots of a quadratic equation. Assume that the answers are integers and that you have a function called `square_root`.

Iteration

Iteration structures or loops are blocks of code that are executed repeatedly. A loop requires a control structure that returns to a statement that has already been executed. Up to this point, all examples of branch instructions have branched forward to code further down the listing, skipping over an unwanted segment. There is no reason that this must be the case. Branching backward (or upward) into the section of code that has already been executed is exactly how loops are constructed in assembly language:

```
top     <action>
        bra     top
```

This generic loop structure seems to create an infinite loop, analogous to

```
while (1)
{
    <body>
}
```

In practice, every loop must have an exit mechanism. Again, the Marina compare and branch pair is sufficient to create the exit mechanism for iteration structures corresponding to those of C++.

Pretest loops The defining characteristic of a pretest (or `while`) loop is that the test for continuation is made at the top of the loop body, before the body is executed. The C++ form of a pretest loop is

```
while ( <test is true> )
{
    <loop body>
}
<next statement>
```

The Marina equivalent is

```
top     cmp     <item1>,<item2>
        beq     out_of_it    ; or other appropriate test
            <loop body>
        bra     top
    out_of_it <next statement>...
```

The test is performed first, comparing the same two values referenced in the C++ test. When the condition is false, the conditional branch exits the loop to the statement immediately following the loop structure. The absolute branch at the end closes the loop by returning control back to the top of the structure.

Example 9.2   Consider a loop to find the sum of the even integers less than 15. This could be written in C++ as

```
total = 0 ;         // running total
counter = 0 ;       // current value to be added
while  (counter < 15)
{
   total = total + counter ;
   counter = counter + 2 ;
}
```

The Marina equivalent is

```
        load    0,R0        ; R0 serves as total
        load    0,R1        ; R1 serves as counter
add_sum_loop
        cmp     15,R1       ; while (counter < 15) do
        blt     continue
        bra     out_of_it
continue
        add     R1,R0       ; total = total + counter;
        add     2,R1        ; counter = counter + 2;
        bra     add_sum_loop
out_of_it  .   .   .
```

Posttest loops The primary characteristic of the posttest (or do) loop is that the test is made at the end of the loop, thus ensuring that the body will be executed at least once. The general form of the posttest loop in C++ is

```
do
    <loop body>
while ( <test is true> ) ;
```

The Marina equivalent is

```
top
    <loop body>
    cmp <operands>
    blt  top
```

Counter controlled loops The counter-controlled loop, written in C++ with a for statement, is really a pretest loop with a built-in counter. Construction of a counter-controlled loop is left as Exercise 9–6.

EXERCISES

9–6 Write a counter-controlled loop to add the sum of the first 100 integers.

9–7 Change the loop in Example 9.2 to a do-while loop in C++; then write its Marina equivalent.

9–8 Write a Marina counter-controlled loop that finds the sum of the squares of n, for all positive $n < 256$.

9–9 Suppose a loop body is executed 100 times. If the loop is a pretest loop, how many branch statements will be encountered? How many branches will actually be taken? What would the answers be for a posttest loop?

*Registers as Index Counters

One common use of counter-controlled loops is as a mechanism for systematically working through an array. In assembly language we normally use a register to create such an index. For example, suppose R0 contains the address of an array of integers, block. We say that R0 points to the array, as shown in Figure 9–5.

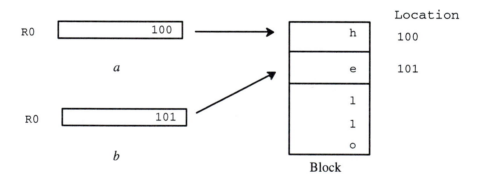

FIGURE 9–5   Register pointing to a location. (*a*) Beginning of block; (*b*) one cell past the beginning.

We can reference the array indirectly using the address register

```
load     (R0),R1
```

which is read as "load the item pointed to by R0 into R1." Since R0 contains the address of (the beginning of) the array block, this statement loads the first element of block into R1 as in Figure 9–5a. But if we added 1 to R0 and repeated the statement:

```
add    1,R0
load   (R0),R1
```

the second element of `block` would be loaded, as in Figure 9–5*b*. Such a reference, called an *indirect reference,* is a very powerful tool in assembly language programming. In particular, it forms the basis for pointers in C++.

EXERCISE

9–10 Suppose a block of 10 integers is stored starting at location 100. Write a loop that will add the contents of the 10 integers.

Subprograms

Imitation of higher-level language subprogram structures requires two additional variations of the branch command. Consider the simplest case: a void function with no parameters and no local variables. In C++, there are two segments of code to consider: the function definition

```
void <name> ()
{
    <body>
}
```

and a calling sequence, or reference

```
        <previous statement>
        <name> ;                  // call the function
        <following statement>
```

Creation of an assembly function definition is reasonably straightforward. Only two new tools are needed: a specialized branch to get to the subprogram and a mechanism to return to the calling program when the function is complete. This mechanism is more complicated since it must always return to the spot from which the function was called. The general form of the function body is

```
<name>    ; Recall that any statement can have a label.
        <body>
      ret
```

The line `ret` means return to the calling program. Return may be thought of roughly as replacing the final `end` statement in a C++ function. More precisely, it is like a branch that returns control to the statement *following* the statement that originally called the subroutine. As an example, a subprogram that counts to 3 might look like

```
count  load    1,R1
        add     1,R1
```

```
add     1,R1
ret
```

The calling statement, or branch to a subroutine, is also straightforward:

```
bsr     <name>
```

For `count`, it would look like

```
bsr     count
```

"Branch to subroutine," is a special form of the absolute branch command, that records its own location. A subsequent return statement within the subroutine body can use that address to branch back (return) to that same spot.

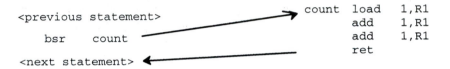

```
                                        count  load    1,R1
<previous statement>                           add     1,R1
                                               add     1,R1
    bsr     count                              ret

<next statement>
```

FIGURE 9–6   Control transfer to a subroutine and back.

Thus if we have a subroutine `star` that prints an asterisk (*), we could call it with the line

```
bsr     star
```

We could use that statement to define a second subroutine, `star3`, that prints three stars:

```
star3
        bsr     star
        bsr     star
        bsr     star
        ret
```

And a reference to `star3` would look like:

```
bsr     star3
```

Functions with parameters and local variables   C++ functions often communicate with their calling programs through parameters. In assembly language the most common technique for duplicating this communication is through the registers: The calling program leaves a value in a register and the called program receives the value by reading that register. For example, a calling program could place values in the registers R0, R1, and R2, and then call a function named add3 which adds the three numbers:

```
load    x,R0
load    R2,R1
load    5,R2
bsr     add3
```

The subroutine itself looks in the same three registers for values:

```
add3 add    R1,R0
     add    R2,R0
     ret
```

Notice several things about this routine. The writers of the calling program and subroutine must agree about which registers will be used to pass the variable. Also add3 is apparently a function. As such it returns a value, which it passes back through exactly the same mechanism: placing it in an agreed-upon register. In this case, each routine has access to exactly the same registers, so coordination is also needed lest the subroutine destroy a value the calling routine expected to have (yet another reason why registers should not be used for long-term storage). In general, great care must be taken when using subroutines.

This technique is limited by the number of registers available. If a subprogram has many parameters an alternate method will be needed. These methods use data structures and pointers, both of which will be discussed in Volume II of this series.

EXERCISES

9–11 Write a function that squares the value stored in R0 (leaving it in R0).

9–12 Assume that you have a function output that prints whatever character is in R0 on the screen. Write a function that writes your name.

9–13 Assume that you have the function star described above. Write a function n_star that writes out n stars, assuming that the value of n is passed in R0.

9–14 Write a function average that computes the average of the values stored in R0, R1 and R2, and leaves the result in R0.

MACHINE LANGUAGE

We have seen that assembly language allows us to write algorithms using the same level of operations supported by the ALU. But we have not seen how the computer takes an entire such program and executes the appropriate sequence of instructions. And we have seen the individual pieces. We saw that an individual ALU could be constructed to execute a specific operation and how a decoder could select one ALU (operation) to execute. But we still may not be able to see the connection between an assembly language algorithm and the operation at the level of the ALUs. More precisely, we need to expand the notion of the *control unit* to one that can recognize the different instructions and then supervise their execution by sending the appropriate coordinating signals. To see this we must first investigate how instructions are actually stored internally.

Although most of the important principles are the same for all machines, the actual internal representation of instructions is highly machine-dependent. We again describe the general principles using Marina as an example throughout.

In a stored program machine, the instructions themselves reside in memory. Therefore, we begin our discussion of machine instructions with a discussion of memory from a machine-level perspective. The addressable unit of memory is the word or byte—in Marina's case a 16-bit word. That is, pairs of adjacent bytes are grouped together to form a word. This allows integers to be in the range –32,768 to 32,767. More relevant to the current discussion, this is just large enough to hold one Marina instruction in the internal format.

Internal Representation of Instructions

We know that information, or data, is represented as patterns of binary digits, or bits. If the machine language instructions are also stored in memory, then the instructions themselves must also consist of patterns of bits. These bits will provide the information to the control unit to select the appropriate ALUs at the appropriate time. Basically, the bit pattern representing some instruction, such as ADD or MULtiply, becomes input to the signal lines of the ALU just as the bit patterns representing the numbers to be added or multiplied become inputs to the operand input lines of the ALU. The bit patterns representing the various available instructions and options must be decoded, and the whole process must be coordinated. We first look at the internal representation and then see how the control unit uses that representation.

The machine-level program is not stored internally in the assembly language format. Like all information, it is stored as a series of bits. In theory, it could be stored as the ASCII representation of the individual characters for each command. But that has several disadvantages. Most notably, it would be very wasteful of machine space. Marina has 15 distinct instructions (it may look like more, but we will see that there are only 15). Most of them have a 3-byte mnemonic name. But 3 bytes is 24 bits—enough storage to represent 2^{24}, or about 16 million possible operation codes. Specification of the details of specific instructions, such as the operands, would require even more storage. On the other hand, 16 distinct instructions require only $\log_2 16$, or 4, bits. Internally, instructions are stored in a compact form known as *machine language*. In Marina, each machine language instruction requires exactly 16 bits or one word. Figure 9–7 shows the schematic format of Marina's machine language instructions. (Note that bit positions—like digits in a binary number—are numbered from right to left, and start with zero).

opcode	mode	reg	addr

bits: 15–12   11–9   8–7   6–0

FIGURE 9–7   Marina's machine instruction format.

Next, we examine the individual fields of Marina machine instructions.

Opcode   The 4-bit *opcode* field specifies the specific instruction, as illustrated by Figure 9–8. The opcode is stored in the leftmost 4 bits (15–12) of the instruction. Virtually every assembly language instruction has a unique machine language equivalent. In Marina, the sole exception is the set of branch instructions. The entire family of branch instructions maps to the single opcode 1110. The mechanism for distinguishing between the various forms of branch is discussed later.

Example 9.3   We will use a running example in the next few sections. We will slowly translate the assembly language code to machine language, and then use the machine language version to see how the control unit manipulates code. We start with the assembly language segment

```
        load    a,R0      ; Copy the value of a to R0
                          ;   where it can be worked on
        add     b,R0      ; Add the value of b to it.
        sto     R0,Sum    ; Save the result in Sum.
        halt              ; It is all done.
Sum  ds                   ; 3 variables placed out of the way.
a    ds
b    ds
```

which is roughly equivalent to the C++ statement

```
    Sum = a + b ;
```

The opcodes for the statements are

Opcode Mnemonic Meaning

```
0000    no-op     does nothing
0001    add
0010    sub
0011    mul
0100    div
0101    and
0110    or
0111    not
1000    rot
1001    bsr
1010    ret
1011    load
1100    sto
1101    cmp
1110    bra       branch unconditionally
                     (mode=000)

        blt       branch on less than
                     (mode=010 and n=0, and z=0)

        beq       branch on equal
                     (mode=100 and z=1)

        ble       branch on less than or equal
                     (mode=110, either z=1 or n=0)

        berr      branch if arithmetic error
                     (mod=001 and o=1)
1111    halt      halt execution
```

FIGURE 9–8   Marina's machine language opcodes.

```
        load    1011
        add     0001
        sto     1100
        halt    1111
sum     ds      (no code generated)
a       ds      (no code generated)
b       ds      (no code generated)
```

Address   The *address* field (bits 6–0) normally designates the RAM address of operand 1. Since this field contains 7 bits, it is just sufficient to specify any one of $128 = 2^7$ memory locations—exactly the size of Marina's RAM. In each instruction this field contains the address corresponding to the named main memory operand of the assembly language command.

Example 9.4   If we assume the example program will be stored starting at location 10_{16} (= 10000_2), sum will be stored 4 locations later at 14_{16} =

10100_2, with a and b at 10101_2 and 10110_2. The machine language equivalents are thus:

```
load    1011 xxx xx 0010101
add     0001 xxx xx 0010110
sto     1100 xxx xx 0010100
halt    1111
ds
ds
ds
```

where the x's indicate that we still need to figure out the mode and reg fields.

Register Marina requires that at least one of the operands be a register rather than a main storage address. We saw in Chapter 8 that this enabled faster instructions. The *register* field specifies that register operand. Since it has two bits, it can specify any one of the four registers R0 through R3. The register field is much smaller than the address field. Thus, Marina's register-operand requirement also reduces the size of the instruction.

Example 9.5 The only register used in the example is R0, so we can specify two more bits:

```
load    1011 xxx 00 0010101
add     0001 xxx 00 0010110
sto     1100 xxx 00 0010100
halt    1111
ds
ds
ds
```

*Special Addressing Modes

Recall that operands come in various forms: register, RAM variable, or immediate. The *mode* field, shown in Figure 9–9, contains three bits that further describe the operands with respect to these properties. These bits distinguish between the various types of operands that the assembly language permits.

Example 9.6 All the instructions in the example have the simplest addressing modes. Their mode bits are therefore all zero. Adding in the three mode bits to our sample instructions, we get

```
      load    1011 000  00   0010101  ;
      add     0001 000  00   0010110  ;
      sto     1100 000  00   0010100  ;
      halt    1111 000  00   0000000  ; no operands so all zeros
sum   ds      0000 000  00   0000000  ; just reserved space
a     ds      0000 000  00   0000000  ; just reserved space
b     ds      0000 000  00   0000000  ; just reserved space
```

Bit	Interpretation of a 1 bit
11	Indicates that the operand is immediate
10	Indicates an indirect operand
9	Indicates that both operands are in registers

FIGURE 9–9 Marina's mode bits.

Register operands If mode bit 9 is 1, there is no RAM operand but two register operands instead. In that case, bits 1 and 0 of the addr field specify the second register operand. Even though it specifies a register in that case, we still refer to it as the addr field. For example, the machine language equivalent of the assembly language statement

```
add    R0,R1
```
is
```
0001 001  00   0000001
```

Immediate values If an operand will never change, the immediate mode is useful in much the same way as are C++ constants. An immediate operand is stored in place of the address in the address field (for example, a register cannot hold an immediate). The machine language equivalent of the assembly language statement

```
add    7,R1
```
is
```
0001 100  01   0000111
```

Indirect operands For situations which call for pointers such as array indexing, indirect operands provide a standard technique. The instruction

```
add    (R1),R2
```

should be interpreted as "add the contents of the location pointed to by R1 to the actual contents of R2." The presence of the indirect address is indicated by bit 10 of the Marina machine language instruction:

```
0001 010  01 0000010
```

Mode bits and branch instructions   As we saw in Figure 9–8, a single branch opcode (1110) refers to an entire family of branch instructions. On the other hand it has only a single operand—one for which the terms "immediate" and "indirect" do not seem directly applicable (although such interpretations are possible). Marina takes advantage of these otherwise "wasted" bits. For the branch operation, the mode bits indicate the conditions under which the program should branch, as summarized by Figure 9–10. That is, the four

```
Mnemonic     Bits        Interpretation
             11/10/9
bra          0  0  0      branch   unconditionally
blt          0  1  0      branch   if less than
beq          1  0  0      branch   if equal
ble          1  1  0      branch   if less than or equal
berr         0  0  1      branch   if arithmetic error
```

FIGURE 9–10   The mode bits for branch instructions.

conditional branch instructions are distinguished from one another and from the unconditional branch instruction bra by the settings of bits 11 and 10. The branch on error is distinguished by bit 9.

Recall that the compare command leaves information in the condition code register describing the result of the comparison: operand 1 is equal to, less than, or greater than operand 2. The decision to branch may be based on any combination of these results. For example, we can see from the figure that mode bits of 000 indicate an absolute branch and 110 indicates a branch if the comparison was less than, or if it was equal.

The Condition Code Register

The system maintains a special register for keeping track of important aspects of its current status. In particular, the various branch instructions all use the current contents of CC. The actual results stored in the CC are not the obvious equal, not equal, etc. This is due, in part, to the actual comparison mechanism and, in part, to additional uses of the condition code register. The compare ALU makes its comparison by subtracting operand1 from operand2 (without changing the contents of the actual operands). This yields a positive, negative, or zero result depending on whether operand2 is greater, less than, or equal to operand1. It is the result of the subtraction which is actually stored in the CC register.

One bit (called "z") of the CC records whether the result of this subtraction was zero (all bits of the result were 0); a second (N) records whether it was negative (sign bit = 1). In Figure 9–11, these are the first two bits of the CC register. If operand1 > operand2, the subtraction results in a negative number

relation of opnd1 to opnd2	result of opnd2 - opnd1	CC bits set (ZNCO)
opnd1 = opnd2	result = 0	10xx
opnd1 > opnd2	result < 0	01xx
opnd1 < opnd2	result > 0	00xx
	error	xxx1
	(overflow or zero divide)	

FIGURE 9–11   Condition code values for Marina.

and the N bit is set to 1. If the subsequent branch instruction is branch less than (BLT; opcode is 1110, with mode bits 01), then the branch is taken because the CC contains a 1 in the N bit.

One reason for the Z-N representation is that it allows other instructions to set the CC bits. In fact many instructions do so. For example, an instruction could branch if the result of the last arithmetic operation yielded a result less than 0. A careful assembly language programmer could take advantage of this to improve efficiency. Shortcuts such as this lead some programmers to prefer assembly language; they also provide considerable opportunities for error!

Marina's condition code register contains two more bits. The "O" bit is set if any operation results in an overflow (result of operation did not fit in the allotted space). For example, the sum of 20,000 and 20,000 will not fit in a 16-bit two's complement word. Adding those two values will set the O bit. The programmer can take advantage of this using the BERR (branch on error) instruction. The carry bit ("C") contains a copy of any value that carries out of during an operation. For example adding –1 and –1 produces

```
      1111 1111
 _    1111 1111
    1 1111 1110
```

The one carried out and is copied to the C-bit. It is useful for creating arithmetic operations on larger numbers, for use with the rotate operation, and for comparison of two's complement numbers.

EXERCISES

9–15 Translate the following instructions from assembly language to machine language. You may assume that a and b are stored at locations 100 and 101.

```
ble      b
div      a,r3
not      r2
bra      b
```

9–16 Translate the following Marina machine language instructions to assembly language

```
1010 000 00 0000000
1011 000 11 0001111
1110 001 00 0010000
```

THE INSTRUCTION CYCLE

The instruction cycle was described earlier as having three steps: fetch the instruction, decode the instruction, and perform the operation. We can now explore those steps in more detail.

The Instruction Fetch

Since the entire description of an operation is contained in the machine language instruction, each instruction is fetched from memory before it is performed. The control unit needs to have direct access to the exact machine language instruction. This operation requires two special-purpose registers.

Instruction register The instruction register (IR) is a special register that holds a copy of the current instruction. Like any data, an instruction can be processed quicker if it is contained in a register. Before each instruction is executed, it is first copied into this register, from where it is decoded. Since Marina's instructions are all 16 bits long, the IR is also 16 bits.

The program counter When the computer executes a program, it reads each instruction from memory. In order to fetch any value from memory, the CPU must request it by address. Therefore, the control unit must keep track of the location in memory of the next instruction. A special register called the *program counter* (*PC*) serves this purpose. It always contains a pointer to the current instruction, that is, a number specifying the address of the instruction. Since Marina has 128 memory cells, its PC contains $\log_2 128 = 7$ bits. Since the default order of the instructions is sequential, this value can also be used to calculate the next location needed.

Using the IR and the PC, the fetch operation can be described a little more formally as

- Copy the memory location pointed to by the PC to the IR.

Before we look at the execution of instructions, let's consider the PC a little further. Once execution of the current instruction is complete, the next instruction to be executed will usually be the instruction stored in the sequentially next memory location. For example, if the processor is currently executing the instruction stored in location 100, there is a good chance that the next instruction will be the one in location 101. To fetch that instruction, the PC will need to contain 101—one more than its current value. The control unit will need to increment the PC by 1, as shown in Figure 9–12 . Thus a second step is needed in the fetch process :

- Increment the PC.

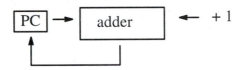

FIGURE 9–12   Incrementing the program counter.

An improved instruction fetch   As we have noted, fetching a data item from main memory is much slower than accessing a register. In fact it is one of the slowest actions the computer will execute. On the other hand, once the instruction is in the IR, its address really is not needed for the actual execution, so the PC can be updated as soon as the fetch is complete. Actually it can be incremented even sooner. Marina uses two more special-purpose registers to accomplish this.

The MAR and MBR   Data is accessed from memory using the two special registers: *memory address register* (MAR) and *memory buffer register* (MBR). When the CPU wants to fetch a particular storage location, it first copies the address into the MAR. The MAR is then used as input to the memory address decoder. The memory fetch copies the content of the selected location into the MBR. From there, the CPU can copy the value to its final destination (for example, the IR). For storing data, the CPU places the address in the MAR and the value in the MBR before sending the store request to memory.

Example 9.7   If the MAR is 16 bits wide, the maximum address space is $2^{16} = 65,536$ storage locations, with addresses from 0 to 65,535. If each address points to an 8-bit byte, then the MBR only has to be 8 bits wide.

The use of the MAR and MBR registers may seem like an unneeded complication; two steps have been added to both fetch and store operations. But it actually results in a significant savings of time. Recall that memory fetches and stores are among the slowest operations in a computer. Without the MAR and MBR registers, the CPU would have to continue sending the address to memory until the result of the fetch was received. With the two extra registers, the CPU can copy the address to the MAR, request a fetch from memory, and continue processing while waiting for the result to be received.

The steps of the instruction fetch are thus:

1. Copy PC to MAR.

2. Request memory fetch.

3. Copy contents of MBR to IR.

4. Increment the PC.

The first three steps of the process are illustrated in Figure 9–13. Once the instruction is in the IR, the control unit may decode it and execute the appropriate actions.

*An improvement One specific improvement resulting from the use of the MAR and MBR is the overlap of the increment step with the fetch. Since memory access is so slow, and since at the time the fetch begins the address of the instruction has already been copied to the MAR, there is no problem with changing the PC immediately. The PC can thus be updated while waiting for the instruction to be fetched—before the MAR is copied to the IR. The first four steps of the instruction cycle therefore can be reordered as:

1. Copy the PC to the MAR.

2. Fetch the next instruction from memory.

3. Increment the PC.

4. Copy the MBR to the IR.

By the time the `load` instruction is fetched in our example, the PC will hold the value 11_{16}, which points to the `add` instruction. At this point the IR contains a concise and structured machine language representation of the assembly language `load` instruction. The control unit can now use that information to perform a single step in the algorithm.

Executing the Instruction

The remainder of the cycle decodes the instruction and performs the operation. That is, the control unit must first figure out what the instruction is and then

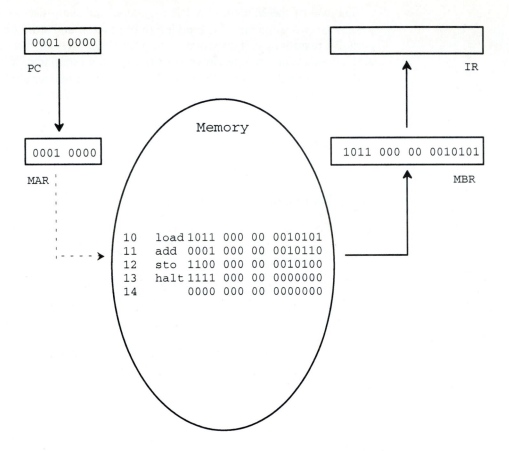

FIGURE 9–13 An instruction fetch.

perform the appropriate action. Although it sounds like a single step, this, too, can be broken down further. To see this, consider the processing of an add-immediate instruction

```
add   6,R1
```

which corresponds to the machine instruction

```
0001 100 01 0000110
```

In an immediate instruction, a value itself—rather than its address—is stored in the instruction. Assume the instruction is stored at location $11_{16} = 001\ 0001_2$. If this is the next instruction to be executed, the PC contains 11_{16}. At the end of the instruction fetch, the machine code `0001 100 00 0000110` in the IR and the PC will point to the (next) instruction at 12_{16}.

The operation code for the current (add) instruction is in the leftmost 4 bits of the instruction register, and the mode fields are in the next 3 bits. The control unit now decodes the opcode (the contents of the bits 15–12 of the IR). The control unit sends the opcode to a decoder as described in Chapter 8. The decoder sends a single positive signal to the add ALU, as in Figure 9–14. So the instruction decode really needs only a single step:

5.   Decode the instruction.

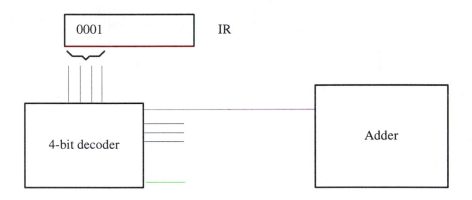

FIGURE 9–14   Decoding the instruction.

To perform the actual operation, the ALU must add two operands. Where does it find them? In this case, one is in register 1 and the other is immediate—that is, part of the instruction. Figure 9–15 shows the process. The control unit copies the two operands to the adder ALU. It first copies the immediate operand (6) from the rightmost 7 bits of the IR (at 1 in Figure 9–15). Then it finds the register number (1) of the second operand in bits 7–8 of the IR (at 2). A 2-bit decoder can select the appropriate register. The contents of register 1 (the 5 placed there by a previous instruction) is copied to the ALU (at 3). Once it has a value for each operand, the adder ALU performs the actual addition process (at 4) using the logic described in Chapter 8. Finally the result (the sum) is copied back (at 5) to the destination register, in this case, register 1. When the cycle repeats, it will fetch a new instruction, which is the one stored at location 12_{16}.

These steps are very uniform, with only minor variations from instruction to instruction. We can thus complete the steps of the instruction cycle as:

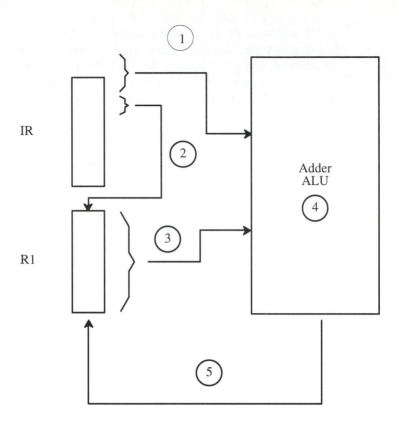

FIGURE 9–15 The steps of the perform cycle.

6. Fetch operand 1 to the ALU.

7. Fetch operand 2 to the ALU.

8. Perform the operation.

9. Store the results in the destination register.

The system clock synchronizes these steps. Each clock pulse designates a step in the process. Its signal is combined with the opcode or mode bits to select the specific action.

Other Operand Types

We just claimed that the instruction cycle is very uniform. Yet it is clear that there must be differences between the operation of the various instructions.

There are three kinds of operands, and each must be treated differently. Worse yet, not all instructions seem to follow this pattern. For example a branch instruction does not appear to fetch, manipulate, or store operands at all. But this single model does indeed account for all these variations. Let's use another example to illustrate the difference between an immediate instruction and a "from memory" instruction. Consider the execution of

```
add a,R1
```

which, if we assume that a is stored at location 21_{16}, is equivalent to the following machine instruction:

```
0001 000 01 0100001   or 10A1₁₆
```
or $10A1_{16}$

The fetch and decode parts of the machine cycle proceed as in the previous example. The instruction is loaded into the IR and the PC incremented to 22_{16}. The actual execution is only slightly more complex: This time, the address field does contain an address. The control unit recognizes this from the mode bits. Unlike the immediate operand of the previous example, this address cannot be copied directly to the adder ALU. Instead, it is a RAM address—the location of an operand that must be fetched. The process here is essentially the same as the steps for fetching an instruction:

- Copy the desired address (bits 6–0) from the IR to the MAR. Bits 6–0 contain the entire address.

- Request a memory fetch operation.

- Copy the contents of the MBR to the ALU.

Other than the original source and ultimate destination of the information, the fetch operation is identical for instruction and operand. The MAR receives the address from the IR rather than the PC, and the MBR delivers it to the ALU rather than the PC. That provides an additional reason for the use of the MAR and MBR: They allow a single operational unit to perform memory fetches for any situation.

The remainder of the cycle proceeds as in the earlier example. Operand 2 creates no problem: It is in a register just as before. The perform and store steps are also exactly the same. The entire difference created by the RAM operand is confined to the fetching of that operand.

Instructions with two register operands are also fairly simple. Both operands are copied using transfers like those of steps 3 and 4 of Figure 9–15. One operand is identified by bits 8–7 and the other by bits 1–0. The remainder of the process proceeds in an identical manner.

Operations with a RAM operand require two memory accesses, one to get the instruction itself and a second to fetch the operand specified by the instruction. Since RAM accesses are expensive, we see immediately that they must be slower operations than those with either immediate or register operands.

EXERCISE

9–17 Suppose a main memory address was specified as the destination (and that this was legal). What impact would this have on the total machine cycle?

Branching

The description of the instruction cycle seems directly extendable to the eight arithmetic and logical operations. But at first glance, it does not seem to explain how any of the branch operations work. Amazingly, this same simple cycle explains those operations also. To understand branch operations, let's extend the program segment from Example 9.2 to include an unconditional branch

```
Location       Assembly code
10         top  load   5,R0
11              add    6,R0
12              sto    R0,Sum
13              bra    top      ; the new line!
14              halt   1111
```

and turn it into a (rather silly) infinite loop, equivalent to the C++ loop

```
while (1)
    sum = 6 + 5 ;
```

A branch instruction works by changing the value in the PC, which causes a different instruction to be fetched next. Assume that the computer has already begun executing instructions and that the PC now holds the value 12_{16}. The CPU fetches the instruction at location 12_{16} (sto) and copies it to the IR. Execution of the store proceeds completely normally. In particular, the PC is incremented so that it contains 13_{16} (i.e., it points to the branch, Figure 9–16a). In the instruction fetch of the next cycle, the branch instruction is fetched, and the PC incremented to 14_{16} (Figure 9–16b). But this is exactly where it should not point if it is going to branch—to the halt instruction.

The control unit decodes the opcode in the IR, recognizing it as a branch instruction. The branch instruction works by changing the contents of the PC. It places a new value (the operand from the instruction) into the PC, so that the next instruction executed will not be the halt. Thus, during the execution part of the cycle, the operand (the destination of the branch) is fetched from the last

7 bits of the IR. No manipulation is needed, so the operand is the result stored in its destination—the PC (Figure 9–16c). The next instruction will be taken

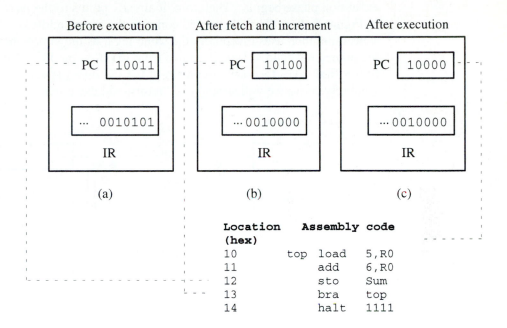

FIGURE 9–16   Execution of a branch instruction.

from the location now specified in the PC, namely 10000, creating the needed loop.

Conditional branches   Conditional branches use exactly the same logic as does the unconditional branch. However, they employ one extra step to check the condition code register. The execution phase can thus be described as

```
if CC matches specified test
    then copy address field to PC
    otherwise do nothing
```

That is, when the test is satisfied the conditional branch behaves exactly like the unconditional branch. When the test is not satisfied, the branch has no impact on the code at all. The condition code register acts like a message holder, saving information from the compare for use by the conditional branch.

*Subroutines   There is one significant difference between the results of a branch to subroutine and a simple branch: Control must eventually return to the location of the calling statement. Thus the bsr command must provide a mechanism for that return. In particular it must record the *return address*. Notice that control should always return to the *next* instruction—the instruction sequentially following the `bsr`. Fortunately, the PC is incremented before the execution phase begins. Therefore, it already points to the next instruction, as in Figure 9–17a. That is, the PC contains the return address. The branch-to-subroutine then uses essentially the same logic as the simple branch. As with the branch the address field is copied from the IR to the PC. However, the controller first saves the current content of the PC into a special storage location, which, for now, we will simply call "return-address-holder".

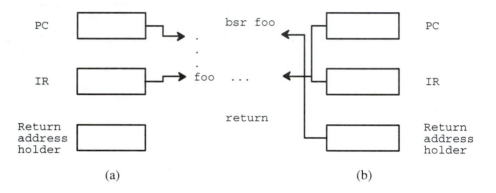

FIGURE 9–17   The branch to subroutine command. (*a*) Before execution; (*b*) after execution.

So the PC is simply copied to return-address-holder. The execute steps can be described as

- Save the return address (copy PC to return-address-holder).

- Branch (copy address from IR to PC).

The return command simply undoes the work of the `bsr`, by copying the saved return address to the PC, as shown in Figure 9–18. The value copied from the return-address-holder is precisely the address of the instruction following the branch to subroutine. It has no other operands; its only operand was implicitly held in the return-address-holder.

The observant reader may notice one very large problem with this explanation: What if the subroutine calls a second subroutine (for example, in an earlier example, function `star3` called function `star`)? The second `bsr` (contained within `star3`) will destroy the value placed in return-address-holder by the first `bsr` (to `star3` from the calling program). This problem is circumvented by a data structure known as a *stack*, which will be covered extensively in *Volume II* of this series.

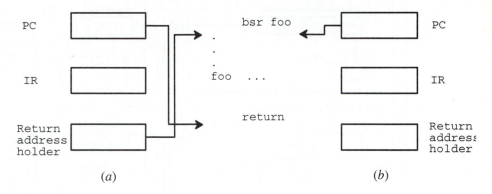

FIGURE 9–18 The return command. (*a*) Before execution; (*b*) after execution.

*The system bus

We have developed the memory unit and the ALU and have seen how they are coordinated by the control unit. Now we want to bring it all together (see Figure 9–19). In order to do this, we need one more thing—a means of facilitating the flow of information among all the components we have described. We use a *bus*, a parallel data path between two or more components of the computer. In reality, a bus contains more than just the lines for the data path, since it also transmits signal and timing information along with the data. The bus connects all registers, and virtually all data transfers between the registers flow through it. Since there is only one system bus, if two registers were to transmit their data simultaneously, the values would conflict with each other. Therefore the system clock provides a sequence of clock pulses to coordinate these transfers, which are combined with the data as described in Chapter 8.

In summary, we have systematically designed a hypothetical working computer. Using logic gates as the basic parts, we designed and built operational components to effect fundamental operations such as addition and subtraction. Then, using the operational units as basic parts, we constructed an ALU. Similarly, we built the memory unit and the control unit. Then, using the memory unit, the ALU, and the control unit, we put together our computer! The process ought to sound familiar. It is analogous to the way we build algorithms and computer programs from routines. We have learned not only the details of how to write programs and how computers work but also a *design process*—a process for dealing with the complex by successively breaking it down into smaller and smaller parts so that we never have to deal with an overwhelming clutter of detail. It remains to make this all a little more real; that is, we would like to

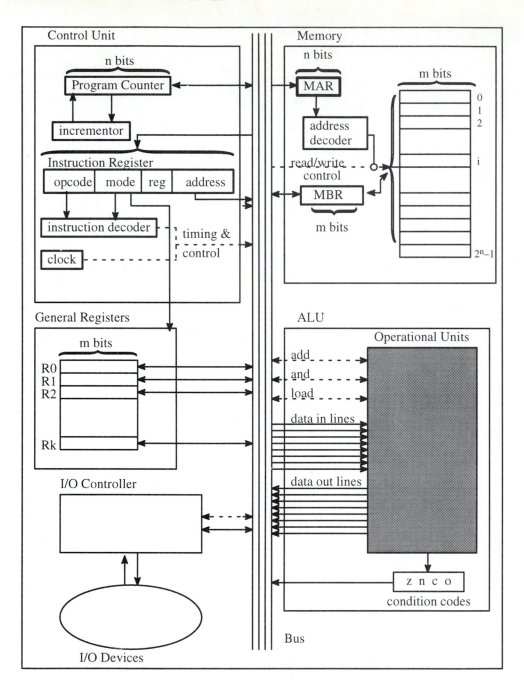

FIGURE 9–19 Component connections and data flow patterns.

see our little computer, to touch it, and even to program it. The lab manual contains a model of Marina.

EXERCISES

9–18 Use **and** and **not** gates to construct a four-line decoder; a circuit that takes a single input line and directs it to one of four output lines q_0, q_1, q_2, or q_3 based on the value of two selection lines s_1 and s_2. If both selection lines are 0, the input should be directed to q_0; if s_1 is 0 and s_2 is 1, the input should be directed to q_1; and so on.

9–19 To compare two 8-bit integers for equality, an elementary circuit called a *comparator* is used on each pair of corresponding bits. That is, suppose we have two integers $P = 5$ and $Q = 13$, whose binary representations are as follows:

```
P = 00000101
Q = 00001101
```

Note that the rightmost pair of bits in P and Q are both 1, the next pair are both 0, the next pair are both 1, and all other pairs are both 0 except for the pair in the fourth position from the right.

a. To design a comparator, we want its input to be a single bit from P, say p, and the corresponding bit from Q, say q. We want its output to be 1 (**true**) only if $p == q$, and 0 (**false**) otherwise. Give a truth table definition for this function.

b. Find a proposition that is equivalent to that truth table.

c. Draw a simple circuit diagram for the comparator that realizes this function.

d. Show how eight of these comparators can be combined to realize an 8-bit comparison.

The Assembler

It is nearly impossible for humans to interpret and understand the meaning of instructions when they are written in machine language—long strings of binary digits. On the other hand, the symbolic form is much too large for the machine to use. Thus, a symbolic assembly language is almost indispensable if we are to create or follow even the most simple programs at the machine level. Since this type of help is so obviously useful, we would like a method for writing programs in this symbolic form, letting the computer take care of the details of translating from the symbolic form to the binary machine language. Indeed, there is such a method: the *assembler*.

The advent of assembly language in the early 1950s was considered a giant step forward in the development and utilization of computers. Prior to that time, programming a computer to do anything at all interesting was extremely tedious and time-consuming. In fact, prior to the development of assembly languages, programmers created programs by first writing down the symbolic form of a program and then *hand-translating* it to the binary codes needed for computer execution. While this was clearly more effective than trying to write binary programs directly, the process was tedious and, worse yet, error-prone.

The first step in dealing with the difficulty of reading binary code was the recognition that binary codes could be abbreviated using another number system such as hexadecimal (actually, octal was more common at that time). For example, the simple program from Example 9.2 can be represented alternatively in hexadecimal form, as shown in Figure 9–20.

	Command	Binary Address	Binary Code	Hexadecimal Address	Hexadecimal Code
	load	10000	1011 0000 0001 0101	10	B805
	add	10001	0001 0000 0001 0110	11	1806
	sto	10010	1100 0000 0001 0100	12	1014
	halt	10011	1111 0000 0000 0000	13	F000
sum	ds	10100	0000 0000 0000 0000	14	0000
	dc				

FIGURE 9–20 Binary and hex version of counting program.

The hexadecimal version of the program is shorter and consequently less cumbersome to read than the binary version. Furthermore, since it is easier to remember that the load instruction is B in hexadecimal than to remember the binary equivalent 1011, most programmers use the hexadecimal representation for machine language programs.

Programming was especially difficult in the early years. There were so many details to keep track of, such as the meaning of the mode bits that follow the opcode in the machine instruction. The invention of assembly language thus marked a major improvement in programming. But an assembly language provides much more than a nicer set of symbols. It facilitates many aspects of the programming process:

1. The use of mnemonic opcodes instead of binary (or even hexadecimal) opcodes. Thus, we write `add` rather than `0001`.

2. The use of symbolic names in place of absolute addresses. Thus, a program may refer to a data value or program instruction as X rather than by its memory address, say `000 0101`.

3. The use of automatic assignment of memory addresses to instructions and data values, thus alleviating the need to hand-assign binary addresses to these items and remember those addresses whenever we need to refer to them. In fact, the programmer does not need or even want to know the internal location of the data value named A. Without symbolic addresses, any change in the program could require that all addresses be recalculated.

4. Representation of addressing modes.

None of this happens automatically; selecting a new language representation does not mean that the computer can understand it. We need some way to assign addresses to the various storage locations, to recognize the various opcodes and symbolic references, and to transform them all into the binary representation, which is still the only representation the computer understands. We have represented the computer as a symbol manipulator, and a program written in assembly language is certainly a series of symbols; it thus seems natural to use a computer to translate its own programs into a language it can really understand.

This process of storage allocation and translation is performed by a program called an *assembler*—a sort of superprogram that takes as its input the text of a program written in assembly language and produces as output an equivalent program in machine language, ready for the computer to execute, as shown in Figure 9–21. Essentially the assembler takes the assembly language state-

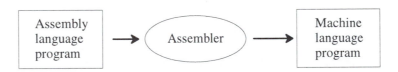

FIGURE 9–21 The assembly process.

ments, one at a time, and generates the corresponding machine language code. It performs roughly the operations of Examples 9.3 through 9.6, substituting the appropriate bit pattern for each field of each instruction. It determines the opcode, address and register operands, and the mode bits, storing these values in the next available location. It maintains a *symbol table* containing the addresses where it stored each labeled statement. It consults this table whenever it translates a statement containing a symbolic name.

The concept of an assembler helps us understand the relationship between code and data. Whenever the assembler encounters a variable directive (DS in Marina), it simply reserves the appropriate amount of storage before translating the next statement. Data and code are all represented as binary strings within a single data space. Similarly a DC directive reserves space and inserts the appropriate value.

The process has actually become more complex in modern computers. For example, the author of one program may want to use a subroutine created by another programmer. In other cases, the programmer may not know where in the machine's memory the program will eventually lie. For these reasons, the role of the assembler is now shared with other software, such as a *linker* which links multiple functions together into a single whole and a *loader* which places (loads) the code at the needed location.

A final but important observation about assemblers is that they tell us something about C++ programs. C++ programs are translated into machine language by a compiler, which can be thought of as an assembler for higher-level languages. Although the initial constructs are much more complex, the compiler must ultimately generate the same machine code as an assembler. C++ does not make any new form of program possible. Every single C++ construct has a machine and an assembly language analog. This must be, because otherwise the C++ program could not run. But it does make the task simpler for the human programmer. That is, higher-level languages make complex tasks more practical—not possible.

EXERCISE

9–20 What language do you suppose the assembler is written in? What implications does this have for the first assembler?

PROGRAMMING IN ASSEMBLY LANGUAGE

Hopefully, the discussion of these last two chapters provides some insight into the actual operation of digital computers and the execution of algorithms. Although it certainly did not provide sufficient detail for you to create extensive programs, you could write some simple algorithms in assembly language and follow their execution.

A Simulation of the Marina Computer

A simulator is a program that, in effect, turns one computer into a different machine, complete with its own memory, registers, and machine language. Because an understanding of the underlying principles of computer organization is so important, we have provided a simulator for Marina. The simulator allows you to load a Marina assembly language program, assemble that program into machine language and run the machine language version. You may run the entire program or step through it. As it runs it displays the contents of all registers so that you can follow the exact execution. You can see the display in figure 9–22. Its use, and several sample programs are described in the lab manual.

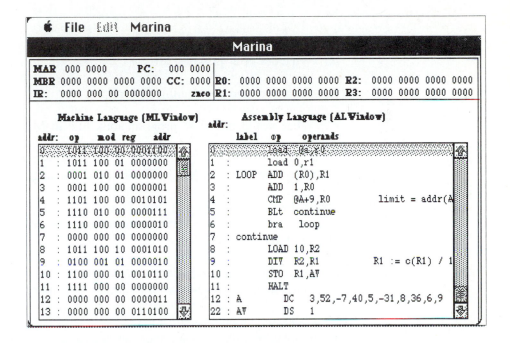

FIGURE 9–22 The screen of the Marina simulator.

EXERCISES

9–21 What is "assembly?" What effect does assembly have when it is applied to the Marina assembly language program in Figure 9–1?

9–22 Briefly compare C++ with Marina assembly language. That is, to what extent do they share common features and how do they differ as programming languages?

9–23 Design an assembly language program for the Marina simulator to rearrange three numbers from smallest to largest. Assume that the three numbers are defined by the dc instruction as in Example 9.2.

9–24 Below is a simple C++ program.

```
void main () ;
{ int i, j ;
  i = 3 ;
  j = i*i*i ;
}
```

a. What does this program do?

b. Write pre- and postconditions for it.

c. What would the same program look like in Marina assembly language?

d. What would it look like in Marina machine language?

9–25 Using the instruction format from Figure 9–3, the opcodes from Figure 9–2, and condition code settings from Figure 9–11, assemble the program in Example 9.2.

9–26 Design a Marina assembly language program to analyze three numbers stored by the dc instruction as in Example 9.2, and set R0 to

0   if all three numbers are different
1   if any two of the three numbers are the same
2   if all three numbers are the same.

9–27 Design a Marina assembly language program that will swap the contents of two previously defined locations A and B.

THE SOCIAL CONTEXT
OF COMPUTING

In this chapter we take an entirely different view of the discipline of computing. This view represents the interests of individuals and organizations that *use* computers and computer software in their daily activities—that is, the *social context* of computing. This "user's view" affects many of the design decisions that accompany the development and distribution of computer technology.

In this discussion we address two fundamental questions:

1. How can quality, reliability, and effectiveness be incorporated into the design and implementation of computers and software so that the interests and goals of users and society at large are optimally served and their rights are simultaneously protected? In other words, what are the *duties of the programmer-designer* that will maximize the *benefits to the user*?

2. Conversely, how can computers and software be protected against the various misuses that individuals can intentionally or unintentionally perpetrate against them? In other words, what are the *duties of the user*?

These two points of view are represented in Figure 10–1.

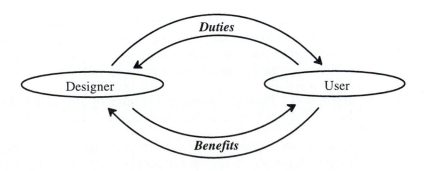

FIGURE 10–1 Duties and benefits: Incorporating the user's view.

The first question involves human factors, health and safety, database accuracy, protection of individual privacy, and software error control. The second question involves system security, intellectual property, and computer crime. Because serious study of any one of these issues would require extensive discussion, we concentrate on just two of them in this chapter: software error control (i.e., risk management) and intellectual property.

Why should we study these issues? There are a number of reasons. First, the dramatic increase in computer use throughout society requires that people who design computers and software for future users have a higher level of understanding of social issues. Many future designers are now students in introductory computing courses. Second, most of us will inevitably become future computer users, usually by way of our professions. Third, as computer technology proliferates throughout modern society, so do the opportunities for its misuse. Computer crime is estimated by some to exceed the combined levels of all other kinds of crime in today's society. We should therefore understand the legal and ethical dimensions of computing so that we will be well prepared to deal constructively and responsibly with such issues when they arise.

Why are the issues of intellectual property and software error control relevant to us? As we shall see, these issues are especially relevant to the topics that were introduced in Chapters 2 through 9. Intellectual property considerations apply to the programs we developed during laboratory sessions as well as to the C++ system and von Neumann machine simulator that supports these laboratory sessions. Software error control is a serious contemporary problem, and it is directly related to the technical discussions of verification and testing that were studied in Chapters 6 and 7 and prominent in all the laboratory exercises.

Many of the other social and ethical issues that surround the discipline of computing are equally important; they are addressed in later volumes of this series.

INTELLECTUAL PROPERTY

What do we mean when we use the term *intellectual property*? Intellectual property is not physical property, like a car or a house, but is instead an idea, an expression of an idea, or a representation of an idea in any of a variety of media. Formally, the definition can be given as follows:

> **Definition**   *Intellectual property* is property that is not physical but nevertheless has rights that can be assigned, licensed, or used as collateral.

This definition suggests that conventional means for protecting physical property rights apply also to intellectual property and that is exactly the case. There are currently four commonly used ways in which property rights can be identified, and hence protected: *copyright*, *patent*, *trademark*, and *trade secret*.

These four means of protection for property rights are discussed in the following sections, paying special attention to their application to computer software as intellectual property. Some computer scientists argue, however, that the application of these forms of intellectual property protection to software is harmful. We conclude this section on intellectual property with a presentation of this perspective.

Software as Intellectual Property

Computer software is a term that applies to the collection of all computer programs that are designed and distributed to facilitate computer use by practitioners and students in any of a wide range of disciplines, professions, and organizations. For example, computer software facilitates computer use by banks and people who have bank accounts, by publishers and people who use word processors to create manuscripts for publication, and by government agencies like the Internal Revenue Service and people who submit federal income tax statements. Thus, the number and variety of computer programs that fall into the realm of software is immense.

We have had firsthand experience in the development of computer software, albeit for a much simpler kind of algorithmic problem than the development of a word processor or a banking system. Our own software has the basic characteristics of intellectual property. That is, as the authors of software we are its owners, in the same sense that we are the owners of economics term papers, musical compositions, or works of art that we create. Thus, we have implicit property rights to the software we create if we want to exercise and/or protect those rights.

For the purpose of the following discussion, we define a *software product* as having three complementary aspects: a source program, an object program, and a user interface. If we write a simple C++ program that displays the message "Hello!" on the screen, then this software product's three aspects can be identified as shown in Figure 10–2. These aspects are intimately related. That is, we know already that any C++ source program must first be compiled, or translated, into a machine language object program before running the program. From Chapter 9, we also know that it is the object program whose steps are actually executed to produce the message "Hello!" on the screen at run time.

When a software product such as a word processor or a C++ compiler is developed for commercial use, its constituent source program is usually not distributed. Only its object program is distributed (along with some documentation and tutorial information). This is a significant fact in situations where we view a software product as intellectual property. (A major exception to this pattern is in the world of education and research in computer science and engineering, where many software products are freely distributed in their source form.)

Software user interfaces are many and varied. Their style and capabilities depend on the nature of the application, the skills of the intended user, and on the particular computer for which the software is designed. In general, a software product's user interface consists of the information presented on the screen by the software along with the keyboard, mouse, and other corventions for interaction that are required if users are to effectively apply the software to their problems. For example, the user interface for a word processor (like WordPerfect) on a particular computer (like the IBM PC) includes all the text creation, insertion, saving, deletion, and other functions that users must assimilate when they type a manuscript using that software product. This is also a significant fact when we consider the intellectual property rights that accompany a software product.

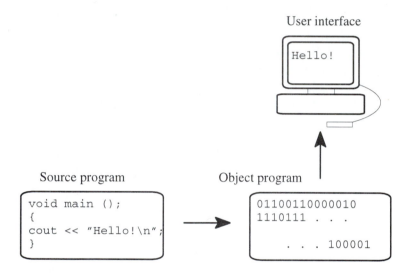

FIGURE 10–2   The three aspects of a software product.

In the computer laboratory you have learned about the user interface that attends a particular C++ system. If you have been using Turbo C++ on an IBM PC, you are now familiar with certain conventions for creating a C++ program text, saving the text, compiling the program, finding and correcting errors, running the program, and so on. If you have been using Symantec C++ on the Macintosh, you have become familiar with a different suite of conventions for accomplishing these tasks. Each of these is a user interface, and as a C++ programmer you are the user.

The dual interpretation of software   When viewed as intellectual property, we can look at an item of software in either of two different ways. On the one hand, if we look at only the object program and the user interface, the software can be viewed as a *process or machine*. On the other hand, if we consider the source program and the object program together, the same software takes on the appearance of an *original work of authorship*. These two interpretations run parallel to the notions introduced in Chapter 5, where a program was shown to simultaneously serve the two roles of mechanism and explanation. This duality of interpretation is illustrated in Figure 10–3.

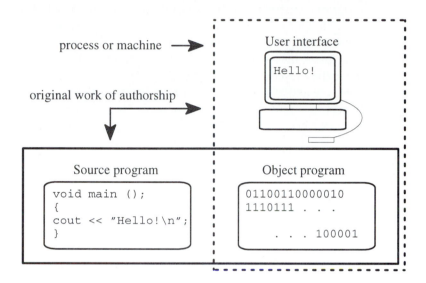

FIGURE 10–3　　The dual interpretation of software.

Applying Intellectual Property Law to Software

Let's review the details of intellectual property law, paying special attention to its applicability to software.

Software copyrights　Because the source program in a software product is an original work of authorship, it is protected by copyright law. Copyright law protects all original works of authorship (historically, literary manuscripts, paintings, and musical compositions) against unauthorized copying. The law was amended in 1980 to explicitly cover computer programs, or software.

Note that in all these cases, the law *protects the expressions themselves* (that is, the verbatim text of the program) but not the ideas that underlie the expressions. For example, suppose we develop an original C++ program that solves the revenues problem posed in Chapter 5. Then the C++ text of our program is protected by copyright law, but the underlying idea (algorithm) that our text represents is not protected. Thus, someone else can independently arrive at the same algorithm, then express it in a different programming style. For example, another person's program might use different variable names or use a `while` loop that has the same effect as our `for` loop. That person's program is therefore technically not in violation of our program's property rights. The second program would violate the first program's copyright protection only if the programmer derived it from the first by changing a few variable names or other program constructs (perhaps by using `while` loops where we used `for` loops).

A simpler example that illustrates different expressions of the same idea is shown in Figure 10–4. If the three programs in Figure 10–4 were independently created, they would not be in violation of each other's copyright protection, since they represent different expressions of an idea. However, if either *b* or *c* were created as a derivative from program *a*, then *a*'s copyright would be violated.

```
#include <iostream.h>   #include <iostream.h>   #include <iostream.h>
void main ();           void main ();           void main ();
{                       {                       {
cout << "Hello!\n";     cout << "Hello!";       cout << "He";
}                       cout << "\n" ;          cout << "llo!\n" ;
                        }                       }

         (a)                     (b)                     (c)
```

FIGURE 10–4   Three different expressions of the same idea.

Any piece of academic work involving computer programs is governed by the same rules of plagiarism as a written term paper. *Plagiarism* is defined as the failure to acknowledge another author's work when that work is included in one's own written work. Computer programs fall into the category of written work in this sense. Therefore, the use or adaptation of another's program without proper written acknowledgement usually constitutes plagiarism. College and university instructors, especially in computer science and engineering, usually make an explicit definition in their syllabi of what constitutes plagiarism for assignments that involve programming.

Copyright law applies to an original work of authorship immediately from the day it is created until 50 years after the owner's death. It also applies *automatically*: The author or owner does not have to affix a copyright notice explicitly to the work. However, many copyright owners prefer to post explicit notice of copyright on all printed copies of the work (the C++ program listing, in our case), and that is suggested though not required by the law itself. Thus, our revenues program was copyrighted immediately, and copyright protection will continue for 50 years after the authors die. It behooves us to affix the following kind of notice to all printed copies of this program if we intend to protect the property rights that apply to it:

Copyright protection means that the owner of the copyright has the exclusive right to make, use, and/or sell the original work.

Software patents Because the object program and user interface in a software product can also be interpreted as a "process or machine," software can also fall into the realm of patent protection. Patent law explicitly protects processes, machines, manufactured items, or compositions-of-matter inventions from unauthorized reproduction, use, or sale by anyone besides the owner. The Supreme Court has ruled that software-related inventions can be judged for patentability in the same way as non-software-related inventions. Thus, patent law now can be fully applied to software.

Unlike a copyright, however, patent rights do not automatically apply to a piece of software at the time it is created. Instead, a software patent must be obtained by application to the U. S. Patent and Trademark Office, just like inventors apply to patent any other process, machine, or invention. Once obtained, a patent remains in force for a period of 17 years, after which the patented process or machine falls into the public domain. That is, it becomes freely available for use, adaptation, or sale by anyone.

The scope of a patent is wider than that of a copyright. Patent protection extends to the whole family of processes *that have the same effect as* the original patented product. Copyright protection, in contrast, applies only to one particular expression or realization of the process. Patent protection gives the owner of the patent the exclusive right to make, use, or sell the process.

Some algorithms can be patented. One famous one is Karmarkar's algorithm for solving certain types of problems which involve large numbers of simultaneous linear equalities and inequalities. In these problems there are typically infinitely many "feasible" solutions—the problem is to find one that maximizes a given function of the variables. For many years these problems were solved with the "simplex algorithm" which used one variable at a time to step toward an optimal solution. Because of the number of equations and inequalities involved, this algorithm was often very slow. Karmarkar devised a much faster way to find the optimal solution, which involved changing several variables simultaneously. This was a truly unique and original algorithm, and the U.S. Patent and Trademark Office awarded a patent for it. The algorithms in this text, however, all use well-known techniques that are in the public domain and thus are not patentable. The main advantage to the patent holder is that now, if someone were to discover Karmarkar's algorithm independently, without knowing that it already exists, he or she could not use it without being in violation of the patent—no matter how the algorithm is expressed.

Software trademarks The Lanham Act defines a *trademark* as "any word, name, symbol, device, or any combination thereof adopted and used by a manufacturer or merchant to identify its goods . . . and to distinguish them from those manufactured or sold by others." Trademarks for software products are many and varied. Some examples are shown in Figure 10–5. Unlike copyrights and patents, trademarks have a direct effect on the market impact of a product as they exploit the idea of "name recognition" to maximize sales. Their major purpose is to create a unique basis for product recognition in the form of a single unforgettable symbol. Technically, when a registered trademark is referenced in a text or document, it must be affixed with the trademark symbol ™ to acknowledge that fact.

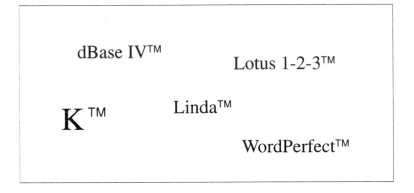

FIGURE 10–5   Some software trademarks.

Like patents, trademarks are obtained by applying to the U. S. Patent and Trademark Office. After a trademark has been registered, the trademark's owner has the exclusive right to affix it to all product(s) to which it applies. In the case of computer software, the law was revised in 1989 to allow owners to affix their trademarks to reference manuals and other documentation for the software product, in addition to the software product itself. Since software is distributed on magnetically encoded media, its trademark would not be visible without this provision.

Software trade secrets   A *trade secret* is generally any item of knowledge or characteristic of a product that makes it unique or valuable in comparison with the competition but which is generally kept secret from the competition. In the special case of a software product, any feature that makes it especially efficient or unique in its capabilities, in comparison with its rivals in the marketplace, can be declared to be a trade secret. For example, a very fast spelling checker built into a word processor might be worth protecting as a trade secret if it makes that word processor unique in contrast with all others on the market.

A trade secret is easy to obtain, and no application procedure is required—in fact, that would be impossible, since the item is a secret! Trade secrets have unlimited life, but they are difficult to protect. Trade secrets often arise by contract, as through an employer-employee relationship. Many software developers require their employees to sign a "nondisclosure agreement" at the time they are hired. Under such an agreement, employees are bound not to reveal any of the software designs or implementations with which they come into contact. A nondisclosure agreement thereby protects the secrecy of a software trade secret. Given the high degree of software portability and employee mobility in the industry, this type of agreement is very difficult, if not impossible, to enforce—especially when an employee terminates employment with a company and begins working for a major competitor.

Software Licenses and Piracy

We see that a software product is an item of property that can be protected under copyright, patent, trade secret, and trademark laws. Most of the currently popular software products are, indeed, protected in one or more of these four ways by their owners, the software manufacturers (often called software houses), against unlawful copying or misuse.

By purchasing a software product, such as a word processor or a C++ compiler, a person automatically obtains a license to use that software. Such licenses come with specific restrictions that are designed to protect the manufacturers' rights to the software product. A software product is typically distributed in its object program form so that the ideas contained in its source program are not easily read or transmitted. Thus, software products have a built-in trade secret aspect to them.

What are the restrictions that appear on software licenses? Licenses usually specify, in one way or another, the following conditions of purchase:

1. The software product can be used only on one computer.

2. Neither the software product nor its documentation can be copied, modified, or transferred to any computer other than the one for which it was purchased.

3. The software can be copied once for the purpose of creating a backup copy to be used if the original copy is lost or damaged.

4. The software cannot be modified and cannot be used in the creation of a derivative work.

5. The software is provided in "as is" condition, without warranty of any kind as to its quality, correctness, reliability, currentness, or efficiency on the computer for which it was purchased. Users effectively rely on the software and its results at their own risk.

6. The manufacturer is not liable for any damages arising out of the use of the software.

The license is automatically canceled by the manufacturer if any of conditions 1 through 4 are violated by the purchaser. However, it is not clear whether conditions 5 and 6 would hold up in court in all cases. That is, if a software error causes severe damages to the person or the activities of the user, the software manufacturer may indeed be held liable for such damages. This issue is discussed further in the next section.

Several variations on this single-user license are also widely used. *Site licenses* are usually purchased by an institution like a college or university. Site licensing allows the purchaser to copy the product and make the copies available to its large community of users at a lower cost than the single-user price multiplied by the total number of users.

Public domain software (also called "freeware") is distributed essentially for the cost of the diskette and postage. Users who are pleased with the quality of the software so obtained are encouraged to make a voluntary contribution to help defray the high development cost of the software on the part of the manufacturer. Public domain software is often distributed with its source code, in the interest of widening the dissemination of technological ideas and improving the quality of future versions of the software.

Although it is a minority activity in the software world, the development and distribution of public domain software has raised an important issue in the ongoing debate over the extension of intellectual property rights to computer software. There is a natural conflict of interests between the users and the developers of innovative computer software. Users want maximal freedom to reuse, reapply, copy, and otherwise exploit the product that they have purchased (usually at a high price) from the developers. Developers want to maximize their profits from their development of new computer software products. So, to what extent should the profit motive in the software market be protected at the expense of technological progress? Said in the opposite way, to what extent should software developers' time and creativity be exploited in order to create an environment in which technological inventiveness and progress can flourish?

Software piracy   Some software users obtain software products illegally. Illegal copying of software (*software piracy*) is a direct violation of copyright law, as well a violation of the terms of the license agreements that accompany software. Why does piracy occur? How widespread is it? How can software manufacturers protect themselves against widespread piracy of their products?

Software piracy probably occurs for three main reasons: the cost of the software, the ease with which it can be copied, and ignorance of copyright laws. Until recently, software manufacturers distributed their products with "copy protection" built into the software. The software was intentionally designed not to perform correctly if an illegal copy were made or used. Manufacturers found many ways to protect their products against illegal copying, but most of these ways were outwitted by clever users. Many manufacturers have essentially given up this battle with the software pirates raising their prices to include an allowance for a certain amount of illegal copying to take place.

There is not a great deal of agreement on how widespread the software piracy problem is. A July 10, 1986, article in the *Wall Street Journal* [14] surmised that piracy is widespread on college and university campuses, stating, "College students are a poor market for software due to piracy and the proliferation of student-written programs." Green and Gilbert [4] disagreed with this assessment, noting that colleges and universities have taken the following steps to help limit the incidence of software piracy:

- Colleges have established written policies on computer access and unauthorized software duplication.

- College faculties have acknowledged that they have a moral responsibility to promote legal and ethical behavior with respect to computer software. That is, at the very least software piracy is considered to be as reprehensible as plagiarism.

- Computer center directors have realized that their ability to negotiate favorable discounts with software manufacturers is directly related to their ability and willingness to control piracy.

- Other college administrators worry about institutional liability for software piracy abuses on their campuses.

- Student-written programs are generally an inadequate substitute for commercially developed software.

These observations notwithstanding, it is nevertheless clear that software piracy remains widespread, not only on college campuses but throughout all public and private institutions that use computer software in their own domains of work.

A solution to the software piracy problem is not near at hand. Its achievement will require software manufacturers and users to arrive at a new relationship. One essential component of this new relationship would be a policy on pricing and licensing that both is realistic for users and guarantees a fair return on investment for manufacturers. Current pricing and licensing practices are often viewed as excessive and unreasonably rigid, and they usually provide no recourse for users in the event they are dissatisfied with the product. Another essential component is a new level of awareness and sensitivity on the part of users to the real costs of manufacturing and distributing software, as well as to the legal and ethical ramifications of piracy itself. At the present time, it's not even clear that many judges and lawyers—let alone that the general population of software users—understand the status of software with respect to the intellectual property laws. A great deal of education will be required before software manufacturers and users can begin to arrive at a new relationship and work to resolve the problem of software piracy.

The "Look and Feel" Debate

When discussing the intellectual property aspects of a software product's user interface, we must first try to define what it is that makes a user interface valuable, or unique, in comparison with other user interfaces. Consider the C++ compiler that you have been using. You have developed a certain level of skill in typing programs, running the compiler, finding and correcting syntax errors, and running programs. Much of that skill depends upon the effectiveness with which the software's user interface makes appropriate commands available to you as you need them. If you are running Turbo C++ on an IBM PC, for example, you use certain control key combinations to initiate these different kinds of operations. Moreover, the system keeps you informed about the status of your work by displaying certain messages on the screen as it completes the tasks you have designated. Similarly, if you are running Symantec C++ on a Macintosh, you perform operations through an entirely different kind of user interface—one that depends upon your skill at using a mouse, opening windows, making menu selections, and so on. These alternative C++ systems present to the user a different "look and feel" when they are applied to the task of developing and running programs.

Some software manufacturers have claimed that this look and feel of a software user interface is protectable under intellectual property laws. The term *look and feel* was actually coined in 1985 by two lawyers, Russo and Derwin. They defined the *look* to mean the appearance of a user interface's screen displays and *feel* to denote how the software interacts with the user (i.e., the sequence of commands, keystrokes, mouse operations, and on-screen responses that occur when the software's various functions are performed by the user).

The validity of the look and feel argument for copyright protection has been tested in two recent court cases. Lotus Development Corporation successfully sued Mosaic Software in 1987 for copyright infringement of the Lotus 1-2-3 spreadsheet software product on the grounds that Mosaic copied the look and feel of that product's user interface. The second case involved a suit by Apple Computer Corporation against Microsoft Corporation in 1988 for copyright infringement of the graphical and visual elements of its Macintosh user interface. In an important ruling in August, 1992, Apple's claim of infringement was largely rejected in court. The main reason the judge gave for rejecting Apple's suit was that it had not made plain what aspects of its interface it was claiming were protected apart from a number of specific interface elements which were either unprotectable or were part of a license Apple had previously granted to Microsoft.

Look and feel cases are difficult to prosecute, for several reasons. First, the originality of the user interface for which copyright protection may apply is difficult to determine. Recall that copyright protection applies only to an *original* work. In the case of Lotus 1-2-3's user interface, one can argue that it is a derivative of an older spreadsheet system called VisiCalc (circa 1982). It can similarly be shown that the Macintosh user interface is a derivative of an earlier system known as the Xerox Star system (circa 1980).

The second problem that surrounds look and feel arguments is that the notion itself has no standing, or at best ambiguous standing, in the law. Thus, some would argue that the alternative term *total concept and feel* may be applicable to copyright cases involving software user interfaces. Yet copyright law makes clear distinctions between the representation of a concept (which it does protect) and the concept itself (which it does not protect).

The third problem is that recent court cases reveal that judges do not understand the nature of user interfaces particularly well. It is not difficult to understand the artistry that is involved in creating a unique image on the screen, but nonprogrammers often do not understand the more complex ideas that encompass the interactive functionality of the software.

The fourth problem is the larger issue of confusion about boundaries between patent law and copyright law, as they apply to software in general and user interfaces in particular. Many patent lawyers believe that the look and feel of a software user interface is patentable. There are some precedents for this opinion. For example, IBM has a patent on a certain method of *highlighting* text on a word processor. Apple has a patent on the "pulldown menu" process, used with a mouse, which is a central aspect of its Macintosh user interface. Yet many judges are unaware that patents are available for software user interfaces; thus they tend to overinterpret the scope of copyright law in cases that involve look and feel arguments.

As of this writing, the legal climate seems to be becoming increasingly chilly toward the protection of look and feel based on copyright law. However, it will probably take a few more years before a clear consensus emerges.

Legal and Ethical Choices for Software Developers and Users

Two major surveys of software developers on the question of copyright and patent protection for software in its various aspects were reported in the May 1990 and the June 1992 issues of *Communications of the ACM* [9, 10]. The first survey polled 667 developers from various parts of the software industry—computer manufacturers, R&D organizations, universities, software vendors, and others. More than 80% of the respondents opposed the extension of copyright protection for the look and feel of software user interfaces, although they strongly supported copyright and patent protection for source programs and object programs. The second survey polled 345 attenders at a conference on computer graphics in August 1991. In this survey, 94% of respondents opposed look and feel protection.

The main reason for their opposition is the view that copyright protection for look and feel would have a negative effect on the user interface design community, stifling creativity and adversely affecting the climate of open exchange and discussion of innovations that marks progress in the field. Yet 93% of the first respondents believed that source programs ought to fall under copyright or patent protection, and 85% thought that object programs ought to be so protected. On the second survey, 86% favored copyright protection for source code, and 2% supported patent protection; 65% supported copyright protection for object code and, again, 2% supported patent protection.

An important additional aspect of these surveys is that they exposed the fact that a large number of software developers do not understand the legal issues surrounding the look and feel argument or the other aspects of intellectual property laws that apply to computer software.

No such survey data is available for the larger population of software users. However, there is anecdotal evidence which suggests that software users do not understand the legal and ethical dimensions of software use any better than the software developers or the lawyers themselves. For a variety of reasons, many individual users copy whatever software they need in order to configure their computers to do useful work. Institutional users—corporations, colleges and universities, government agencies, and so on—are probably more cautious than individuals in this regard, perhaps because managers fear the possibility of institutional exposure, embarrassment, and lawsuits.

Several factors contribute to illegal copying of software, including cost, objection to the law, uncertainty about performance, convenience of copying, low level of use, and ignorance. Some have compared software copying in colleges and universities with plagiarism. Some users think that software product prices are unreasonably high and that vendors are gouging the public in the interest of making windfall profits. Others object to the fact that software is protected under the law in this way; they think that software is not "real" property, so the act of copying software is just copying and not stealing. Some people are uncertain whether a certain product is appropriate or effective for their needs, and they would prefer to have the software on a trial basis. However, vendors do not generally make their products available on this basis. Still other people justify illegal copying merely because it is convenient or because they expect to use the software only occasionally. And some people are simply ignorant of the intellectual property laws that protect software. In this sense, the software copying black market is similar to that which exists for videotaped movies.

Nevertheless, unauthorized software copying is illegal and unethical, and it can be detrimental to future progress in computing technology. The U.S. patent law gives the inventor of a product the right to make a profit from his or her invention. Software developers need to recover the costs of inventing and distributing their products. If copying becomes widespread, it can deprive vendors of a fair return on investment. This, in turn, can discourage future investment in new software products by innovative firms. Furthermore, society needs a vehicle for holding developers responsible for software errors, and software that does not enter into the normal stream of commerce cannot be so regulated.

There are consequences to breaking the laws. Anyone who makes 10 or more copies of copyrighted software within 6 months having a collective value of $2500 or more is subject to criminal prosecution. A first offender can be sentenced to up to 5 years in jail and fined up to $250,000. Even if less than 10 copies were made, a first offender can be sentenced to up to a year in jail and fined up to $25,000. Software copiers also have a higher risk of obtaining contaminated or otherwise dysfunctional software when making illegal copies. Illegal actions are sometimes defended on grounds of conscience. Individuals and institutions must weigh these and other tradeoffs if they are seriously contemplating making an illegal copy of a software product.

Case Study: An Interesting Dilemma

Jane Petoskey has a PC in her home. She is a free-lance programmer who has taken consulting jobs for a number of commercial and industrial firms in her area. She often tests programs to see whether they would be of use to her clients. Petoskey also presents frequent oral and written reports to clients and potential clients. She prepares these reports using two software products on her PC: a word processor and a presentation graphics editor. She also uses a spreadsheet program for keeping track of all her business expenses and a database program for keeping track of present and potential clients. Her children occasionally use the PC to play games and run educational software.

Sometimes Petoskey purchases software for her PC. For example, she recently bought a $75 spelling checker for use with her word processor. However, she has copied most of the software that she uses or tests from friends' versions. Questions:

- Should Petoskey stop using software that she hasn't purchased?

- Is there a difference between testing software for clients and using it for one's own work?

- Which software items should she have purchased, and which (if any) need not have been purchased?

A strict interpretation of the copyright law would require Petoskey to purchase all the software that is on her PC, except for products that are explicitly marked to be in the public domain (freeware).

Yet, if we take into account the fact that she uses many of these software items only once, for the purpose of an evaluation, it is not obvious that she should be subject to the same pricing policy as people using the software continuously in their work. Sometimes, though not often, users can obtain a software product on a trial basis for this purpose, and they do not have to pay the full price of the product until after deciding whether or not it will be useful on an ongoing basis. Alternatively, some software products are available in a stripped-down trial version, so that users can get a feeling for the product's capabilities. That policy gives additional leverage to the vendor, who is not "giving away the store" if the person decides to keep the abbreviated version for permanent use.

Although this case study points out some of the issues and gray areas in the application of current intellectual property law to computer software, there are many other questions. The readings listed at the end of the chapter give more information regarding this important social issue in computing [2, 3, 4, 10].

The Perspective of the Free Software Foundation

Richard Stallman has been the most prominent spokesperson for a different perspective than the one we have discussed so far in this chapter. He is the founder of the Free Software Foundation and the principal author of GNU Emacs (a text editor), C++ and other language compilers, and other software, much of which is widely used. Stallman gives all this software away with the proviso that recipients may not subsequently charge others for it. Here are some of his statements [13]:

I consider that the golden rule requires that if I like a program I must share it with other people who like it. Software sellers want to divide the users and then conquer them, making each user agree not to share with others. I refuse to break solidarity with other users in this way. I cannot in good conscience sign a nondisclosure agreement or a software license agreement . . . So that I can continue to use computers without dishonor, I have decided to put together a sufficient body of free software so that I will be able to get along without any software that is not free.

Many programmers are unhappy about the commercialization of system software. It may enable them to make more money, but it requires them to feel in conflict with other programmers in general rather than feel as comrades. The fundamental act of friendship among programmers is the sharing of programs; marketing arrangements now typically used essentially forbid programmers to treat others as friends. The purchaser of software must choose between friendship and obeying the law. Naturally, many decide friendship is more important. But those who believe in law do not feel at ease with either choice. They become cynical and think that programming is just a way of making money.

By working on and using GNU rather than proprietary programs, we can be hospitable to everyone and obey the law. In addition, GNU serves as an example to inspire and a banner to rally others to join us in sharing. This gives us a feeling of harmony which is impossible if we use software that is not free. For about half the programmers I talk to, this is an important piece of happiness that money cannot replace.

Copying all or parts of a program is as natural to a programmer as breathing, and as productive. It ought to be free.

Note that Stallman is not advocating the illegal copying of software—rather he is denying the wisdom of laws which make copying illegal. He has acted consistently with his convictions on this matter by writing high-quality software and not copyrighting it; perhaps his most popular piece of software—the text editor EMACS—is used in academic and industrial settings all over the world. The fundamental question he raises is critical—should software be treated as property in the same sense as a chair, a house, or a car? Furthermore, the economic implications of Stallman's perspective need to be considered—that is, would removing legal protection for software advance computing as he suggests, or would it be a setback? You are asked to consider these questions in the exercises for this section.

EXERCISES

10–1 From your library, obtain and read the article by Green and Gilbert cited at the end of the chapter. What is EDUCOM? What is EDUCOM's policy on intellectual property rights? What are site agreements?

10–2 Argue the case in favor of software piracy. Argue the case against software piracy.

10–3 What methods do colleges and universities use to control illegal copying of software? Are you familiar with some additional methods from your own educational experience? Can you suggest other methods?

10–4 Identify the user interface of the revenues program in Chapter 6. Discuss the effects of making this program user-friendly, as suggested in Chapter 6, on its user interface: That is, how would these changes alter the look and feel of the user interface for the original revenues program?

10–5 What is the difference between a software patent and a software copyright? Explain how any differences would affect a particular software product, such as the revenues program of Chapter 6 or the Marina simulator of Chapter 9.

10–6 Respond to the following critique of Stallman's perspective: "Any author, artist or other creative person should have the right to decide how his or her creations are used. Thus if Stallman wants to give his software away, that is his privilege. But if others want to profit from their creations, that is their privilege. The law needs to protect the rights of those who want to profit."

10–7 Suppose there were no legal protections against the copying of software. Do you think this would advance the profession of computing or harm it? Why?

LIABILITY FOR SOFTWARE ERRORS

The following story is based on an actual situation. The names and a few details have been changed to protect the confidentiality of everyone involved. In January 1987, Payroll Systems, Inc. (PSI) signed a contract with the Theron Corporation to manage Theron's employee benefits. One of these benefits was a retirement package. Before signing with PSI, Theron employees had a single retirement fund; however, PSI allowed employees to invest their funds in one of three options. One was a fixed income fund, which was very secure and provided a return of about 7% per year. The second was a bond fund, which provided a variable rate of return—it averaged above 7% but could be substantially more or less. The third choice was an equity fund which invested in common stocks; it was the most risky but potentially the most profitable of the three funds. Employees were allowed to distribute their retirement benefits over the three funds as they wished. Furthermore, employees were allowed to reallocate their previous retirement accumulation to the three new funds in any proportion they chose.

Each employee was given a form on which to indicate his or her allocation (see Figure 10–6). About 1200 of these forms were sent to PSI for entry into the Theron payroll system. Note that the percentage to be allocated to each fund was entered, not the dollar amount.

Election Form

Indicate the %age of your future retirement contributions which you want invested in each fund:

_____Fixed Income Fund
_____Bond Fund
_____Equity Fund

Indicate the %age of your present retirement account balance which you want invested in each fund:

_____Fixed Income Fund
_____Bond Fund
_____Equity Fund

FIGURE 10–6   Election form for employee retirement accounts.

One of PSI's programmers wrote a special utility program to allow addition of this information to the employee database. The screen displayed to the data entry clerk contained the information in Figure 10–7. The number 36 refers to the present account balance field in the employee's record; 37 refers to the future contributions; 1, 2, and 3 refer to subfields corresponding to the fixed income fund, bond fund, and equity fund, respectively.

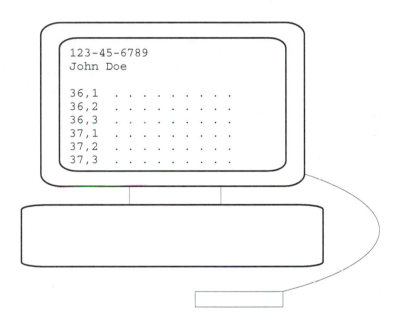

FIGURE 10–7   Data entry screen for Theron retirement accounts.

If you look carefully, you can see that the fields for the present and future allocations on the screen appear in the opposite order from their presentation on the election form. The data entry clerk did not realize this, nor did the the individual who checked the clerk's entries.

On August 25, 1987, the Dow-Jones industrial average reached a high of 2722.42. It then began a gradual retreat which culminated in a precipitous crash of 508 points on October 19. In December 1987, the PSI accountant who was in charge of the Theron account was checking her end-of-the-year reports to the Theron employees. She noticed that the values of some of Theron employees' largest retirement funds were substantially less than what she remembered the values to be when PSI established the accounts in January. She subsequently discovered the error that had been made. A number of employees had chosen the safe fixed income fund for their present retirement accumulation but had selected the more risky equity fund for their future contributions. After 2 months of work, the accountant was able to establish what the value of each account for each employee would have been had the allocations been assigned correctly. The net loss to Theron employees was $193,000.

Ultimately, the loss was paid by PSI's insurance company under an "errors and omissions" clause in its policy. The PSI accountant who discovered the error graciously accepted responsibility for it, which cost her 2 months of commissions. But liability for the error was never clearly established. A strong case could be made that the principal fault rested with the programmer on two grounds: The programmer designed a user interface which was so cryptic that the data entry clerk could not see that data was being entered into the wrong fields and the input sequence did not match the sequence on the election form. But some liability rested with both the data entry clerk and the checker for not inquiring about the meaning of the fields and ensuring that the meaning corresponded to the data. Some responsibility also rested with the designer of an election form on which reading from top to bottom put future before present. The main responsibility for the problem in this case, however, would appear attributable to the programmer whose interface design invited such an error.

Types of Computer Errors

There are hundreds of documented cases in which a software error has resulted in problems ranging from inconveniences, such as the loss of a few hours of one person's time, to the loss of life (in the case of a malfunction of an x-ray machine).

There are three types of computer errors: hardware errors, software errors, and user errors. A *hardware error* is the failure of a piece of equipment—perhaps a memory chip fails or a bit is dropped while a document is being transmitted from one computer to another. *Software errors* are of two kinds: design errors and coding errors. PSI's problem was the result of two *design errors*. One was a poorly designed user interface, and the other was an input specification which did not match the anticipated input. *Coding errors* occur when a program or subprogram does not give output which satisfies the postcondition even though its input satisfies the precondition. *User errors* occur when inaccurate data is entered as input. For example, if a bank manager forgets to give a customer the overdraft protection requested on a new checking account, the data record describing that account is in error. Bounced checks and damage to the customer's credit rating could result. If PSI's program for entering the retirement allocation had been written before the election form, the error would have been a user error rather than a design error, since the error would have occurred in the design of the form rather than the design of the program.

The Relationship between the Programmer and the User

Because software errors are so common, so potentially harmful, and so easy to make, let's clarify the responsibilities of software developers.

Developing software for a user is quite different from developing software for oneself or for a course. When we develop a program for a user, we enter into a certain kind of relationship with that user. This relationship has legal as well as ethical aspects. Some benefits the developer may receive from this relationship are money, self-esteem, the satisfaction of meeting an intellectual challenge, and the satisfaction of doing work that helps another person. The developer also assumes certain obligations, and these obligations are the principal subject of this section. The legal term for the developer's obligation is *duty of care*. This is a basic legal concept "which expresses social approval of deeds which help other people and disapproval of deeds which are harmful" [9]. The particular meaning of the duty of care depends on the relationship involved. For examples, parents have different duties to care for their children than vendors have to care for their customers. For the moment we will assume we are talking only about software which is sold, not freeware. But we will return to freeware again.

We can identify the following duties the developer has to the user:

1. *To produce appropriate software.* This means identifying clearly what the user's needs are and developing software which meets those needs. This duty applies more obviously to developers who write custom software for individual customers than to producers of packaged software. The dynamics of the marketplace tend to enforce this duty for producers of packaged software, but vendors of packaged software are not free of this duty. Some vendors are very responsive to their users and some are quite unresponsive.

2. *To produce quality software.* Quality has been defined in various ways for software. However, some typical factors are conformity to specifications, portability, reliability, efficiency, user-friendliness, and maintainability. *Portability* means that the software can be moved easily from one system to another; this is especially important when the user wants to upgrade to a larger computer without having to rewrite software. *Reliability* means more than working correctly when users enter correct data; the software must be reasonably resistant to users' errors as well. For example, a user should not be able to crash a program with a typographical error. It is not possible, however, for a developer to anticipate every possible combination of incorrect data a naive or inept user might enter. Although there is no precise definition of "reasonably resistant," a useful guideline is that an entry outside the acceptable range should be met with a suitable error message and the user should subsequently have an opportunity to change the entry. No user error should be allowed to crash a program or damage files. Writing *efficient* software shows respect for the user's time and money; efficient programs consume fewer resources than inefficient ones. *User-friendliness* is clearly important, as it makes the software more accessible to potential

users. *Maintainable* programs are more easily modified and thus serve the user's future needs as well as present ones; they also show consideration for future developers who may work on a piece of software.

3. *To represent software honestly.* Vendors cannot ethically induce users to buy a piece of software on the basis of false claims for what it can do. This duty also means that developers of custom software must fulfill any promises made to a potential user.

4. *To represent one's qualifications honestly.* The meaning of this duty is clear. Like the duty to produce appropriate software, this duty applies especially to developers who write custom software. However, it also applies to firms that sell packaged software.

5. *To respect the proprietary rights of other developers.* Software that is copyrighted or patented cannot be used without the owner's permission and, most likely, the payment of royalties. Anyone who fails to check whether there is a patent on an algorithm can be charged with "willful infringement" of the owner's right. If established in court, triple the normal damages are assessed.

Let's look at some of the specific tasks involved in preparing a piece of software for sale and see how these duties apply to each task. (For more information on the software life cycle, see the next chapter.) We address only custom-designed software here and leave packaged software for the exercises.

1. *Needs analysis.* The analyst who investigates the user's needs and subsequently writes the specifications is the person most responsible for producing appropriate software. One estimate is that 60 to 80% of software errors are built into the design before coding even begins. No amount of verification or testing is going to make an improperly specified program satisfy the user's needs. Listening to the user may be difficult, however, especially when the user may not know his or her own needs or may not understand the capabilities of computers well enough to know what a program can do. Thus, many designers today are advocating a design methodology based on prototyping. This means including the user in every phase of the software development process. A typical procedure is to design the user interface first and then code software to manage it. This is tested by the user and subsequently revised. The program itself is then designed for easy modification; as parts of it are written, they are tested by the user and again revised.

2. *Design.* The designer has substantial responsibility for ensuring the program's reliability, maintainability, and user-friendliness. A well-designed modular program with simple interfaces between modules and with unambiguous pre- and postconditions is far more likely to be reli-

able and maintainable than a poorly designed program. The designer must give a lot of thought to the design of the user interface as well as to the design of the programs themselves.

3. *Coding.* The principal concerns in coding are portability, reliability, efficiency, and respect for proprietary rights. The developer needs to understand the pre- and postconditions properly and to verify the code written. Many software errors can be avoided by careful coding. If a developer is working in an area where software has been patented, he or she must investigate whether patents exist for this particular application. The developer must obtain permission before using someone else's patented or copyrighted code. The developer also needs to make sure that the code is efficient and portable.

4. *Testing.* Ensuring reliability rests primarily with the tester, who designs appropriate test data to exercise the program in a reasonable number of cases that are likely to arise when the software is used. At the present time, there is no universally accepted definition of "appropriate test data." If a program fails and the vendor is sued and accused of inadequate testing, a court would most likely call in several professional software developers and ask them whether the testing done was within the bounds of current professional practice. However, courts hold developers to a much higher standard of testing for software which can cause physical injury if it fails. Thus the extent of testing required depends on the nature of the application.

5. *Software sales.* Although not often directly involved in the programming process, the software salesperson is the principal link between the developer and the user who buys the program. The salesperson's principal duty is to represent the software honestly. Another duty some writers have identified is not to coerce the buyer. Oftentimes a private consultant will serve as both salesperson and designer. In this case the duty to represent one's own qualifications honestly also applies.

6. *Software support.* The support people are the ongoing link between the developer and the user after purchase of software. The principal support duty is to provide appropriate software, in the sense that support people help users apply the software to their problems most effectively. But there is also a responsibility to represent one's qualifications honestly by not trying to provide help one is not qualified to provide. Support people also have a responsibility to communicate users' experiences (both positive and negative) back to the designers so that they can improve the design.

The Legal Context in Which the Developer Works

Even the most conscientious developer will make inadvertent errors. And even the most thoroughly tested and verified software may fail. What, then, is the legal context within which the developer works?

The principal tool software vendors use to protect themselves from damage suits resulting from software errors is the disclaimer. A *disclaimer* is a statement to the purchasers of the software acknowledging the possibility of errors and informing users that they are taking a risk in using it. The disclaimer declares the vendor free of responsibility for failure of the software and any damage that failure might cause. Figure 10–8 shows a typical disclaimer.

> **LOTUS MAKES NO WARRANTY OR REPRESENTATION, EITHER EXPRESS OR IMPLIED, WITH RESPECT TO THIS SOFTWARE OR DOCUMENTATION, THEIR QUALITY, PERFORMANCE, MERCHANTABILITY, OR FITNESS FOR A PARTICULAR PURPOSE. AS A RESULT THIS SOFTWARE AND DOCUMENTATION ARE LICENSED "AS IS" AND YOU, THE LICENSEE, ARE ASSUMING THE ENTIRE RISK AS TO THEIR QUALITY AND PERFORMANCE. IN NO EVENT WILL LOTUS BE LIABLE FOR DIRECT, INDIRECT, SPECIAL, INCIDENTAL, OR CONSEQUENTIAL DAMAGES ARISING OUT OF THE USE OR INABILITY TO USE THE SOFTWARE OR DOCUMENTATION.**

FIGURE 10–8 A typical software disclaimer. *Source*: Lotus Development Corporation.

Disclaimers are very important to software vendors, since without one a vendor could be held legally responsible for virtually any inadvertent error and for consequential damages—losses caused by failure of the software, such as loss of employee time or financial losses. Anyone interested in selling software would do well to employ a lawyer familiar with computer law to help write an appropriate disclaimer.

However, disclaimers do not exempt software developers from all responsibility. Courts regard certain disclaimers as "unconscionable" and will uphold lawsuits against vendors even if a disclaimer has been made. The principal law regulating the sale of property in the United States is the Uniform Commercial Code (UCC). In essence, the UCC protects customers by providing an implied warranty on products; it asserts that any product sold must be "merchantable"—fit for its intended purpose. Thus, if a vendor's program is not capable of performing according to its intended purpose, the vendor can be held liable for refund of the purchase price and for consequential damages.

In practice what this usually means is that any attempt to disclaim responsibility for physical harm is regarded as unconscionable, whereas courts will usually uphold a disclaimer if the damage is only financial. The practical consequences of this interpretation is that software that affects people's physical well-being (such as programs that control an x-ray machine, pharmacy database software, or robotics software used in an environment where people could be harmed) is held to a substantially higher level of accountability.

Software that does not do physical harm can be found unfit for its intended purpose and thus have its disclaimer voided if the failure is serious enough. In order for this to happen, the software must be incapable of accomplishing its main purpose and must be unrepairable within a reasonable length of time. A developer who is not writing software that can do physical harm and who is attentive to the duties we have discussed in this section is relatively safe from liability for inadvertent errors. Even so, anyone planning on selling software would be wise to do as PSI did and purchase an errors and omissions insurance policy.

Two other issues tie in with the subject of liability for software errors. First, some people have attempted to make a distinction between packaged and custom software. They consider packaged software a product and thus subject to the UCC, but they consider custom software a service and thus exempt from the UCC. However, courts have not upheld this distinction. The principle that has evolved is that if there is a viable software product and money changes hands, the UCC applies. Thus, private consultants and other custom developers do need to be careful to write disclaimers. Second, even authors of freeware can be held responsible for damages caused by their software in certain circumstances. Suppose a firm distributes a C++ compiler free of charge to anyone who wants it. It is distributed with a disclaimer declaring it to be free and informing the users that they take the risks in using it. Even so, if a user writes a program to control a piece of medical equipment and the program fails because of an error in the C++ compiler, it is possible that the compiler's author could be held liable for damages.

EXERCISES

10–8 What are the duties of care in each of the stages of preparing a packaged program (rather that custom-designed software) for sale?

10–9 Which duty of care is more likely to be neglected, the duty to produce appropriate software or the duty to produce reliable software? Why?

10–10 Arthur has been hired by a small firm to customize a set of accounting programs. Because the modifications required are fairly extensive, Arthur estimates the task will take him about a year. The programs are well-written and he finds the work challenging and enjoyable. About 6 months into the project, Joyce, the chief accountant, asks Arthur to write a special program for her. Arthur sees immediately how to write it and realizes it will take him about 2 days, but it will be boring and tedious work. Joyce tells him that it will save her about 2 hours per week. He is unsure whether to write the program or not. Arthur and Joyce are peers in the organization and both report to a vice president. The last time Arthur faced a similar situation, the vice president refused to decide, saying that Arthur knew best what needed to be done. What are the duties of care Arthur faces in this situation? On what bases should he make his decision?

10–11 Consider the following scenario as described in Miller [6]:

In 1986, at least two people died and at least one other was maimed after receiving excessive radiation form a linear accelerator radiation machine called the Therac 25 (Joyce, 1986). The first death occurred after a treatment on March 21. Technicians and doctors carefully examined the equipment and the incident, and concluded the machine was safe. On April 11, however, a second patient was given what proved to be a fatal overdose from the machine. After this incident, the problem with the machine was finally discovered: a bug in the assembler language program which controlled the machine.

The Therac 25 has two modes: x-ray mode and electron beam mode. In x-ray mode, a very high powered beam strikes a heavy metal plate; that plate gives off x-rays which are focused on the patient. In electron beam mode, the plate is retracted, and a much lower powered beam of electrons is focussed directly on the patient. A technician controls the Therac 25 using a PDP-11 mini-computer. An assembler program on the PDP interprets the technician's commands, and controls the radiation machine as a peripheral. The software includes two different methods for correcting a mistake when entering commands: retyping the command completely, or using the up-arrow to edit the mistaken command. Under one particular set of circumstances, when the technician used the up-arrow edit to change from the x-ray mode to the electron mode, the assembler program retracted the heavy metal plate (a correct action) but did not lower the power of the beam (an incorrect omission). Thus, the high power beam was focused directly on the patient, delivering a lethal dose of radiation. Whenever this situation occurred, a sensor detected the large amount of radiation and flashed a warning on the monitor, "MALFUNCTION 54." The significance of this warning was not understood until after April 11.

What responsibility do each of the following have in this situation: the assembly language programmer, the manager in charge of programming, the company which manufactured the machine, the hospital, the technicians who ran the machine, and the engineers who tested it after the first accident?

10–12 Consider the following "fictional case study" based on a scenario presented by Nancy Leveson (Leveson, 1986) and reported in Miller [6]:

Following a detailed English specification from a systems analyst, a programmer produces code that controls safety features in a nuclear power plant. One part of the specification states:

"Whenever one of the plant sponsors discovers a potentially dangerous situation, the task monitoring these sensors should shut down all plant systems. When plant personnel have rectified the situation that caused the exceptional sensor condition, the program will allow a manual override that will restart the plant systems."

The programmer tests the code, and installs it at the plant. The systems analyst views the programmer's test results, and attests to the correctness of the program. The program is installed and runs for six months without incident.

One component of the nuclear power plant controls fuel rods and flow of water into the the reactor in order to regulate the temperature of the reaction. One of the sensors in the reactor has a hardware failure, and gives a false, abnormally high, reading. The program controlling safety immediately shuts down all reactor systems. Unfortunately, at the moment the sensor fails, the valve for the cooling water had begun to open because the temperature was starting to rise in the reactor; insufficient water gets to the reactor because of the shut down, and the temperature continues to rise. While the sensor in the reactor is being replaced, the reactor overheats, and some radioactive steam is emitted into the atmosphere as the pressure builds up. A technician notices the problem, and, even though it is against safety procedures, manually overrides the safety system so that the cooling water valve opens. The communities surrounding the plant are aroused both by the radioactivity that was released and the potential disaster that was narrowly avoided.

Where does responsibility for this (fictional) disaster lay? With the physicist who signed off on the specifications, with the analyst who wrote them, or with the programmer for not testing more? Could a formal proof of correctness of this program have prevented this disaster? Why or why not? What does this tell us about the role of formal proofs of correctness?

SUMMARY

Our brief study of computing in Chapters 1 through 9 has, for the most part, dealt with the technical aspects of the discipline; it was primarily directed toward learning about the design and use of algorithms and computers to solve problems. In doing this, we have introduced powerful tools. Indeed, the algorithmic process is a tool simple enough for problems like averaging revenues and complex enough to analyze the content of a satellite photograph of the earth.

As computing practitioners, we have a responsibility that is not limited only to technical competence but includes also the ability to understand basic issues and the ramifications of technical and managerial decisions we make about the use of computers. In Chapter 10, we have studied some aspects of this social context of computing. The scenario is the relationship between computer professionals (who design and develop computers and their software), computer users (who purchase and use computers and software), and other members of society who are somehow affected (say as consumers whose credit ratings are in a computer database or as patients whose treatments are under computer control) by the decisions of computer professionals and computer users. The issues are enormous and pervasive; only a small example was studied here.

In the first section, we considered the issue of software as intellectual property. As such, software can be owned, sold, and stolen. We looked at the applicability of protection by copyrights, patents, trademarks, and trade secrets. The use of software licenses and piracy was studied. The issue of exactly what constitutes copying was considered in the review of the recent look and feel debate. Improvement upon someone else's ideas is technical progress—copying someone else's ideas is morally and legally wrong—where does one draw the line?

The second section studied the issue of liability for software errors. Our work on even the simplest of programs in the laboratory accompanying this course is probably enough evidence to demonstrate how difficult it is to produce error-free software. However, the implications of errors in commercial software, especially in such areas as complex as medicine or space exploration, are indicative of the seriousness of the matter. But errors happen. Who is liable and how do the developer and the user protect themselves?

The importance of social context issues cannot be over-emphasized. They're hard and complex, and they will continue to persist as the complexity and range of computer applications continue to grow.

SELECTED READINGS

1. Peter J. Denning, *Computers under Attack: Intruders, Worms, and Viruses*, ACM Press, 1990, 113 pages.

2. Peter J. Denning, "Educating a New Engineer," *Communications of the ACM*, **35(12)** (Dec. 1992)

3. Tom Forrester and Perry Morrison, *Computer Ethics: Cautionary Tales and Ethical Dilemmas in Computing*, MIT Press, 1990, 193 pages.

4. Kenneth Green and Steven Gilbert, "Software Piracy: Its Cost and Consequences," *Change*, Jan.-Feb. 1987.

5. Deborah Johnson, *Computer Ethics*, Prentice-Hall, 1984, 110 pages.

6. Keith Miller, "Integrating Computer Ethics into the Curriculum," *Computer Science Education*, **1(1)**, 1988.

7. Frederic W. Nietzke, *A Software Law Primer*, Van Nostrand, 1984, 157 pages.

8. Pamela Samuelson, "Why the Look and Feel of Software User Interfaces Should Not Be Protected by Copyright Law," *Communications of the ACM,* **32(5)** (May 1989).

9. Pamela Samuelson, and Robert J. Glushko, "Survey on the Look and Feel Lawsuits," *Communications of the ACM,* **33(5)** (May 1990).

10. Pamela Samuelson, Michael Denber, and Robert J. Glushko, "Developments on the Intellectual Property Front," *Communications of the ACM,* **35(6)** (June 1992).

11. Pamela Samuelson, "The Ups and Downs of Look and Feel," *Communications of the ACM* **36(4)** (April 1993).

12. Eugene H. Spafford, *Computer Ethics*, Acorn Publishers, 1990.

13. Richard M. Stallman, "The GNU Manifesto," *GNU Emacs Manual*, 1987.

14. *Wall Street Journal*, July 10, 1986.

15. Alan R. White, *Grounds of Liability, An Introduction to the Philosophy of Law*, Oxford University Press, 1985, 128 pages.

16. E. Robert Yoches, "Legal Protection of Computer Software," *Communications of the ACM,* **32(2)** (February 1989).

COMPUTING AS A DISCIPLINE

As promised, this text has presented a broad and vigorous introduction to the discipline of computing. We have provided a comprehensive, integrated look at the discipline as well as a basic and rigorous introduction to the art and science of problem solving and programming. We have emphasized the union of abstract ideas with practice. The essence of this approach has been to help readers establish a tight coupling between an understanding of the principles of the discipline and a mastery of technical skills.

Chapter 1 reviewed the historical foundations for the discipline; Chapters 2 through 6 developed a precise methodology (MAPS) for problem solving and C++ programming. Chapter 7 addressed the issue of program verification. The principles of logic, problem solving, and programming served as the basis for a study of elementary circuits and computer organization in Chapter 8 and 9, using a simulated computer (Marina). The landscape for all this is the idea that computing is ultimately a human and social enterprise, as outlined in Chapter 1 and studied in some of its particular aspects in Chapter 10. Thus, we have portrayed computing as the study of algorithmic problems, solutions, and machines, all in the context of a society that requires their efficient and humane utilization.

The purpose of this chapter is to provide additional perspectives on computing as a discipline and a profession—perspectives that join what we have covered in this text together with what we have not covered. That is, this chapter will complete the overview of computing—to see how the material in this text fits into the whole discipline and to see what remains to be encountered in later courses of study. To this end, we explore in more detail each of the nine subject areas of computing that were identified in Figure 1–5. The nine subject areas will provide a structure for this overview. Many of the remaining topics in these areas are covered in later volumes of this series. The goal, therefore, is to provide a good sense of where we, as computing professionals, have been, where we are today, and where we seem to be headed.

THE DISCIPLINE OF COMPUTING

Computing is a relatively young academic discipline. In characterizing the role of computing, it is important to distinguish between *applications* of the computer within the other disciplines (and society in general) and the *nature* of computing itself. To be sure, the use of computers to process vast amounts of data and to solve long and complex mathematical problems is invaluable in the sciences and engineering, the humanities, and the professions. Furthermore, the computer has opened up new areas of research that had been impossible to study in the past. However, this observation does not explain the nature of the discipline of computing any more than the application of statistical and other mathematical methods to the natural and social sciences explains the nature of the discipline of mathematics.

Knuth and others have suggested that the central core of computer science is the algorithm [8]. Recall the definition of an algorithm from Chapter 4:

> **Definition**   An *algorithm* is a list of instructions specifying a precise description of a step-by-step process that is guaranteed to give the answer to any problem of a given type and terminate after a finite number of steps have been completed.

Algorithms are thus characterized by several fundamental properties. First, they are deterministic, in the sense that identical inputs will always yield the same outputs. Second, they are finite, so that they may be performed mechanically in a finite amount of time (either by humans with pencil and paper or by machines). Finally, algorithms are general, in the sense that they yield the answer to a specific instance of an entire class of problems.

Using this definition, the discipline of computing would be defined as the study of algorithmic problems and methods for their solution. The basic algorithmic approach to problem solving includes analysis of the problem, development of a global or systems view or perspective, followed by successive refinements by subdividing the problem ultimately leading to development of a correct algorithm for solving a particular class of problems. Thus, computing professionals (computer scientists and computer engineers) are concerned with:

1. Analysis of algorithmic problems

2. Invention or discovery of algorithms

3. Description of algorithms

4. Understanding algorithms

5. Proving or otherwise establishing the correctness of algorithms

6. Analyzing the behavior of algorithms, including efficiency of operation under worst-, average-, and best-case conditions and the interaction of algorithms with one another

7. Identification of classes of problems to which algorithms may be applied

8.   The theoretical potential and limitations of algorithms

But the discipline of computing has evolved to encompass a far wider range of intrinsic and related concerns.

In defining computing, then, we need to look to more circumspect and contemporary sources. One source is an article by Peter Denning, a past president of the Association for Computing Machinery (ACM) and a widely recognized educator and scholar in the field. Denning gave the following broad, historically based definition of the discipline:

> *Computer science is the body of knowledge dealing with the design, analysis, implementation, efficiency, and application of processes that transform information. The fundamental question underlying all of computer science is "what can be automated?"* [3]

In this article, Denning identifies 11 general subject areas that combine to make up the discipline of computer science. These areas have evolved over the last four or five decades. Denning lists these areas and their approximate dates of emergence into a coherent body of knowledge as shown in Table 11–1. (The date of 1986 that Denning gives for the emergence of Artificial Intelligence, or AI, as a coherent subject area has been controversial—most believe that Artificial Intelligence has its origin in the 1950s.)

TABLE 11–1   Subject Areas in Computing

Area of computer science	Date of emergence
Theory	1940
Numerical computation	1945
Architecture	1950
Programming languages and methodology	1960
Algorithms and data structures	1968
Operating systems	1971
Networks	1975
Human interface	1978
Database systems	1980
Concurrent computation	1982
Artificial intelligence	1986

In 1986, the ACM established the Task Force on the Core of Computer Science [4], which was given the charge of developing a contemporary and extensive definition of computer science, accompanied by recommendations for teaching an intensive three-semester introductory sequence that would leave students with a comprehensive understanding of the entire field—especially those aspects of the field that go beyond the development of programming skills. The result differed considerably in both substance and presentation from previous efforts. In addition, the task force concluded that "no fundamental difference exists between the two fields [of computer science and computer engineering] in the core material." Therefore, it coined the phrase "discipline of computing" to represent the union of both fields.

In addition to changing the domain of the definition, the task force presented the definition itself in a comprehensive two-dimensional form (Table 11–2). This is almost identical with the definition of the discipline of computing that appears in Chapter 1 (see Figure 1.1). The two definitions differ only in the absence of a *social context* paradigm, which would add a fourth column alongside the Theory, Abstraction, and Design columns in Table 11–2.

TABLE 11–2 The Array of Subject Areas in Computing

	Theory	Abstraction	Design
Algorithms and data structures			
Programming languages			
Architecture			
Numerical and symbolic computation			
Operating systems			
Software methodology and engineering			
Database and information retrieval			
Artificial intelligence and robotics			
Human-computer communication			

As we recall from Chapter 1, the columns of Table 11–2 represent the paradigms, or processes, that characterize distinct methods of approach that different points of view bring to the discipline. Since this aspect of the definition is somewhat new and unique, we quote the explanation from the Report itself [4].

> *"The first paradigm, theory, is rooted in mathematics and consists of four steps followed in the development of a coherent, valid theory:*
>
> *(1) characterize the objects of study (definition);*
> *(2) hypothesize possible relationships among them (theorem);*
> *(3) determine whether the relationships are true (proof);*
> *(4) interpret results.*
>
> *A mathematician expects to iterate these steps (e.g., when errors or inconsistencies are discovered).*

The second paradigm, abstraction (modeling), is rooted in the experimental scientific method and consists of four stages that are followed in the investigation of a phenomenon:

(1) form a hypothesis;
(2) construct a model and make a prediction;
(3) design an experiment and collect data;
(4) analyze results.

A scientist expects to iterate these steps (e.g., when a model's predictions disagree with experimental evidence). Even though "modeling" and "experimentation" might be appropriate substitutes, we have chosen the word "abstraction" for this paradigm because this usage is common in the discipline.

The third paradigm, design, is rooted in engineering and consists of four steps followed in the construction of a system (or device) to solve a given problem:

(1) state requirements;
(2) state specifications;
(3) design and implement the system;
(4) test the system.

An engineer expects to iterate these steps (e.g., when tests reveal that the latest version of the system does not satisfactorily meet the requirements)."

The fourth paradigm, *social context*, was not defined explicitly in that report [4]. (It was added in the 1991 report of the ACM/IEEE-CS Joint Curriculum Task Force [12], which used all the other elements of the original report [4] as a basis for developing a comprehensive set of curriculum recommendations for undergraduate programs in computing.) The social context, as we learned in Chapter 10, deals with the effect of computing on human beings, human relationships, and the environment. Unlike the other three paradigms, it does not follow a four-step pattern. Rather, the social context of computing is concerned with three tasks:

(1) Identifying human relationships in which computers have a role
(2) Understanding ways in which computers affect these relationships
(3) Clarifying the rights and responsibilities of the parties in these
     relationships

For instance, some scholars have studied the ways in which computers affect the relationship between employers and employees. In Chapter 10 we discussed issues related to intellectual property and liability for software errors.

Our concern there was to clarify some of the rights and responsibilities involved in the programmer-user relationship. It is important to emphasize that the rights and responsibilities that surround such relationships are intimately connected with the technical content of the discipline itself. For example, in order to consider liability for software errors, we must have a good conceptual and technical grasp of the software methodology and engineering and architecture subject areas.

The four approaches to the discipline of computing are uniquely interconnected. Other related ideas which might at first appear to be subject areas are not listed separately in Table 11–2 because their content transcends several or all of the other subareas. For example, parallelism appears in the form of parallel algorithms, parallel languages, parallel architectures, and computer performance evaluation; this topic is thus relevant in nearly all the subject areas.

SUBJECT AREAS IN THE DISCIPLINE

This section completes the overview of the discipline of computing. The subsection headings correspond to the nine subject areas of the discipline listed in Table 11–2. The new subjects are briefly introduced in order to indicate the breadth and richness that students of computing will encounter in further study.

Algorithms and Data Structures

A major theme in this text is the study of algorithms and their use in problem solving including problem analysis; algorithm design; and implementation, evaluation, and verification. We have seen that the realization of an algorithm is first a *program*. Indeed, the principles of programming methodology introduced in Chapters 2 through 6—precise specification, algorithm discovery, program coding, and testing—are recurring themes throughout the text. Ultimately, an executable realization of the algorithm—that is, a *process*, running on a computer provides the solution to an algorithmic problem.

Recall from Chapter 8 that computers are basically data processors. Thus, the data and the form that it takes are also an important part of using computers to solve problems. The term *data structures* refers to methods of organizing, storing, sorting, and searching significant amounts of data. As we have seen in Chapters 2 through 6 and in the laboratory exercises, the use of effective methods for representing and organizing information is a key factor in determining effective solution functions for problems. The fundamental data structures that we have encountered in our study so far are the list and the array. Other, more complex data structures, such as queues, stacks, strings, trees, and graphs, will be introduced in later volumes of this series.

For example, an interesting and useful kind of data structure is called the *tree*. Intuitively, a tree can be visualized as a way of organizing information in a hierarchical fashion. As shown in Figure 11–1, a tree looks like a sketch of an upside-down natural tree. Its single entry point, the *root*, is at the top, and the root is connected to a series of paths, each fanning out vertically to a "subtree" of successively lower points (*nodes*), and ultimately ending at points called *leaves*.

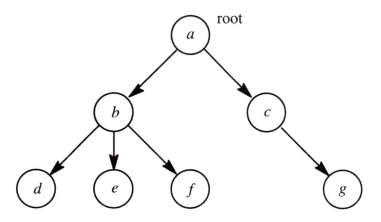

FIGURE 11–1   A tree. (*a*) The root; (*a, b, ..., g*) the nodes; (*d, e, f, g*) the leaves.

Trees are useful in a wide variety of applications in computer science. They are used to facilitate searches of large files of data that are maintained in lexicographic order. For example, consider the problem of searching a dictionary for a particular word. If the words in the dictionary are ordered in a treelike fashion, this search process can be greatly simplified. For another example, trees are useful in the process of translating programs written in a high-level language (such as C++) into a sequence of machine language statements (such as Marina) that represent the individual operations to be performed.

Computer scientists are interested not only in the formulation of algorithms and the study of data structures but also in the evaluation of algorithm efficiency and the limits of algorithmic methods in general. We want to be able to measure the execution time for complex algorithms and see that different algorithms, even for the same problem, have different "levels of complexity" or efficiency of execution. In searching a dictionary containing, say, 32,000 words, a particular word can be found after at most 15 comparisons using a binary search algorithm (this is developed in Volume II), whereas as many as 32,000 comparisons are required using a simple linear search of the dictionary from beginning to end. While these two algorithms solve the same problem, they have considerably different efficiencies. We characterize the efficiency of the simple linear search as $O(n)$, read "order n," since the basic operation—the number of comparisons—varies exactly as the number of words (n) in the dictionary. The efficiency of the binary search, on the other hand, is $O(\log_2 n)$, since the number of comparisons varies as the logarithm of the size of the dictionary. The measures $O(n)$ and $O(\log_2 n)$ are examples of what we call the *computational complexity* of an algorithm.

The algorithms we have studied in this volume have complexities that can be measured in $O(n)$ or $O(n^2)$ *execution steps*. That is, their execution times are bounded by a polynomial of degree n^2 or less. There are many other common algorithms whose complexities greatly exceed these bounds. Algorithms with complexities bounded by a polynomial n^k have *polynomial complexity*. For example, a straightforward algorithm for matrix multiplication has complexity $O(n^3)$, where n is the number of rows and columns in the two matrices being multiplied. In general, the class of all deterministic algorithms—like the ones in this text—that have polynomial complexity is known as the class *P*. The class of all nondeterministic algorithms with polynomial complexity is known as the class *NP*. The difference between determinism and nondeterminism in algorithmic behavior is difficult to explain briefly and is not covered here. This, and other matters concerning the theory of algorithms and their behavior, is a subject that will be covered in Volumes II and IV of this series.

There are many algorithms whose complexities exceed the bounds of any degree of polynomial. These algorithms have execution times that grow exponentially with the size of their input—that is with complexities such as $O(2^n)$, $O(n^2 2^n)$, etc. This important class of algorithms requires such extraordinary execution times as to make their use impractical if not impossible on conventional machines. Unconventional computer architectures, such as parallel and array processors, are being designed to help solve these highly complex problems. The study and characterization of these algorithms and computer architectures is also an important topic in Volume IV.

There are also problems which, although describable, are provably *unsolvable* by any algorithmic method. That is, we can define a problem which is so difficult that *no* algorithm (i.e., no program whose execution terminates for all possible inputs) can be devised to solve it. Here we are at the limit of computability, and computer scientists are interested in characterizing this class of problems precisely, so as to determine which problems are solvable in this sense and which are not.

The classic example of an unsolvable problem is the *halting problem*, which was discussed briefly at the end of Chapter 7. It can be stated as follows:

Find an algorithm H *that will determine, for an arbitrary program* P *and input* I*, whether* P *will halt after a finite number of steps or enter an infinite loop.*

It has been proved that such an algorithm H does not exist; that is, the halting problem is unsolvable. The idea of unsolvability and the characterization of unsolvable problems constitute an important topic in computer science, addressed in Volume III of this series.

Programming Languages

In this text, our work has been limited to a single high-level programming language, C++. Our reason for this choice is that C++ is becoming a dominant language in the computer science curriculum. In the broad discipline of computing and its application areas, however, many different programming languages are in use. Most of these are designed explicitly in favor of the needs of professional programmers and thus are less than adequate for a first course.

In the scientific and engineering area, for example, there is a premium on the use of efficient and powerful tools for the numerical and statistical analysis of data. Scientists and engineers rely heavily upon FORTRAN (*for*mula *trans*lator), one of the oldest programming languages (developed in 1956). The main reasons for this choice are FORTRAN's extensive support for mathematical analysis and its efficient implementation on very fast scientific computers and supercomputers. Recently, scientific programmers have begun to migrate toward other languages, like C and Pascal. More recently, social scientists prefer to use commercially available packaged data analysis programs such as SPSS, (*Statistical Package for the Social Sciences*) and SAS (*Statistical Analysis System*) instead of programming languages.

In data processing and information systems applications, COBOL has been the dominant programming language. This dominance arises from COBOL's extensive support for large data file definition and processing; its relative ease of learning; and its widespread implementation and standardization since its origination in the late 1950s. Recently, however, the COBOL programming community has begun to migrate toward the use of *fourth-generation languages* (4GLs) for many data processing applications. These languages are useful in many specialized applications and have more expressive power than conventional programming languages. For example, many 4GLs contain powerful "query" commands for selectively searching and retrieving information from a database. In a conventional language like COBOL, such queries are not directly supported in the language.

LISP is an important programming tool in *artificial intelligence* (AI) applications. PROLOG is another programming language which is especially useful in AI applications where the simulation of logical reasoning, or rule-based systems, is required. Some of these applications are called *expert systems* because they attempt to simulate the deductive reasoning process of a human expert. For example, an early expert system known as MYCIN simulates the reasoning of a medical diagnostician in deducing one or more possible diseases in a patient who shows a particular group of symptoms.

Another important general area of programming applications is *systems programming*. Systems programmers produce operating systems, programming language compilers and interpreters, text editors, real-time embedded software systems, and all other software elements whose reliability and efficiency are most crucial in the effective utilization of computers by the applications programming communities. As indicated in Chapter 9, most systems programming has traditionally been done in the assembly or even machine language of the host machine where the software systems were to be used. This choice, although arguably efficient, places serious constraints on software reliability and portability. The emergence of the high-level languages C, Ada, and Modula-2 has provided an effective means for systems programmers to address the reliability and portability problems while maintaining acceptable levels of software efficiency.

Another aspect of the subject area of programming languages concerns the basic difference that, you will recall from Chapter 7, exists between a program statement as it appears in a C++ program and the corresponding series of machine instructions representing the statement as it is interpreted and executed by a computer. The resolution of this difference—a translation—is accomplished in one of three different ways: compilation, interpretation, or direct execution.

Compilation is the translation of a program written in a high-level language (such as C++) to a machine language (such as Marina) *prior* to execution. A *compiler*, which is a piece of software (not a separate computer or peripheral device), has four major stages. First, the C++ program to be translated passes through a phase called *lexical analysis* where individual *tokens* (constants, identifiers, operators, reserved words, punctuation marks, etc.) are identified and separated out. The second stage, called *syntactic analysis* or *parsing*, takes this list of tokens and transforms it into a meaningful, treelike structural description of the program. This structural description, often called a *parse tree,* unambiguously represents the meaning of the program. Thereafter, in the *code generation* stage of compilation, an equivalent machine language program is developed. Finally, in the *optimization* stage, the efficiency of execution of the program being translated is improved. Thus, after a C++ program is compiled, an entirely separate and later step is required in order for the equivalent machine language program to be executed.

In contrast, the process of *interpretation*, also performed by a software program, scans the original program in a step-by-step fashion, translating and executing each step immediately as it is encountered. No prior translation of the *entire* program takes place; instead, each step is directly interpreted (and in cases where the step is inside a loop, repeatedly *re*interpreted) whenever it is encountered. As our intuition would suggest, compilation requires less time than interpretation. However, interpretation is often preferred in program development, since this process generally provides the programmer with more information related to the text of the original program than does compilation. Important languages which are widely implemented by interpreters include LISP, PROLOG, and BASIC.

Recently machines have been designed that directly (and, hence, interpretatively) execute the statements of a program in a particular language such as LISP. For instance, "LISP machines" are widely used in AI research because they combine the conceptual advantages of interpreters with the run-time efficiency of compilers. Under direct execution, the machine is no longer bound to the basic von Neumann architecture that was discussed in Chapter 8. Instead, the machine has an architecture that directly mirrors the underlying primitive functions and execution structure of the language it is interpreting. That is, its instructions and data types are matched with those of the LISP language itself.

Object-oriented languages represent a recent attempt to address problems in software reliability, development, and maintenance by providing a distinctive methodology and powerful libraries that can be more directly associated with the application itself than can conventional "procedural languages." While procedural programming—such as most of the C++ work we have done in this course—uses the function as the building block for decomposing a problem into its algorithmic solution, object-oriented programming uses the "object" as the point of focus. We have had a brief introduction to objects and classes in Chapter 5, as we used the lists and grids class libraries to construct powerful programs. We saw there the idea that "Objects" combine data structures and functions. For example, a programmer who is developing software for a bank could have an object such as an ACCOUNT. Typical banking functions include OPEN an account, DEPOSIT some money, WITHDRAW some money, and CLOSE an account. The data structure used to represent ACCOUNT and these functions would be bundled together to form the ACCOUNT object.

The application of object-oriented languages and methodologies to design software systems is the subject of much recent interest and attention in the computing field. These methodologies hold great potential for improving software quality, maintainability, and portability. Examples of object-oriented languages include Eiffel, C++, Smalltalk, and extended versions of Pascal. We shall study the principles and uses of object-oriented design more intensively in *Volume II* of this series.

Architecture

In Chapter 7, we studied computer organization in order to understand how data is represented and programs are executed by contemporary computers. In a more comprehensive study of computer organization and architecture, different levels of computer organization are exposed and related: the digital logic level, the microprogramming level, the conventional machine level, the assembly language level, the operating system machine level, and the application program level. More advanced study in computer architecture introduces topics such as interrupt handling, logic design, integrated circuits, and very large-scale integration (VLSI), multiprocessing, and highly parallel architectures. Many of these topics appear in sections B and C of the Computing Review Categories list in Appendix E.

Two recurring concepts in the design of computers are control and efficiency. By *control*, we mean the design and machine realization of techniques that effectively manage and respond to the myriad different events that occur during the operation of a computer in executing programs. The simplest and oldest control model is the familiar von Neumann machine, such as Marina, in which the instructions of a single program are executed in a sequential, one-at-a-time fashion. Variations and improvements upon the von Neumann architecture have been introduced over the last three decades, such as use of overlap, pipe-lining, and cache memories, all in the interest of gaining efficiency over the simpler model.

Designers gain additional efficiency by going beyond the von Neumann ar-chitecture and its variations, developing computers and programming lan-guages that facilitate execution of several instructions at a time, several programs at a time, and/or several data streams at a time—that is, machines that operate *in parallel*. This is an exciting and challenging area; a significant amount of research remains to be done before the natural parallelism in algo-rithms is fully exploited for day-to-day applications. There are several compet-ing theories and processor models that represent parallelism in different ways, each one making quantum gains in efficiency over the conventional von Neu-mann machines and sequential programming styles. All these theories come under the general heading of parallelism and concurrency.

Theories of concurrency usually assume the availability of several proces-sors, any number of which may be simultaneously executing a different func-tion, or *process*. One way to enable cooperation and information sharing among such processes is to use common (shared) variables called *signals*. This general model is depicted in Figure 11–2. In this setting, each signal is used to synchronize processes by signaling the occurrence of a specific event. In-formation can be transferred from one process to other processes by means of a SEND operation. Moreover, other processes may suspend activities and wait for the occurrence of an event by using the operation WAIT. These special opera-tions thus serve to prevent the confusion that can occur from the uncontrolled sequencing of events by two or more processors that are executing asynchro-nously.

Processes themselves can be represented as functions. Within the body of such a function, any number of SEND and WAIT instructions may be included as

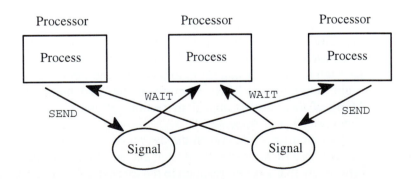

FIGURE 11–2   Concurrent processes and processors.

needed to send or wait for a particular signal before continuing. Communication among a collection of concurrent events can be accomplished by writing a *monitor*, a program module in which one or more signals are declared globally and shared among its constituent functions (representations of processes) for the purpose of coordinating control as certain classes of events take place.

Parallelism, in the context of computer architecture, refers to the design and implementation of computer systems able to realize and control concurrency—that is, the execution of several functions in a single algorithm simultaneously. A classification scheme was developed in 1966 by Flynn [5] to characterize the various alternative designs for parallel machines and prototypes. Thus, in addition to the sequential von Neumann architecture, called SISD (*single instruction stream, single data* stream) in that classification scheme, there are other classes representing alternative parallel computer architectures. For instance, SIMD (*single instruction stream, multiple data* stream) architecture includes the so-called vector supercomputers and array processors, such as the Illiac IV, the Cray, and the Connection Machine. MIMD (*multiple instruction stream, multiple data* stream) architecture refers to the multiprocessors such as hypercubes, Transputers, and the Ultracomputer.

Other recent developments in computer architecture include the RISC machines mentioned in Chapter 7. The Sun Microsystems SPARC and the MIPS R2000 and R3000 are perhaps the most popular examples. Volume III of this series addresses hardware and architecture issues in greater detail.

Numerical and Symbolic Computation

The area of numerical and symbolic computation is an important part of the discipline of computing. It serves a wide range of engineering and scientific R&D activities that depend critically upon mathematical methods—applications which rely principally upon the computer's ability to perform rapid and accurate mathematical calculations, often involving very large numbers of individual data values and calculations.

The challenge here comes from the fact that the digital computer is a discrete device (it represents **real** numbers with a *finite* number of significant digits), whereas many physical and biological phenomena actually have continuous mathematical representations (that is, some real numbers such as π would require infinite precision for accurate representation). Thus, the calculus of continuous variables provides theoretical foundations for a large class of mathematical algorithms.

The computer scientist must understand the ramifications of using inexact computer representations for scientific and statistical phenomena which have exact mathematical characterizations. The field of *error analysis* seeks to analyze errors in the computer representation of real numbers (called *representation errors*) and errors in the computer execution of arithmetic functions (called *propagation errors*). In order to acquire a proper basis for studying errors and their control in mathematical algorithms, computer science students should develop proficiency in calculus.

Suppose a program requires a computation involving the decimal number 1.1. To represent this number in the computer as a **real**, it is converted to an equivalent binary value (recall the discussion in Chapter 7). However, the *exact* equivalent binary number has an *infinite* number of binary digits, forming the repeating pattern

```
1.00011001100110011001100110011...
```

But the computer cannot accommodate values which require an infinite number of bits for their representation. Instead, such values are *truncated* to the maximum number of significant bits that the computer representation will allow. That number varies among the different computers, but it is often 24 (using a 32-bit word for the entire value, including sign and scale factor), 56 (for "extended precision," which is required by many mathematical algorithms), or more. In any event, that number is always *finite*. Thus, the 24-bit binary *approximation* of the decimal number 1.1 is

```
1.00011001100110011001100
```

which is 1.099999914628568359375 in base 10. The difference between this value and the true value, 1.1, is called the *representation error*.

Errors are also propagated during the computer execution of arithmetic operations, such as multiplication or division of two **real** values. For example, the real values 11.0 and 10.0 have *exact* real representations, but their exact quotient (1.1) cannot be represented exactly.

Because of the potential for uncontrolled growth of representation and propagated errors during a computation, the computer solution of complex mathematical and statistical problems is always an approximate process. A great deal of effort, therefore, goes into estimating and controlling the *degree* of such errors, which themselves vary widely among different classes of problems. Part G of the Computing Review Categories in Appendix E lists the major areas of computing where numerical analysis and error analysis are used.

In numerical analysis, the notion of interpolation suggests a general process of iterative refinement of an approximate solution to a problem. Iteration continues either until a tolerably small error (difference between the approximate solution and the exact solution) has been achieved or until it is discovered that such a small error cannot be achieved. The classic example of interpolation is Newton's method for iteratively arriving at an approximation to a mathematical function (such as the square root of a real number) that cannot be computed directly.

The area of numerical linear algebra includes a broad spectrum of mathematical problems that require the solution of a series of simultaneous linear equations. With two variables x_1 and x_2, these equations have the form

$$a_{11}x_1 + a_{12}x_2 = b_1$$
$$a_{21}x_1 + a_{22}x_2 = b_2$$

Here, the problem is to find values for x_1 and x_2, given any particular set of values for the a's and b's. For some such sets the solution is exact, while for others the solution may only be approximated. Moreover, there are some sets of values for the a's and b's which lead to either *no* solution or *infinitely many* solutions to these equations.

Any effective computer algorithm for solving sets of linear equations must gracefully accommodate each of these different possible outcomes; it must find solutions or reasonably accurate approximations for the exact solutions when they do exist, and it must detect and report the nonexistence of solutions in all other cases. A widely used algorithm for this problem is known as Gaussian elimination; its mastery requires some mathematical maturity as well as programming skill.

The area of *optimization* encompasses algorithms which represent the process of mathematical modeling of economic systems, in which different sets of strategic decisions lead to different levels of profit or loss. Finding optimal strategies leads to maximization of profit (or minimization of loss). Optimization methods are used in simulation of other kinds of strategic and physical systems as well. For example, in fine-tuning the performance of an operating system in a particular application environment (such as a bank), the programmer would like to determine the optimal amount of memory and online disk space and the optimal number of interactive terminals for managing the daily average and peak numbers of transactions that the operating system will have to accommodate. Here the systems programmer needs to minimize computing costs (by using the minimum amount of memory and/or disk space) while ensuring a reasonable response time to users during peak periods of activity.

Recently, significant strides have been made in the area of *symbolic computation*—the use of computer programs to accomplish symbolic manipulations of algebraic formulas. For example, software packages have been developed which will perform factoring of an algebraic expression or differentiation and integration of mathematical functions, and make graphic plots of equations. Systems such as Mathematica and Maple V may dramatically change the way mathematics is taught at both the secondary and college levels.

Operating Systems

The operating system is the fundamental software component which, when executed by the hardware, creates the "virtual computer" which we use today. It is our interface with the hardware; indeed, it is that "superprogram"—or, more properly, that group of superprograms—which makes the computer hardware accessible and usable.

Definition   An *operating system* (OS) is a collection of programs that together provide the interface between computer hardware and computer users by facilitating the coding, debugging, maintenance, and use of software. Simultaneously, the operating system provides appropriate control and allocation of system resources to ensure reliable and efficient operation.

The operating system has a nucleus that contains fundamental components that reside in main memory. In addition, the OS has routines for memory management, input-output, file maintenance, control of system resource allocation and scheduling, protection for both the system and its users, and maintenance of system reliability and integrity. Each of these is a complex topic itself. Together, they form the outline for an advanced course in the curriculum that will be essential for most majors.

Contemporary operating systems research addresses issues of concurrency, distribution of system resources over networks of cooperating computers, and sophisticated user interfaces involving graphics, mice, and windows along with a natural command language. Traditional ASCII terminals are rapidly being replaced by more modern bit-mapped graphics workstations, with powerful interfaces that facilitate efficient and reliable software development.

One widely used operating system is called UNIX. Users communicate with the UNIX operating system by means of a *shell* programming language. This language allows programmers to combine different commands from the library of UNIX utilities in creative ways to solve problems which would normally require many times the effort in a conventional programming language. Although these solutions are not always efficient in a production sense, they do provide powerful tools to help rapidly develop prototype solutions to problems (especially in the domain of text processing) and demonstrate their feasibility.

Volume II in this series, along with a later course in the curriculum, contains more detailed treatments of the principles of operating systems and their applications to contemporary hardware environments.

Software Methodology and Engineering

In Chapters 4 and 5 we learned that the effective use of abstractions can help us avoid repeating the design of common utility functions and data structures when solving complex algorithmic problems. Knowing when a particular routine or data structure is appropriate for solving a given problem is often a matter of style and judgment gained from experience with other similar problems. Once the usefulness of a given routine or data structure is determined, however, the ability to reuse it should be second nature for the computing professional.

The process of analyzing problems and designing, implementing, and maintaining effective software solutions is called *software engineering*. An important element of software engineering is the mastery of tools (program modules, such as the averaging function, and data abstractions, such as the `list`) and their effective use in problem solving. Most real-world problems are considerably bigger than those we encountered in Chapters 2 through 6. In order to effectively tackle these much larger and more complex problems, an even more organized approach is needed.

The entire process of realizing an engineered software solution to an application problem is called the *software life cycle*. There are several different versions of the life cycle; one common version, called the *waterfall model*, consists of the following steps (which turn out to be generalizations of the different stages in our MAPS methodology, as identified below):

1. *Needs analysis* determines the set of requirements that the software should fulfill (i.e., the application is defined). This is a generalization of the dialogue stage in the MAPS methodology.

2. *Specifications* are formally drawn for all the input, output, and functional processes to be embodied by the software, and is a generalization of the specifications stage in MAPS.

3. *Design* takes place, in which the major data types and operators (i.e., data abstractions) are identified, along with the major functional modules of the solution, their interfaces, their individual functional requirements, and their algorithms. This is an extension of the ideas in the breakdown and abstractions stages in MAPS.

4. *Implementation*, or programming of these modules in a programming language (such as C++), then takes place. This is called coding in MAPS.

5. *Installation and testing* of the resulting programs verifies their correctness and adequacy for meeting the original specifications that were derived in step 2. This encapsulates the ideas found in the testing, verification, and presentation stages in MAPS.

6. *Maintenance* of the programs, after they have been placed into productive use, involves the regular evaluation of their performance and adequacy, the discovery and correction of errors as they appear, and the modification of the programs as changes in the application occur. This step has no analogy in MAPS, though it is by far the most costly one in the software life cycle.

An important element of software engineering is the process of design itself. Though design has been a recurring concept throughout this volume and the accompanying laboratory manual, we have emphasized understanding and use of basic tools (the programming language C++, programming techniques, routines, some simple data types and structures, and effective techniques for program testing and verification) in the implementation of predesigned solutions. (More deliberate attention to design itself is manifest in later courses in the curriculum, such as a compiler course, a database course, or a course in software engineering itself.)

A certain trend has emerged as we moved through this volume and the accompanying laboratory exercises. That is, we have tended to tackle increasingly complex problems, building upon experience with relatively easier problems from earlier chapters and laboratories. To solve these more complex problems, we have relied on *assimilation*, which is simply identifying the problem at hand as a variant or combination of other related problems that we have previously solved. Technically, we coined this activity as the breakdown and defining abstractions stages within the MAPS methodology. Generally speaking, we used a sort of "top-down design" methodology, which is based on the premise that arriving at a solution to a problem is a hierarchical process, in which each stage represents an elaboration of a set of general specifications into sets of relatively more detailed specifications until a complete and usable program solution is found.

Another design technique, sometimes called "bottom-up design," begins with the most detailed parts of a solution and works upward in the hierarchy to increasingly more general levels of design until the top of the hierarchy is reached. It is virtually the opposite of top-down design in its development of the problem solution.

Object-oriented design represents an entirely different strategy from the top-down and bottom-up design strategies. It relies on the preexistence of powerful sets of tools (data types and routines, such as `Lists` and its operations) in libraries and begins by asking the questions: "How can I best describe (or model) the situation at hand using objects?" and "Which of these objects are already in my library?" Once the appropriate objects and operators are known, the dynamic relationships among the objects are identified. When this design methodology is properly utilized, substantial gains in software productivity and reliability can be realized.

Our discussion of software engineering here is necessarily cursory. A more careful treatment of the subject can be found in *Volume II* of this series, as well as in texts by Pfleeger [9], Booch [1], and Pressman [10].

Database and Information Retrieval Systems

One of the most significant applications of the computer is the storage, retrieval, and maintenance of large volumes of information using hardware-software entities known as *information systems*. There are three basic types of information systems: (1) transaction processing systems, such as student record systems (used to organize, store, and make available student grades) and library information systems (used to locate and keep track of various library materials); (2) management information systems (used to store and retrieve critical information to assist business managers in their decision making); and (3) decision support systems (which provide mathematical models of certain decision-making situations along with access to information relevant to the problem).

The information to support these information systems is generally held in a database. A *database* is a collection of logically interrelated files. The database software which facilitates its creation, maintenance, and use is called a *da-*

tabase management system (DBMS). A DBMS is organized into two constituent parts: one that allows the programmer to design and implement the database maintenance activities (addition, deletion, and modification of records in its constituent files) and one that allows the user to retrieve information effectively from the database. The programmer's activities are often supported by so-called data definition and data manipulation languages, which have many of the characteristics of an ordinary programming language such as C++. The user's activities are often supported by a so-called query language. Query languages are styled to facilitate use of the DBMS by nontechnical personnel—managers and professionals in the application areas that use the database, such as hospital administrators or librarians—to write statements, or queries, that allow effective and efficient retrieval of information from the database.

Organizing a database is a difficult and complex matter. There are several general strategies. In the 1970s, the two popular strategies were the *network* and the *hierarchical* models. As their names imply, these models follow a distinct structure, which requires design and implementation of a "navigation program" to handle queries on the database. Changes in the nature of the desired queries require reconstruction of the query program. Nevertheless, these systems are popular; IBM's Information Management System (IMS) is a hierarchical DBMS, and the CODASYL model represents a class of network models.

The more recent *relational database* organization allows significantly greater flexibility and generality in information retrieval applications. In the relational model, the data is perceived to be organized into tables, and operations exist which facilitate rearrangement of the data into new tables (relations). The user may query the database through a nonprocedural query language (i.e., the user describes *what* is wanted rather than *how* to find it—the query language works out how best to find it). The nonprocedural language is significantly easier to use, facilitating access to the system by nontechnical personnel. Examples of relational database systems are INGRES (on many UNIX systems), ORACLE, Informix, IBM's System R, dBase (on PCs) and Paradox (also on PCs).

All these DBMSs are designed to facilitate management of many files of information and to make that information secure and selectively available to a variety of users for a variety of purposes. Design, implementation, and use of database systems requires important technical considerations and perhaps even more important social context issues, such as reliability, security, and privacy. We study database systems in more detail in Volume III of this series.

Artificial Intelligence and Robotics

The area of computing known as artificial intelligence has evoked widespread interest and discussion. *Artificial intelligence* is the study of the use of computers to simulate various aspects of intelligent behavior. These aspects include deductive reasoning, vision, natural language understanding, speech, problem solving, modeling human behavior, and various associated mechanical or robotic activities that make up intelligent behavior. The subfields of AI are broken out in part I of the CR Categories List in Appendix E. AI has received much attention in recent years, not only as an important field of research but also in areas of industry and government where many of its theories and models have been brought into productive use.

The LISP programming language and recursion are central to the study of AI, as are problems related to the combinatorial explosion of alternatives and knowledge representation and acquisition. That is, in order to simulate even the simplest aspects of human intelligent behavior, an AI system must be designed to manage efficiently the large number of elementary decisions that occur. How can an AI system acquire, store, and maintain the knowledge elements and structures that are needed for governing such decisions? These are difficult problems; some skeptics believe, in fact, that they are not solvable. Researchers in AI have developed programs that can play championship chess and assist in the diagnosis of a disease. Yet they have not been able to design a robot that can recognize a tree. Seemingly simple human capabilities we take for granted turn out to be quite complex when we attempt to mechanize them. Clearly, much remains to be done in this exciting field. Excellent readings on the philosophical as well as the practical issues surrounding AI are abundant; readers are referred to Weisenbaum [13], Rich [11], and the two books by Haugelund [6, 7].

The 1980s saw a new academic field emerging: *cognitive science*. This field is based on the belief that the focus of AI research and development is too narrow for effectively studying and modeling human intelligent behavior. Cognitive science combines certain areas of psychology, philosophy, linguistics, and AI itself into a coherent intellectual discipline. A prominent scholar in this new field is John Searle, and his writings on the subject are strongly recommended for the interested reader. Undergraduate and graduate programs in cognitive science have evolved at some of the nation's leading colleges and universities.

Human-Computer Communication

During the short history of computing, a great deal of effort has been spent searching for ways to effectively bridge the gap between our natural, human modes of communication and the computer's unnatural, nonhuman modes of communication. Although some progress has been made, this human interface problem remains largely elusive. That is, professionals in various fields who need to use computers cannot yet directly communicate their needs to these machines without some kind of intermediate restatement of these needs in a form and style that the computer can assimilate.

Sometimes, that restatement can be made after the professional has directly learned the artificial language of an application package, such as Lotus 1-2-3 which is used for solving spreadsheet problems that appear in all kinds of accounting applications. Many writers (including the authors of this text) have learned the details of desktop publishing and typesetting software, so that they can prepare, revise, and publish articles and books in various fields of science, engineering, and the humanities.

Other applications, however, require the intervention of an intermediary programmer between the professional and the computerization of his or her problem. Small accounting firms, medical organizations, and other businesses have data processing requirements that exceed the limited capabilities of a simple spreadsheet program. Additional design and interface development by an experienced systems analyst is required before these users can take full advantage of computing in their day-to-day operations.

Software products tend to use the language of the professional fields served. Ideally, software is designed to be both easy to learn and efficient to operate by people in that profession. Ease of use and efficient operation are well served when the language at the interface is mostly English and the software effectively integrates the technology of mice, graphics displays, and the conventional keyboard at the user's terminal. (Voice and touchscreen systems are also designed for this purpose, and they are beginning to find widespread use in some professions.)

So, what can be said about the use of English as an interface with computers? On the surface, this would appear to be the ultimate medium of communication between English-speaking people and computers. In fact, that goal has emerged at various times during the short history of computing. Originally, the designers of COBOL fashioned its syntax after the syntax of pidgin English, identifying paragraphs, sentences, clauses, and so forth in the structural hierarchy that makes up a COBOL program. However, the ultimate goal—that COBOL would allow the widest range of professionals to intelligibly read and understand computer programs—was naive in its conception and was not even closely approximated at any time during its 30-year life. That rather negative conclusion does not diminish COBOL's substantial contribution to the use of computers in the field of data processing.

Recent efforts to develop models and systems that simulate computer understanding of English have appeared within the field of AI. The goal here is to concentrate on a relatively narrow subject area, such as weather forecasting, and develop tools that exploit the computer's ability to simulate the understanding of utterances in that area. These tools can serve as an aid to a person developing a weather forecast. One AI system can even translate the text of a weather forecast between English and French (TAUM—METEO is used regularly by the Canadian government to provide bilingual weather forecasts). The development of computerized natural language understanding systems is in its infancy; this field shows rich promise as a research area for the foreseeable future.

COMPUTING: THE DISCIPLINE AND THE PROFESSION

Our study of the fundamentals of computing in this text enables us to draw some conclusions about the essential nature of computing as an academic and professional discipline, including both what it *is* and what it *is not*. First, this experience allows us to dispel some common myths about the nature of the discipline:

1. Computing *is not* programming. An accurate characterization of the role of programming in the field of computer science can be drawn by equating it with the role of narrative writing in the study of English or history. Programming is indeed pervasive as a medium of expression in computing but as we have seen, the discipline encompasses a far broader and richer range of subject matter.

2. Computing *is not* the use of computers by those professionals in other fields who need computer services. Those professionals sometimes tend to see computing from this self-serving point of view; that is, some view "computing" as "whatever computers can do for us." For example, the fact that the largest single application of computers is in business information processing leads some business professionals to wrongly characterize computing as the design and implementation of management information systems. This sometimes leads to misunderstandings between business and academia over the choice of subject matter that should be taught in an undergraduate curriculum.

3. Computing *is not* a subdiscipline of electrical engineering, on the one hand, or a subdiscipline of mathematics on the other. This does not mean that the discipline does not draw heavily in its design methodology from engineering or in its theory from mathematics; the body of this text testifies to the fundamental importance of both these perspectives to the unique discipline of computing.

Our experience suggests that the following are generally more accurate statements about the nature of computing as a discipline and a profession:

1. Computing *is* the study of algorithms and computers—their theories, their abstract models, their mechanical realizations, their reliability and verification, their measurement and efficiency, their linguistic description, and their social context.

2. Computing *is* a mathematical discipline, in the sense that its theories and style of investigation and communication are necessarily rigorous in the same way that mathematics is rigorous.

3. Computing *is* a scientific discipline, in the sense that its theories and abstractions are continually evaluated and tested in an experimental laboratory setting.

4. Computing *is* an engineering discipline, in the sense that design, analysis, efficiency, reliability, and correctness are central in all of its nine subject areas.

5.   Computing *is* a discipline that has a direct and profound impact on the quality of life and society at large.

A computing professional, therefore, is a person who understands computing in its depth and breadth and who conducts his or her research, design, or application development activities in one or more of its nine major subject areas.

Professional Engagement: A First Look

Having now seriously begun the study of computing, some readers may want to begin exploring the possibilities for direct personal involvement in this field outside the classroom. One way to do this would be to become a student member of the Association for Computing Machinery (ACM) or the IEEE Computer Society, the discipline's two principal professional societies. Many colleges and universities have student chapters of ACM, with membership open to undergraduates who want to develop their interests in this field.

As members of ACM, students receive a subscription to the *Communications of the ACM*, its major monthly journal. This journal not only contains technical articles and reports on contemporary issues in computer science but also keeps an up-to-date calendar of conferences, reports, and current events in the computer industry and publishes classified advertisements for employment in the computer industry and academia. Similar benefits accompany a student membership in the IEEE Computer Society, through a regular subscription to its monthly publication, *Computer*.

Academic degree programs are available in computer science and computer engineering at the bachelor's, master's, and doctoral levels at most leading colleges and universities throughout the nation and the world. This rapid evolution of the discipline in the academic community has taken place mainly during the last two decades. During this period, the academic curriculum in computer science has also become better understood and implemented. A catalyst in the evolution of strong undergraduate and graduate curricula has been the ongoing development of curriculum standards, under the sponsorship of the ACM, the Computer Society, and other interested groups of computer scientists and engineers.

Undergraduates who major in computer science or computer engineering have a wide range of options for further study and professional growth upon completion of their degrees. A good reference for these different postgraduate study and professional opportunities can be found in the two *Peterson's Guides* that are published on an annual basis and are available in the reference section of most college and university libraries. One lists employment opportunities in the computer industry; the other lists graduate school opportunities in computer science. The ACM also publishes an annual *Graduate Assistantship Directory* [2], which gives comprehensive and detailed information on many computer science graduate programs—the number of faculty members, their research areas, the number of graduate assistantships, research computer support, etc.

Graduate programs leading to the M.S. and Ph.D. degrees in computer science and engineering vary widely in their areas of emphasis. Major areas include theory (formal languages, automata, computability); hardware systems (architecture, networking, parallel processing, VLSI design); software systems (operating systems, compilers, interpreters, human interfaces, graphics); AI (natural language understanding, vision, robotics, speech, expert systems); and database and information systems.

EXERCISES

11–1 Summarize your ideas about the nature of the discipline of computing by writing a one- or two-page essay in which you describe the aspects of the discipline that you find most interesting for further study, as well as those aspects you find least interesting, and why.

11–2 Find a current issue of *Communications of the ACM* in your library, and read it from cover to cover. Do the same for the IEEE *Computer* magazine.

11–3 Use the list of subject areas (rows) and paradigms (columns) in Table 11–2 to classify Chapters 1 through 10 of this book. Explain how you determined the location of each chapter's topics in that table.

SUMMARY

Chapter 11 completes the first course in this breadth-first introduction to computing. Our purpose in this chapter has been to provide a forward look—some introduction beyond that of the first 10 chapters—into each of the nine subject areas of computing. We have tried to engage your interest and increase your knowledge about the general nature of the discipline. We hope that some of you have been enticed by this experience to pursue further study by taking the second course in the curriculum. Others will have gained a useful overview of computing. This field promises to remain young, dynamic, and exciting for the foreseeable future. We hope that during the course of this study you, too, have felt some of that excitement.

We began this chapter with a retrospective on the dynamic evolution of the discipline by way of its recent definitions and redefinitions. You ought to be able to discuss the field of computing with others who are interested in it. At the very least, you have gained a strong impression that *computing* is a much more richer and broader concept than *programming*.

The second section of this chapter reviews and extends those subject areas that were covered earlier in the text and introduces the remaining areas. For instance, you should understand what data structures are and should have some sense of what is likely to be contained in a course entitled "Analysis of Algorithms." Also, you should have some ideas about which areas of the discipline are more central and which are more peripheral. These mini-surveys of the nine subject areas are intended to stimulate your interest but also to help you begin thinking about future courses of study.

The final section provides a perspective on the profession and professionalism. This section also emphasizes that computing is a dynamic field, characterized by rapid conceptual and technological changes. Keeping current is essential for success in any field, though it is especially important in computing by its rapid rate of growth and development. The best that we can do at the outset is to develop a solid academic foundation upon which to build future curricular and professional growth.

REFERENCES

1. Grady Booch, *Software Engineering with Ada*, Benjamin Cummings, 1983, 502 pages.

2. Robert D. Cupper (ed), *Graduate Assistantship Directory*, Annual Editions, ACM Press, 1991, 97 pages.

3. Peter J. Denning, "The Science of Computing: What Is Computer Science?" *American Scientist 73*: 16–19 (January 1985).

4. Peter J. Denning, Douglas E. Comer, David Gries, Michael C. Mulder, Allen B. Tucker, A. Joe Turner, and Paul R. Young, "Computing as a Discipline," *Communications of the ACM 32, 1*: 9–15 (January 1989).

5. Michael J. Flynn, "Very High-speed Computing Systems," *Proceedings of the IEEE 54, 12*: 1901–1909 (December 1966).

6. John Haugelund, *Artificial Intelligence: The Very Idea*, MIT Press, 1985.

7. John Haugelund, *Mind Design*, MIT Press, 1981.

8. Donald E. Knuth, "Computer Science and Mathematics," *American Scientist, 61*: 707–713 (November–December 1973).

9. Shari Lawrence Pfleeger, *Software Engineering: The Production of Quality Software*, Macmillan, New York, 1987, 443 pages.

10. Roger Pressman, *Software Engineering: A Practitioner's Approach*, McGraw-Hill, 1987, 567 pages.

11. Elaine Rich, *Introduction to Artificial Intelligence*, McGraw-Hill, 1991.

12. Allen B. Tucker (ed), Bruce H. Barnes, Robert M. Aiken, Keith Barker, Kim B. Bruce, J. Thomas Cain, Susan E. Conry, Gerald L. Engel, Richard G. Epstein,

Doris K. Lidtke, Michael C. Mulder, Jean B. Rogers, Eugene H. Spafford, and A. Joe Turner, *Computing Curricula 1991: Report of the ACM/IEEE-CS Joint Curriculum Task Force*, ACM Press and IEEE Computer Society Press, 1991, 154 pages.

13. Joseph Weisenbaum, *Computer Power and Human Reason*, W. H. Freeman, 1976.

14. Terry Winograd, Fernando Flores, *Understanding Computers and Cognition*, Ablex, 1986.

The ASCII Character Set

Leading Digit(s)	Right-Hand Digit									
	0	1	2	3	4	5	6	7	8	9
0	nul	soh ^a	stx ^b	etx ^c	eot ^d	enq ^e	ack ^f	bel ^g	bs ^h	ht ^i
1	lf ^j	vt ^k	ff ^l	cr RET	so ^n	si ^o	dle ^p	dc1 ^q	dc2 ^r	dc3 ^s
2	dc4 ^t	nak ^u	syn ^v	etb ^w	can ^x	em ^y	sub ^z	esc ^[	fs ^\	gs ^]
3	rs ^`	us ^_	sp SPC	!	"	#	$	%	&	'
4	(	)	*	+	,	-	.	/	0	1
5	2	3	4	5	6	7	8	9	:	;
6	<	=	>	?	@	A	B	C	D	E
7	F	G	H	I	J	K	L	M	N	O
8	P	Q	R	S	T	U	V	W	X	Y
9	Z	[	\	]	^	—	`	a	b	c
10	d	e	f	g	h	i	j	k	l	m
11	n	o	p	q	r	s	t	u	v	w
12	x	y	z	{	|	}	~	del ^?		

The C++ expression int(c) can be used to retrieve the decimal representation of each character c in this table, while the expression char(n) delivers the character value equivalent to the integer n. For example, the value of int('A') is 65 and the value of char(65) is 'A'.

In the preceding table, the notation ^ denotes typing the <control> key and the character on its right simultaneously. For instance, ^a means that the ASCII character with decimal value 1 (and known obscurely as "soh") can be entered by holding down the <control> key and typing the letter a simultaneously. Readers should note that not all keyboards are set up in this particular way. However, some simple experimentation with the above C++ expressions can decypher the various encodings for ASCII characters that don't normally show on the screen. Those are the ones whose decimal values are less than 32, which itself represents the space (SPC) or the blank character. Also, the notation RET denotes the <return> key on most keyboards.

C++ SYNTAX SUMMARY

This appendix summarizes the syntax of the C++ subset that is used in the text and the lab manual. While this subset is not a complete description of C++, it is designed to cover all the programming questions that may arise while doing the labs in the manual and reading the text. More detailed explanations of the meaning and uses of each construct described below are given throughout the lab manual.

Keywords Certain words have reserved uses and meanings in C++ programs and as such cannot be used as variable names, function names, or any other purpose than that for which they are reserved. These are called "keywords," and a list of these is given below for GNU and ANSI C++:

asm	continue	float	new	signed	try
auto	default	for	operator	sizeof	typedef
break	delete	friend	private	static	union
case	do	goto	protected	struct	unsigned
catch	double	if	public	switch	virtual
char	else	inline	register	template	void
class	enum	int	return	this	volatile
const	extern	long	short	throw	while

Turbo C++ (version 3.0) has the following additional reserved words:

_asm	_ds	far	interrupt	_pascal	_ss
_cdecl	_es	_huge	_loadds	pascal	
cdecl	_export	huge	_near	_saveregs	
_cs	_far	_interrupt	near	_seg	

Think C++ has the following additional reserved words:

direct	indirect	inherited

Predefined functions The C++ libraries provide many predefined mathematical, string, and input/output functions. The following list describes the principal ones. In these descriptions, x and y denote double values; i, j, and n denote int values; s and t denote references to strings; and f denotes a text file. These mathematical, string, and i/o functions are linked to a program that uses them by writing one of the following

```
#include <math.h>
#include <string.h>
#include <iostream.h>
```

at the top of the program, accordingly.

```
acos(x)
// pre: -1 ≤ x ≤ 1
// post: result == the angle (in radians) whose cosine is x

asin(x)
// pre: -1 ≤ x ≤ 1
// post: result == the angle (in radians) whose sine is x

atan(x)
// pre: x is a number
// post: result == the angle (in radians) whose tangent is x

ceil(x)
// post: result == ⌈x⌉

cos(x)
// pre: 0≤x≤2π radians
// post: result == the cosine of x

cosh(x)
// pre: 0≤x≤2π radians
// post: result == the hyperbolic cosine of x

cin >> v₁ >> v₂ >> ... >> vₙ
// pre: input has at least n values c₁ c₂ ... cₙ to be read and
// the v's are variables of the same types as those values, from
// left to right, or else the input has no values remaining
// post: input has n fewer values && v₁ == c₁ && v₂ == c₂ && ...
// && vₙ == cₙ && result == 0 || the v's are unchanged and
// result !=0

cout << e₁ << e₂ << ... << eₙ
// pre: e₁ == c₁ && e₂ == c₂ && ... && eₙ == cₙ && the e's are
// expressions && the c's are their values
// post: output has new values c₁ c₂ ... cₙ

exp(x)
// pre: x is a number
// post: result == eˣ

fabs(x)
// post: result == |x|
```

```
fclose(f)
// pre: f is an open file
// post: f becomes no longer accessible to the program

floor(x)
// post: result == ⌊x⌋

log(x)
// pre: x > 0
// post: result == logₑx

log10(x)
// pre: x > 0
// post: result == log₁₀x

fopen(f, s)
// pre: f is a text file and s is a string naming a disk file
// post: f is ready for program reading or writing

pow(x, y)
// pre: x is a number
// post: result == xʸ

sin(x)
// pre: 0≤x≤2π radians
// post: result == the sine of x

sinh(x)
// pre: 0≤x≤2π radians
// post: result == the hyperbolic sine of x

sqrt(x)
// pre: x≥0
// post: result == √x

strcat(s, t)
// pre: s and t have values
// post: result == s == the concatenation of s and t

strcpy(s, t)
// pre: t has a value
// post: result == s == a copy of the value of t

strncpy(s, t, n)
// pre: t has a value
// post: result == s == a copy of the first n characters of t

strcmp(s, t)
// pre: s and t have values
// post: s and t are identical && result == 0 ||
// result != 0
```

```
strncmp(s, t, n)
// pre: s and t have values
// post: the first n charcters of s and t are identical &&
// result == 0 || result != 0

strlen(s)
// pre: s has a value
// post: result == the number of characters in s

tan(x)
// pre:  0 ≤ x ≤ 2π radians
// post: result == the tangent of x

tanh(x)
// pre: x is a number
// post: result == the angle (in radians) whose tangent is x
```

C++ syntax diagrams   On the following pages is a summary of syntactic rules for writing C++ programs, in the form of syntax diagrams. These disgrams represent a subset of C++ that is appropriate for this text, rather than the entire language. Many of the more advanced or complex C++ features are therefore not included in this summary.

The idea of an *identifier* runs through many of the definitions that follow. An identifer can be any sequence of letters (A–Z, a–z), digits (0–9), and underscores (_) and is designed by the programmer to "identify" or "name" something, such as a variable or a function. Thus, when terms such as *library name*, *structure name*, *type name*, *function name*, *variable name*, and *field name* appear in the following syntax diagrams, they will be understood to denote a particular instance of the general idea of an *identifier*.

program

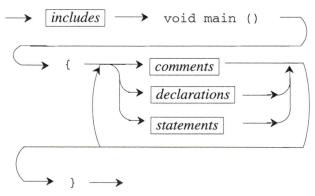

includes

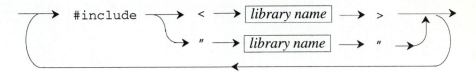

comments

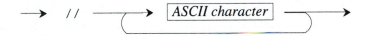

declarations

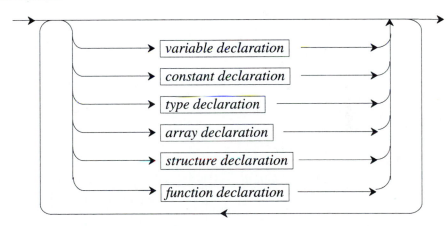

variable declaration

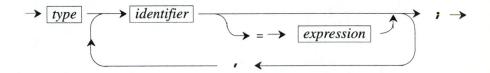

constant declaration

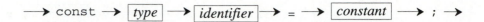

type declaration

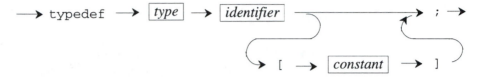

array declaration

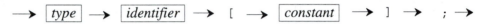

structure declaration

identifier*

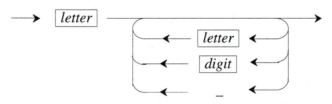

* A *letter* is any ASCII character in the range 'A' − 'Z' or 'a' − 'z';
A *digit* is any ASCII character in the range '0' − '9'. (See Appendix A.)

constant

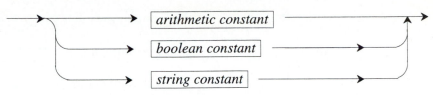

arithmetic constant

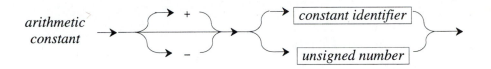

unsigned number

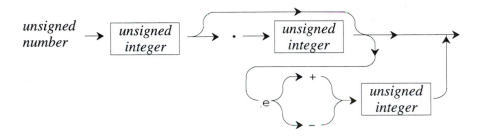

unsigned integer

boolean constant

1

0

string → " *any ASCII character except* " → " →
constant

type

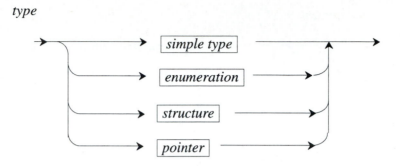

simple type

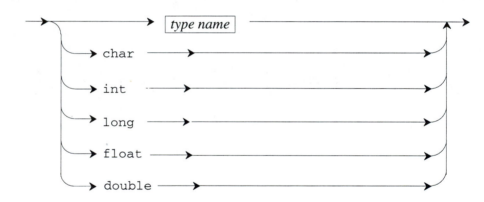

enumeration

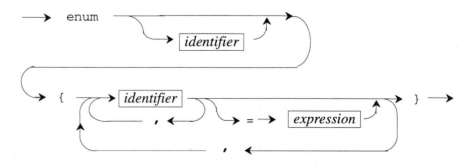

structure

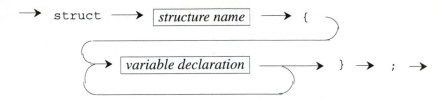

pointer

function declaration

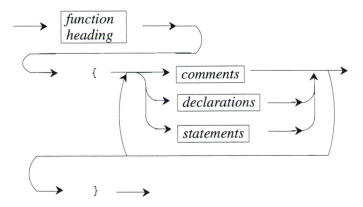

function heading

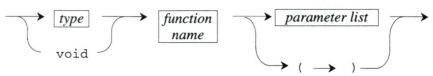

parameter list

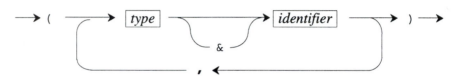

statement

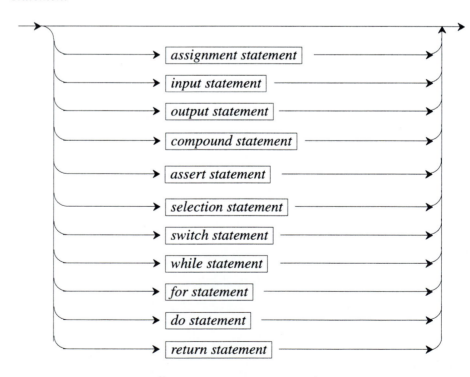

assignment statement

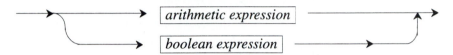

expression

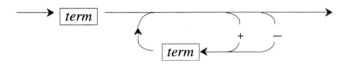

arithmetic expression

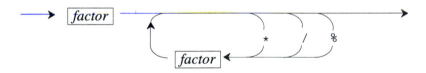

term

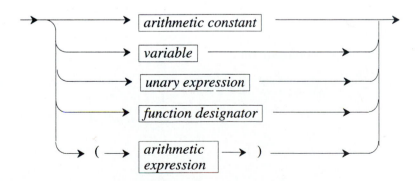

factor

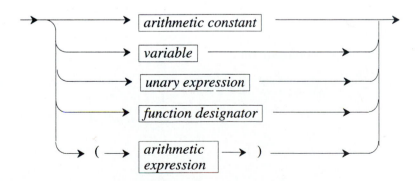

unary expression

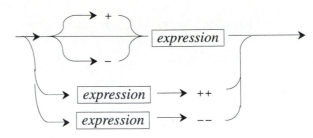

variable

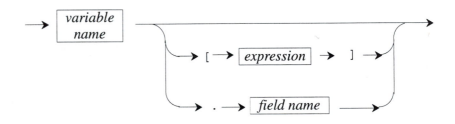

boolean expression

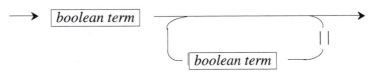

boolean term

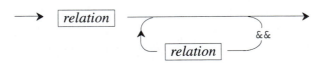

relation

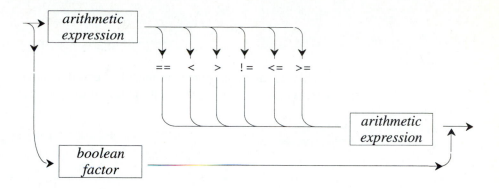

boolean factor

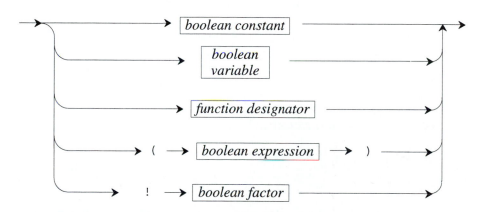

function designator

input statement*

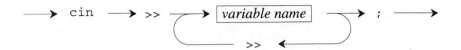

* This statement and the next must be accompanied by an
#include <iostream.h> at the top of the program.

output statement

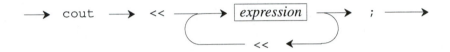

compound statement

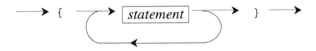

assert statement*

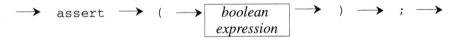

* This statement must be accomapanied by an #include <assert.h>
at the top of the program.

selection statement

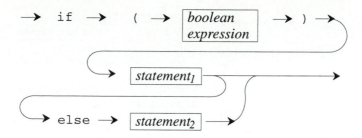

switch statement

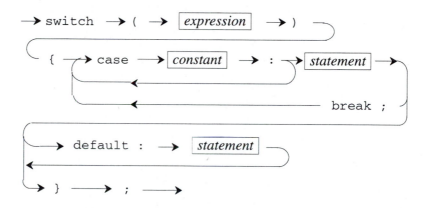

while statement

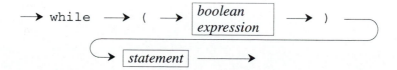

for statement

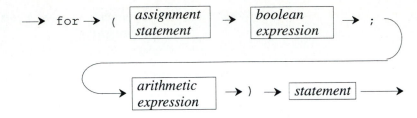

do statement

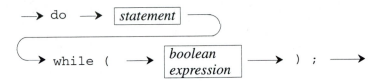

return statement

The List Class

```
// This is the header file "ListClass.h" for the list class
// and its member functions.  Developed by Brian Davies, 7/93.
// Revised by Allen Tucker, 5/94.

const int max_size = 256;
typedef float element_type;

class list
{
  public:
    list();

    int length ();
    // pre: L == (e[1] e[2] ... e[n]) && n >= 0
    // post: result == n.

    void empty ();
    // pre:
    // post: L == () and error == false).

    int is_error ();
    // pre:
    // post: result == error

    void read ();
    // pre: input == (e[1] e[2] ... e[n]) || (input == filename
    //     where the named file contains one or more lists)
    //        && n <= max_size && ctrl-d signals end of input
    // post: L == (e[1] e[2] ... e[n])

    void write ();
    // pre: L == (e[1] e[2] ... e[n])
    //     and output == anystream
    // post: output == anystream (e[1] e[2] ... e[n])

    void remove (int);
    // pre: L == (e[1] e[2] ... e[i] ... e[n])
    //        && 0 < i <= n
    // post: L == (e[1] e[2] ... e[i-1] e[i+1] ... e[n])
```

```
            void insert (element_type, int);
            // pre: L == (e[1] e[2] ... e[i] ... e[n])
            //     && 1 <= i <= n+1 <= max_size
            // post: L == (e[1] e[2] ... e[i] ... e[n])

            int pos (element_type e);
            // pre: e exists, L == (e[1] e[2] ... e[i] ... e[n]) n >= 0
            //    and 1)  e == e[i] for some i where 1 <= i <= n.
            //     or 2)  e != e[i] for all i where 1 <= i <= n
            // post:  1) result == i
            //     or 2) result == 0, respectively

            element_type element (int);
            // pre: L == (e[1] e[2] ... e[i] ... e[n])
            //     && 1 <= i <= n
            // post: result == e[i]

            int end_of_input();
            // pre:
            // post: input is at its end (ctrl-d for keyboard input)

            int has_error();
            // pre:
            // post: result == error

      private:
            element_type elements[max_size];
            int size;
            int error;
            int get_token(char *);
            float to_float(char *);
      };
```

The Grid Class

```
// This is the header file for "GridClass.h", its member
// functions, and other associated functions that implement the
// text and graphics output windows.  Brian Davies and Allen
// Tucker -- 5/94.

const int min_grid_size = 1;
                       // limits on rows and columns for a grid
const int max_grid_size = 50;
const int min_cell_size = 4;
                       // limits on pixels for a cell in a grid
const int max_cell_size = 120;

void open_text ();        // open the text and graphics windows
void open_graphics ();
void close_text ();       // close these windows
void close_graphics ();

class grid
{
  public:

      grid (int, int, int, int, char *);
      // pre: the parameters are grid size, cell size,
      //   left edge location, top edge location, and label.
      // post: if the parameters are within bounds, then
      //   each cell of the grid is set to ' ', and the grid is
      //   displayed.

      char cell (int, int);
      // pre: int, int describes a cell in the grid.
      // post: ((error == 0) and (returns cells[row, col]))
      //    or (sets error == 1).

      void set_cell (int, int, char);
      // pre: int, int describes the row and column of a cell in
      //   the grid, and char == 'x', 'o', ' ', or '.' ('.' means
      //   shade the cell black).
      // post: cells[col, row] == char && error == 0, or
      //   error == 1 and the cell is unchanged.

      void set_cell_display (int, int, char);
      // pre: int, int describes the row and column of a cell in
```

```
        //    the grid,
        //    and char == 'x', 'o', ' ', or '.' ('.' means shade
        //    the cell black).
        // post: cells[col, row] == char && error == 0 && the cell
        //    is displayed, or error == 1 and the cell is unchanged.

        void get_click (int &, int &);
        // pre:  a mouse click in the graphics window will occur
        // post: retrieves the x, y pixel coordinates for the
        //    position on the graphics window where the mouse is
        //    clicked.

        int locate_cell (int &, int &);
        // pre:  the integers x, y represent a pixel in the
        //    graphics window
        // post: if the pixel is inside the grid, x and y are
        //    converted to an equivalent row and column in the grid
        //    and result == 1, or else x and y are unchanged and
        //    result == 0.

        int grid_size ();
        // pre:
        // post: returns size.

        void display_grid ();
        // pre:
        // post: the grid is displayed.

    private:
        int size;
        int cell_size;
        int left_edge_loc, top_edge_loc;
        char cells[max_grid_size][max_grid_size];
        char grid_label[30];      // the grid's identifying label
        int error;

};
```

TAXONOMY OF THE COMPUTING LITERATURE

One way to comprehensively view the broad subject matter of computing is to look at the ACM's subject classification scheme. The ACM maintains this scheme as a basis for cataloging, reviewing, and retrieving information from the steady flow of scholarly work that appears in books, journals, and conference proceedings. This scheme is called the "CR Categories," and is the basis for organizing information in the monthly publication of ACM's *Computing Reviews* of this literature.

This classification scheme is elaborate, but overall it has a hierarchical structure. Below is a partial display of the CR Categories. The particular categories shown here are only the ones for which *actual* citations appeared during the period extending from January to July 1990. Students interested in the complete list of CR Categories should browse a recent issue of ACM's *Computing Reviews* in the local library.

Some of these topics should be already familiar to you. However, most of the topics in this list are not addressed in a first course in computing. They are gradually revealed either through additional courses in the curriculum or through outside reading or professional experience.

A. General Literature
1. Introductory and Survey
2. Reference

B. Hardware
1. Control Structures and Microprogramming
1.1. Control Design Styles
2. Arithmetic and Logic Structures
2.1. Design Styles
2.3. Reliability, Testing, and Fault-Tolerance
3. Memory Structures
3.2 Design Styles
3.3 Performance Analysis and Design Aids
4. Input/output and Data Communications

4.2   I/O Devices
4.3   Interconnections (Subsystems)
4.4   Performance Analysis and Design Aids
4.5   Reliability, Testing, and Fault Tolerance
5.   Register-Transfer-Level Implementation
5.1   Design
5.2   Design Aids
5.3   Reliability and Testing
6.   Logic Design
6.1   Design Styles
6.2   Reliability and Testing
6.3   Design Aids
7.   Integrated Circuits
7.1   Types and Design Styles
7.2   Design Aids
7.3   Reliability and Testing

C.   Computer Systems Organization
1.   Processor Architectures
1.1.   Single Data Stream Architectures
1.2.   Multiple Data Stream Architectures (Multiprocessors)
1.3.   Other Architecture Styles
2.   Computer-Communication Networks
2.1.   Network Architecture and Design
2.2.   Network Protocols
2.3.   Network Operations
2.4.   Distributed Systems
2.5.   Local Networks
3.   Special-purpose and Application-based Systems
4.   Performance of Systems
5.   Computer System Implementation
5.1   Large and Medium ("Mainframe") Computers
5.2   Minicomputers
5.3.   Microcomputers
5.4.   VLSI Systems

D.   Software
1.   Programming Techniques
1.1.   Applicative (Functional) Programming
1.3.   Concurrent Programming
2.   Software Engineering
2.1.   Requirements/Specifications
2.2.   Tools and Techniques
2.3.   Coding
2.4.   Program Verification

2.5.   Testing and Debugging
2.6.   Programming Environments
2.7.   Distribution of Maintenance
2.8.   Metrics
2.9.   Management
2.10. Design
3.   Programming Languages
    3.1.   Formal Definitions and Theory
    3.2.   Language Classifications
    3.3.   Language Constructs
    3.4.   Processors
4.   Operating Systems
    4.1.   Process Management
    4.2.   Storage Management
    4.3.   File Systems Management
    4.4.   Communications Management
    4.5.   Reliability
    4.6.   Security and Protection
    4.7.   Organization and Design
    4.8.   Performance
    4.9.   Systems Programs and Utilities

E.   Data
1.   Data Structures
2.   Data Storage Representations
3.   Data Encryption
4.   Coding and Information Theory
5.   Files

F.   Theory of Computation
1.   Computation by Abstract Devices
    1.1.   Models of Computation
    1.2.   Modes of Computation
    1.3.   Complexity Classes
2.   Analysis of Algorithms and Problem Complexity
    2.1.   Numerical Algorithms and Problems
    2.2.   Nonnumerical Algorithms and Problems
    2.3.   Trade-offs among Complexity Measures
3.   Logics and Meanings of Programs
    3.1.   Specifying and Verifying and Reasoning about Programs
    3.2.   Semantics of Programming Languages
    3.3.   Studies of Program Constructs
4.   Mathematical Logic and Formal Languages
    4.1.   Mathematical Logic
    4.2.   Grammars and Other Rewriting Systems

4.3. Formal Languages

G. Mathematics of Computing
1. Numerical Analysis
  1.1. Interpolation
  1.2 Approximation
  1.3. Numerical Linear Algebra
  1.4 Quadrature and Numerical Differentiation
  1.5 Roots of Nonlinear Equations
  1.6. Optimization
  1.7. Ordinary Differential Equations
  1.8. Partial Differential Equations
  1.9 Integral Equations
2. Discrete Mathematics
  2.1. Combinatorics
  2.2. Graph Theory
3. Probability and Statistics
4. Mathematical Software

H. Information Systems
1. Models and Principles
  1.1. Systems and Information Theory
  1.2. User/Machine Systems
2. Database Management
  2.1. Logical Design
  2.2. Physical Design
  2.3. Languages
  2.4. Systems
  2.5. Heterogeneous Databases
  2.6. Database Machines
  2.7. Database Administration
  2.8 Database Applications
3. Information Storage and Retrieval
  3.1. Content Analysis and Indexing
  3.2. Information Storage
  3.3. Information Search and Retrieval
  3.4. Systems and Software
4. Information Systems Applications
  4.1. Office Automation
  4.2. Types of Systems
  4.3. Communications Applications

I. Computing Methodologies
1. Algebraic Manipulation
  1.1. Expressions and Their Representation

1.2 Algorithms
1.3. Languages and Systems
2. Artificial Intelligence
   2.1. Applications and Expert Systems
   2.2. Automatic Programming
   2.3. Deduction and Theorem Proving
   2.4. Knowledge Representation Formalisms and Methods
   2.5. Programming Languages and Software
   2.6. Learning
   2.7. Natural Language Processing
   2.8. Problem Solving, Control Methods and Search
   2.9. Robotics
   2.10. Vision and Scene Understanding
3. Computer Graphics
   3.1 Hardware Architecture
   3.2. Graphics Systems
   3.3. Picture/Image Generation
   3.4. Graphics Utilities
   3.5. Computational Geometry and Object Modeling
   3.6. Methodology and Techniques
   3.7. Three-Dimensional Graphics and Realism
4. Image Processing
   4.1 Digitization
   4.2. Compression (coding)
   4.4. Restoration
   4.6. Segmentation
   4.7. Feature Measurement
   4.8. Scene Analysis
   4.9. Applications
5. Pattern Recognition
   5.1. Models
   5.2 Design Methodology
6. Simulation and Modeling
   6.1 Simulation Theory
   6.2 Simulation Languages
   6.3. Applications
   6.4. Model Validation and Analysis
7. Text Processing
   7.1. Text Editing
   7.2. Document Preparation

J. Computer Applications
1. Administrative Data Processing
2. Physical Sciences and Engineering
3. Life and Medical Sciences

4. Social and Behavioral Sciences
5. Arts and Humanities
6. Computer-Aided Engineering
7. Computers in Other Systems

K. Computing Milieux
1. The Computer Industry
2. History of Computing
3. Computers and Education
   3.1. Computer Uses in Education
   3.2. Computer and Information Science Education
4. Computers and Society
   4.1. Public Policy Issues
   4.2. Social Issues
   4.3. Organizational Impact
5. Legal Aspects of Computing
   5.1 Software Protection
6. Management of Computing and Information Systems
   6.1. Project and People Management
   6.2. Installation Management
   6.3. Software Management
   6.4. System Management
7. The Computing Profession
   7.1. Occupations
   7.2. Organizations
8. Personal Computing

Answers to Selected Exercises

1–1 *a.* design
     b. theory
     c. design
     d. abstraction
     e. design
     f. design
     g. abstraction
     h. design

1–4 *a.* Input for braised chicken is flour, salt, pepper, celery salt, paprika, a large fryer, and water. Output is a plate of braised chicken.

     b. Input for the ATM machine is a series of entries for the customer's account number, selection of a withdrawal or deposit, and the amount of money to be withdrawn or deposited. In case of a deposit, input includes the money to be deposited itself. Output is a receipt showing the transaction and the account's balance. In case of a withdrawal, output includes the withdrawn cash itself.

1–5 yes: a, b, d; no: c, e

2–1 Preparing for an exam can be cast as an algorithmic problem. One solution is to carry out the following steps:

    Step 1.   Read class notes.
    Step 2.   Read assigned text material.
    Step 3.   Collaborate with classmates and do sample problems.

    Other algorithms for preparing for an exam can be easily conceived. For instance, any one or two of the above steps can be viewed as an alternative algorithm for this problem.

2–3 *a.* { x | x is a series of 4 or fewer 0's and 1's, and x contains either one or two 0's }
     b. { ..., –4, –2, 0, 2, 4, ... }
     c. { a, b, c, ab, ac, bc, abc }

> d. { 012, 021, 102, 120, 210, 201 }
>
> e. { $p \mid p$ is a polynomial of the form $ax^3 + bx^2 + cx$ and $c <> 0$ }

2–6 $S = \{\varepsilon\}$ and $T = \{\varepsilon\}$, or else $S = \{\ \}$ and $T = \{\ \}$.

2–7 b. $(A \cup B)' \cup (A \setminus B)$

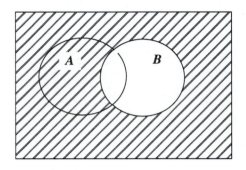

2–9 c. true
  e. true
  i. true

2–11 a. {0, 2, 4, 6, 8, 10}
  b. {012, 021, 102, 120, 201, 210}

2–12 a. i == 2 && j == 2

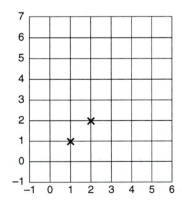

2–15 b. Domain = {−2, −1, 0, 10, 15} and range = {true, false}
  d. Domain = {−1, 0, 1, −49.5, $\frac{\pi}{6}$} and range = {1, 0, 1, 49.5, $\frac{\pi}{6}$}

2–13

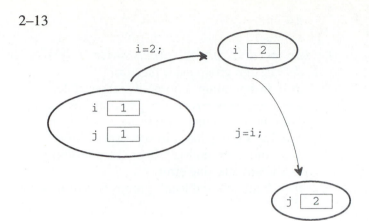

2–17 *a.*   Domain = **R**
  b.   Range = {true, false}

2–19   The decoded message is OH TO BE IN NARNIA (spaces added for clarity). This is not a one-to-one function on characters, since two different characters can be encoded as the same character. It is a one-to-one function on strings, since no two different strings can be encoded as the same string, yet every string has an encoding.

2–20
```
Step 1.  Obtain the input list of grades.
Step 2.  Compute n = the number of grades in the list.
Step 3.  Compute Sum = the sum of the grades in the list.
Step 4.  Compute GPA = Sum / n.
Step 5.  Compute NumberAbove = the number of grades that
         are greater than GPA.
Step 6.  Report the resulting value of NumberAbove.
```

Here, the new steps are 5 and 6. The additional variable needed is NumberAbove, which is used to keep track of the number of grades that are greater than the value of GPA, which was computed in Step 4.

3–1

  a.   proposition
  c.   proposition, given that x has a value; not a proposition otherwise
  g.   not a proposition

3–3

  a. $p \wedge q \wedge r \wedge s$
    $p = -1 \leq x$
    $q = x \leq 1$

$$r = -1 \le y$$
$$s = y \le 1$$

f. $(de \Rightarrow (dr \wedge ebd)) \wedge (pce \Rightarrow (tr \vee lr)) \wedge (te \Rightarrow frr)$

  de = design group made the error
  dr = design group is primarily responsible,
  ebd = everyone except design group has secondary responsibility
  pce = programming team made a coding error
  tr = Ted's group has primary responsibility
  lr = Louis's gropu has primary responsibility
  te = it was a testing error
  frr = FouSen's and Rita's groups have primary responsibility

3–5

a.

p	q	$((p \Rightarrow q) \wedge p) \Rightarrow q$		
true	true	true	true	true
true	false	false	false	true
false	true	true	false	true
false	true	true	false	true

3–7

  p = Reds are better than the A's.
  q = Pirates are better than the Reds

3–9

a. result = (i < 10) && (j < 10) ;
c. result = (i + j) > k ;

3–11

Note: we can't check for domain N since the int data type is finite; instead we will check only from 0 through some constant MaxValue.

```
a.    result = 1 ;
      i = 0 ;
      while (result && i <= MaxValue)
      {    if ( ! (i < i + 1) )
              result = 0 ;
           else
              i = i + 1 ;
      }
```

(Actually, a loop isn't needed, since we know that i<i+1 is always true!)

e.
```
result = 0 ;
i = 0 ;
while (! result && i <= MaxValue)
{
    j = 0;
    while (! result && j <= MaxValue)
        if (i*i + j*j) <= 25
            result = 1;
        else
            j = j + 1;
    if (! result)
        i = i + 1;
}
```
g.
```
max = -1;
for (i = 1; i<=100; i++)
    if (i + 2 == 101 && i > max)
        max = i;
```
l.
```
Sum = 0;
for (i = 1; i<=10; i++)
    Sum = Sum + (i - 5);
```

3–13   (Note: p(Row, Column) = WQ, etc., is not proper C++, but it is used here for illustrative purposes.)

a.
```
Queen = 0;
Row = 1;
while (! Queen && Row <= 8)
{
    Column = 1;
    while (! Queen && Column <= 8)
        if (p(Row, Column) == WQ)
            Queen = 1;
        else
            Column++;
    if (! Queen)
        Row++
}
```
e.
```
RowBQ = 1;
FoundBQ = 0;
while (! FoundBQ && RowBQ <= 8)
{
    ColumnBQ = 1;
    while (! FoundBQ && ColumnBQ <= 8)
        if (p(RowBQ, ColumnBQ) == BQ)
```

```
                        FoundBQ = 1;
                else
                        ColumnBQ++;
            if (! FoundBQ)
                RowBQ++;
    }
    Attacking = 0;
    ColumnWR = 1;
    while (! Attacking && ColumnWR <= 8)
        if (p(RowBQ, ColumnWR) == WR)
            Attacking = 1;
        else
            ColumnWR++;
    RowWR = 1;
    while (! Attacking && RowWR <= 8)
        if (p(RowWR, ColumnBQ) == WR)
            Attacking = 1;
        else
            RowWR++;
```

3–15

    a. $s(1,2) = X \wedge s(1,3) = O \wedge s(3,2) = X$

    d. $\exists i \in \{1,\ldots,3\} : s(i,2) = O$

    e. $\forall j \in \{1,\ldots,3\} : \exists i \in \{1,\ldots,3\} : s(i,j) = O$

3–17

    a.   The program will read an integer value and then place the sum of that many real values, read from input, in the variable Addem.

```
cin >> N;
Addem = 0.0;
for (i = 1; i<=N; i++)
{
    cin >> x ;
    Addem = Addem + x ;
}
```

4–1
```
EvenSum = 0;
OddSum = 0;
for (i=1; i<=L.length(); i++)
{
    if (i % 2 == 0)
        EvenSum = EvenSum + L.element(i);
```

```
        else
           OddSum = OddSum + L.element(i);
     }
```

4–5   ```
for (i=1; i<=L.length(); i++)
    if (i % 2 == 1)
        if (L.element(i) % 2 == 1)
            L.element(i) = 0;
```

4–9   *Ancestors*(*n*)  =    2                          if $n = 1$
                  =    2*Ancestors*(*n*–1)        if $n > 1$

4–11   The problem breaks down into three major steps; one to initialize the grids, one to process a customer's transactions, and one to finalize the process by displaying the message "Have a nice day."

   *b.*   The variables needed by this program are declared and documented below:

```
grids deposit, withdrawal, balancecheck, and nomore
     // Each of these is a 1x1 grid, in which a mouse
     // click signals one of the four transaction types
char TransactionType;
     // 'w'=withdrawal, 'd'=deposit, 'c'=balancecheck,
     // 'n'=no more }
float balance;
     // The account's running balance and the amount of
     // a single transaction }
int i, j;
     // auxiliary variables used to index the coordinates
     //of a mouse click in a grid }
```

   c.   The following Grids functions will be needed by this program:

`StartGrids;`	To open the graphics and text windows
`grid`	To initialize each of the four grids. E.g.,
	`grid deposit(1, 10, 10, 30, "Deposit");`
`get_click(i,j)`	To wait for and receive a mouse click
`locate_cell(i,j)`	To find the grid where the click was made. E.g.,
	`if (deposit.locate_cell(i, j))`
	`    TransactionType = 'd';`

4–12   *a.*   1
   f.   –3
   h. $x + 1$
```

4–13   *a.* $\displaystyle\sum_{i=1}^{10} 2^{i-1} = \sum_{i=0}^{9} 2^i = 2^{10} - 1 = 1023$

     c. $\displaystyle\sum_{j=m}^{n} a_j = a_m + a_{m+1} + \ldots + a_n$

4–15   *c.*   The first odd integer is 1, the second is 3, and so forth, so that the ith odd integer is $2i - 1$. So we have:

$$\sum_{i=1}^{500} (2i - 1) = 2\sum_{i=1}^{500} i - 500 = \ldots = 250,000$$

4–16   *a.* $\displaystyle\pi \sum_{r=1}^{10} (100r + 25)^2 - (100r - 25)^2$

4–17   *a.* $\displaystyle\sum_{i=1}^{25} i = 25(26)/2 = 325$

     c. $\displaystyle\sum_{i=6}^{12} 3i^2 = \sum_{i=1}^{12} 3i^2 - \sum_{i=1}^{5} 3i^2 = 3[12(13)25/6 - 5(6)11/6] = 1785$

     g. $\displaystyle\sum_{i=2}^{5} i^2 = \sum_{i=1}^{5} i^2 - 1^2 = 5(6)11/6 - 1 = 54$

5–3

A void function can be converted to a nonvoid function if it has one reference parameter with a simple type (e.g., int or float). A nonvoid function can always be converted to an equivalent void function by adding a single reference parameter and assigning the returned result to it.

5–5

```
int IndexOfMin (list AnyList, int n)
// Returns index of a minimum element in a list of length n
// pre:
{
  int i = 2;
  int IndexOfMinSoFar = 1 ;
  while (i <= n)
    {
```

```
        if (AnyList.element(i)<AnyList.element(IndexOfMinSoFar)
            IndexOfMinSoFar = i;
        i++;
      }
    return IndexOfMinSoFar ;
// post: for all i in {1,...,n}:
//          AnyList[i] <= AnyList[IndexOfMin]
}
```

5–7

a.
```
int Fib(int n)
// pre: n >= 0
{
    if (n < 2)
        return n ;
    else
        return Fib(n-1) + Fib(n-2) ;
// post: result == the nth Fibonacci number
}
```

b.

c.

```
int Fib(int n) ;
{
// pre: n >= 0
  int i, X = 0, Y = 1, result;
  for (i=2; i<=n; i++)
    {
```

```
                result = X + Y;
                X = Y;
                Y = result ;
            }
          if (n < 2)
             return n ;
          else
             return result ;
       // post: result == the nth Fibonacci number
       }
```

5–11

```
    int pos(float x, list l)
    {
    // pre: L = (e[1] e[2] ... e[n]) && x is a number
        i = 1;
        found = 0;
        while (i <= L.length() && ! found)
            if L.element(i) = x
                found = 1 ;
            else
                i++ ;
        if (found)
            return i ;
        else
            return 0 ;
    // post: there is i in {1,...,n}: x == e[i] && Result == i
    //       or
    //       for all i in {1,..., n}: x <> e[i] && Result == 0
    }
```

5–15

```
    #include <iostream.h>
    #include "ListClass.h"
    int IsBigger (list L)
    {
    // pre :
        int result = 1;
        int i = 2;
        while (result && i <= L.length())
            if (L.element(1) > L.element(i))
                i++ ;
            else
                result = 0 ;
        return result ;
```

```
// post: result ==
//         for all i in {2,...,L.length(): L[1] > L[i]
}
void main ()
{
  list TestL;
  TestL.read();
  if (IsBigger(TestL)
      cout << "First element is bigger than the rest\n";
  else
      cout << "First element isn't bigger than the rest\n";
}
```

5–18

```
if (n < 0)
    m = -n ;
else
    m = n ;
```

5–21

```
#include <iostream.h>
void main ()
{ int Number = 0;
  int i, n;
  for (i = 1; i<=100; i++)
  {
    cin >> n ;
    if (n % 5 == 0)
        cout << n << " is divisible by 5\n" ;
  }
}
```

5–24

Calculation of a^b for a == 5 and b == –4:

Step	a	b	Result	i
1	???	??	???	???
2	5	–4	???	???
2.1	5	–4	???	???
2.2	5	–4	5	1
	5	–4	25	2
	5	–4	125	3
	5	–4	625	4
3.	5	–4	0.0016	???

5–27

```cpp
#include <iostream.h>
void main ()
{
  // pre: input == aword1 aword2 ... awordn
  int Count = 0 ;    // total number of 'and's in word s
  int CurrentPos ;   // position of the current 'and' in s
  char s[30] ;       // next word from input stream
  while (cin >> s)   // input the next word
  {
    CurrentPos = 0;    // look for "and" in s
    while (CurrentPos <= strlen(s)-2 && s[CurrentPos]=='a'
        && s[CurrentPos+1]=='n' && s[CurrentPos+2]=='d')
    {
        strcpy(s, s[CurrentPos+3]); // remove "and" from s
        Count++ ;
    }
    cout << "The count is " << Count << '\n' ;
// Output == number of times 'and' appeared in input
}
```

5–29

```cpp
// nwords == 1 for "Able " && 1 <= 6 <= 26
// nwords == 2 for "was " && 1 <= 9 <= 26
// nwords == 3 for "I " && 1 <= 11 <= 26
// nwords == 4 for "ere " && 1 <= 15 <= 26
// nwords == 5 for "I " && 1 <= 17 <= 26
// nwords == 6 for "saw " && 1 <= 21 <= 26
// nwords == 7 for "Elba." && 1 <= 25 <= 26
```

5–31 Below is a revision of Step 3 in the program:

```cpp
board.get_click(row, col);
while (board.locate_cell(row, col))
{
  if (board.get_cell(i, j) == ' ')  // see if cell occupied
  {
    if (move_number % 2 == 1) // determine turn: 'x' or 'o'
      current_player = 'x';
    else
      current_player = 'o';
    board.set_cell_display (row, col, current_player);
    move_number++;
  }
  else        //  move was attempted onto an occupied square
    cout << "Invalid move; try again\n" ;
```

```
    board.get_click(row, col);
}
```

6–1 Yes. No. For example, it does not prevent one player from using the square already used by another. More such examples could be given.

6–3 *a.* `// pre: input == a series of 9 or fewer mouse clicks on`
    `//        the 3x3 tic-tac-toe board, such that each click is`
    `//        on an empty square`

6–5 This is a fairly simple program, so it doesn't need a lot of enhancement. However, a more extensive set of opening documentation for the user could be given. Another possible enhancement would be to describe, e.g., what it considers to be a legal "word."

6–7 To create an autodriver for tic-tac-toe, the program must be modified to monitor a series of games, rather than just one. A convention must also be adopted for the program to recognize when it is at the end of the last game in the series (as opposed to the end of an intermediate game).

6–9 (0.0 0.0 0.0 0.0 0.0 0.0 0.0 0.0 0.0 0.0 0.0 0.0)
    (1.0 2.0 3.0 4.0 5.0 6.0 7.0 8.0 9.0 10.0 11.0 12.0)
    (1.0 2.0 3.0 4.0 5.0 6.0 7.0 8.0 9.0 10.0 11.0 –12.0)
    (1.0 2.0 3.0 4.0 r.0 6.0 7.0 8.0 9.0 10.0 11.0 12.0)

This is a fairly simple program to test—there are no `switch` statements, the loops are `for` loops (and hence execute a fixed number of times) and there are only two conditionals. Also, the loop at the beginning excludes any data list that is not of the right length. Both conditionals are tested in both the true and false cases and the above data tests likely user errors.

6–11

```
months below average:
Highest month(s):

February
March
April
May
June
July
August
November
December
```

6–18
```cpp
int strpos (char * s, char * t)
{
// pre: s and t are strings
   for (int i=0; i < strlen(t) - strlen(s) + 1; i++)
    if (strcmp(s, t[i]) == 0)              // found a match
       return 1;
   return 0;                  // loop finished; no match found
// post: s appears in t and result == the index in t of the
//       leftmost occurrrence of s in t, or result == 0
}
```

6–21 Part *a* of 6–23 (below) is a terminal state. So is the empty grid.

6–23 Generation 2

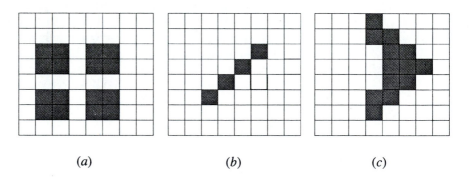

(*a*)   (*b*)   (*c*)

7–1 *a.*

p	*q*	*r*	*p* $\vee$ (*q* $\wedge$ *r*)		(*p* $\vee$ *q*) $\wedge$ (*p* $\vee$ *r*)		
true	–	–	true	–	true	true	true
false	false	–	false	false	false	false	–
false	true	true	true	true	true	true	true
false	true	false	false	false	true	false	false

7–3 *a.* 1 . $[(p \Rightarrow r) \wedge (r \Rightarrow q)]$ Assumption

2 . $p \Rightarrow r$ $\wedge$ – simplification

3 . $r \Rightarrow q$ $\wedge$ – simplification

4 . $[p]$ Assumption

5 . r Modus Ponens

6 . q Modus Ponens

7 . $p \Rightarrow q$ $\Rightarrow$ – introduction

8 . $((p \Rightarrow r) \wedge (r \Rightarrow q)) \Rightarrow (p \Rightarrow q)$ $\Rightarrow$ – introduction

7–6 *d.*

$((p \vee q$

$((\sim p \wedge$

$((\sim p \wedge$

$(F \vee (\text{-}$

$\sim p \wedge$

$\sim (\sim p$

$\sim \sim p$

$p \vee T$

T

7–7 *a.* 1 . $[(\sim p \vee q)]$ Assumption

2 . $q \vee \sim p$ Commutativity

3 . $(\sim p \vee q) \Rightarrow (q \vee \sim p)$ $\Rightarrow$ – introduction

7–10 Let *A*, *B*, and *C* denote the propositions that Abigail, Bridget, and Claudia drink coffee after dinner, respectively. Thus, ~*A*, ~*B*, and ~*C* denote that Abigail, Bridget, and Caludia drink tea, since we know that each one drinks either coffee or tea. The facts given in the statement can be rewritten as propositions. For instance,

$B \Rightarrow (A \Leftrightarrow \sim C)$

means "If Bridget orders coffee, then Abigail orders the drink that Claudia doesn't order."

Now, the question "Which one (if any) of the three always orders the same drink after dinner?" asks whether *A*, *B*, or *C* is a tautology or a contradiction. *Hint:* Start by assuming that *A* is a tautology.

7–12 Hint:

Base case: $f(0) = 1 = 2^0$.
Induction step: Assume that, for some $n>0$, $f(n) = 2^n$.

7–13 Hint:

Base case: $\displaystyle\sum_{i=1}^{1} 2i - 1 = 1 = 1^2$

Induction step: Assume that, for some $n > 0$, $\displaystyle\sum_{i=1}^{n}(2i - 1) = n^2$.

7–15 *a.*

Base case: $\displaystyle\sum_{i=0}^{0}(i(i + 1)) = 0 = \frac{0(1)(2)}{3}$

Induction step: Assume that, for some n,

$$\sum_{i=0}^{n}(i(i + 1)) = \frac{n(n + 1)(n + 2)}{3}$$

Then, for $n + 1$, we have

$$\sum_{i=0}^{n+1}(i(i + 1)) = \sum_{i=0}^{n}(i(i + 1)) + (n + 1)(n + 2)$$

$$= \frac{n(n + 1)(n + 2)}{3} + \frac{3(n + 1)(n + 2)}{3}$$

$$= \frac{(n + 1)(n + 2)(n + 3)}{3}$$

7–16 *a.*
```
// i ≥ 0
   i = i+1 ;
// i > 0
```

e.
```
// x = 12
   cout << x ;
// output == 12
```

7–20 *a.*
```
// a == 0 || a == 1
   if (a == 1) b = a; else b = a + 1;
// b == 1
```

7–21
```
int IsSorted (list A)
{
  int result = 1;
  for (i=1; i<=A.length()-1; i++)
// inv:result==1 && for all j in {1,...,i-1}: A[i]≤A[i+1]
//      || result == 0
    if (A.element(i) > A.element(j))
```

```
        result = 0 ;
    return result ;
  }
```

Note that when the loop terminates, the invariant resolves itself to a post-condition that defines whether or not the list A is entirely sorted.

8–1 *a.* $177_8 = 64 + 56 + 7 = 127_{10}$
     d. $AEC_{16} = 10*256 + 14*16 + 12*1 = 2796_{10}.$

8–3 *a.* $200_8 = 128_{10} = 80_{16}$
     c. $ABC_{16} = 10 \times 4 \times 8^2 + 11 \times 2 \times 8 + 1 \times 8 + 4 =$
            $= 5 \times 8^3 + 2 \times 8^2 + 7 \times 8 + 4 = 5274_8$

8–5 The
```
54  68  64  20
01010100  01101000  01100100  00100000
```
quick
```
71  75  69  63  6B
```
. . .

8–7

	01001101 =	77
+	10101010 =	−86
	11110111 =	− 9

8–8 The largest integer would be all 1s. Therefore it would be the sum of all powers of 2 from 2^0 to 2^{15} $= 1 + 2 + 4 + ... + 32768 = 65535.$
$2^{16} - 1 = 65535.$

8–10

$(b \wedge \sim a) \vee (a \wedge \sim b) \equiv$
$((b \wedge \sim a) \vee a) \wedge ((b \wedge \sim a) \vee \sim b) \equiv$
$((b \vee a) \wedge ((\sim a \vee a)) \wedge ((b \vee \sim b) \wedge (\sim a \vee \sim b))) \equiv$
$(a \vee b) \wedge \sim (a \wedge b)$

8–15

The leftmost carry output from an addition cannot be ignored in all cases.

8–18 Suppose a and b are numbers with opposite signs. Without loss of generality assume a is positive and b is negative. Then A+B is A − |B|, where |B| is the absolute value of B. A − |B| is less than A. If it is positive then it must fit in the allowed space (since A fit) so there is no overflow. If A−|B| is negative then it must be less then B. and the same argument holds ...

8–19 Assuming that the following functions compare, shift left (one bit) and add arrays of int (as defined in Lab 8), the function is given below.

```
int compare (word A, word B)
void shift(direction dir, word & dummy)
void add(word A, word & C)

void multiply (word A, word B, word & C)
{
// This version assumes unsigned integer arithmetic
  int position;
// initialize C to zero
  for (position = 0; position < 16; position++)
  c[position] = 0 ;
// for every positive digit in B add A*2^current position
  while (! (compare(zero, B)))
// zero is a global constant of all 0's
  {
    if (B[0])
      add(A, C);
    shift(left, A);      // multiply A by 2
    shift(right, B);     // check next digit of B
  }
}
```

8–24 c becomes true, then
Q becomes false, then
a becomes false, then
b becomes true, and
c remains true

8–26 The third byte in this message is in error.

9–1
```
load      first,R2       start with one value
add       second,R2      add the other two
add       third,R2
div       3,R2           leave the result in R2
halt
first     dc    10
second    dc    15
third     dc    20
end
```

9–3 *a.*
```
load      a,R1
```

```
          cmp       b,R1
          blt       action_label
```

9–5
```
          load      B,R1
          mul       R1,R1
          load      A,R2
          mul       C,R2
          mul       4,R2
          sub       R2,R1
          bsr       square_root
          load      A,R2
          mul       2,R2
          load      0,R3
          sub       B,R3
          load      R3,R0
          add       R1,R3
          div       R2,R3
          sub       R1,R0
          div       R2,R0
```

9–9 In each pass through a pretest loop, one branch statement will be encountered at the top and one at the bottom. In addition one branch moves control out of the loop. So 101 branch statements will be encountered. But in every successful iteration, the exit branch at he top will not be taken, so 101 branches will be taken. For a posttest loop exactly 100 branches will be both encountered and taken.

9–11
```
     mul r0,r0
     ret
```

9–13
```
     n_star
     top bsr star
         sub 1,r0
         cmp 0,r0
         blt top
         ret
```

9–15
```
          ble b                = 1110 110 00 1100101
          div a,r3 =   0100 000 11 1100100
          not r2      =        0111 000 10 0000000
          bra b           =        1110 000 00 1100101
```

9–17 The total instruction would require one more memory access for a total of three memory cycles: one to fetch the operation, one to fetch the operand and one to store the result.

9–21 Assembly is the translation of a (symbolic) assembly language program into a (binary) machine language program. Applying assembly to the MARINA program on the righthand side of Figure 9–1 results in the machine language program on the lefthand side. Assembly itself is performed by a program called an "assembler."

9–23 *a.* This program computes the cube of the number 3.

b.
```
// pre:
// post: i == 3 && j == i³
```

c.
```
    LOAD R1,I
    MUL  R1,I
    MUL  R1,I
    STO  R1,J
    HALT
I   DC   3
J   DS
    END
```

d. The best way to determine what this program will look like in MARINA machine language is to type it and assemble it.

9–27
```
    LOAD A,R0
    LOAD B,R1
    STO  R0,B
    STO  R1,A
A   DS   1
B   DS   1
    END
```

INDEX

A

abs, 440

absolute value function, 52
    in C++, 53

abstraction, 11, 14, 43, 139, 227, 415
    defining, 237, 246

abutment, 181

Ada, 202, 420

adder, 319

addition, circuit, 316

address space, 333

Aiken, Howard, 7

al-Khowarizmi, 3

algorithm, 3, 22, 412

algorithmic problem, 22
    solving, 61

algorithms and data structures, 13,
    14, 416

alphabet, 33

and, 313
    in C++. *See* conjunction

and gate, 313

architecture, 13, 14, 421

Aristotle, 2

arithmetic
    operations, 43
    progression, 158

arithmetic-logic unit (ALU), 312

artificial intelligence, 419, 429

ASCII character set, 33, 57, 202,
    310, 437
    in C++, 57
    memory representation, 310

assembler, 376, 377

assembly language, 10

assertion
    intermediate, 105

assignment, 43

associativity, 253
    sets, 33

Atanasoff, John, 8

ATM problem, 149

automatic teller machine (ATM),
    16

B

Babbage, Charles, 4, 12